Turkey, Egypt, and Syria

Middle East Literature in Translation
Michael Beard and Adnan Haydar, *Series Editors*

Select titles in Middle East Literature in Translation

All Faces but Mine: The Poetry of Samih Al-Qasim
Abdulwahid Lu'lu'a, trans.

Arabs and the Art of Storytelling: A Strange Familiarity
Abdelfattah Kilito; Mbarek Sryfi and Eric Sellin, trans.

The Elusive Fox
Muhammad Zafzaf; Mbarek Sryfi and Roger Allen, trans.

Felâtun Bey and Râkim Efendi: An Ottoman Novel
Ahmet Midhat Efendi; Melih Levi and Monica M. Ringer, trans.

Gilgamesh's Snake and Other Poems
Ghareeb Iskander; John Glenday and Ghareeb Iskander, trans.

Jerusalem Stands Alone
Mahmoud Shukair; Nicole Fares, trans.

The Perception of Meaning
Hisham Bustani; Thoraya El-Rayyes, trans.

32
Sahar Mandour; Nicole Fares, trans.

For a full list of titles in this series,
visit https://press.syr.edu/supressbook-series
/middle-east-literature-in-translation/

Turkey, Egypt, and Syria

A Travelogue

Shiblī Nuʿmānī

Translated from the Urdu by
Gregory Maxwell Bruce

Syracuse University Press

Syracuse, New York 13244-5290

First Edition 2020

20 21 22 23 24 25 6 5 4 3 2 1

Originally published in Urdu as *Safarnāmah-i Rūm o Miṣr o Shām* (Agrah: Mufīd-i ʻĀm Press, 1894).

∞ The paper used in this publication meets the minimum requirements of the American National Standard for Information Sciences—Permanence of Paper for Printed Library Materials, ANSI Z39.48-1992.

For a listing of books published and distributed by Syracuse University Press, visit https://press.syr.edu.

ISBN: 978-0-8156-3656-4 (hardcover)
978-0-8156-3654-0 (paperback)
978-0-8156-5481-0 (e-book)

Library of Congress Control Number: 2019948327

Manufactured in the United States of America

Contents

Translator's Preface

Turkey, Egypt, and Syria: A Travelogue (*Safarnāmah-i Rūm o Miṣr o Shām*), by Shiblī Nu'mānī (1857–1914) was first published in July of 1894. It records the experiences of the author while traveling in the Ottoman Empire and Egypt from May to September, 1892. Internal evidence (for example, reference to the death of the Egyptian scholar 'Alī Pāshā Mubārak [d. November 1893]) suggests that Shiblī wrote much of the travelogue in the first half of 1894. Advertisements for the book were published by the *Aligarh Institute Gazette*, the widely circulated biweekly organ of Mohammedan Anglo-Oriental College, where Shiblī was professor of Arabic and Persian. The book was also promoted by prominent scholars closely tied to the college. It sold well enough that a second edition, including a few minor changes, was published from Delhi in 1901. All subsequent editions of the text are based on the second edition. During the Khilafat Movement in British India (1919–24), the text came to have new political significance as the figure of the Ottoman sultan and the Turkish Empire became symbols of political and social mobilization against British rule. By the middle of the twentieth century, the text had become a canonical work of travel writing in Urdu and it has rarely, if ever, been out of print. It is often required reading in Urdu literature courses in India and Pakistan. This translation is based on the first edition. Changes reflected in the second edition are noted in the endnotes.

Readers will notice that the section titles in the original Urdu table of contents do not exactly match the headings in the text. This is in keeping with the original text, in which the latter appear in the margins. The text itself divides into sections rather than chapters, though the index of the lithographed first edition hints at major sections by employing a bolder, larger script. I devised the sections in the first table of contents of this translation. In other regards, the translation attempts to mimic as closely as possible the format of the original.

Although the main narrative is in Urdu, the travelogue also includes a considerable amount of Arabic and Persian, as well as a handful of phrases and a royal *farman* in Ottoman Turkish. In the interest of maintaining the multilingual character of the original, I initially considered transliterating all Arabic, Persian, and Turkish passages in roman script and giving translations in the footnotes. This method proved irksome and did little to enrich the experience of reading the text, so I decided to include the English translations of the longer Arabic, Persian, and Turkish passages in the body of the text and to put the transliterations in the endnotes and appendices. It proved impossible to translate all the passages into English in the body itself, since Shiblī often quotes a phrase, sentence, or passage, then translates or explains it to his reader in Urdu. To present both the original quotation and Shiblī's Urdu gloss in English would have been confusing. In these cases, the original is left in transliteration alongside Shiblī's translation, in parentheses. My literal translation is given in the endnotes. Shiblī also quotes from the Quran and the maxims of jurisprudential reason without glossing the meaning for his readers. In order to preserve the allusive nature of the original, I decided to retain these transliterations in the body and to give translations in the endnotes. Where appropriate, I have inserted English glosses into the body of the translation in square brackets. I have also noted some specific terms and proper names in brackets to facilitate comparison—for example, "Military Academy [Maktab-i Ḥarbiyah]." The original travelogue includes a handful of footnotes. These are marked by an asterisk and are maintained as footnotes in the translation. All numbered notes, which appear as endnotes, are my own and are intended to provide historical context. To facilitate comparison with the original Urdu, I have also included the page numbers of the 1894 first edition in brackets.

The travelogue contains a handful of English words transliterated into Urdu, some of which Shiblī glosses in parentheses. It also includes a large number of technical or specialized Urdu (and Arabic, Persian, and Turkish) terms now current in English. In keeping with the literalism of the translation, I decided that, where appropriate, Urdu words that are adequately glossed in the *New Oxford American Dictionary* (*NOAD*) should be left in transliteration in the travelogue. Readers are thus directed to *NOAD* for definitions of technical terms not included in the glossary, such as amīr (amir, emir), *fiqh*, ḥājī (hadji, haji, hajji), *namāz*, pāshā (pacha), qiblah (kiblah), ʿulamā (ulama, ulema), and *żikr* (*dhikr*), as well as nonspecialist terminology, such as crore, lākh, sāḥib, and *ustād*. In a few cases, standard American English spellings have been used to facilitate the use of the dictionary (e.g., *crore* instead of *karoṛ*).

In addition to the annotations, I have also included five appendices. Appendix 1 comprises biographies of (mostly) recent and contemporary figures mentioned in the text. Many of the figures have not been studied in English. Short biographies of the historical figures mentioned in the text are given in the endnotes. Appendix 2 comprises English translations of Urdu letters sent by Shiblī during and shortly after his travels. The letters shed light on the context of Shiblī's travels, offer details concerning institutions and networks in Istanbul not mentioned in the text itself, and hint at networks connecting archives, scholars, and literary cultures in South Asia to those in the Ottoman Empire and Egypt at the end of the nineteenth century. Appendix 3 translates three Urdu reviews of the travelogue written shortly after its publication. Appendix 4 includes English translations of a series of short newspaper reports, mostly in Urdu, but also including a short letter from Shiblī in Arabic, concerning the purpose, circumstances, and timeline of the journey. The notices were published in the college's organ, the *Aligarh Institute Gazette*. Appendix 5 comprises English transliterations of the one short and two long Persian poems that Shiblī wrote and included in the travelogue. The glossary comprises technical and specialist vocabulary either absent from or inadequately glossed in *NOAD*. The translator's afterword discusses the text in context. Points of focus include, inter alia, relevant biographical information about the author and broad discussions of Arabic literature, intellectual networks, Islam, and travel writing in Shiblī's world.

The translation adheres as closely to the literal meaning and form of the original as possible. It attempts to strike the elusive balance between readability and fidelity, to render the text both enjoyable and reliable. As an academic trained in Urdu literature and South Asian history, I place great value on literal translation. This is especially true in the case of the travelogue, since I consider it not only an enjoyable work of literature but also a historical document. As will be clear from the text, Shiblī wrote with a purpose. He aimed to educate and inform, and his prose evinces a concern with truth and accuracy. I have therefore attempted to adhere as closely as possible to the literal meaning of the text at the risk of occasional awkwardness.

This is the first complete translation of the travelogue into English. The only other full-length translation I am aware of is the Modern Turkish translation by Yusuf Karaca, which omits some passages of the original and includes some interpolations.[1] An abridged summary of the travelogue in Arabic has also recently been published.[2]

Acknowledgments

This project has benefited from the ideas, criticisms, and wisdom of more scholars, colleagues, students, friends, and family members than I can possibly hope to thank here. For their guidance on the translation and their help with the annotations, I wish to thank specifically Ahmad Agbaria, Muhammad Ilyas Azmi, Mardin Aminpour, Cemil Aydin, Douglas Brookes, Lisa Jardine Bruce, Samuel Frederic Coggeshall, David Commins, Aria Fani, Jim Grehen, Carol Hakim, Syed Akbar Hyder, Rishi Kant, Sara Lane, Adnan Malik, Gail Minault, Lynn Nyhart, Hussein Omar, Jeannette Okur, Ricardo Rivera, Devika Saxena, Kathryn Schwartz, Erkan Serçe, Wasim Shiliwala, Himmet Taskomur, and Sibel Zandi-Sayek. This project would not have been possible without their guidance and support. I am also grateful to the editors and staff at Syracuse University Press, especially Meghan Cafarelli, Suzanne Guiod, Brendan Missett, Kay Steinmetz, and Fred Wellner for their meticulousness, patience, and vision. All errors and shortcomings are, of course, my own.

Note on Transliteration

Turkey, Egypt, and Syria: A Travelogue is a multilingual text that reflects both the background of its polyglot author as well as the many languages and linguistic communities and traditions that he encountered during his travels. Shiblī wrote the main narrative in Urdu, but peppered it with excerpts from Arabic literature, phrases that he heard or spoke in Modern Turkish and Arabic, and original poetry in Persian. In the journalistic sections of the text, he records in detail and at length the names of scholars, journals, academic institutions, printing presses, cities, landmarks, urban districts, and monuments whose names are tied to Arabic, English, Italian, Persian, Turkish, and Urdu.

The multilingual and multiregional nature of the text compounds the difficulties of transliterating proper names into English. A great number of words and names in the text are shared among linguistic traditions, in which they are pronounced differently, and therefore conventions for rendering names into English differ among scholars of Arabic, Persian, Ottoman Turkish, and Urdu. Orthographical conventions in Modern Turkish further complicate the problem. Shiblī's name is a case in point. Urdu pronunciation suggests that it should be written *Shiblī Nomānī*. Arabic classicization requires *Shiblī Nuʿmānī*. Modern Turkish transliterates his name as *Şibli Numani*. The name of the bookseller in Beirut whom Shiblī met would be spelled *Abdul Basit* according to standard Urdu pronunciation, but *ʿAbd al-Bāsiṭ* in the *Encyclopaedia of Islam*, while Darwesh Pāshā's name is spelled *Derviş Paşa* in Modern Turkish.

To maintain consistency, I decided to transliterate all personal names according to an adapted standard that reflects, to the extent possible, Urdu pronunciation, but also adapts the schema of standard journals and encyclopedias, such as the *International Journal of Middle Eastern Studies*, the *Annual of Urdu Studies*, the *Encyclopaedia of Islam*, and *Encyclopaedia Iranica*. I prefer to spell the author's name *Shiblī Nomānī* to reflect its proper pronunciation in Urdu, but in this case, aesthetic and phonetic standards have been sacrificed for the sake of accuracy and consistency. Ottoman Turkish names and titles are thus transliterated according to the following scheme. Modern Turkish spellings are listed in Appendix 1 and cross-referenced in the index.

The goal of this system of transliteration is to represent as closely as possible the Urdu pronunciation of vocabulary while facilitating comparison among Arabic, Persian, Turkish, and Urdu. Thus, where it is common in Arabic to render ذ as *dh* and ض as *ḍ*, because neither of the Roman letters accurately represents the pronunciation of these letters in Urdu (in which they are homophones and pronounced *z*), I have instead used *ż* for ذ and *z̤* for ض. This system is both effective and readable, but it is also imperfect. For example, when the consonants ک (*k*), ز (*z*), and س (*s*) are succeeded by ہ (*h*) without an intervening vowel, the resulting transliterations will be indistinguishable from خ (*kh*), ژ (*zh*), and ش (*sh*), respectively. Such cases are rare, and it is hoped that context will resolve any ambiguity.

The first edition of the travelogue, like many Urdu texts of the late nineteenth century, does not always follow what have become standard Urdu spellings in the twentieth and twenty-first centuries. For example, it uses the aspirated h ہ and unaspirated h ھ interchangeably (e.g., لکہنا [*likhnā]* for the now standard لکھنا [likḣnā; to write]; but the standard بھی [bḣī; also]). It does not use the nasalized *n*, ں; instead, the non-nasalized ن (e.g., ہان for ہاں [yes]) is used throughout. Transliterations in the translation follow the spellings in the first edition of the Urdu. The transliteration scheme used in the translation is as follows.

آ	ā	د	d	ص	ṣ	ل	l
ا	a; i; u	ڈ	ḍ	ض	z̤	م	m
ب	b	ذ	ż	ط	ṭ	ن	n
پ	p	ر	r	ظ	ẓ	ں	ṅ
ت	t	ڑ	ṙ	ع	ʿ	و	o; au; ū; w

ٹ	ṫ	ز	z	غ	gh	ہ	h
ث	ṡ	ژ	zh	ف	f	ھ	ḣ
ج	j	س	s	ق	q	ء	’
چ	ch	ش	sh	ک	k	ی	ī; y
ح	ḥ			گ	g	ے	e; ai
خ	kh					*iżāfat*	-i
اً	an, un, in						
یٰ	ā						
ة	t, h						

Turkey, Egypt, and Syria

A Travelogue

COMPILED BY

Maulānā Shiblī Nuʿmānī

ENTITLED

Shams al-ʿUlamā' [Sun of the Scholars]

Professor of Arabic at the Madrasat al-ʿUlūm, Aligarh

Fellow of the University of Allahabad

Printed at the Mufīd-i ʿĀm Press in Agrah

First Printing (1,000 copies)

سفرنامۂ روم

و

مصر و شام

مرتبہ

مولانا شبلی نعمانی

المخاطب بہ

شمس العلماء

پروفیسر عربی مدرسۃ العلوم علیگڈھ۔ و فیلو آف یونیورسٹی الہ آباد

در مطبع مفید عام آگرہ طبع شد

طبع اول (۱۰۰۰ جلد)

Turkey, Egypt, and Syria

A Travelogue

In which, in addition to the small, interesting incidents that have arisen in the course of the narrative, the following circumstances related to Constantinople, Beirut, Jerusalem, Cairo, and so on, have been written in detail—that is, general circumstances of the city, sights worth visiting, famous buildings, the administration of the Department of Education, academies and madrasas, boarding houses and students, women's education, writers and their writings, libraries, newspapers and journals, encounters with famous pāshās and people of achievement, and the morals and habits of the Turks and Arabs. In the end, there is a very brief lexicon of the newly fashioned terms that have come into use in Egypt and Syria today, without knowledge of which, people cannot take advantage of Arabic newspapers.

Compiled by Shiblī Nuʿmānī

List of Subjects

List of Subjects

List of Subjects

List of Subjects

Note: On line 3 on page 230 [in the Urdu original], the word *ḥawāyaj* should be read instead as *awā‘ī*, and this word should be counted among the words in the alif [*a*] section.

Preface

In the Name of God, the Compassionate, the Merciful

With Praise and Prayers[1]

Although we did not reach the land of roses in the season of roses
We did not let the spectacle of autumn fall from our hand.[2]

The journey that I made to Constantinople, and so on, in auspicious Ramžān, 1309 Hijrī / [March/April] 1892 was purely a student's journey, and because it was neither an extraordinary affair, nor was there much rareness in the happenings of the journey, I had absolutely no intention of writing a travelogue. However, after I returned from there, the elders and friends whom I had occasion to meet all demanded a travelogue. I thought that since the custom of travel and journey stopped in our community some time ago, and for this reason absolutely no acquaintance with the true circumstances of the Islamic regions is acquired, this demand by the people was not out of place. I was reminded of my own situation when, before the journey, any time I met a traveler from Constantinople, and so on, I would spend hours asking about the circumstances of that place. [3]

These were the reasons that persuaded me to give order to these scattered pages. Otherwise, to record the circumstances of such a hasty and ordinary journey, and to give it the name *safarnāmah* or *kitāb al-riḥlat*,[3] would not have been devoid of small wit. The kind of information that is necessary and required in a safarnāmah, that is, the general circumstances of the region, the method of administration, the principles of the court, the particularities of business and commerce, and sketches of buildings; not even one of these is found in this safarnāmah. Of course, there are a substantial number of incidents related to social life and intellectual-scientific circumstances, although they too are not as detailed as they should be. In sum, whoever desires to see the *Safarnāmah* as a safarnāmah will not be able to derive full pleasure from this book. Still, this potluck of whatever was at hand can be presented at the table setting of people who take pleasure in even the ordinary events of Islamic regions, for *mā lā yudrak kulluh lā yutrak kulluh.*[4]

Although I have not discussed the civilizational and regional circumstances of the Turks in this book, nor was a discussion of this kind appropriate with respect to my position and status, the degree of cultural refinement and propriety of the Turks that will be established in the hearts of readers will be different from that which is expressed by the general literature of Europe.

The thoughts against Muslims that Europe formed in some age in the past were, for a time, expressed openly in such a way that the hue of religious prejudice was clear to see, and at that time this was an excellent means of general acceptance. But when the [4] power of religion declined in Europe, and religious anthems became entirely ineffectual, that policy took a turn. Now it was not thought to be so beneficial to write such clearly prejudiced words about Muslims. Instead, the learned, scholarly practice was adopted that the flaws of Islamic governments, Islamic nations, and Islamic society be laid bare in historical ornament, and these have become so absorbed in the literature by means of common writings, stories, novels, and proverbs that they cannot be separated even by a chemical solution.

Although this practice is employed with all Islamic nations, at this time our discussion lies with the Turks in particular. Not having contemptuous thoughts about Turks after reading European literature is precisely like not feeling drowsy after taking a soporific drug.

The circle of scholars in Europe is quite extensive, and for this reason there are people of every degree and class among them: prejudiced and good hearted, superficial and discerning. But in discussion of the Turks, this difference of degrees collapses entirely, and the same sound issues from every instrument.

For example, the straightforward and honest account of the truest of true European writers of today is that, in mentioning the Turkish government, he writes entirely straightforwardly of the heaviness of debt, the insufficiency of industry and technology, the absence of the expanse of education in the provincial districts, the dependency on Europe for weapons and armaments—all of this. But he so avoids mentioning the reforms that have taken place of late that it is as if reform does not exist at all. The administration of the treasury, the establishment of agricultural banks in all the provincial districts, [5] the progression of the number of *rushdiyah* schools from 96 to 405, the establishment of many large and great colleges, the extensiveness of the railway, the arrangements for discharging debt, the development of military power—he does not write about these events,* not even by mistake.[5]

An extremely easy method of proving a nation or a person praiseworthy or contemptable is to paint a one-sided picture of its circumstances and happenings, and the just truth of the matter is that Europe has used this deceptive method more than all other nations in the world.

No doubt, there are also beneficent people in Europe who have nothing to do with prejudice, but even their lack of prejudice is ineffective when confronted with the kind of thoughts among which they have been raised since childhood, the sources of information all around them, and the voices that enter their ears from all directions. One gentleman, who is an extremely unprejudiced and learned person and whom I have the honor of serving, returned from a journey to Constantinople and Egypt, and I asked in the course of conversation, "Did you also visit the Azhar Congregational Mosque in Cairo?"[6] He said, "I was very keen to visit it, but my guide said that Christians were not permitted to go there;" although this fact is purely erroneous. [6] I myself resided in the Azhar Congregational

* A separate book has been written and published in Constantinople detailing the intellectual-scientific and practical developments that have taken place in the time of the present sulṭān, and the tract by Rāsim Bey Āfandī discussing naval progress in particular has been published, the name of which is *Daur-i taraqqī* [The Age of Progress].

Mosque for more than one month, and my Christian friends used to come to meet me right in the masjid without any trouble. But because in Europe the prejudice and narrow-mindedness of Muslims is very nearly axiomatic knowledge, how could that ṣāḥib have had any hesitation in believing the words of his guide?

To crown all, if anyone says or writes something that deviates from the common thoroughfare, his voice is thought to be the voice of a parrot in the drum chamber of Europe. An English princess, having lived in Constantinople for fifteen or sixteen years, wrote a book by the name of *The Twelve-Year Governance of ʿAbd al-Ḥamīd the Second.*[7] Although to be taken as credible—the intellectual capability of the authoress, the experience of fifteen or sixteen years, the authentic means of discovering information—all the attendant requisites were present; still, because it was not of one voice with Europe in speaking of the faults of the Turks, it was not able to obtain the status of reliability and trustworthiness. We have heard educated people say of it, "It would be no wonder if the Turks themselves wrote the book under the name of an assumed author, or if favors from the sulṭān compelled the British princess to write such a book!!" But if the same book had been about the faults of the Turks, then (according to these people) every letter of it would have been absolute and certain. Even the essays that Professor Vámbéry has written drawing from his scholarly investigations into the cultural refinement and propriety of the Turks remained ineffectual for the very reason that the aforementioned professor had acknowledged the present intellectual-scientific progress of the Turks.[8]

Although this is the state of the common literature of Europe concerning the Turks, with respect to the occasion, we should [7] mention in particular the travelogues of Turkey, for it is from these very travelogues that the resources of European historical writings have also largely been taken. Although the travelogue is an interesting part of the historical tradition, it is as replete with erroneous suppositions as it is interesting.

A major error that commonly befalls the writers of travelogues is establishing generalizations from particulars. Human beings establish a general view of an entire nation from the character, habits, and ideas of the people whom they encounter on a journey, even though it is possible that these matters are exclusive to those few people alone. Similarly, they desire to derive a general conclusion from every occurrence, and neither desire to spend time in search of the specific causes of each occurrence nor have occasion to do so.

One major cause of error is that the person who travels to some country already has friendly or opposing ideas about it. After arriving there, whatever he sees and hears at first is purely superficial, and because such cursory familiarity is not sufficient for the derivation of conclusions, and he cannot wait long to form conclusions, he therefore interposes conjectures with every incident. While making such conjectures, the positive or negative notion that already existed in his heart continues to act in silence and the person is completely unaware. Although erroneous supposition of this kind is connected with all the nations of the world, the people of Europe enjoy special superiority in it, the reason for which is that no other nation is [8] as impatient to derive conclusions as the Europeans. It is the effect of this that when a common European traveler or politician happens to turn up in Hindustan, on the basis of the experience of just a week or two, he publishes major articles in European newspapers and magazines claiming that it is as if all the secrets of the society and civilization of Hindustan have been revealed to him.

Another major reason is that because the traveler is extremely eager to discover information, he desires to acquire some resource or means of information from every person he encounters. In this generalizing, he does not care to discern if the person is trustworthy or untrustworthy, enlightened or prejudiced, or someone with an eye for finer points or who only sees the apparent, and even if he does desire to do so, he cannot do so successfully. Europeans are even more incautious in this regard. Most European tourists who travel to Constantinople typically have occasion to stay in the hotels of Bayoghlī [Beyoğlu] and Ghalatah [Galata].[9] Wherever they want to go, a *gāyaḋ* (guide) is with them who not only takes them on a tour of the buildings and places, but also answers all the questions that they ask from time to time as needed.[10] These guides are generally Christian, and their rate is a rupee or two per day. Everyone can estimate for oneself what kind of information these guides can have.

Fāṭimah Khānam* has written in the preface of her book, "When the esteemed European women [9] whom I had occasion to meet would recount something relating to Turkish women as fact, I used to suspect that they were discussing some other nation or they were stories in the style of a novel." Fatimah Khānam has also given the opinion that, "It is not the fault of these poor people. They are compelled to believe whatever guides say to tourists." A guide also deceived our friend, who was deprived of a visit to the Azhar Congregational Mosque.

In sum, it was inevitable that my travelogue would be different from European writings and travelogues, although it would not have been befitting to go into such excessive detail in describing the reasons for this difference that it became its own separate subject or section.

It is not at all necessary to express here the impression that the journey to Turkey has left on my heart. This can be learned by reading this safarnāmah. Of course, it is necessary to say at the very least that if the status of the sultanate is set aside, then the condition of Muslims there, too, is not worthy of much joy or satisfaction. Rather, one should say that in a great many matters, it is very close to that of Hindustani Muslims. They have nothing to do with industry. They have very little share in commercial trade. Even the ordinary shopkeepers are Jewish or Christian. The old education is extremely defective [10] and continues to become more and more so. The complaint concerning new education that is made here is also made there. There is still enmity between the old culture and the new culture, and no composite temperament has been produced by mixing the two. Those of the old way of thinking are still unaware of the

*This is an extremely esteemed and educated lady who, in addition to Arabic, Persian, and Turkish (which is her mother tongue), knows French extremely well. In order to reform the kind of erroneous information about Turkish women that Europe possesses (see page 9) [8–9] she has written a book in the form of novel whose name is *Nisā' al-Muslimīn* [*The Muslim Women*]. This book has been translated into Arabic, and, having been presented at the American exhibition, has been translated into English under the care of that place. [The 1901–2 edition adds, "It has also been translated into Urdu, and has been published at the Muhammadan Press at Aligarh."] [Fāṭimah Khānam, *Nisā' al-muslimīn*, trans. Sa'īd Aḥmad (Aligarh: Muhammadan Press, n.d.)]

pace of the times. Those of the new taste do not do as much as they say. Instead of courage, dignity, passion, resolve, and fortitude, something like despondency has spread over the entire nation (predominantly). People are content with whatever circumstance they find themselves in. The present situation is, *laʿallallāha yuḥdiṡu baʿda żālika amran.*[11]

IT ENDED WELL

The Intention to Travel and Beginning of the Journey

The Reason for the Intention to Travel. At the time when the idea for the Heroes of Islam[1] occurred to me, the thought also occurred to me that the historical material that existed in our country could not in any way suffice for this purpose. It was this thought that initially produced the motivation for this journey in my heart because I was certain that such a series of compositions could surely be prepared from the balance of Islamic writings that remains in Egypt and Turkey.

Although this resolution had already become firm, for various reasons there continued to be a delay. So much so that for obvious reasons I became somewhat hopeless, and the resolution remained nothing more than a feeble idea. Last year, by a strange coincidence, this intention was set in motion, and, with that motion, was completed. I was often ill last year. So much so that, having grown weary of the treatments, I intended to have a change of climate. Accordingly, I wrote numerous letters to friends in Almora and Kashmir to arrange for a house, and so on. Meanwhile, I learned that Mr. Arnold, who is professor of philosophy at the academy and my ustād (I have learned French from him), was planning to go to Europe in the coming days.[2] At once the thought occurred to me that the journey to Egypt and Turkey, the change of climate, the company of Mr. Arnold—all these things had happened to come together; this moment should be considered an extremely great blessing. [2] Thus, right then I went to see the aforementioned gentleman to say, "I will go with you." He expressed extreme happiness and said, "As far as possible, I shall give you sufficient assistance in the necessary tasks of the journey."

At that time, only three or four days remained before the departure of the ship. When friends and dear ones heard, they were utterly astonished, and most tried to make me understand, "Such a great journey with such haste and lack of means; what kind of wisdom is this?" I said:

har chih bādābād man kashtī dar āb andākhtam.[3]

Summer vacation at the college is typically three months long. As per my period of employment, I was entitled to privileged leave of three months. Thus, putting both together, I had six months' leave, and on April 26, 1892, I left Aligarh. Mr. Arnold had departed for Jhansi a day or two before to meet with a friend of his. We met at Jhansi station, and the entire trip was spent in great pleasure and enjoyment. Mr. Arnold had informed Hājī Raḥmatullāh bin Da'ūd, who is an esteemed and enlightened merchant in Bombay, of his arrival by a means of a letter, in which my company was also mentioned. Because, as it happened, our prior arrangements had changed to some extent, we arrived at Bombay two days after the scheduled date. Mr. Arnold took his and my things to the Western hotel.[4] I was strolling around the market when I encountered a boy. I asked him, "Do you know Ḥājī Raḥmatullāh?" He asked, "Aren't you Maulawī Shiblī?"[5] I was amazed by this intuitive perception of his, which was nothing short of revelation. He said, "We have been wondering about you for two days," and said, "Please, come with me. Ḥājī ṣāḥib is expecting you." [3] Ḥājī ṣāḥib called Mr. Arnold, too, from the hotel, and we both stayed in his garden.

Our ship was to depart on the day after we arrived at Bombay. Thus, we spent all our time making the necessary preparations for the journey and were not able to tour the Islamic madrasas and societies that are in Bombay. We bought our ticket through the Cook Company.[6] The rate of a second-class ticket from Bombay to Port Said on the ship on which we were going was 210 rupees. I made the terrible mistake of not buying a return ticket, the result of which was that I was compelled to pay twenty-one pounds, that is 335 rupees, upon my return from Port Said to Bombay. We boarded the ship at nine o'clock on the morning of the first of May. At approximately twelve o'clock, the ship raised anchor and, reciting *bismillāh majrīhā wa-mursāhā*,[7] we said goodbye to Hindustan. There were only five travelers in second class, and by a curious coincidence all of them were from a different nation and a different race.[8] That is, one Muslim, one English, one Parsi, one Spanish, and one Siamese.

The Ocean Air. The motion of the ship did not seem too disagreeable at first. But around evening, my constitution began to change for the worse. I ate dinner and went to sleep. When my eyes opened in the morning, I was in a strange state. The discomfort from dizziness and nausea was too severe to describe. For two days, I remained in a state like that of fainting. The ship attendant sometimes brought tea, biscuits, and tangerines, telling me to eat something. But upon seeing those things, I would begin to retch. Mr. Arnold always drank tea. Even though it did not stay down, [4] one felt some relief by vomiting. At his insistence, I, too, drank tea a few times and vomited, and felt some benefit. On the third day, we all recovered and sprang to life. I had always heard that sea air was extremely beneficial for one's health and fitness. Truly, travel by ship stands out as one treatment among a hundred treatments. I was weak and feeble up to the time that I boarded. But with each passing day I became haler and heartier. My constitution was always cheerful and I had quite an appetite. We were given food five times a day, that is, tea, milk, and biscuits at eight o'clock in the morning; ordinary food at eleven o'clock in which there were dishes of numerous kinds; tiffin at one o'clock; dinner at five o'clock, in which, in addition to ordinary meat, there were chicken, duck, pigeon, puddings of every kind, and wet and dry fruits. Sometimes there was even *kulfi*.[9] Tea and butter at nine o'clock at night. We ate our fill at every meal and everything was digested.

A Christian's Prejudice against the Arabic Language. I kept busy all day, walking along, taking in the view of the sea. Mr. Arnold had begun learning Arabic. The Spanish Christian who was with us used to become heated about Mr. Arnold's reading Arabic. He would often come to him and pronounce the Arabic letters contemptuously in an extremely nasty voice, and would say, "This language is the language of camels." Although I was offended by these actions of his, such treatment of Arabs and the Arabic language by a nation that had lived with disgrace for a time under the hand of Arabs was not inappropriate.

Winged Animals Were Slaughtered in Accordance with Żabḥ. Because it is generally reported that winged animals are not slaughtered according to *żabḥ* on ships,[10] and Maulawī Samī'ullāh Khān ṣāḥib[11] [5] has even confirmed this in his travelogue, I abstained from eating fowl meat for a few days. Mr. Arnold asked me the reason for this. I said, "In our religion, an animal killed by strangulation is haram." He told me, "On this ship, fowl are slaughtered with żabḥ. They are not killed by wringing their necks." Because, according to sharia, his testimony alone was not sufficient, I went and confirmed this myself. The person doing the żabḥ was a Christian. He did not recite anything at the time of żabḥ. He just slid the knife across the throat. Although an animal slaughtered by this method of żabḥ is not halal among the Ḥanafīs, for a few days I became a Shāfi'ī on this issue, according to whom every kind of *żabīḥah* is permissible.[12]

On the ship, Mr. Arnold was no longer the Arnold that he was in Aligarh. Neither was there that seriousness, nor that standoffishness. He would often laugh and joke, play with children, and skip and jump on the deck. I began to write an ode[13] about the circumstances of the trip, and in fact the atmosphere of the ocean was so appealing and pleasant that a man of suitable and balanced nature could not help but break into a hum on a journey by ship.

The Despicable Actions of the Somali Nation. On May 7, 1892, the ship arrived at Aden and dropped anchor at a distance from the shore. A very interesting thing in Aden is that a great many boys of the Somali nation aboard dinghies come close to the ship and make all kinds of strange, disgraceful movements for reward from the people on the ship. Some dance and sing. Some come together and say a few meaningless words as they play their armpits. The remarkable thing is that people toss whatever they wish to reward them, *do-annī, chau-annī*, paise, into the ocean, and the boys dive in and retrieve it. Most Europeans were engaged in the spectacle, and Arnold, too, enjoyed it. But [6] my state was something different, for I mistakenly thought that this place was generally populated by Arabs. For this reason, it was natural that I should look at them with eyes of respect and affection. But they made such unbefitting and disgraceful movements for reward that my nature could in no way endure it. It was like a cautionary lesson that the state of the Arabs was now such that they were not ashamed to act this way in front of others. These thoughts filled my heart with grief. So much so that tears flowed from my eyes and *qumm yā 'Umar*[14] spontaneously issued from my tongue. Arnold was nearby. He noticed the change in my state. I described the condition of my heart and the reasons for it. Raising his eyes once, he looked at me and fell silent. When, having gone into the city to investigate, it was proved by all accounts that the Somali nation is not Arab, I was to some extent reassured. This very anger and offense was the reason that I have harshly ridiculed this wretched nation in my travel ode and, in truth, it deserves it.[15]

Because time was short, I could not see the interior parts of the city. I dispatched letters to Hindustan. On the heading of one letter I wrote these couplets, which were composed just then:

> When, intent on this journey, I girded my loins, with this intent of mine
> I cast both enemies and friends into writhing and twisting.
> All wondered: What is to be gained by it?
> For what have I cast myself into such affliction?
> Everyone gave me advice, and all said that I had,
> With these words, cast a mask from the cheeks of meaning.
> When they carried their insistence over the limit, I said, "Enough!
> Let come what may! I have cast my boat into the water."[16]

The Language of Aden. The language of Aden is generally Arabic, and the Parsis, Hindus, and Bengalis, [7] who live here on account of commerce or service, speak Arabic effortlessly. Because I had never heard the words of this sacred language from the tongue of a Hindu, I felt a strange pleasure seeing merchants and grocers[17] saying, "*Aina tarūḥ? Mā tabghī?*"[18]

The language here is Arabic, but it is extremely base and ineloquent. Although classical Arabic no longer exists in any of the regions where Arabic is spoken these days, the language of Aden is the most peculiar. Except for a few ordinary words, I could not understand anything. Most likely, the language of this place has reached this state after a period of continual degradation because of admixture with foreigners. 'Allāmah [very learned] Muqaddasī,[19] who was a renowned traveler of Arabia and who traveled the world at the beginning of the fourth century, writes in his geography, “The nations that reside in Aden are mostly Persian.” The aforementioned very learned scholar has also written, “They commonly say *kāf* [*k*] instead of *jīm* [*j*] here, and *rujlīnah* instead of *rujliyah*,[20] and so on.” When such was the state of things in the age of the ʿallāmah, what complaint can be made about the language of this place after the mixture of Marhaṫṫas and Gujaratis?

Strange and Wondrous Monkeys. In Aden, a German boarded our ship who is an employee at a famous German museum and is returning to Europe after living in these environs for some time.[21] By virtue of travel and trade, he was able to speak effortlessly in numerous languages. When he conversed with the ship’s officers in Italian, Arnold in English, and me in Arabic, I was seriously astonished and envious. When we all gathered at the dinner table, he was the one who acted as everyone’s interpreter. [8] He has collected many strange and wondrous animals from the jungles of Arabia and Africa. In one large cage, there were African monkeys whose appearance was somewhat different from ordinary monkeys. The most wondrous thing about them was that when, seeing someone coming toward them, they would cry out, and several letters seemed to come from the sounds that they made. At first, I thought that they were made-up words of some kind, just as we interpret the sound of cats as *miyā’on*, for example. But several times, when I listened closely, I clearly sensed the sound of *l* and *yāyā*. So much so that if some person had heard it from behind a curtain, he could never have thought that it was the voice of a monkey. When I mentioned this to Mr. Arnold, he, too, confirmed it. Probably because of examples of this kind, the idea has occurred to several people in Europe that monkeys, too, can speak. Thus, it is famously noted that after a period of experiment and research, one ṣāḥib has discovered several letters of this language.[22]

An Unpleasant Incident and Mr. Arnold’s Steadiness. Because in Aden new things of interest had been found, we were traveling with great pleasure. But the very next day, a dangerous incident occurred which kept me seriously worried for a while. When I awoke on the morning of May 10, a fellow traveler said that the ship’s engine had broken. When I looked, the captain and the ship's employees were indeed worriedly pacing about and were devising strategies to repair it. The engine had become completely useless, and the ship was moving along extremely slowly because of the wind. I became terribly worried, and some extremely disagreeable thoughts began to enter my mind. What else could I have done in this state of panic? I ran to Mr. Arnold. At that time, he was reading a book with extreme calm and composure. [9] I said, "Haven't you heard the news!?" He said, "Yes, the engine has broken." I said, "Aren't you panicked? What kind of time is this to read a book?" He said, "If the ship is to be lost, then this little bit of time is even more precious, and it is total stupidity to squander such precious time." Because of his steadiness and boldness, I also felt reassured and regained composure. Eight hours later, the engine was repaired and began to run as usual.

The ship arrived at Suez on May 13 and stayed for three or four hours. Egyptian Arabs brought paneer, dates, and bread to sell. One of them, understanding me to be Hindustani, began to speak with me in Urdu. I was surprised, and when I learned by inquiry that he had never seen the face of Hindustan, I was even more surprised at the worldwide reach of Urdu. On May 14, we arrived at Port Said, and with much regret I was forced to separate from Mr. Arnold. I had purchased a ticket to Brindisi from Bombay. Having arrived at Port Said, I thought, "I am with Arnold as far as Brindisi, but it is a week's journey from there to Constantinople. During that time, because I will have to deal with strangers and the foreign language and country, I will face difficulty in every task." On the basis of this thought, I changed the previous scheme entirely and decided that I would go to Constantinople by way of Syria.

When the ship anchored, a Cook Company employee came aboard to take care of his travelers. The ship stands at a bit of distance from the shore. Thus, a very small boat provided by the Cook Company is always ready to carry travelers ashore. [10] An inexperienced person faces serious difficulty when disembarking the ship at these ports. With the anchoring of the ship, coolies and sailors attack from every direction and seriously harass the travelers. Amid their throng, noise, shouting, and the snatching and seizing of luggage, travelers completely lose their senses. When, with a thousand difficulties, one finally reaches the shore, the debate and dispute over the rate lasts for hours. An excellent way to remain safe from these troubles is not to have any dealings with anyone except for the employees of the Cook Company.

When we arrived on shore, Shemūyal [Samuel], who was already standing waiting for us, stepped forward and shook hands with us. This man is of the Jewish nation and is appointed to look after travelers and to render them assistance of every kind. He knows numerous languages and speaks Arabic, English, and French extremely effortlessly. The best part is that he can speak in Urdu with extreme ease, the reason for which is that he has lived for some time in Hindustan. We went with him to his office. The office building is on the edge of the water and is nicely appointed with a table and chairs. On the desk are always found a great many newspapers, in which there is mostly news and advertisements related to ships. First, we spoke with him about having the ticket changed, meaning that if we disembarked here and bought a new ticket for Constantinople, could we receive the additional rate that we had already paid as far as Brindisi as a deduction or not? Because he could not answer the question himself, he went into the company's main office, and, upon returning, said, "You can go to Constantinople on the same ticket. You will only have to pay two pounds, meaning thirty-two rupees, more." I was very pleased and in reward for his good service gifted him eight rupees. [11] It was also a happy coincidence that the ship going to Constantinople was ready at that time. Otherwise, I would have had to remain at Port Said for fifteen days.

Port Said. Port Said is a small, beautiful port. The populated area has two parts. European merchants generally live in the part that adjoins the sea, and there are many large hotels, coffeehouses, theatres, and so on. One coffeehouse is right on the seashore and is quite spacious and atmospheric. Many small tables made of slabs of marble stone, and around them chairs, have been arranged with extreme attention to order and detail. Coffee, chai, toast, and butter are always available. The shops in this area are in abundance, and they are extremely grand and well appointed. The original residents of this place reside in the other part. But unfortunately, everything is in an extremely poor state. Instead of hotels, there are the dirty shops of cooks.

Initially, when I left to tour the city, I viewed everything with eyes of great interest and wonder because this was the first occasion on which I saw a populated area of the sultanate of Islam. (I had already had the honor of pilgrimage to Mecca and Medina, but that was the country of God, and I am talking about a worldly sultanate and government).[23] Whenever I saw a tall and magnificent building, I would become happy at the thought that "Praise be to God! In these regions, Muslims are prosperous and wealthy!"[24] But upon inquiry, I would learn that the building belonged to a European merchant. Not one excellent store or tall building in the entire city belonged to a Muslim. Alas!

In every land we reached, the sky is found.[25]

[12] Of course, there is a royal masjid at the end of the European settlement, and it is quite lofty and magnificent.

After wandering around the marketplace for a little while, I boarded the ship to Constantinople. Shemūyal and Mr. Arnold were with me. Because it was the time for ḥajj to Jerusalem, first and second classes were both filled with Christian ḥājīs. Mr. Arnold said, "I fear lest you be troubled. These people are strict adherents to their religious tradition, and therefore they are certain to hold some prejudice. You are of another religion, another nation. How will these people tolerate your company?" But from experience, I learned that Mr. Arnold was mistaken. Those people were adherent to religion, but they were French and Italian. They were not English. Thus, they lacked entirely the qualities of aloofness and the distinction between conqueror and conquered that are the special characteristics of a conquering nation. Mr. Arnold departed after a little while. I said goodbye to him, and, along with that, had the worrisome thought, "Let's see how it goes now, all alone."

On May 15, the ship arrived at Jaffa. Most of our European fellow travelers disembarked here. Jerusalem is only a night's journey from here. Because time was short, I could not disembark here.

On May 16, we arrived at Beirut. The ship generally does not stop here for less than two watches [six hours]. Because this is a historical place, and it is an extremely ancient city, I was very keen to see it. Having arrived on shore, I was faced with the great difficulty that they did not let anyone disembark there without a *tażkirah*, meaning a passport.[26] I had left Hindustan in such a hurry that I did not have an opportunity to obtain a passport. First, I became very worried that I would miss out on the visit. But then an idea came to me, and I said to the people, [13] "I do not want to stay here. My intention was only to visit." One of them, God knows how, recognized that I was from Hindustan. Thinking me to be far from home, he treated me kindly and sent a person with me: "He will take you on a tour of the city."

A Visit to Beirut. Because it was already my intention to stay here for a day or two on my return from Constantinople, I only cursorily toured the marketplace, and so on, this time. I looked through bookstores. There was a coffeehouse on the main thoroughfare. I stopped there for a little while and watched the passersby. Whenever a person passed in front of me in a carriage or on horseback with great glory and grandeur, I would ask my guide who it was, and he would mostly respond, "Christian."

The thing I liked most here was that all the shop owners and professionals, even the coolies and laborers, were extremely well dressed and clean clothed. After strolling around for three or four hours, I returned. I gave the guide an eight-anna tip, and, having taken leave of him, boarded the ship.

From Port Said, a Change in the Condition of the Journey. The novelty that occurred in the circumstances of the journey from Port Said was that, from Bombay to Port Said, there was no Muslim on the ship. Having arrived here, I caught a glimpse of one or two Muslims, and, in Beirut, the entire ship filled up with Syrian Arabs. Unfortunately, this honor did not fall to the lot of first and second class, but in third class there were Muslims and only Muslims in every direction. I had longed to see the faces of Muslims since the outset of the journey. Upon seeing this crowd, my happiness knew no bounds. The deck of first class was an extremely clean and spacious place, and I often sat there and took in the ocean view. But when this company fell to my lot, I did not set foot there again, not even by mistake. [14]

Initially, I met with severe difficulty in making friends with these people. These people were spread out all around the deck, and there were separate groups of two to four people each. I very eagerly approached them, but they paid absolutely no attention to me. Whomever I stood near raised his eyes toward me once and lowered his head. I was seriously stunned at this rudeness. I said in my heart, "And I had heard such praises of the hospitality of the Arabs! They have trouble making even casual conversation." Among them were several students from the Military College who had come to their homeland on break and now were going to Constantinople.[27] They sometimes read an Arabic dīwān, and so on, to amuse themselves. I thought that I should produce some acquaintance with them by means of our sharing a field of learning. Thus, I went to them and began to make a show of my *maulawiyat* and knowledge. Even then, they did not pay attention to me. I returned, feeling foolish and at a loss. But I was certain that there must be some reason for this. As it happened, one person asked me my religion. I said, "Islam." He said, "*Lā*! *Wa-Allāh*! *A hāżā ṭarbūsh al-Muslim*?"[28] meaning, "No! Would a Muslim ever wear such a cap?" Unfortunately, there was an Iranian cap on my head, and for this reason all the Arabs thought I was a Magian. When this mystery was solved, I removed the suspicion from their hearts and we became as inseparable as milk and sugar. So much so that they did not want to be apart from me for even a single breath. I mostly kept company with the students of the Madrasah-i Ḥarbiyah. From them, I learned some very important things about Constantinople, and, in truth, I benefitted greatly from the information.

The Effect of Islamic Government. The effect of our now being in the Islamic world was also noticeable on the ship. From Bombay to Suez, [15] the travelers in third class were treated like coolies. But in these regions, the situation changed entirely. Whatever the ship's officers and employees, who are generally European, thought of the travelers in their hearts, they could not mistreat them outwardly. There were numerous occasions on which I saw that it was the Muslims who were out of line, but the officers of the ship were forced to turn a blind eye.

Cyprus. On May 17, the ship arrived at Cyprus.* This is a small island, which is located in the Sea of Turkey, and which they call Qubruṣ in Arabic. This island is a monument of the classical conquests of Islam. Amīr Mu'āwiyah attacked it in the time of Ḥaẓrat 'Uṡmān (ra) in 27 Hijrī [647–48].[29] The people of the city signed a treaty declaring that, "Just as we give tribute to the sultanate of Turkey, we shall give you, too, 7,200 dinars per year, and if ever there is war between you and the Romans, we will not have any involvement with anyone." Amīr Mu'āwiyah accepted this condition. But in 32 Hijrī [652–53], those people, against their promise, gave assistance to the Romans against the Muslims. The aforementioned amīr attacked again with a fleet of five hundred ships and conquered it with extreme ease. Still, he allowed the amount of tribute and the conditions of the truce to remain the same. On his order, twelve thousand Arabs went and settled there and built buildings and masjids. After some time, this island fell from the hand of the Muslims, and, having been conquered several times, was lost again. At last, the Turks took it back from the Christians in 1570, and it was in their control until recently. In the last war between Turkey and Russia, the English took it on the condition [16] that the sulṭān would continue to receive the yearly tribute that he used to receive.[30] Thus, now there is English rule and English administration there.

Larnaca [Larnakah] and Limassol [Limāmūn] are two large cities on this island, and the ship anchors at both places for a short while. I visited Limassol. Because there is English governance here, there was no passport inquiry and inspection. When I entered the city, I was wearing an Iranian cap on my head and a *shirwānī achkan* on my body.[31] The people there probably had never seen this fashion. Wherever I passed by, people would look at me in wonder, and wherever I stood, a crowd of spectators would form. I first went into the congregational masjid. There is a

* It is written in books of geography that in the classical age there were 9 districts, 12 cities, 805 villages, and 10 lākh residents on this island. The Turks seized it in 1570. Now there are seventy thousand inhabitants. Larnaca's wine is extremely famous, and its silk, too, is quite excellent.

school adjacent to the masjid. There, a *maulawī* ṣāḥib, who was extremely dignified and well dressed, was giving lessons to the elementary ranks. I greeted him with *salām ʿalaik* [peace be upon you]. He stood up and, responding to my greeting with extreme kindness, indicated for me to sit. The boys were seated on tripod stools. I, too, sat down beside them. At the maulawī's indication, one boy read several verses of the Holy Quran. A wondrous effect came over my heart. I thought, "How could one even compare that desert of Hijaz with the distant islands in the Sea of Turkey?! What effect was there in this sacred word (the Quran) that, like electric force, it raced from the East to the West and still remains today?" That innocent boy also had a nice voice and read in accordance with the principles of recitation. As it happened, the verses were also effective. These things rendered me half-conscious, and for a while I was overcome by a strange, wondrous state.

Although the English have been ruling here for fifteen or sixteen years, they have maintained a great many old things in the style of administration with regard to policy. [17] The department of *qażā* is entirely separate, and the English government has no involvement with sharia cases.[32] I happened to pay my respects to the qāżī ṣāḥib. He is a very polite and dignified person. The method of education, too, is entirely in accordance with the Turkish system. In all the schools and madrasas, the books of the Turkish Department of Education are taught. In the school that I just mentioned, the Holy Quran, an introductory tract on fiqh [jurisprudence], history, and geography are included in the course, and instruction takes place in an extremely fine manner. I also visited this school when returning from Constantinople. It was in the morning, and the instructor ṣāḥib had not yet come at that time. Two or three boys were present. They treated me with extreme respect and good manners. One asked me, "Where is your homeland?" I said, "Hindustan." He said, "Hindustan is a vast region. Please tell me the name of the city, specifically." I mentioned Aligarh. He began to say, "I will see on the map where it is located." A map of Hindustan was hanging in front. He took a brief look at it and immediately set his finger on Aligarh and said, "Yes, this is it!" He was not more than nine or ten years old. Accordingly, I was surprised by his sharpness and memory. I asked, "Who is your king?" He said, "*Āfandim.*"

In Turkish, *āfandī* is synonymous with "lord and master." And when the first-person *m* is affixed, then the sulṭān is generally meant. I said, "But the English are ruling here." He said, "Yes, they have taken it on lease and they pay an annual tribute." The policy and practical philosophy [18] of the British is extremely wise, that when they seize control of a region, they do it so gradually and mildly that the people of the region are not even aware of the regime change.

The language of this place is Turkish, and this is also the language of every city and town from here to Constantinople. One can estimate the dominance of the rule of the Turks from the fact that they changed even the language of the conquered regions. Asia Minor is such a vast region, and an abundance of Christians reside in it whose language at some time was Greek or Latin, but now Turkish is spoken throughout the entire region. Although the maulawī ṣāḥib and qāẓī ṣāḥib of Cyprus, whom I mentioned, knew Arabic well, they could not speak it. Of course, they could understand ordinary sentences, and I spoke with them relying on these.

What accurate estimate of the state of the Muslims of this place could I have gained in such a short time? But by appearances one can reason that it is not good. Upon inquiry, I learned that whatever tall buildings and fine stores I saw all belonged to Christians.

The ship reached Rhodes on May 18 and stayed for three or four hours. This is a very small island whose extent our classical historians have described as sixty miles, and in the geography translated by the Aligarh Society, the length is written as forty miles and the width fifteen miles.[33] This, too, is among the classical conquests. It was conquered in the time of Amīr Mu'āwiyah in 52 Hijrī [672], and at that time many Muslims went and settled there. I was eager to visit it on account of its antiquity, but unfortunately it was nighttime [19] and none of the people on the ship would go with me. An even greater misfortune was that, as it happened, the same reasons confronted me on the return trip, and I was left entirely deprived of a visit to it.

On the morning of May 20, we arrived at Izmir. Because this is a very large port, the ship remained here for two days. I disembarked with my Syrian friends. There was the same tażkirah inquiry on the shore, but thanks to my companions, I did not have much trouble. This city, which in English they call Smyrna, is the headquarters of Asia Minor, and no city in this district is more expansive and populous. It is also a monumental location with regard to antiquity and historical events. The grave of Homer, who was a famous poet of Greece and about whom the thought of Europe is that he was the greatest poet in the world, is right here. One of the seven churches that are mentioned in the Book of Revelation in the New Testament was in this city. The vicissitudes of time have destroyed it ten times. Still, its current population is greater than one lakh. The land in the area is extremely fertile, and the city itself is a major center of trade. Scores of steamships and sailboats are always present in the port. The rail, too, runs here, and the train departs from here twice a day.

Islamic monuments are in abundance. People have recounted to me that the number of masjids is no less than three hundred, among which some are of great glory and grandeur.

When we disembarked the ship, we saw a series of extremely tall and glorious [20] buildings that stretched far into the distance in a straight line along the sea. These buildings are hotels, coffeehouses, dance houses, and the shops of Christian traders, and are extremely beautiful, spacious, and full of atmosphere. At night, it always seems that there is some festival or a wedding party. In addition to the coffeehouses and the dance houses, there is always a large crowd on the street, and wherever you go, you hear the sound of singing and sarod. Behind this series of buildings is the neighborhood of the Christians, and there are such tall and glorious buildings as I had never seen before. All the lanes and alleys of this neighborhood are extremely clean and level.

Having finished my tour of this neighborhood, I turned toward the city. Although the city is extremely vibrant and seems like a festival because of the large number of people, all the streets are uneven and unclean, and it is difficult to walk down the street because of the filth and mud. The reality is that in all these regions, the administration of the municipality is extremely bad, and this matter is extremely worthy of the attention of the Turkish government. As we were walking, our Syrian friends became hungry, and we went and sat at the shop of a *nān-bā'ī* [baker]. I did not have an appetite, but I joined at their insistence. By the word *baker*, our readers will probably have thought of the bakers of India and their vile shops. But this supposition is not correct. The look of the appointments at the most ordinary of ordinary shops here is that numerous small tables, and chairs around them, are arranged. An extremely clean sheet is spread on the tables. A tap is set up in one corner of the wall, and beneath it a basin, and to the right side, soap and a towel are laid out. This is the condition of extremely ordinary shops, and the large shops, [21] which can be called hotels [restaurants], are extremely elaborate and magnificent. But all the hotels of this kind generally belong to Christians.

I tried to tour the madrasas, but because it was Friday, all the madrasas were closed. I performed namāz at the Hisar Congregational Mosque [Jāmiʿ Ḥiṣār].[34] This masjid is ceremonious and decorated. There is gilt ornamentation on the ceiling. The great virtue of this masjid is that bells are set on two large pillars on both sides of the courtyard because of which, in addition to knowing the timings of namāz, the masjid is also decorated. It would be good if this were imitated in our Hindustan. There are several innovations in the sermons and namāz here, but neither do they have any basis in the sharia, nor are they suitable in their own right. When the preacher reads the sermon, he regularly stops in the middle, and at that time several people recite something in unison. When they become silent, the preacher begins again, and this happens several times. They generally read short sūras in namāz, which are not more than three or four *āyats*, even though throughout the entire world it is customary to read long sūras in Friday namāz.

After finishing with namāz, I went into the library. This is not a large library. It is a very small room in the corner of the masjid, and there are three or four small cabinets of books. After namāz, most ʿulamā and authors come and sit here. When I arrived, the following people were present: Maulānā Muṣṭafā Āfāndī, imam of the Congregational Masjid and instructor at the madrasa; Ṣabrī Āfandī, teacher at the *iʿdādī* school;[35] Maulānā Saʿīd; Shukrī Bey; and Ḥusnī Afandī, former secretary of education.[36] [22] After salām and standard greetings, one ṣāḥib declared, "We were just talking about an issue. If you wish, let the issue be raised again." I gladly agreed. It was a debate about *mutʿah*,[37] and the same famous point of uncertainty was before us that it is proven by the word of Ḥazrat ʿUmar (ra) himself that the custom of temporary marriage was current in the lifetime of the Prophet (saas). I discussed it in some detail and everyone present agreed. These people did not understand Arabic, so I spoke in Persian. This custom of debate and discussion is commonly practiced in these regions and is an extremely polite and proper custom. A foreign person has no easier and more beneficial means of meeting a group of ʿulamā and producing a connection and intimacy with them. Its great virtue is that disputation does not take place by reason of egotism and arrogance; rather, if during the discussion they come to know, by means of the addressee's manner, that he cannot successfully discharge his duty in the debate, then they purposefully bring up another topic. Intellectual-scientific assemblies of this kind were a major means of my success on this journey, and, in some places, thanks to them alone I obtained deliverance from difficulties from which there was no other means of escape.

The ship raised anchor around evening on May 21. There is no large station from here to Constantinople. The ship stopped at a few places for a short time each, but we could not disembark. These places are mostly for the necessities of war, and at each place the instruments of war are assembled in abundance. Chanāq Qilʿah [Çanakkale] is one place where there is an extremely secure fort. People recounted to me that when Muḥammad Fātiḥ[38] decided to conquer Constantinople, [23] cannons and cannonballs were not generally in use, and Muḥammad cast cannons himself and had clay cannonballs made, some of which have survived as memorials. These cannonballs are well built and extremely strong, and it is recounted that they are no less than iron cannonballs. From Izmir to Constantinople, such secure fortresses and barrier walls have been set up on both sides of the sea, and the provisions of war are in such abundance, that even the most powerful of powerful sultanates cannot attempt to attack the capital by this route. All these fortresses and fortifications are from the age of Muḥammad Fātiḥ. When this renowned *emperor* went forth with the plan to capture Constantinople, he had military cantonments built all around and had fortresses and barrier walls prepared. (But all the details in this section are peoples' oral reports. I have not confirmed this in the history.)

Moving beyond Chanāq Qilʿah, we saw a strange spectacle. The ship was moving quickly when from afar something appeared to be erupting like a fountain in the water. After a little while, I learned that four or five fish were racing toward the ship. When they came near, they joined the ship. One could clearly see their body through the surface of the water. Although the ship was going extremely fast, they kept right along with it. Sometimes, when they would gasp, they would hiss loudly, and at that time one could see something like a fountain erupting in the water. They raced alongside the ship for nearly two miles. All the people watched the spectacle in wonder. Several had the idea, "These fish have never seen the form of a ship. Thus, they thought it was some animal, and, in the passion of competition, [24] did not want the ship to be able to outrun them." During my return trip, too, just such an incident occurred, and at that time I discovered that the fish had happened to come to this place one time, and the ship's employees tossed something into the sea for them to eat. Greedy for this, whenever a ship passes through here, these fish often appear and race alongside the ship for a distance.

We arrived at Constantinople in the morning on May 23. The ship anchored. This was a time at which I should have been extremely happy to arrive at my destination, but in the commotion and shouting of the coolies and boatmen, I lost my senses; and the boatmen surrounded the entire ship. With their shouting, pushing, and shoving, a strange commotion had arisen. I had not determined beforehand, nor could I, where to go after disembarking the ship. A hotel was not appropriate to my situation (the reason for this will be made known later), and because of my foreignness and unfamiliarity, I could not be assured of or rely upon serais. The serious difficulty was that my Syrian friends, from whom assistance of every kind could have been expected, were in a hurry to reach the college. Thus, they could not wait for me. Finding me alone, the boatmen and coolies began to harass me even more. My distress continued to grow from the thought that if I had this much trouble on the ship on account of the foreignness of the language, how would things be in the city? It became later and later in this dawdle and delay. Most of the travelers had disembarked the ship and continued to disembark. Finally, I turned my luggage over to the steward and told him, "I shall return having toured the city." My intention was first to go into the city to make some arrangement for my stay, [25] then to remove my things from the ship. Some Arabs from

Syria had rented a boat. I, too, went along with them. There was passport inquiry and inspection on the shore. I showed my English papers, but they asked for a passport. In short, with a thousand difficulties, I was released. Now I was confused as to where I should go. On the boat, I was introduced to a Syrian Arab whose name was ʿAbd al-Fattāḥ.[39] I described my distress to him and said, "Please, tell me some reasonable way to proceed." He said, "My situation is nearly the same as yours. Thus, it is best that we stay together." Although this course of action was opposed to caution, I had to adopt it because of my unfamiliarity and the foreignness of the language. And if you ask the truth, this chance company was the preface of all my future success.

Hotels, Serais, and Places for Rent. There are several manners of lodging for travelers here. The greatest surety and ease is in hotels. However, firstly, their rate is no less than one pound, that is, fifteen rupees, per day. And second, most—rather, nearly all—the excellent hotels are in the European area, which is far from Istanbul, and all the congregational masjids, libraries, madrasas, and schools are in Istanbul.

After hotels there are *khānāt*, that is, serai, but these serais have no relation to Hindustan. Here, all the rooms in large serais are generally large, spacious, and attractive, and a bed made of woven strips, *toshak* mattress, sheets, blanket, and necessary things are always furnished in them. [26] There are several beds in each room, and the rate is eight or ten annas per bed.

The third method is rental houses. These houses are typically two or three stories. On each level are numerous rooms, and in each room, a table, chair, couch, lamp, carpet, bed, mattress, pillow, and blanket are provided. The rent per room is typically from ten rupees per month to twenty or thirty. The owners or leaseholders of these houses are generally Christian. They themselves also live in these houses, and because of them, travelers experience a great deal of ease.

Although, as I have just described, taking a house on rent would have been the easier option, my Syrian friend and I were both unaware of it. Thus, we went and stayed in a khān, meaning a serai. When I was satisfied with this arrangement, I went back onto the ship and had my luggage removed and brought. We lived in that khān for six or seven days. Then we took an excellent house near the *Bāb-i ʿālī* on rent.

The Circumstances of Shaikh ʿAbd al-Fattāḥ. Fortunately, Shaikh ʿAbd al-Fattāḥ, with whom I made friends by compulsion, turned out to be a person from a very esteemed family. Ḥażrat Shaikh Khālid Naqshbandī was a revered elder in Damascus to whom the people here are so devoted that they do not utter his name, rather, they refer to him with the word *ḥażrat* [his majesty].[40] This elder was nurtured in the pure soil of our Hindustan. That is, he was a disciple of Mirzā Jān-i Jānān Dihlawī.[41] Shaikh ʿAbd al-Fattāḥ is his fraternal nephew, and [27] because of this relationship, people hold him in high esteem. Because there is a large group of Syrians in Constantinople, ʿAbd al-Fattāḥ became acquainted with most people within just a few days, and, by means of him, I, too, was introduced to them in turn.

Meeting Shaikh ʿAlī Ẓabyān. One day, Shaikh ʿAlī Ẓabyān, whose father is a famous Ṣūfī, came to meet Shaikh ʿAbd al-Fattāḥ. I, too, was present at the time, and it just so happened that the tract *Iskāt al-Muʿtadī*, which is an old work of mine and is in Arabic, was lying in front of us.[42] Picking it up, he looked at it and said, "Aha! I saw this tract some time ago at my shaikh's place in Damascus, and he said of its author, "*Shakkar Allāh masa*"*iyah*."[43] When Shaikh ʿAlī Ẓabyān learned that the tract was written by none other than me, he stood up and embraced me with passionate warmth and treated me with extreme grace and kindness. I was extremely delighted by the fact that my insignificant writing had come all the way here and people looked upon it with eyes of acceptance, and in the loneliness of the journey, such a means of introduction felt like a great blessing. Shaikh ʿAlī Ẓabyān is a young man. He was educated in fiqh by Shaikh ʿAbd al-Raḥmān, who was the maternal grandson and student of the author of *Radd al-muḥtār* (known as Shāmī [the Syrian]).[44] Although he has aptitude in most of the current sciences, he has the greatest mastery in literature. He presented an undotted *qaṣīdah* in praise of the sulṭān, upon which he received reward and recompense. He has been a guest of Darwesh Pāshā for some time and the aforementioned pāshā treats him as a dear friend.[45] His relationship with me grew stronger by the day. So much so that despite the great distance, he would come to my place nearly every day and sometimes would stay with me for the entire day. [28] Shaikh ʿAbd al-Fattāḥ returned to Damascus after a few days. Alone, I might perhaps have run into hardship at that time, but Shaikh ʿAlī Ẓabyān's sympathies removed all anxiety from my heart.

Although the house that we had taken on rent was extremely spacious, attractive, and elegant, because the landlord (temporary) was extremely dishonest in business and vagrant in temperament, after a few days, I took another house on rent and stayed there until the end. Here, not only was the place very nice, but it was also a great comfort that the landlord was a kind-natured woman. Although she was Christian and was of the Italian nation, she could speak Arabic as needed and had special closeness with Muslims.

We had no need for arrangements for food and drink. Hotels and shops are in abundance, and they are extremely neat and elaborate. To eat in the marketplace is absolutely not a matter of disgrace here. I often saw esteemed officials eating in hotels. These hotels generally belong to Christians. The shops of Muslims, except that there are also chairs and tables there, in all other respects resemble the shops of Hindustan.

The qaṣīdah that I began to write on the ship came to completion upon arrival at Constantinople. Included in it is a summary sketch of the circumstances of the journey, and because readers, having become familiar with the details of all the circumstances, will be able to understand well the allusions in the qaṣīdah that require a backstory and will take more enjoyment and pleasure in it, I copy the qaṣīdah in its entirety here. [29]

Ode[46]

For both the completion of my subject and in search of edification,[47]
For ages it has been my intention to travel.
Having fulfilled the duty of ḥajj and pilgrimage by God's decree,
I desired to journey to Turkey.
Although I burned with desire and was eager to make haste,
By the dictates of fate, postponement continued.
There was such a delay that the spiteful said,

"So-and-so has nothing in his head but half-baked desire.
As if Turkey were just two or three steps away, this dreamer of half-baked dreams
Has, without a care, tightly girded his loins for the journey.
The path is so long and the journey so perilous;
How is it achievable by one who has neither power nor gold?"
I worried and suffered greatly in this frustration and grief.
Suddenly, the manifestation of my desire walked through the door.
There took place a wondrous coincidence which unraveled this knot,
Of which even imagination and thought were unaware.
A couple of months before I beat the drum of departure,
My heart was frail and burnt from the strife of fever.
When I became weak with fever, it occurred to my heart,
"There is no remedy but a change of place, here and now."
I remembered my longstanding intent and thought it would be nice
If the Lord accomplished two tasks in a single act.
Arnold, who is both my colleague and my teacher,
Also planned to travel to England at the time.
I thought to myself, "Such company and such an occasion rarely occur."
Thus, I leapt eagerly from my place, intent on this journey.
When all became aware of my intention,
News also spread to friends and dear ones at home.
The kindness of all was stirred, and hearts ached.
All said, "Do not go to this useless trouble. [30]
Do not set hearts in separation; and do not forsake the way of fidelity.
And if you will not retreat from this path,
Rest a few days, then arrange
The provisions of the journey in a way that is suitable.
Take enough cash and goods with you that
There will be no danger or worry if you stay long.
It is best not to make this journey alone;
You must also bring along a servant."
I said, "All that you have said is a wise counsel,
But the seeker-student is not in the game of profit and loss.
When a man takes a step forth at this stage,

He does not withdraw it, even if it brings death."
In short, it was from the twenty-sixth of Ramžān that I
Rose fervently from my place and set out upon my journey.
For a time I traveled through mountains and deserts,
Then I and other friends boarded a ship.
I endured trouble and hardship for two or three days on the ship,
It so rose and fell at every moment because of the waves.
No one had the power to lift his head from his pillow.
No one had the power to separate his body from his bed.
Nothing on the ship causes torment
Except for this three-day trial, from which there is no escape.
Bread and foods of every kind were available to us,
Lamb kabob and chicken and wine and fruits and sweets.
Although I did not pollute my lip with that pure wine,
Others, by contrast, quaffed from the goblet.
On the seventh of May, when we reached Aden,
The ship came to rest and dropped anchor for a while.
I disembarked and turned toward the city
In order to find information about the desert and towns of this region.
It is a mountainous area, in which, although it is high and vast,
There is no trace of greenery or flowers.
Every place you pass by, there is flowing sand and clay.
Every place you go, there is black dust and stone. [31]
The Guebres and Christians[48] who have settled in this place
Spoke entirely in the Arabic language.
The people of the city, who call themselves Somali,
Are animals. No. In fact, they are even worse than animals.
Wretched, ill-fated, ruinous, black-skinned, and disgusting.
Vile, contemptible, perverse, and bad both by substance and by birth.
They have attached themselves to Arabia, but heaven forbid that
The Lord approve of such base and vile ones!
Because the language of all is Tāzī [Arabic] and, just like the Arabs,
Their name is tied to the title of their ancestors and fathers,
Common people fall into error and incorrectly believe
That they are from the lineage and descent of Ma'd and Mužar.[49]

The seed, and the roots, too, of this tree are from the soil of Ḥabash;[50]
It has bloomed and scattered fruit in this place.
In the evening, our ship set out again
And passed through the Red Sea for a week.
It came to Suez and came to a stop and it happened so quickly
That I was not aware of its condition or state.
This is that wondrous channel, of such a feat
I had never heard except in ancient tales;
It is twenty leagues long and so wide
That two steamships can pass through it.
A Frenchman named Lesseps[51]
Designed it and became famous throughout the world.
When in the beginning that wise man made the claim
That one could bring the task to completion,
The people mocked him and said that this
Was foolishness which no wise person would believe.
It was from the fourteenth of May that we arrived
At Port Said and boarded another ship.
Separation befell Arnold and me,
For my path and his parted at this crossing.
The port is a place filled with skiffs, boats, and steamships
As far as the eye can see. [32]
See a hundred that have raised flag here;
See a hundred that have dropped anchor there.
In the evening, our ship set sail again and passed
By way of Jaffa and then stopped at Beirut.
I went ashore and a man of the sons of Aleppo
Accompanied me and became my guide in every quarter.
It is a nice place where he cannot help but give away his heart
Who has fervor and passion in it.
It is a pleasant place, a fine spot to visit, and an attractive location:
Roads, even; land, clean; buildings, spectacular.
Giaours and Muslims alike, all well dressed and fine in form.
Elite and common, all rose-hued bodies and beautiful faces.
Their clothes resemble Arabia, as do their uniform and dress.

There is no difference between Muslim and nonbeliever.
When I left this place, it was because I had no choice.
I went ahead and my eye turned back once more.
It was the sixteenth of May when we departed.
Then at dawn we reached Cyprus.
This is the ancient place which, in the age of Amīr (meaning Amīr Muʿāwiyah),[52]
An army went to seize, and victory was augured.
At present, the government of England has taken it from the Turks,
But in peaceful treaty, not by aid of sword and hatchet.
I saw the congregational masjid and palace of Cyprus.
My visit to this place gave rise to more wondrous signs.
Rhodes and Chios[53] appeared along the way, and, after that, Izmir.
The ship stopped at Izmir and spent one night there.
I went to the city and saw, one by one,
Masjid, school, market, street, alley, and door.
I performed my Friday duty and, after prayers,
I happened to pass by the *sulṭānī* library.
An assembly of jurisprudents was gathered there.
A discussion of mutʿah and the words of ʿUmar was underway.[54]
One of them turned toward me, "How are you? What are you?
Why have you tied the garment of toil at your waist?" [33]
I said, "I am from Hind, a beggar for crumbs from the table of culture;[55]
I carry away something from every place and country."
He said, "Just now discussion of mutʿah was underway, and you, too,
If you can, should speak a few words and give example."
In response, I knocked on the door of meaning and the audience
Opened lips of praise after debate and deliberation.
Then I departed from Izmir and in the span of two days
This route was traversed, and this volume reached its end.
I have written these letters briefly, and you, too, know
That in this lonely wilderness, the traveler is in straits.
Anyone who seeks the circumstances and details of me and my journey
Should be told to read this poem from end to end.

Summary History and Brief Circumstances of Constantinople

Summary Ancient History of Constantinople. Before I give an account of the detailed circumstances of this place under separate headings, it is necessary that I give an account of its ancient history extremely briefly, and, along with that, its general present circumstance with cursoriness. The initial history of this city (meaning when it used to be called Byzantium) is extremely ancient, but not a very short period of time has passed since its name has been Constantinople.[1] Constantine the Great laid its foundation in 476, and from that time until the age of Muḥammad Fātiḥ [Mehmet the Conqueror], it remained the seat of the throne of the Caesars of Rome [Rūm (Turkey, Byzantium)]. Its circumstances are found in extreme detail in English and present Islamic geographies. It is also mentioned in classical Islamic geographies. However, except for Ibn-i Baṭūṭah, I do not know of any Islamic author who has written an eyewitness account of the events of that time.[2] [34] Ibn-i Baṭūṭah saw this city in 725 Hijrī [1324–25]. At that time, there was a Christian government here. He writes, "This is an extremely magnificent city, and because it is divided by a channel of water, it has been separated into two parts. One part, which is on the eastern shore of the channel, is called Istanbūl, and this is the part in which the Caesar of Rome and the members of government and amīrs live. The other part is named Ghalaṭah. The great traders of Europe generally live in it, whom the Caesar forcibly keeps in his obedience."[3] Ibn-i Baṭūṭah has praised the extent of trade of these merchants and ridiculed their filthiness. He writes, "When I entered this city, in addition to small boats, nearly one hundred large ships were present, but the entire market is extremely dirty and foul, and even the churches are no exception to this."*

Muslims had looked upon it with eyes of conquest in the very first century. Thus, the first to strike a sword on the iron door of the city walls, ʻAbdullāh bin al-Muṭṭalib,[4] was the general of Caliph Walīd bin ʻAbd al-Malik.[5] After that, other caliphs and sulṭāns also attacked it. But the end of the Caesar of Rome was to be at the hands of Muḥammad Fātiḥ, who raised the standard of Islam in place of the cross above this magnificent capital of the sultanate in 857 Hijrī [1453]. The thing about this astonishing conflict that is worth remembering is that because the Christians had blocked the way to the port by sea, the Turks [35] spread out wooden boards for five miles on the rocky terrain that lies between the Bosphorus and the Golden Horn, and, by driving ships to which they had attached wheels across it, conveyed all the armies to the Golden Horn. At that time, the age of this renowned Fātiḥ was twenty-three years. The chronogram of the conquest is *baldatun ṭayyibatun*.[6]

Present Condition. The present condition is that the city is settled on both shores of the branch of the Bosphorus Strait, which stretches far off into the distance, and for this reason it has two parts. One part is called Istanbul, and all the large masjids, libraries, and tombs of the sulṭāns are in this part. The population of Muslims, too, is in abundance here. The second part begins with Perah, and at its far side are located Bashikṭāsh [Beşiktaş], and so on, where the sulṭān's royal palace and the hall of justice are. On the other side of Perah [Pera] is Ghalaṭah [Galata], and because all the major European traders and consuls of the sultanate reside here, it is more appropriate to call it the European settlement.

They say that no city in the world is as scenic as Constantinople, and the truth is that with respect to scenery, one cannot even imagine being more beautiful than this. For this reason, they call its harbor "Golden Horn" in English, meaning *sunahrī sīng*.[7] Here and there, a series of buildings lies

*I have copied Ibn-i Baṭūṭah's description so that you would be able to compare it with the present state of things.

right on the edge of the sea and stretches far off into the distance. The land that is in front of the buildings is extremely level and clean. Its surface is perfectly even with the surface of the sea, and a stunningly beautiful scene has been produced there.

An estimate of the extent and civic development of the city can be made from the fact that in Istanbul alone there are five hundred congregational masjids, [36] 171 bathhouses, 324 serais, 164 classical madrasas, 500 modern madrasas, 12 colleges, 45 libraries, 305 hostels, and 48 printing presses. There is such an abundance of business and traffic that numerous tramways, public cars, twelve steamships, an underground rail, and ordinary rails (which leave after every half hour), run at all times, and despite this, there is still such a crowd of pedestrians on the streets that it seems like a festival at all times. The toll for crossing the bridge that lies between Ghalaṭah and Istanbul is one paisa per person. Its daily income is no less than five or six thousand rupees.

Coffeehouses. Coffeehouses are in extreme abundance. In my estimation, there must be no fewer than four or five thousand. Several of them, whose buildings seem like royal palaces, are extremely magnificent. All kinds of sherbets, chai, and coffee, and so on, are always available in the coffeehouses. Most coffeehouses are on the seashore, and some are right in the sea, for which a wooden bridge has been built. Daily newspapers, too, are available in the coffeehouses. People go on drinking coffee as they read the newspaper. In Constantinople—rather, in all these regions—coffeehouses are counted among the necessities of life. When my Arab friends heard from me that there is no such custom in Hindustan, they used to say in astonishment, *bi-aish yatasallūn*,[8] meaning, how do people amuse themselves there? In these regions, coffeehouses are places for meeting with friends, and for the warmth and passion of company and conversation.

Alas, Hindustanis have no taste for such things. They just do not know [37] how necessary public intercourse of this kind is for the pleasure of life and what kind of effect it has on the uplifting of one's constitution. Friendly assemblies take place in our area, too, the method of which is that a few friends sometimes come to sit together at the house of a friend.

But there are two great defects in this method. First, sessions of entertainment should take place in atmospheric locations so that bodily health can benefit from fresh and fine air. Second, it is a serious flaw that because these sessions are private sessions, no conversation takes place in them except for backbiting, complaint, and nonsense of this kind, as opposed to coffeehouses, where, because of the public gathering, one cannot find occasion for things of this kind. I always sat with friends in coffeehouses in the evening in Constantinople and Egypt, but I never heard discussions of this kind. No discussion except for joking and jest took place there, nor could it have taken place.

Examples of European and Asian Civilization. One great special quality of Constantinople is that if someone wishes to view an image of European and Asian civilization in a single folio, then he should see this place. Tour the shops of booksellers, and on one side is an extremely large shop. There is a floor of marble stone. There are extremely beautiful glass cabinets. All the books are bound, and the bindings are not ordinary, but rather generally gilt and gilded. The owner of the shop is seated, having set up a table and chairs. Two or three young, well-dressed boys are busy at work, moving this way and that. You set foot in the store. A boy brings a chair and sets it in front of you, and hands you the catalogue of books. The price is mentioned in the catalogue, and bargaining for more or less is not permitted. [38]

On the other side, a disorderly pile of books is set on platforms on the side of the street. The carpet for seating is laid out on the floor, and it, too, is so small that there is not space for more than four people. A period of some hours is required to settle on a price.

Similarly, shops of both types, of every profession and industry, are found. The same is true of public cleanliness and elegance. Look at Ghalaṭah, and it seems like a piece of Europe. Stores: tall, appointed, and decorated. Streets: broad and even. There is no sign of dirt or filth anywhere. By contrast, in Istanbul, where the population is largely comprised of Muslims, most streets are unclean and in some places so uneven that it is difficult to walk.

Reason for the Difference in Conditions. Having come to this city, the first thought that will come to the heart of a traveler will probably concern why there is such a difference between the two parts of this glorious capital. Thus, this thought came to my heart at first. I discussed and researched this a great deal. I easily came to know the reason for the difference in the conditions of the residents. That is, the poverty of the Muslims and the wealth of other nations. But ostensibly this could not be considered the reason for the filth and unevenness of the streets and thoroughfares. Thus, I inquired of an esteemed Turkish officer, Ḥusain Ḥasīb Āfandī, police commissioner.[9] He said, "Our municipal taxes are very low. A great many things are exempt from tax collection, but in Ghalaṭah, the European merchants pay high taxes of their own accord. [39] Thus, the municipality can spend those amounts generously." I thought, "This is the same Ghalaṭah regarding which Ibn-i Baṭūṭah has harshly complained of dirtiness and filth. Now they have such care for cleanliness and tidiness that they pay large taxes for it." The fact is that cleanliness and propriety have become the leaven of Europe these days.

The Form of the Buildings and Fire. The buildings here are of a form completely different from the buildings of Hindustan. Houses are usually of three or four stories. There is absolutely no courtyard. All the buildings are made of wood. The homes of major amīrs and pāshās, too, are made of wood, and this is the reason that fire often breaks out here. No month, rather, no week passes without two or three homes burning to ruin, and sometimes entire neighborhoods are burnt to ashes. Extreme care has been taken and arrangements made by the sulṭān for extinguishing fires. Several hundred people are appointed especially for this work. An extremely tall tower has been built on which several workers are present at all times, so when they see fire breaking out somewhere, they immediately sound the alarm. Other small towers of this kind have been set up all around. When fire breaks out somewhere, canons are immediately fired, and fire-extinguishing workers from every part of the city arrive at the site with all their instruments. They have been ordered to continue rushing headlong, so much so that if someone walking down the street is crushed by their onrush, there is no criminal accusation. I asked people why the buildings were not made of stone and learned that they are quite uncomfortable in the wintertime, and bodily health suffers. [40]

Climate. The climate here is extremely excellent. It is extremely cold in the winter, and sometimes it even snows. The warm season, which I experienced myself, is so pleasant that it cannot be described. It is a wonder why the amīrs of our area do not travel to Constantinople instead of Shimlā and Nainītāl.[10] The water comes from the mountains and is extremely agreeable and conducive to digestion.

Fruits. Fruits of every kind are in abundance, and the grapes and melons in particular are incomparable. The melons of Lucknow are perhaps a bit ahead in delicacy, but they cannot equal the melons of this place in sweetness. Guavas, which the Arabs call *injās* [pear],[11] are of a strange conical shape, similar to carrots, not in color, but in form. But they are extremely sweet and delicious. The apples are bigger and sweeter than the apples of Kabul. There is a fruit here they call *mishmish* [apricot].[12] It is somewhat similar to the *jāmun* of our area.[13] Fruits of every kind are extremely inexpensive. Grapes are at most two annas per seer. Apples, the best of the best, two for a paisa. And so on.

Dress and Fashion. The dress and fashion is entirely European. From outward appearance, it cannot be known if a person is Muslim or Christian. Christians and Jews all wear a red cap, which could have been the distinguishing dress of the Turks, and for this reason there is no means of distinguishing between the nations. In one respect this practice is good because the more the traces of difference among different nations are eliminated, the more beneficial it is for civilization. But in matters of social necessity, it leads to serious problems. [41] I often faced difficulties because of it, and I always thought that if Ḥaẓrat ʿUmar gave the order to the Christians to restrict themselves to national clothing, he was right to do so. The astonishing thing is that the religious group here, meaning the ʿulamā and teachers, too, could not escape the effect of Europe. There are buttons on their pajamas, like pants. The only difference is that they are wide and loose on top and are beautifully pleated. Instead of a kurta or achkan, there is only a *wāyiskōṫ* [waistcoat]. They wear a robe on top of the waistcoat, and this is the distinguishing symbol that separates them from other groups of people. The influence of Europe is also found in the fact that they do not fasten the buttons of their robes, and the waistcoat remains open from the front. These people, too, generally use the Turkish cap, but a band of white fabric is wrapped around it, which they call a *laffah* in Arabic, and it is considered the special symbol of the scholars. I shall write details of women's clothing in the discussion of women's culture and society.

Congregational Mosques and Royal Palaces. The excellent buildings and monumental buildings of this place are the congregational masjids and royal palaces. Discussion of the congregational masjids, with some degree of detail, will come later under a separate heading. They call royal palaces here sarāe [serai]. Their number is twenty or twenty-one, and all are located at far-off distances. These buildings are from the time of different sulṭāns and are buildings of extreme grandeur and glory. One palace, which is made of marble from top to bottom, is right on the edge of the sea and is extremely large, lofty, and beautiful. When the emperor of Germany was recently a guest of the sulṭān, this is the palace in which he stayed.

No Town Hall. It is a matter of great wonder that in the entire city there is no town hall. Even the public garden, meaning [42] the *bāgh-i 'āmah*, is so small that it does not befit this magnificent capital.

Courts. The courts (except for one or two) are all located in one place, and they call this collective building the Bāb-i 'Ālī. The office of the prime minister is also here. These buildings are not so magnificent. The High Court, which they call the Maḥkamat al-tam'īz here, is at a distance from the Bāb-i 'Ālī. Although I did not go inside it, from the outside it seems like a very glorious building. The court of the police commissioner is in Ghalaṭah. I toured it well. The building is not so remarkable, but it is extremely orderly and well appointed. A very valuable Turkish carpet is spread out in the assembly room. The chairs, too, are extremely beautiful and elegant. I also saw the office of Maʿārif, meaning the Department of Education. It is an ordinary building, but due to cleanliness and orderliness, it seems attractive.

The Progress of Education in Colleges and Schools

Education. If I could have had any other purpose in this distant journey apart from visiting libraries, then it was to gain an estimate of the style of education and progress of education here. Thus, I paid more attention to it than to all other matters, and, to the extent that I could, I spared no effort. However, readers should not expect that I was also entirely successful in my objectives and that my educational report will be a complete report. The efforts that I was able to make for inquiries were that I went to the office of the Department of Education several times, inquired after matters requiring investigation from the officers of education, [43] went and saw large, important colleges and schools myself, met teachers and professors, and obtained the yearly reports of the colleges. But even with all these efforts, one cannot achieve complete success here. It is a strange practice among the Turks that they look at every single thing from the perspective of politics, and for this reason they do not like for any matter of business to come onto the public scene. The report of the Department of Education that is published with the annual record is extremely brief and purely summary. So much so that the salaries of the professors and teachers are not even mentioned. The reports of some colleges, for example the Maktab-i Ḥarbiyah [Military College] and the Maktab-i Sulṭānī [Imperial College], are published separately, but there is nothing in them except the results of the examinations and the curriculum of instruction.[14]

At first, I thought that I had few means of access, and this was why I could learn very little information, but when I read the book by Khair al-Dīn Pāshā, wazīr of Ṭūnis, I was consoled.[15] Where he has discussed Turkey and has written the state of its civilizational and educational progress, he has employed extreme cursoriness, and has apologized, saying, “The information about Turkey that I have written, I have written by means of English books, and for this reason could not write in detail. But not even this much can be found in the writings of Muslims." After this preface and apology, I begin my principle purpose.

Different Methods of Education. Classical Education. Modern Education. In Constantinople, rather, in all the Islamic regions, there are two methods of education: classical and modern. Classical education began with Turkish rule. Thus, Urkhān (died 761 Hijrī) [1359–60], who was the second emperor in this line, established a madrasa in Iznīq [İznik], and this was the first madrasa that was established in the Ottoman regions.[16] After Urkhān, other sulṭāns attended to education with royal ambition and established hundreds of academies and madrasas. [44] Thus, in my treatise, *Guẕishtah taʿlīm*, a full, detailed account of this can be found.[17] The history of new education begins from the time when Turkish government, having left the Asian mold, entered the European mold. The founder of this revolution was Sulṭān Maḥmūd, who first adopted European fashion and equipped his army in the manner of Europe.[18] This same modernizer[19] laid the foundation of the Military College in 1250 Hijrī [1834–35],[20] which was the first college of modern education. This college still exists and is the center of all military madrasas. After Sulṭān Maḥmūd, in 1261 Hijrī [1845–46], Sulṭān ʿAbd al-Majīd[21] further extended modern education and established the rushdiyah schools.[22] Since then, this education has continued extensively and is making progress daily. Four levels of modern education have been established.

Elementary Education. *Ibtidāʾiyah* [elementary]. Its duration is at most five years, but an intelligent and astute student can progress having finished it in two or three years, rather, in just a year or two. In it, instruction is given in the Glorious Quran, the Turkish language, Arabic spelling, script, and arithmetic up to long division.

Rushdiyah [Secondary Schools]. Duration of education: three years. Instruction is given in Turkish dictation, elements of the Turkish language, Turkish syntax, the tenets of Islam in the Turkish language, all four parts of arithmetic, French, Arabic, geography, geometry, the principles of commercial bookkeeping, and cartography. This level is approximately equal to the "middle" of our area, or somewhat ahead of it.[23]

I'dādiyah [High Schools] and the Number of Its Students. After rushdiyah is *i'dādiyah*, which can be called "entrance." In 1892, the collective number of students of this class was 5,215. This includes the madrasas of all districts as well as the capital itself.[24] [45]

After i'dādiyah are different specialized colleges, for example, the Civil College, the Legal College, and so on, a detailed description of which will come later.[25] The number of general and specialized madrasas of every kind in Constantinople is five hundred,* among which thirteen are major colleges.

The Progress of Education in the Era of the Present Sulṭān. The Annual Expenses of Education. It is generally accepted that education has made extreme progress in the time of the present sulṭān, and continues to do so daily. At the time of the sulṭān's enthronement, the number of rushdiyah madrasas was 96, but now it is 405. The number of new madrasas of every kind that have been founded in the fifteen-year reign of the sulṭān is two thousand. Along with that, the number of students in schools and colleges continues to grow so much that the educational progress report of the preceding year has no relation to the report of the succeeding year. In the lecture on the general progress of the Turks that Professor Vámbéry gave several years ago, the number of students at the Maktab al-Ḥuqūq [Legal College] was reported as three hundred. But when I was in Constantinople, there were 1,200 students present in this college. During my stay in Egypt, I read in Cairo's famous newspaper *al-Muwayyad* that "When the present sulṭān took the reins of the government in hand, the expenses in education were three lakh pounds annually.[26] But now they are eight lakh pounds annually." This amount is equivalent to one crore twenty lakh of our region.

Inviting Students. In truth, the sulṭān has a strange and wondrous attachment to education. The Civil College and the Legal College, which are the

* from *Qāmūs al-Islām* [This footnote first appears in the second edition.]

renowned colleges of Constantinople, were established by the sulṭān himself. [46] The lauded gentleman has such regard for these colleges that he has come to inspect them in person several times. During the time that I was in Constantinople, the lauded gentleman invited the students of all the major colleges to a royal banquet. Kāghaż-khānah [Kağıthane] is a famous place to visit in Constantinople where once a week there is a gathering of spectators.[27] This place was suggested and selected for the banquet and the order was given that the students of each college be called there in turn. First the Military College, then the Civil College (Civil Service College) and the students of other colleges were invited. As the students walked from the college, a royal band played in front of them in accordance with the order of the sulṭān. Because the sulṭān himself could not participate in these assemblies by reason of state considerations, a wazīr always participated in the banquet on his behalf and conveyed the salaam of the sulṭān to the students. At that time, the students would cry out *bādshāhim choq yashā* (meaning may our emperor live for a very long time) with great passion and sincerity of feeling.[28]

In the branch of education, an extremely beneficial invention that recently took place at the special suggestion of the sulṭān is the founding of the Maktab al-ʿAshāyir [Tribal College].[29] Although at this time education is progressing in all the Ottoman regions, up to now, the tribes of Arabia were nearly entirely deprived of this beneficence, the reason for which was their own heedlessness and bedouin quality. The sulṭān gave the order to found a college especially for the Arab tribes and, along with it, a large and well-ordered boarding house. During the time of my stay, farmans were issued in the name of rulers and governors that boys from the esteemed tribes of Arabs in Ḥijāz [Hejaz], Yaman [Yemen], Diyarbakr [Diyarbakır], Baṣrah [Basra], Baghdād [Baghdād], Ṭarābulus al-Gharb [Tripoli], Ḥalab [Aleppo], Mauṣil [Mosul], and Shām [Syria], be selected and sent. [47] The sulṭān approved that their expenses of every kind be paid by the government. On 12 Rabīʿ al-Awwal 1310 [October 4, 1892], it was opened with great glory and magnificence and inaugural ceremonies were performed. One cannot find the equal of such an outstanding effort for the training and cultural refinement of the Arabs in all Islamic history.

The Dār al-Shafaqah Madrasa. Even more proof of royal generosity is to be found in the Dār al-Shafaqah [Darüşşafaka], which has been established especially for orphans.[30] One thousand orphans receive education in this madrasa, and all of them are boarders. The burden of the food, clothing, and all other necessary expenses of this enormous group does not fall on the Department of Education, but rather on the Great Sulṭān himself.

Major Colleges and Schools. Among the colleges and schools, the ones that are most worthy of mention are these:

The Royal Military College The Imperial College The Civil College	I saw these colleges myself and have obtained detailed information regarding their method of education, and so on. For this reason, I shall include them under a separate heading later.
The Legal College, meaning College of Law	The following subjects are taught at this college: fiqh; principles of fiqh; Roman law; law of commerce; principles of trial; punishments; maritime law; political economy, meaning the politics of cities; the laws of the sultanates of Europe; briefly, the history of the creation of law and its developments, period by period. [48] The total number of students is 1,200, among whom 600 are boarders. Those educated here can become a *munṣif* and a *ṣadr al-ṣudūr*.[31] The period of instruction is four years.
The Engineering College	The period of education is six years. This is similar to Roorkee College.[32]
The Language College	German, French, Greek, Armenian, Latin, Italian, and Russian languages are taught in it.

The College of Industries, meaning technical school	The yearly expense is 8,250 pounds, that is, 123,750 rupees. The number of students is 240 and all are orphan boys. Their expenses are paid by the fund of the madrasah itself. Up to now, blacksmithing and carpentry were taught in it, but in the past year the secretary of the madrasa, Taufīq Bey Āfandī, requested that the work of machines be taught.
Deputy College	This college has been established on extremely excellent principles. In the previous period, it was not stipulated for the muftīs and qāẓīs who were appointed to pass a test in a particular course of instruction of any kind. Now the rule has been set that a person who is not educated at this college cannot be appointed to *shar'ī* [Islamic legal] posts. This method [49] has completely obstructed the path to appointments by recommendation. Education in fiqh takes place at an extremely high level at this college. Several things of modern education, too, have been added to bring about familiarity with the necessities of the present age.
Maritime College	Education in navigation takes place here.
Agricultural College	.. ..

Noteworthy Matters Related to the System of Education

A few points related to the method of education are especially noteworthy.

(1) The Compulsoriness of French. That in nearly all colleges and schools, French is compulsory, the result of which is that one cannot find even an ordinary person educated in modern learning who is unfamiliar with French.

(2) Education in Science and the Arts. In all major colleges, education in physics, chemistry, geology, and so on, is compulsory, and practical exercise is given in these sciences. The instruments of these subjects are available in abundance in every college for this purpose.

(3) Education of the Highest Order in History. Education in history is of the highest order. I saw the course of the Civil College. It is in six thick volumes, in which, in addition to other regions, there is a detailed history of Europe in addition to other countries. Along with that, the great virtue is that it contains discussion and refutation of the errors about Islamic history that many authors of Europe have made.

(4) Education in All Modern Sciences Takes Place through the Turkish Language. Apart from the Imperial College, in which Christian students are in abundance, in all other remaining madrasas, [50] arts and sciences of every kind are taught in the regional language, meaning Turkish. All modern sciences have been translated into Turkish and continue to be so from time to time. Although it is debatable whether or not translation is a superior means of education, and the great renowned theorists of Hindustan have taken the negative position in this debate, the debate is probably particular to Hindustan, where the regional language is not the language of governance. The Turkish language is the language of the sultanate, and in the entire world one cannot find an example of a sultanate that has progressed having acquired arts and sciences in the language of another nation. The progress of England began at a time when the arts and sciences were transferred into English from Latin, and there is no doubt that if Turkey's progress, too, is possible, then it can only happen by means of the regional language.

(5) The System of Boarding. The thing that is most valuable and respectable in the matter of education and training is the boarding system. The reality is that Turkey can claim with extreme pride that there can be no better system of boarding than the one that it has adopted. There are boarding houses attached to all the major colleges, and a great many students live in them, but the rule is observed that food, clothing, fashion, living space, and appointments should all be uniform, and that there should be no suspicion of differences in rank in the condition of the students. The cost of clothing is taken along with the rent for boarding and the fees for food, and the clothes of the students are prepared by the college itself. All the students eat at tables and chairs, and extreme care is taken for good manners, cleanliness, and ceremony in all things. The amount of fees is no less than five pounds per year in any college, [51] and in the Imperial College it is forty pounds, meaning six hundred rupees.

It is the wondrous estimable generosity of the Turks that despite the excessiveness of the fees, the poor are not deprived of the benefit of these colleges. In every college, there is a considerable number of poor students. So much assistance is given to them on behalf of wealthy Turks that they can pay all the expenses of the college. At the Imperial College, the fees for which are forty pounds per year, two hundred students are poor and less fortunate. Among them, amīrs and members of the government pay the fees of 150 students, and the sulṭān himself bestows those of fifty from his own pocket. The effect of this is that on the grounds of the college no one can distinguish in any way that such-and-such a student is poor and less fortunate. The uniformity of the students produces an extremely powerful idea of unity and nationhood among them, and for the poor, obtaining the society of the upper class produces in them the material of ambitiousness and high aspiration. In the major colleges of Europe, there is the great shortcoming that less fortunate people do not receive much benefit from their munificence. The Turks have taken measures to redress and guard against this loss, and have done so extremely nicely.

Seeing this manner of boarding, I would recall my own academy and would mourn the different ranks in its boarding house. But my lament was in fact not at the state of the college, but rather at those greats of the nation to whom God has given wealth and fortune but not the guidance to endeavor, by means of their own generosity, that in our educational institutions, the poor and the powerful appear at the same high level. I hereby declare that the thing that is most necessary, [52] and extremely necessary, in our national college is that the dress, fashion, food, living space, and furniture of all the students be made entirely one and the same, and that the different strata that remain in the college today be completely erased. If not, then there is no soul of nationhood in the college.

Student Dress. There is another novelty in the colleges and schools here, and it is extremely beneficial and effective. It is that on the collar of the coat of every student, the name of the college in which he is being educated is embroidered in golden thread. The letters of the silken thread are raised and of the highest order in accordance with the Naskh script. If you go to the thoroughfares of the colleges and schools at around four o'clock, a wondrous, enchanting sight appears. Whole crowds of students emerge from the madrasas, divide into numerous ranks, and walk with such order and regulation that one might say a regulated army is marching. The rosy, pale complexion of the boys, the black coat over it, and the golden monogram of the college on the collar of the coats seems so attractive that it is beyond description.

In addition to decoration and adornment, grandeur and majesty, a great benefit from this practice is that when the students step out into the market for recreation, they cannot engage in any inappropriate behavior. The dress of the college, which is compulsory to be worn at all times, causes one to recognize that they are students. Thus, they have no choice but to be mindful of the reputation of the college. Furthermore, if some boy participates in some disagreeable company or is guilty of any indecency, a policeman will grab him and bring him to the school or college where he is educated.

Many Students Living in Each Room. There appears to be one defect in the boarding system here, and it is that there are not separate rooms; [53] instead, there is one large hall for fifty or sixty boys in which beds are laid out according to their number. At the headboard of each bed is a small cabinet, which holds ordinary clothing and books. When I initially saw the boarding houses here, on the whole the thought of their contemptibleness occurred to me, especially because the ceremonious and well-appointed rooms of the academy were before my eyes. But with further research, I learned that this method is not devoid of benefit. Although there is no doubt that the principle reason for this deficiency is the abundance of the population and the unavailability of sufficient land, with respect to the benefits that cannot be obtained without this particular method, it would not be inappropriate to claim that such had been done intentionally and such alone was appropriate.

The Uniformity of the Social Life of All Boarders. The extremely beneficial use that has been made of this method is that the daily life of all boarders has been fixed upon uniform principles. For example, as dawn breaks, the watchmen, who walk around the sleeping rooms all night, awaken the boarders. Spouts have been attached to the wall in accordance with the number of boys, and beneath them a small watercourse has been made. All the boys went and sat together there. There is such commitment to the boys' arriving together that in some colleges there is a machine that turns to open the mouths of all the spouts together. When all the boys arrive, a servant turns the machine, and, when the allotted time has passed, closes it. If any boy comes late, he will have to turn back because a great deal of water cannot be wasted for just one person. Having washed their hands and faces, [54] all the boys go and sit on benches in the reading room (which is reserved for reading books, and where a supervising instructor remains present), and occupy themselves by memorizing lessons or studying their readings. All the students get up together and go into the dining room. After the meal, the school bell rings, and everyone goes and sits in the college rooms. At night, too, all the students read in a single room (reading room) and, when it is time to sleep, all stand up together and move into the sleeping room. In sum—arising from sleep, washing hands and face, studying lessons, eating, performing namāz, and at ten o'clock at night, each going and lying in his respective bed—the students are required do all these tasks together. By this method, maintain a schedule becomes a habit, and, gradually, it becomes second nature. For this method, it is necessary to arrange for the fifty to sixty boys to live in a single room. Otherwise, arrangement for all tasks to be performed together cannot be made in separate rooms. Our college, Ẓaḥūr Ḥusain Wārḋ, which was just recently established, has been established on this principle.[33]

A Few Things Are Still Lacking in the Progress of Education. Concerning the breadth and progress of education, although such care has been taken, because the new method of education has only recently been put into effect, there is a lack of a great many things, which, it is hoped, will gradually be fulfilled. Among them the fact that there is no debating club or intellectual-scientific society in any college, rather, in the entire city. For this reason, the students do not have the opportunity to develop abilities in public speaking. As a result, those who have obtained degrees from these colleges cannot give a lecture or speech on any topic in a public gathering. The effect of this is also that in the educated group, the liveliness, freethinking, ambitiousness, and high-mindedness that are the requisites of the new education have not been produced. [55]

One very great defect is that the existence of large colleges and schools is limited to the walls of the seat of the caliphate. Although in large cities madrasas have been established in abundance, they are generally elementary or rushdiyah, meaning madrasas of the middle grade. As far as I am aware, in Beirut, Damascus, Aleppo, and Jerusalem there is not even one intellectual-scientific madrasa to which the word *college* can truly be applied.

Even greater is the regret that all the colleges and academies of Constantinople that I mentioned are paid for by the government. The nation has not yet given this any attention. That is, in such a large capital of the sultanate, there is not even one national college. No government, no matter how powerful and wealthy it is, can be the guarantor of the intellectual-scientific needs of the entire country. And even if it were, it is not very beneficial. The mental and spiritual powers of a nation whose every need the government fulfills become dead and useless. To the magnificent intellectual workshops spread throughout Europe, the nation has contributed the largest share. The famous universities of England, Cambridge and Oxford, were founded by national efforts alone, and to this day they have not seen fit to bear the burden of government favor.

After this summary report, we write the detailed circumstances of several colleges.

Military College [Maktab-i Ḥarbiyah]

This is a very large college, rather, it is a very large university, of which the Turks are proud, and, in truth, it is deserving of this pride. Although military education is to some extent detached from the sense of technical education, and in this regard [56] it was apparently not befitting to mention the Military College under the heading of "Progress of Education," still, instruction in physics, chemistry, mathematics, and all the branches of medicine especially, in addition to the military sciences, is given to such an extent in this college that we cannot call it outside the sphere of technical education. Sulṭān Maḥmūd founded this college in 1250 Hijrī [1834–35]. Relative to this time, a good deal of progress has taken place in the building, and the curriculum of education has become so extensive and superior that one might say it has ceased to be a college at all.

The number of military madrasas subordinate to this college is 37, among which 18 are i'dādiyah and 27 are rushdiyah, in which a total of 9,224 students are acquiring an education.

Details will be learned from the following chart:

TYPE OF MADRASA	MADRASAS IN THE CAPITAL		MADRASAS IN THE DISTRICTS	
	Boarder	*Non-boarder*	*Boarder*	*Non-boarder*
A'dādī	1069	0	745	0
Rushdiyah	155	2,425	128	2,225

This college (the Military College) is a college of great magnificence and glory. Although the general rule in Constantinople is that no person can be admitted onto the grounds of a madrasa without the permission of the secretary of the madrasa, there are even more checks and controls at this madrasa. When I attempted to visit it, people said that the *irādah-i sunnah*,[34] meaning the permission of the sulṭān himself, was necessary. [57] Although 'Uṡmān Pāshā,[35] in whose service I had already had the honor of appearing at the time, could easily have had permission granted to me, I did not think it appropriate to trouble him for this undertaking. I was on informal terms with Ḥusain Ḥasīb Āfandī, the police commissioner. I spoke about it with him. He said, "*Dar Ḥarbiyah māżūn nīstam*."[36] Left with no other choice, I had to rely on my own effort. I had already learned that the secretary of the Military College was Żakī Pāshā, who is an extremely capable and highly educated person. I thought that I should meet him myself without any mediation. Shaikh ʿAlī Ẓabyān, too, was of the same opinion. Thus, we both went to the home of the aforementioned pāshā.

Meeting Żakī Pāshā to Visit the Military College. As it happened, he had gone out. The person said, "Please, just wait a short while, he may come back soon." Meanwhile, he arrived. He turned to face us as he stepped out of the carriage. Shaikh ʿAlī Ẓabyān and I were both in Arab dress. Although there was a silken turban on my head and a golden band around my waist, because of my *qafṭān* and my robe, I appeared by my overall appearance to be an Arab. The aforementioned pāshā was in an extreme hurry at the time. As soon as he said "Salām ʿalaik," he thrust his hand into his pocket and took out some *majīdīs* (Turkish coin). First I was severely shocked. Then I thought, "*Naʿūż billāh*! He thinks we are beggars, like common Arabs!" With that thought I became extremely irritated, and along with the irritation, angered, too. I shouted, "*Shū hāżā? Mā jīnā li-hāżā. Lisnā min al-fuqarā'*!"[37] meaning, "What is this? We have not come for this! We are not faqīrs!" Although the pāshā did not understand Arabic, he understood from the look on my face and the tone of my words that the action had offended me. [58] He turned his attention to Shaikh ʿAlī Ẓabyān. "Why is he in a rage? And what does he want?" Shaikh ʿAlī Ẓabyān was able to speak some broken Turkish. He described the purpose and aim of my visit. The pāshā became extremely embarrassed. Along with apologies, he said, "Please, go to the upper gallery. I will come in a little while." There were some esteemed officers gathered on the upper gallery. They welcomed us with extreme reverence. Coffee came as usual. Each person was greeted in turn. When they learned that I was a resident of Hindustan and had come here for the purpose of scientific research, they became so enthralled that interest and affection were expressed by their every word and gesture. It was extremely unfortunate that I understood neither Turkish nor French and they could not converse in any other language. One by one, they came and sat near me, and, along with expressing affection, expressed regret that "We do not understand your language." After a little while, Żakī Pāshā sent word asking extremely politely to be excused: "I have crucial business to attend to, so I cannot come myself; but I have ordered an officer to take you on a thorough tour of the college." The name of that gentleman was Rażā Bey, and he had the rank of *mīr-alāī* [*miralay*].[38] The pāshā's asking to be excused could not have been based on pretense. Indeed, a great many departments really are entrusted to him, and his entire day is spent making rounds. Still, there is no doubt that he felt extremely embarrassed by his behavior and this, too, was one reason for his not coming.

In learning that when 'ulamā and Sūfīs meet some amīr or officer of rank here, [59] they do so with the purpose of getting their hands on some shiny coins, my irritation with Żakī Pāshā's negative suspicion went away, but I felt great anguish at the condition of this group. I used to think that the practice of begging for offerings and oblations was exclusive to Hindustan, but, alas, there is no escape from it here, either.

Going to the Boys' Dining Room. The Cleanliness and Fine Manners of the Boys While Eating. To make a long story short, we went to the Military College with Rażā Bey. There was a guard at the gate. The soldiers saluted us according to military custom. When we entered, it was not just a college, but a proper colony. Rażā Bey first took us into his private room. A few other officers of the college were present there. We were introduced to them. As usual, coffee came. After a little while, Rażā Bey said, "The dining bell has already rung. Come, before anything else, let me take you on a tour of the dining room." Because at that time the *ḍā'ining rūm* (dining room) and the buildings attached to it had been demolished and were being rebuilt anew, a building at some distance from the row of college buildings had been temporarily set up, and a clean and level road had been prepared from the college to the building. When the boys emerged from their rooms and headed toward the dining hall, a wondrous, heart-enchanting scene appeared before the eyes. There were thirty or forty lines of five or six boys each, and they were going along with such order and regularity that you might say a regulated army was marching. Their fashion and dress was entirely uniform, and because all the boys were Turks or Syrian Arabs, there was not much difference in their complexion and appearance. The astonishing thing is that although no officer was with the group, nor did they know about our coming, not a single movement of theirs was opposed to order and arrangement, and there was absolutely no sign of noise and shouting. When we entered the room, all the boys were already seated at the table. The hall was extremely large and beautiful, and there was gilt ornamentation on the ceiling. [60] There were foods of two or three kinds and, in accordance with Turkish custom, one large dish was set in the middle of each group of four boys. There were no forks or knives. There were only spoons. But the boys ate with such fine manners that neither did their hands become soiled nor could a stain have appeared anywhere on the tablecloth. The boys are probably held to strict standards of cleanliness. It seemed as if the four or five hundred boys who were present in the hall had changed their clothes just before coming. Wherever we passed, the boys would stand up and say, "*Tafažžal yā maulānā.*"[39] At their insistence, I ate a few bites. The food was not bad. But I was looking for Hindustani *qormah*. Where was that to be found here?

Having left the dining room, we strolled around for a little while until the college bell rang and the boys moved into the lecture room.

Lecture Rooms. The lecture rooms (rooms of instruction) are not of the same form as those of our Hindustan. Stretching into the distance in a straight line are a great many rooms whose form is like that of common buildings. The professor sits on a high platform. There was even a wooden railing around some platforms. Whichever room Ražā Bey (and we along with him) entered, a boy would stand up and say the word *baq* with a loud cry.[40] With that cry, all the boys would stand up and greet us with a gesture of the hand. I learned that whenever an officer of the college comes, the boys show him respect in this way. Ražā Bey introduced us to all the professors, but unfortunately we could not understand anyone's language. [61]

The hammam, printing house, draftsman house, and a great many buildings of this kind that are on the grounds of the college—we toured them all. There are so many of these buildings that we walked around continuously for nearly two hours before no more remained. The room for instruction in anatomy is extremely large and the implements for anatomical procedures have been collected in abundance. I had never seen examples of cartography and drawing like the ones that I saw here. The innovation that I saw in the printing house was that maps of geography were printed having been made on stone instead of paper. The map that was being prepared at the time was extremely dense and fine, and in truth was work of painstaking detail.

The Moral Character of the Professors. For the amusement of the students, there is a beautiful pond in which fish of different colors live, and benches and chairs are set up all around. For professors and teachers, there is a separate pond a short distance away. Because we had become tired while walking, we took a breather there, and kept company for a while. Rajab Āfandī, who is appointed to teach Turkish composition and knows Persian, joined us on the final tour. I could speak with the esteemed officers of the college through him without any trouble. I cannot describe the quality of the kind manners and Islamic affection with which the professors and students treated me. It was extremely regrettable that the day on which I saw the college was not a day of practical instruction. For this reason, military exercises, that is, drills, marksmanship, horsemanship, preparing trenches, preparing temporary fortifications—we could not see anything of this kind. We could have gone to see them on some other day, but the college was so far from our residence that [62] we could not find the nerve again.

Numerous Branches of Instruction. There are numerous branches of instruction at this college.

(1) Military Officers. Military Officers. This is the highest level, and its duration of study is three years. It has two branches, technical [*fannī*] and military [*'askarī*]. In the technical, the following subjects are taught: land division and cosmography; optics; machines; architecture; the French, German, and Russian languages; the besiegement of fortresses and principles of battle; military telegraph; posts, salaries, and pensions of the military officers; military inventions; practical studies; forms of architecture; the roads of the Ottoman territories and the railway lines of all the territories of Europe; the art of heavy weaponry; the science of geology; the organization and principles of the militaries of Europe; the famous battles of the world and the causes of victory and defeat and the details their occurrence with respect to military principles; geometry; algebra; *palūghrāfiyā*;[41] the art of light weaponry; writing; the history of the art of war; drawing.

Most of the same subjects are also taught in the military[42] branch. Along with this, there are also several modern subjects. Basic instruction in most of the subjects that are taught at both of these levels has already taken place in the rushdiyah and iʿdādiyah. At these levels, they are merely completed, and this is the reason that so many different subjects can be acquired in three years. From the rushdiyah to this level, the total period of education is ten years.

(2) Cavalry. Education in Cavalry. Its duration of instruction is three years, and, in addition to practical exercises, instruction is given in the following subjects: traditional geometry; theoretical and practical palūghrāfiyā; the French, German, and Russian languages; [63] chemistry; the art of weaponry; military inventions; and military geography.

(3) Infantry. Duration of education, three years. In this, in addition to practical exercises, there is education in military geography; the art of weaponry; German, French, and Russian languages; military inventions; light fortifications; and health care.

(4) Baiṭārī, Meaning the Medical Treatment of Animals. *Baiṭārī*, meaning animal medicine. Period of education, four years. Subjects of instruction: common diseases; the art of birth; the art of equestrianism; internal diseases; inborn diseases; the art of surgery; external diseases; the French language; writing; organic chemistry; uncompounded medicine; dissection and anatomy, physiology; botany; biology; inorganic chemistry; and the science of geology, mineralogy, and mining. In all four of these divisions, nearly six hundred students are under instruction, and after obtaining certificates, they are given official posts as per rankings. Beneath them are the classes of i'dādiyah and rushdiyah, whose total period of instruction is seven years, and instruction is given in history, geography, arithmetic and accounting, geometry, machine work, and subjects of this kind. All together, the students who acquire an education in the different branches of this college are 1,500 in number, among whom 1,000 are boarders.

The Number of Professors and Teachers. The professors, assistant professors, and teachers are eighty-seven, among whom most reside right on the premises of the college. Most of the professors are educated at the highest level and are esteemed officers. Among them, six people hold the rank of pāshā, whose names are Ṡarwat Pāshā, secretary; Fāyiq Pāshā, professor of organic chemistry; Hizbar Pāshā, professor of cavalry education; Tafawwuq Pāshā, professor of geology; Shākir Pāshā, professor of the elements of war; and 'Uṡmān Pāshā, professor of German. [64] Nine professors have obtained the rank of mīr-ālāī.

Imperial College [Maktab-i Sulṭānī]

This, too, is an old college, and is more distinguished than all colleges except the Military College.[43] It is located in Ghalaṭah-sarāe [Galatasaray], where European merchants mostly reside, and for this reason there are more Christian boys in it than in all other colleges.

I regret that at the time that I saw this college, it was a time of holiday, and apart from two or three officers, meaning the secretary and assistant secretary, and so on, no other officer was present.[44] The college building is two stories. The boarding house and lecture rooms are all on the upper level. There is an extremely large room for instruction in biology, in which there are many dead animals of every kind and very large skeletons of animals. I had never seen the skeleton of a whale before. For experiments in chemistry and electricity, expensive instruments have been made abundantly available.

I very much liked that an extremely large hall is furnished for ill boarders in which there are many beds, and so on, and numerous attendants are present at all times. In this way, the doctor finds ease in diagnosing and treating the boys, and he can see all the ill at the same time. Otherwise, if there were separate rooms, then coming to see each ill person one at a time and sufficiently visiting and making inquiries after each patient would be seriously difficult.

The expense of this college is eighteen thousand pounds, meaning two lakh, seventy thousand rupees annually, [65] but this also includes the amount of the scholarships for poor students. The collective number of students is eight hundred, of whom most are boarders. The room of the sleeping quarters of the boarders is extremely large. It is magnificent and of pleasant atmosphere. A summary of a few items from the regulations of the boarding house is included below:

1. The food, clothes, bedding, books, paper, pens, and so on, of all boarders will be provided by the college.
2. Forty pounds per year (six hundred rupees) will be taken as fees from the boarder.
3. Such students will also be admitted who can pay two-thirds or one-third of the fees, or who cannot pay them at all, but their number will be fixed, which will be determined at the beginning of each year following an inquiry by the office of director of public instruction. (One should remember that the remainder of the fees of such students are paid by the sulṭān and the amīrs of the city, and for this reason, with respect to food, dress, and furniture, and so on, no difference of any kind between them and the fortunate students can be sensed.)
4. At the time of admission, 15 pounds, meaning 225 rupees, will be taken from every student for the sake of clothing.
5. The fees of students who do not stay in the boarding house at night are twenty pounds per year and cannot be reduced under any circumstances.
6. The fees of nonboarders are ten pounds per year and cannot be reduced under any circumstances. [66]
7. Boarders shall receive permission to go home only once per week, and when they come and go it is necessary for a trusted servant to be with them.

8. No boarder can keep more than ten qurush (one and one quarter rupees) with him in one week.

With respect to education, the distinctive quality that is in this college is that all the arts and sciences are taught in French, and for this reason most of the professors are either French or German. Along with that, education in the Turkish language is of an extremely high level. Education in Arabic and Persian, too, is compulsory, though it is not at the highest level. The remaining languages, Greek, Armenian, English, German, Italian, and Latin, are included in the curriculum, and many students study them, too. But education in them is optional, not compulsory.

The subjects that are taught in Turkish, Persian, and Arabic, apart from the literary sciences and the Glorious Quran are as follows: tenets, fiqh, ethics, history of the Ottoman Empire, recitation of the Quran, and hadith and Quranic exegesis. But education in recitation and hadith and Quranic exegesis begin in the fourth year and take place only once per week. French is taught from the very beginning and continues regularly until the conclusion of instruction, meaning seven years. Along with syntax, morphology, and literature, the principles of composition and the art of rhetoric are taught up to the highest level, and the following subjects, too, are taught by means of this language: arithmetic and accounting, algebra, geography, geometry, chemistry, biology, physics, botany, [67] electricity, acoustics, geology, engineering design, and imitative design.

The Number of Professors and Teachers. The total number of teachers and professors is seventy-four, among whom twenty-six are German and French, and the remainder are Turks.

The reality is that with respect to the extensiveness of the building, the provision of intellectual-scientific instruments, the breadth of instruction, and the excellence of administration, no college in all of Constantinople is more excellent. Of course, it is regrettable that the people receiving education in the high classes are mostly Christians. The number of Muslims is very small. Shaikh ʿAbd al-Fattāḥ Āfandī kindly gave me the current annual report of the results of examinations. In it, all the people who passed examinations at the highest level are mostly Christian. I bear no malice toward the progress of Christians. By God I do not. But I certainly feel anguish at the decline of Muslims.

Civil College [Maktab-i Mulkiyah]

This college, which is the civil service college of this place, has been established by the sulṭān himself, and the lauded gentleman pays special attention to it. Thus, he has already twice graced it with his presence for inspection.

The Subjects in Which Instruction Is Included in the Curriculum. The Number of Students. Before, there were five levels in it, three lower and two upper. Thus, the period of instruction was five years. But two more levels have been added in order to establish a high standard, and the total duration of education has been set at seven years. Along with French, education in the Greek and Armenian languages is also compulsory in this college. Arabic and Persian, too, are included in the curriculum of education, but are not compulsory. [68] The subjects that are taught are as follows: history and geography; electricity, and so on; physics; political economy; the principles of law; the laws of Europe. Education in all these subjects is at an extremely high level. I saw the history course myself. It was in six thick volumes. Those educated at this college are appointed to very high offices. Accordingly, so far more than two hundred have already been appointed to regional offices, some of whom hold offices of an extremely high rank. The number of students who are receiving education in the college at this time is more than six hundred.

The Cleanliness and Furnishings of the Dining Room. I toured the college thoroughly. Although the manager of the college, who is an esteemed Turk, does not understand Arabic, because there was an interpreter with me, we were able to communicate without difficulty. In the colleges here, I generally noticed and liked very much that the manager was a man of esteemed rank, and respect and dignity were expressed by his social comportment. The manager's room, too, was organized and well-arranged, as usual. When I arrived at the college, it was break hour, and the boys were busy playing cricket. After a little while, when the boys came back to class, the manager ṣāḥib took me on a tour of all the rooms of the college. The dining room was arranged with extreme propriety. There was an extremely clean cloth spread on the table, and elaborate dishes had been beautifully set out. The carafes, which were in accordance with the number of students, were generally made of glass and, one might say, served to decorate the table. In the room for education in chemistry, and so on, there were instruments of the highest degree, [69] and they were in abundance. In the same series of buildings there is a very small masjid. Its building is not very remarkable, but because a Turkish carpet of extremely superior grade was spread inside and out, it seemed beautiful and adorned. On one side, an excellent fragment of writing in Naskh script was hanging on the wall. By inquiry, I learned that it was written by the hand of the deceased Sulṭān ʿAbd al-ʿAzīz.[45] It is extremely excellent script.

Preparation for Namāz. Meanwhile, it came time for midday prayers. The Muslim boys (there is no shortage of Christian boys, too, here) prepared for namāz. They were generally wearing coat and pants, and their performing ablutions with respect and resolution in that dress, and going into the masjid line by line with dignity and reverence left a wondrous impression on my heart. The truth is that if Muslims make progress having been freed from religious influence, then decline is a thousand degrees better than such progress. After namāz, a sermon took place for a little while, but very few boys participated in it.

Classical Education and Classical Madrasas

As we have already written above, education among the Turks began along with the start of the sultanate. This was the very education that today is remembered by the name "classical education." No doubt, in some era it was at the highest level. Thus, the original writings of Afẑal al-Dīn Khūnajī, ʿAllāmah Qūshjī, Chalabī, Khwājah-zādah, Ḥājjī Khalīfah, and so on, exist even today as monuments to it.[46] But the present education has reached such an extreme of baseness that the education in our Hindustan is a blessing in comparison with it. The thought that laid waste to all my joys and happinesses [70] on this journey was the miserable state of classical education. This issue is touched upon in Hindustan, too, these days, and anguish and regret are felt generally at the miserable state of classical education, but my regret was a regret of a different kind. The anguish and regret that the new-educated of our country express at the old education is in reality not anguish at all, but rather derision and delight in the suffering of others. Although I like new education, and I like it from my heart, I am still a staunch supporter of old education, and my thought is that old education is necessary, and seriously necessary, for maintaining the nationhood of Muslims. Along with that, when I see that the way this education is put into practice is completely profitless and meaningless, I cannot help but feel extreme anguish. In Hindustan, I managed to endure by the thought that a lack of patronage and resources for something that is not under the government's shadow of benevolence is a natural matter. However, seeing this situation in Constantinople, Syria, and Egypt, I often felt severe anguish.

The Number of Students. The Livelihood of the Students. Boarding. To make a long story short, classical education is abundantly prevalent here, and because students of this kind are clearly recognized by their fashion and dress, one can easily gain an estimate of their abundance in masjids and common thoroughfares. Some people told me that in Constantinople itself their number is no less than twenty thousand. Their means of living is not only regrettable, but shocking. In all the (classical) madrasas of this place, there is a continuous holiday of three months which begins with auspicious Ramžān. In these months, the students leave Constantinople and acquire zakāt in the villages and rural towns. This zakāt is their income for the entire year. [71] In some madrasas—and they are few and far between—they receive some bread, too, but there is absolutely no arrangement for clothes, and so on. For living, there are the madrasas' rooms, which are extremely small, cramped, and dark.

The layout of the madrasas is as follows. There is a very small courtyard, and on three sides of it there are small rooms. In the courtyard, there is a cistern where they sit and perform ablutions. The rooms in the large madrasas that the sulṭāns (Muḥammad Fātiḥ and Sulaimān, and so on) built and are still standing today are extensive and spacious, but the rooms of all other madrasas are so small and confined that one suffocates as one goes inside. Despite all these things, I should acknowledge the generosity of the Turks in promoting knowledge because, even if of a low degree, at least hundreds of intellectual-scientific monuments exist today, and the fair truth is that with respect to the period which these madrasas memorialize, they are not unsuited to the culture and civilization of the time. In our Hindustan, which, with its vastness and breadth, is itself a clime in its own right, not a single intellectual-scientific monument of the six-hundred-year period of the rule of Islam is found.

Curriculum of Instruction. The biggest complaint about classical education is that the standard of education has been set extremely low. There is no trace of the science of literature. *Īsāghūjī* and *Shamsiyah* are the concluding books in logic and philosophy.[47] It is difficult to find a madrasa in which the *ṣiḥāḥ sittah* are taught.[48] The science of meaning and rhetoric, and the principles of jurisprudence, too, are in the same state. Of course, there is a great deal of attention paid to fiqh, but education in it, too, is not innovative.[49] Rather, it is extremely common and imitative. [72] I came to know several maulawīs. They always talked about such trivial and general issues that I felt both surprise and disappointment.

The Scientific State of the Turks

The Scientific State of the Turks. The Translation of Books into the Turkish Language. If the regional languages in the parts of the world where Islam ruled did not completely disappear, then it certainly happened that their scientific status was snatched from them and given to Arabic. Although the regional languages of Hindustan, Persia, Spain, and Afghanistan were completely different, Arabic alone remained the intellectual-scientific language at each place, and is so even so now. The Turks, too, are no exception to this general influence. But they are distinguished among all Islamic nations by the particular characteristic that, along with submission to Arabic, they also did not allow their own language to be deprived of intellectual-scientific treasure. In the age in which the classical sciences ruled, an entire series of those sciences existed in the Turkish language, and still does. I saw with eyes of wonder that the histories of Ibn-i Khaldūn, Ṭabarī, Ibn-i Khallikān, Maqrīzī, and so on, which are extremely thick books, and among which some are in seven volumes each—translations of all of them exist in Turkish.[50] By contrast, one cannot find even a single example of this in Fāris or Afghanistan. If mention were made of translated books apart from original compositions in Turkish, one would have to prepare a large catalogue.

A Turkish friend of mine, who is an expert in numerous languages, recounted to me as a factual account [73] (not a boastful one) that histories, dramas, novels, travelogues, and books on stylistics and rhetoric in the French language have been translated in such abundance into Turkish that it is no exaggeration to say that France's entire field of literary studies and has entered the Turkish language. Hundreds of books of modern arts and sciences, too, have already been translated, and it is for this reason that in all the colleges of Turkey, except for the Imperial College, education in these arts and sciences takes place in the Turkish language, and takes place at the highest level.

Historical Writings in Turkish. The practice of original, independent writing, too, is not lacking. Books on all the branches of the arts and sciences are being written in abundance, and the books that are taught in colleges and schools are generally original writings, not translations. How could I have found the time and opportunity to acquire acquaintance with all modern original writings? Of course, in accordance with my taste, I did look at books on history and *rijāl*, on the basis of which I can say that, besides Arabic, such historical material does not exist in any language of Asia.[51] Rather, in one respect, it is superior to Arabic. All the histories in the Arabic language are a collection of simple facts and events, and whatever effort and care there is, it is only related to the principles of narrative transmission. By contrast, Turkish histories are written in accordance with the principles and rules that are the principles of historical philosophy, and on the basis of which Europe has taken this subject to the peak of perfection. I took a cursory look at the history book that is included in the course of studies at the Civil College. In all points of fact, it has carefully considered the chain of causation, made judgments by weighing evidence, and employed discernment and criticism throughout. Along with that, at the end of each period of rule, the civilizational, moral, and intellectual-scientific state of the period has been shown in detail. [74]

Biography, Meaning *Rijāl* and *Tarājim*.[52] *Qāmūs al-aʿlām*. There is an extremely useful series of biographies the name of which is Mashāhīr-i Rijāl [The Famous among Men]. They have written information about the lives of famous people of achievement extremely finely and in a pleasing style. Unfortunately, this series was left incomplete. Otherwise, it would have been an extremely useful collection. A special kind of very large encyclopedia, the name of which is *Qāmūs al-aʿlām* [Dictionary of the Sciences], is in preparation these days.[53] In addition to biographical studies of men, it also includes entries on famous cities, buildings, and historical places. A list of the writings in Arabic and French, and so on, on which the author has relied is included with it. I read the names of the Arabic books. They are extremely rare and reliable books and are not available anywhere except Constantinople. This book is arranged in alphabetical order and, at this time, has come to the letter *ze*.

The Progress of Geography. Along with history, geography, too, has enjoyed extreme progress. A great many useful books have been written. So many large maps and charts of the entire world and different populated areas have been prepared that it is unlikely that so many exist in any part of the world other than Europe. The maps are extremely standardized, beautiful, and elegant, and are not inferior to the maps prepared in Europe in any regard. Turks have a special interest in this field.

The Abundance of Turkish Writings. I cannot tell you the sufficient standard of the majority of Turkish writings, but one time in the office of the Department of Education, I took a cursory look at the catalogue of books that were published in Constantinople alone in just the period of a single month. Their number was nearly two thousand. Although among them were also books in Armenian, Greek, French, and other languages, [75] the Turkish writings had the largest share. Still, it is regrettable that among them novels and dramas were more numerous, and this is the same affliction that is spread throughout our unfortunate region.

Turkish Literature. Turkish literature, too, has made extreme progress, and it is a strange thing that, in many characteristics, it resembles our Urdu. Turkey's classical literature, in the manner of classical Urdu, was colorful, elaborate, filled with metaphors, and restricted to rhyme. But now, like new Urdu, there is regard for simplicity, clarity, and an apropos quality, and new original compositions are written in exactly this style. The inventors or masters of this new style are Kamāl Bey, Ḥāmid Bey, Professor Nājī, and so on.[54] When I began studying Turkish, I intended to read classical compositions. But my friends, who were also my teachers, said that the difference between classical and modern Turkish is that of the earth and the sky, and learning the classical language would not be sufficient for the new language. Professor Vámbéry,[55] in the lecture that he has given on the present civilization of the Turks, having compared classical and modern Turkish, has acknowledged with astonishment the attractiveness, clarity, and simplicity of the present language.

Turkish Writers. Among Turkish writers, these are the names of the most renowned and distinguished figures of the day: Aḥmad Midḥat, Jaudat Pāshā, Professor Nājī, ʿAbū al-Żiyā, Sāmī, ʿAlī Nuṣrat. Professor Nājī is a poet, and you might say he is the poet of the capital. There is no office of *malik al-shuʿarā* here.[56] Otherwise, he would have received this title. Still, he is considered the poet of the capital. Aḥmad Midḥat is a major author.[57] [76] He has written an extremely detailed history of the Turkish government, which is in twelve volumes. In response to the objections that are made against Islam, he has written a detailed book, which is in three volumes and is named *Mudāfaʿah-i Islāmiyah.*[58] In addition to Turkish, Farsi, and Arabic, he has mastery in the French language. He was appointed as a representative on behalf of Turkey in numerous sessions of the Oriental Conference that has been established in Europe, and in the Stockholm Conference it was he to whom official authority over the departments of Arabic, Farsi, and so on, was given. Aḥmad Jaudat Pāshā is an extremely esteemed person, and is a member, meaning he is a wazīr and *yāwar*, of the assembly of wazīrs.[59] His age is close to sixty or seventy, and because, along with being aged, he is weak in body and frail, he participates less in the assembly of wazīrs.[60] Among his writings, *Qawā'id-i 'Uṡmāniyah*, which is on Turkish morphology and syntax, is included in the course. I met him. We kept company for a while. He can speak in Arabic and Persian without difficulty. He spoke to me in Arabic.[61] The great praiseworthy thing about him is that despite his wealth, power, and office of wazīrate, he lives an extremely simple life and mostly keeps busy with intellectual-scientific activities.

Newspapers and Journals. In mentioning Turkish literature, it is also necessary to discuss newspapers and monthly journals, because these things are considered a major part of literature these days. I say with regret that, in this respect, Turkish literature is in a state of baseness. Turkish-language newspapers are not few in number. There are a great many daily newspapers, and they come out with great luster and splendor. The diction, too, is very simple and polished. [77] A taste for newspapers has also spread throughout the entire region. A great number of coffeehouses are specifically for newspapers, where newspapers are always found in abundance, and for this reason they are called a *qir'at-khānah* [reading room] instead of *qahwah-khānah* [coffeehouse].

There is all this, but the thing that is the life of a newspaper, that is, freedom, it does not exist here at all. There is nothing in all the newspapers except for official ordinances and everyday news. The result of this is that the Turkish language is completely deprived of a political style of writing and the power of reasoned argument. And the reality is, how and by what means can loftiness of thought, power of description, force of diction, passion, and efficacy come into a language in which the element of freedom does not exist? Look at Arabic. As long as it was the period of the righteous caliphate and natures were free and headstrong, Arabic was brimming with passion and efficacy. From the time that the foundation of autocratic government was laid and the family of the Banū Umayyah trampled and crushed the freedom of Arabia with great power and force, neither that efficacy nor that passion remained. No doubt, because of an abundance of information, the literature of the subsequent period is extremely extensive and rich. But sift through all the writings of that period. No trace of a free style of writing, political passion, or efficacy is found.

The Reason for the Lack of Freedom in Newspapers. Along with all these things, it is necessary for me to acknowledge that the newspapers' lack of freedom is necessitated by Turkey's political circumstances. The difference of religion among the citizens, the antagonism of foreign powers, interferences by adversaries, sensationalism in the newspapers, the proximity of European governments—these are circumstances in which even the freest of free governments would do the same as Turkey has done. [78] Having seen the orders that the republican government of France just recently implemented in Tunisia concerning the freedom of newspapers, who is unjust enough to make accusations against Turkey?[62]

Obstruction in Printing Books.[63] Of course, the obstruction that exists here concerning the printing of books is somewhat objectionable. The general rule here is that when some person wants to publish a classical or modern book, the book is first presented in the Department of Information. There is a separate bureau of inspection and investigation there. The officers of this bureau read the entire book from beginning to end, and, in accordance with their report, sometimes the printing of the book is stopped, or erasure and emendation is made. The need for this rule arose because some people act in extremely bad faith in printing books. For example, when the Christians in Beirut printed *Alfāẓ al-kitābiyah*,[64] wherever there were āyats of the Pure Quran and, in accordance with Islamic practice, the headings were *qāl Allāh*[65] or *kamā fī al-Qur'ān al-majīd*,[66] they changed them everywhere and made them *kamā qīl*[67] or *kamā qāl al-Qur'ān*,[68] whereas such words about the Glorious Quran could not have issued from the pen of a Muslim. More than that, these same Christians have printed a selection of the Quran, and wherever in some āyat there is mention of an event that opposes Christian narratives, they have written in parentheses that "it is wrong and this way is correct." No doubt, an Islamic sultanate cannot tolerate interpolations of this kind, and this is the reason that extreme caution and investigation is employed by the sultanate when publishing books. [79]

But it is regrettable that these days its method of application has transgressed moderation. This department was established with the purpose of stopping distortion and alteration, but sometimes it has acted on distortion and alteration itself. *Sharḥ-i ʿAqāʾid-i Nasafī* was being printed in front of me in a printing house.[69] The Department of Information had censored all the text in the book in which there was discussion of the caliphate and the hadith *al-aimma min Quraish* is mentioned.[70] The people at the printing house were compelled to print this censored copy. I saw the original copy on which the Department of Information made this manipulation, and I recall that I lost control of myself because of frustration and anger at that time. These people probably made this manipulation in the passion of, in their own minds, well-wishing for the sulṭān, but if the acclaimed gentleman had been informed of it, he would never have approved of it.

As I have recounted above, the newspapers, at least, are not worthy of attention, but the magazines and monthly journals that are issued in the Turkish language are extremely valuable. The most famous and renowned among them is *Maʿārif*, which is issued weekly.[71] Articles of the highest order are always written in this journal, and the people who are masters of the modern sciences among the Turks nowadays mostly demonstrate their achievement and perfection by means of this journal. Articles are generally related to natural science and modern instruments, and no issue is without illustration. The amount of distribution is not small, either. When I inquired from the owner of the printing house, I learned that five thousand copies are issued. Apart from *Maʿārif*, there are other intellectual journals, and they are published extremely capably. [80] Among them, *Rasamlī Ghazatah*, *Muṣawwar Jahān*, and *Śarwat-i Funūn* have passed before my eyes.[72] In terms of paper, script, clarity, in short, in external splendor, all of these journals compete with the renowned journals of Europe.

There is no doubt that with respect to the daily progress that the arts and sciences have made in Turkey, and the abundance with which new writings continue to be published in each field, it has acquired the rank of preeminence over the entire Asian world.

Printing Houses

The printing houses are in extreme abundance here, and they are unexcelled in fineness of script, clarity, and elegance. The Arabic script type that exists, and which is the invention of the Turkish intellectual 'Abū al-Żiyā, is considered incomparable throughout the world.[73] Wherever Arabic books are printed in the world today, the books printed in Beirut are regarded as the most excellent. But the people in Beirut themselves recounted to me that "in fact this type is the invention of the Turks, and we are their imitators." Because Turkish books are typically printed in Constantinople, and they do not come into these regions, Beirut alone has gained general renown. It is either the effect of affluence or general appreciation that all the books printed in Constantinople are printed on extremely excellent and expensive paper, as opposed to Egypt and Hindustan, where paper for cleaning shoes is used for books. There is no other reason for this except that in these regions, people still do not understand the value and worth of knowledge. [81]

It is a matter of regret that there is no printing house here that is as prominent and prosperous as is the Nawal Kishorī printing house in Hindustan.[74] Along with that, it is another matter of regret that most printing houses belong to other nations. Even the owner of *Ma'ārif*, which I have just discussed, is a Christian. Among the printing houses that belong to Muslims, Tarjumān-i Ḥaqīqat, Matba'-i 'Uṡmāniyah, and Shirkat-i Ṣaḥāfiyah are the most distinguished. I toured all of them. Shirkat-i Ṣahāfiyah is remarkable with respect to the fact that it has been founded on shared capital, and all its shareholders are Muslims. The sum of its capital is eighteen thousand pounds, meaning nearly two lakh rupees. All the work is done by an engine. The engine is very large and runs ten or twelve machines. Just as I arrived, *Sharḥ-i Bukhārī* by 'Ainī was being printed.[75] Two thick volumes had already been prepared by that time. The people at the printing house said that there were eight more just like it. In all of Constantinople, this is the Muslims' only shared workhouse. Otherwise, first, why would Muslims touch commerce at all, and even if by some chance they had, why would a few people have come together to do it? In this respect, this printing house, in a way, is an extraordinary occurrence.[76]

Libraries

Because of thematic arrangement and discursive order, I have reached this heading late; otherwise, with respect to personal interest and the purpose of the journey, this was the topic that I would have written first and in the most detail. The truth is that among the intellectual achievements of the Turks, the most worthy of pride are these libraries. The parts of the Islamic world in which there is talk of education and learning today are [82] Hindustan, Arabia, Egypt, Syria, the countries of the Maghrib, Persia, and Iran. I have seen the intellectual-scientific resource of most of them with my own eyes, and those that I have not seen I know by such strong means that it is as good as seeing them. On this basis, I can say with sufficient certainty that Constantinople is the largest center of Arabic writings in the entire Islamic world.

The Number of Libraries and Books. The number of all the libraries that are in this city is forty-five. The royal library, which is in the Qaṣr-i Humāyūn [Royal Palace] and is extremely old, is in addition to them.[77] These libraries house a total of eighty-five thousand books. Although this number is not such a large number—there are probably more books than that in our Hindustan—Constantinople is superior in terms of the excellence and rarity of the books. Among these libraries, the names of a few are recorded as follows: Jāmi‘ Āyā Sofiyah Library; Jāmi‘ Bāyazīd Library; Yol Jāmi‘ Library; Old Ḥamīdiyah Library; ‘Āshir Āfandī, Shaikh al-Islām, Library; As‘ad Āfandī, Naqīb al-ashrāf, Library; Jāmi‘ Muḥammad Fātiḥ Library; New Ḥamīdiyah Library; ‘Alī Pāshā Shahīd Library; Nūr ‘Usmāniyah Library; Lālah Bī Library; Ḥakīm Ughlī ‘Alī Pāshā Library; Muḥammad Pāshā Kūprulī Library; Qalīch ‘Alī Pāshā Library; Walī al-Dīn Āfandī Library; Salīmiyah Library; Faiżullāh Āfandī Library; Sulṭān Muḥammad Qażī-zādah Library; Wālidah Sulṭān Mosque Library; ‘Āṭif Āfandī Library; Shāh-zādah Dāmād Ibrāhīm Pāshā Library; Khusrau Pāshā Library; Mihrshān Library; [83] Muḥammad Āfandī Library; Muṣṭafā Āfandī Library; Taufīq Āfandī Library; Sulaimāniyah Library; Muḥammad Āfandī Murād Library; Rāghib Pāshā Library.[78] Detailed catalogues of fourteen of these libraries have been printed and published, and the remaining catalogues, too, will probably be published in time.

Endowments for Libraries. As their names themselves express, these libraries were founded by former pāshās and amīrs, and all of them are public endowments. Along with each library, property, too, is endowed, from which its ordinary expenses—meaning renovations and repair of the building, carpet and ordinary furniture, and the salary of employees—are paid. With regard to these matters, one must acknowledge that the rank of the Turks in the generous support of knowledge is superior to all Islamic nations. In India, an Islamic government lasted for ages and was prosperous and glorious. Great renowned wazīrs and amīrs came and went, but today not even one intellectual-scientific monument of theirs exists.

In these libraries one also finds proof of the fact that among the Turks, the group of amīrs (which in other nations is in generally a relatively illiterate group) is educated, and educated at the highest level. In most libraries, there exist the personal writings of the endowers, or books written in their hands, which bear witness to their taste and breadth of vision. Additionally, from the kind of excellent and rare books that have been sought out and collected, one gains an estimate of the fact [84] that the intellectual-scientific taste of the collectors was no ordinary taste.

The External State of the Libraries. These libraries are of an ordinary grade with respect to the fineness of the building and other resources and provisions. So much so that in some libraries, there are not even cabinets. They have piled books on a platform around which there is an iron enclosure. In all the libraries, seating is on the floor. Of course, there is just this much formality: benches are arranged in front, on which they set books and read. Although the Ḥamīdiyah Library, which has recently been established and is a monument to the auspicious age of the Great Sulṭān, is of greater magnificence and glory—the building is beautiful and large; there are silken pillows on all the desks, chairs, and couches; in sum, it is an exception to other libraries in all matters—still, it cannot compete with the Allahabad Public Library.[79]

The Administration of Endowments. Because the administration of all endowments is connected with the state, the libraries, too, are under the care of the government, and this is the reason that, despite the length of time, the books are so carefully protected that not even a single page has been lost. The employees, despite their meager salaries, are extremely honest and of upright character. The endowment of the 'Āshir Āfandī Library is so small that the librarian cannot receive more than ordinary food and two rupees per month. But the person who has been appointed librarian is so honest and so observant of his duties that it is not possible to be more so. Grapevines have grown on the walls of the library. One day I said to him, "If you just sold all the grapes, you could have a reasonable income." He said, "According to the condition of the endower, [85] these grapes are only for the people who came to the library for the purpose of reading books, so I cannot gain any kind of benefit from them." Because of his meager salary, the poor fellow has not even married, nor does he have a place to live. He sleeps right there in the library at night.

Several Characteristics of the Libraries. The characteristics and summary details of the libraries will be known by the following facts:

(1) The Soundness and Excellence of Manuscript Copies. The greatest distinction is that the books that are found here are generally in old script, authentic, and corrected by past masters. The authenticity of classical and rare books of which there are only a few copies in the world takes precedence over all else. Otherwise, one cannot rely on them. There is no lack of old books in the libraries of Egypt, too, but most have been written in the present period, and for this reason they are not very authentic or reliable. Having seen the books at Constantinople, one wonders from where have such wondrous copies of these books been gathered? I had been searching for 'Abd al-Qāhir al-Jurjānī's *Asrār al-balāghah* for some time.[80] I found only one copy in Hindustan, but it was extremely erroneous and unreliable. I saw numerous copies of it in Constantinople, and all of them were extremely sound and in old script. Similarly, copies of *al-Bayān wal-tabyīn* by al-Jāḥiẓ, *Tażkirah* by Ibn-i Ḥamadūn, *Mu'jim al-Udabā'* by Ya'qūt Ḥamawī, *Kitāb al-ashrāf* by al-Balāżurī, and *Tārīkh-i kabīr* by Imām Bukhārī all exist and are extremely authentic and reliable.

(2) The Excellence of the Script and the Paper's Being *Zar-afshān*. In some libraries, for example in the Old Ḥamidiyah, there is the distinction that the paper of most books is *zarīn* or zar-afshān,[81] and there are golden flower and vine designs in the margins. Along with these formalities, the script is of an extremely high order. Because books of the classical age could rarely be found with such formalities, the founder of the library has had most of them prepared with care. I had numerous books, which even included a complete copy of *Shifā* by Bū ʿAlī Sīnā, taken out, and I looked at them and spontaneously praised the refinement of the owner of the library.

(3) The Translation of Greek Books. I thought that the translations that were made of Greek and Egyptian books in the period of Abbasid rule had disappeared from the world. But when I came here, the falsehood of this idea was proven. Although relative to the large amount of translations that were made, the existing material may as well be nonexistent, still, what little does exist is a blessing.[82]

It seems that the Turks paid special attention to classical writings. Thus, in this matter, they took advantage of European efforts, too. Ibn-i Rushd had written an extremely beneficial and comprehensive summary of Aristotle's writings. This original summary has been lost. But a translation of it was made in Latin, which is still found in the libraries of Europe. Asʿad Āfandī, a Turkish intellectual, translated the Latin summary into Arabic and made some additions throughout. I saw this translation in the library of Rāghib Pāshā. It is a very large collection and is an excellent specimen of the intellectual-scientific endeavors of the Turks.

(4) Rare Works of History and Literature. In the fields of history and literature, I saw several writings in which the innovation that I had been seeking for some time was found and, apart from the present writings of Europe, no trace of this kind of writing style had been found anywhere. For example, many books have been written on the circumstances of qāẓīs, [87] but no one thought to copy their rulings and decrees along with their life circumstances so that one could compare this with today's method of deciding cases. A book of this kind exists in the Library of the Yanī Congregational Mosque. The author of the book is Abū Bakr

Muḥammad bin Khalaf Wakīʿ,[83] an author from an extremely ancient period, who recounts all events with an unbroken chain of authority. In the book, he has observed the rule to copy, along with information about each person, a great many rulings and judgments, and has recounted the specifics of the cases.

I had never seen a book of this kind in the field of literature; rather, I did not even think that a Muslim would ever have written a book in which there was a history of poetic themes; that is, such-and-such a poet first wrote such and such a theme, then, gradually, such and such a poet made this and that addition, or changed its forms thus. In the Library of ʿĀshir Āfandī, I saw a very thick book specifically on this topic. The author has claimed that the pre-Islamic Arabs invented themes of every kind, then later poets developed them and came up with various new embellishments. The entire book is in proof of this claim. The author copies one poem by a pre-Islamic Arab for each theme and tells us that among the Islamic poets, such and such a poet changed this same theme a bit and wrote it thus. Then the poets of the Umayyad and Abbasid governments produced even more forms from it. Having read this book, one is astonished by the author's breadth of vision and discernment of subtle detail, and, along with that, one regrets that later authors could not follow in the footsteps of [88] rare compositions of this kind so that numerous books on this subject might exist today.[84]

(5) The Writings of Philosophers and the Leaders of Their Fields. The abundance in which the books of renowned philosophers and leaders of their fields are found here cannot be found anywhere else. The rare writings of Imām Ghazālī, Bū ʿAlī Sīnā, Fakhr-i Rāzī, and Fārābī, whose names are known only by means of Ibn-i Khallikān, and so on, are found here in abundance. The correspondence and letters related to gnosis and truth that occurred between Abū ʿAlī Sīnā and Ḥaẓrat Sulṭān Abū Saʿīd Abū al-Khair from time to time are available in the form of short treatises.[85]

Regarding Ibn-i Sīnā, it has long been a matter of debate whether or not he added anything to Greek philosophy. He has written in *Kitāb al-shifā*, "Whatever I write is the philosophy of Aristotle. I have written my own philosophy in *Ḥikmat-i mashriqiyah*." Europeans are desperately seeking this book, meaning *Ḥikmat-i mashriqiyah*. And because they cannot find this book, Professor Munk has written in his book, *Rabṭ falsafat al-Yahūd wal-Islam*, that we cannot find *Ḥikmat-i mashriqiyah*, and from the books we can find, it is proven that Ibn-i Sina did not add anything.[86] An extremely excellent copy of this rare book is found in the Library of the Āyā Ṣofīyah [Hagia Sophia] Congregational Mosque. Would Muslims ever have taken the trouble to read it and to compare it with Greek philosophy? But if Europeans had found this book, there is no doubt that a conclusive decision in the debate as to whether or not Muslims added anything to Greek philosophy would have been made. Because time was short, I looked only superficially at this book. It did not appear that there was any innovation in it. [89] If there had been an opportunity to look at it with eyes of minute examination, then some opinion could have been formed.

The Names of Some Books of History and Literature. Among the rare books of history and literature that I saw here, the names of some of them are as follows: *Tārīkh* by Khaṭīb Baghdādī, whole and complete; *Tārīkh-i Islām* by ʻAllāmah Żahabī, eight volumes; *Tārīkh al-ḥukamā* by Jamāl al-Dīn Qifṭī;[87] *Tārīkh-i kabīr* by Imām Bukhārī, three volumes; *Tajārib al-umam* by Ibn-i Miskawaih;[88] *Muntaẓam* by Ibn al-Jauzī; *Mira't al-zamān* by Sibṭ ibn al-Jauzī; *Masālik al-abṣār* by Ibn-i Fażlullāh, twenty volumes; *ʻIqd al-jumān* by Badr al-Dīn al-ʻAinī, eighteen volumes; *Mukhtaṣar-i Tārīkh-i Dimashq-i Ibn-i ʻAsākir* by Jamāl al-Dīn bin Mukarrim al-Anṣārī, four volumes; *Riḥlah* by Ibn-i Khaldūn; *Nihāyat al-arab* by al-Nuwairī; *Tabaqāt al-udabā* by Yāqūt al-Ḥamawī;[89] *Tabaqāt al-kubrā* by Ibn-i Saʻd;[90] *Tabaqāt al-umam* by Ibn-i Ṣāʻid al-Andalūsī; *Kitāb al-ashrāf* by al-Balāżurī, whole and complete; *Sīrat al-ʻUmarain* by Ibn-i Jauzī;[91] *Kitāb al-bayān wal-tab'īn* by Jāḥiẓ;[92] *Ṣināʻatain* by al-ʻAskarī; *Dalā'il al-iʻjāz* by ʻAbd al-Qāhir al-Jurjānī;[93] the *Tażkirah* by Ibn-i Ḥamdūn; *Sharḥ-i Tabrīzī bar Dīwān-i Abū Tammām;*[94] the *Dīwān* of Abū Nuwās, complete; *Sirqāt al-Mutanabbī* by Ibn al-ʻUmaid;[95] *Majmūʻah-i risā'il* by Abū Isḥāq Ṣābī.[96]

The People[97] of This Place Do Not Take Advantage of the Libraries. In mentioning libraries, I am forced say with extreme regret that these rare books are entirely useless here. First, these libraries open for only a few hours in the day. Along with that, there is a continuous holiday for a few months in the year. Along with these things, there is such a lack of superior taste that rare and classical books just lie there, unused. No one even picks them up to look at them. In the libraries, whenever I saw people engaged in studying books, I always sought to discover what kind of books they were reading. But I never saw any books other than *Mukhtaṣar-i ma'ānī*, *Īsāghūjī*, *Sharḥ-i waqāyah*, *Jalālain*, and so on.[98] [90] Of course, renowned scholars from foreign countries appear from time to time, and they are always in search of rare and excellent books.

The reality is that in the entire Islamic world, the method of education has become so debased that, apart from a few textbooks, no one has any inclination toward modern knowledge of any kind, the result of which is that the material of novelty and innovation is being stripped away from the nation, and there is no hope in the future for whatever little remains.

Note: The detailed account that I gave in description of the libraries, I made for a specific purpose, and I want to call the nation's attention to it. In Europe, numerous societies have been established whose aim is to collect classical, excellent books and print and publish them. It is by virtue of these societies that classical and rare Arabic books have become available to us which we had never thought obtainable. These are the societies that compiled a complete copy of *Tārīkh-i kabīr* by Abū Ja'far Jarīr Ṭabarī and have printed and published a great number of volumes of it,[99] whereas the scholars of Egypt and Turkey had lost all hope of finding this rare historical treasure, and Shāh 'Abd al-'Azīz sāḥib had assured us that it had been lost from the world.[100] Without a doubt, Europe has done us a great favor, and we should acknowledge it openly. I beseech the elders of the nation to form a grand society of this kind. Sufficient capital should be collected by means of public donations. Capable and qualified authors should be appointed as members for the selection of books. Books should be copied and ordered from Constantinople and Egypt, and they should be printed and published. [91] Such an undertaking may appear overwhelming and, with regard to the present state of the nation, impossible. But in reality it is not. If among four crore Muslims, even one hundred Muslims are prepared to give a small amount in subscription, then it is no difficulty for this task to be accomplished.

We hope that the society that has been established in Hyderabad by the name of Dā'irat al-Ma'ārif al-Dakaniyah, of which one esteemed member is Nawāb Iqbāl Yār Jang Bahādur, will attend to our request.[101] We recognize with gratitude its generous support of science and knowledge, but we require more generosity than this, and our hope is that the Dā'irat al-Ma'ārif will attend to this purpose with even more attention and care.

Zawāyā or Hostels

Hostels, which they call *takyah* or *takāyā* here, are in abundance.[102] The names of 305 hostels, along with details of their locations and other information, are recorded in the latest report that has been compiled. But the word *khānqāh* [retreat for dervishes] does not carry the same meaning that is used in our region. In these regions, this is a wondrously beneficent practice that is, in truth, amazing. In all major cities, there are separate hostels for every region and every group. When a traveler from that region and group turns up there, he can enter the hostel without hindrance of any kind and can stay there as long as he desires. Food and one serving of tea each day are free. This generosity is so widespread that despite the remoteness of the distance and the lack of connection, in Constantinople, Damascus, Jerusalem, Aleppo, Mosul, Diyar Bakır, all these places, there are separate hostels for Hindustanis, [92] and an appropriate quantity of meat and grain is designated for them.

Amīrs and elites have established these hostels and have endowed enough property that regular expenses are always paid. There is a shaikh in every hostel who receives a reasonable salary and board, and the entire administration of the hostel depends on him. I visited numerous hostels. The buildings of some of them were of pleasant ambiance and elegant. The type and quantity of food is also sufficient. The yearly expenses of the hostels in Constantinople alone cannot be estimated at less than four or five lakhs. In truth, this is very great proof of the generosity of the Turks and there is no doubt that, with regard to the time when this practice was established, it was neither unsuitable nor inelegant.

You have probably read in Arabic histories that there always remained a steady stream of travelers and students throughout the Islamic regions.

This was on account of these hostels and *zawāyā*. Ibn-i Baṭūṭah was aided by this practice on his worldwide journey. Thus, he wrote the names of these hostels in his travelogue. But it is a fact of nature that when bad days befall a nation, beneficial practices become harmful. Muslims lost the taste for travel, geographical research, and the acquisition of knowledge. For this reason, this custom has become nothing more than a means of laziness, freeloading, and pauperism, and it is doing extreme harm to national life. I went into and saw many hostels myself. Some travelers have been there for several years. They have neither any occupation nor any work. Here, one can see with one's own eyes the condition of the officers of Lucknow that we always used to hear about.[103] [93] The shaikhs to whom the administration of the hostels is entrusted, and the cash and commodities in their care, are generally double-dealing and dishonest. They live in extreme ease and luxury themselves and do not give the travelers half, a third, or even a quarter of the amount that is designated for them. The shaikh of the Indian hostel is a Kashmiri gentleman. He has taken several wives. He has built a house separate from the hostel for himself. He often stays there. The two and a half seers of meat that are allotted for the hostel each day come into the possession of the gentleman, and even ordinary food does not fall to the lot of the travelers. The building of the hostel is crumbling. There is always a pile of trash and filth sitting in the courtyard. In brief, it is a complete picture of savagery and desolation. Although the other hostels that I saw were better than the Hindi hostel in every respect, no trace of honesty and integrity is found. In this way, an amount of several lakhs annually is squandered in an extremely bad way.

Congregational Masjids and Famous Places

With respect to the abundance of congregational masjids and their fineness of construction, magnificence, and glory, Constantinople has no equal in the world. From the time of Muḥammad Fātiḥ, who was the first to sit on the throne in this capital city, up to today, a congregational masjid of all the rulers who have passed (with a few exceptions) is found, and each is of great grandeur and glory. Among them the most distinguished are the Jāmi‘ Fātiḥ, the Jāmi‘ Sulaimān, the Jāmi‘ Bāyazid, the Jāmi‘

Wālidah-i Sulṭān, the Jāmi' Sulṭān Aḥmad, and the Jāmi' Āyā Sofiyah, and among these the Jāmi' Āyā Sofiyah is the most glorious and magnificent. [94] The construction of these masjids is completely different from the masjids in our place. There is neither a hall nor arches nor a courtyard. There is only a single dome, but so large that several thousand people can fit under it. Although with respect to Hindustani taste, one cannot call these masjids beautiful and elegant, the boundless largeness of the dome and the loftiness of the building immediately fill a person with wonder, rather, render him awed and wonderstruck. There are metal chandeliers of several hundred candles in each masjid. It seems as if the tradition of the chandelier exists from a very ancient time. In the Arabic histories of Spain, this kind of chandelier is probably meant by the word *śurayyā*.[104] Of course, the difference is that they were made of glass and crystal there, and they are made of metal here. Generally, in all masjids there is a special compulsory element from which it seems that the sulṭāns were extremely excessive in Sunnism and made a display of it at every turn. Generally, in every masjid there are four large shields in all four corners, and, on them, written in gold in extremely fine calligraphy and large, bold letters, are *Abū Bakr, 'Umar, 'Uśmān,* and *'Alī,*[105] in entirely the same way that they hang calligraphed fragments written by masters on walls for decoration and adornment.

The Decoration of the Masjids. All masjids are elaborate and decorated. Ordinarily, reed mats, and on Friday and both Eids, excellent and highly valuable carpets are laid out on the floor. On one side of the masjid, some land is reserved on which there is a place for ablutions with flowing water. I was extremely pleased by the fact that pools are absolutely not in use here.

The Āyā Ṣofiyah [Hagia Sofia] Mosque. The Āyā Ṣofiyah Mosque is the most glorious, and all masjids are built on its example. Originally, it was a very large church, which Constantine constructed in 325. Its construction took seven years, and one hundred architects and ten thousand laborers worked on it. [95] Muḥammad Fātiḥ, having altered it somewhat, turned it into a masjid. Ibn-i Baṭūṭah had seen it as a church. He writes, "This is the largest church of the Romans, and because no outsider can go inside it,

I cannot describe the quality of its interior. From the outside, its features are that there is a compound of one mile, and the entire ground is covered in marble flooring. In the middle is a canal on both shores of which there is a wall of marble one arm's length high. On the wall is excellent mosaic work, and extremely excellent flowers and vine patterns have been made. The gate of the church is covered in gold leaf and silver leaf. It became clear from peoples' accounts that several thousand priests and monks live in the church, day and night."

The features that Ibn-i Baṭūṭah described, alas, no longer exist. The enclosure, in which there was a canal, is completely outside the masjid, and has been turned into a coffeehouse.

Truly, this building is wondrous and astonishing. The diameter of the middle dome is 115 feet, and the elevation of the ceiling is 180 feet. There are 170 columns, and all the stones are marble and porphyry stone. The diameter of these columns is no less than three or four arm's lengths each. On the gate, which is from the time of Constantine and is made of copper, some images from the classical age are made, and they are still standing. Even remnants of the images of Jesus, peace be upon him, and Mary that were on the ceiling still exist.

Places Worth Seeing. Places worth seeing are many. For example, ancient temples of the Greeks; the armory; the treasury, meaning where there are full-sized images of all the Ottoman sulṭāns along with original dress, weapons, and jewelry; the factory for casting canons; [96] *mūzah khānah*,[106] meaning the ancient museum where there are rocks and inscriptions of an extremely ancient period. In it, there is even the coffin of Alexander the Greek, and so on, and so on. But I could not visit most places. Thus, I shall content myself with those places that I toured myself.

Shipyard [*Tars-khānah*]. That is, the factory for building ships. It is a very large, magnificent factory, and because it is connected with the Military Department, no one can go there without the written permission of the Naval Office. Fortunately, one esteemed officer in the Naval Office was an acquaintance of our friend Shaikh ʿAlī Ẓabyān. He kindly sent an officer along with us, who took us on a thorough tour of the entire factory.

This ṣāḥib understood and spoke Arabic well, and for this reason we could inquire about everything in detail. This factory is divided into different parts whose headquarters are a very large, rectangular, two-story building, where there are large engines, and by means of them hundreds of machines run. Our guide first took us on a tour of the upper level. First he took us into a large room. There, several esteemed officers seated around a long table were preparing the plan of a ship. When the diagram is prepared, it is sent into another office, where a small model of the ship is prepared in accordance with the diagram. This model is made of wood, and despite being small, it is a complete image of the ship. This model is first presented to the sulṭān for consideration, and, after approval, a ship is prepared in accordance with its example. How could I have understood the subtleties and finer points of these replica ships? But in appearance, it seemed to be work of extreme precision and mastery. [97]

Torpedo Ships. Having seen these things, we went down below. Here, hundreds of machines were running, and different jobs were being done. On one side, parts were being cast. On another side, a hammer weighing hundreds of maunds repeatedly fell onto many thick iron bars and turned them into sheets. Ahead of this building there is a very large, long enclosure. There, was a nearly complete ship there. All that remained was to clad the sheet. Here, I saw many torpedo boats that had been prepared in this very factory and had been launched into the ocean. There is nothing in the upper level of these ships. The entire ship looks like a large wooden board. The instruments of war and necessary things of every kind, that is, the kitchen, sleeping chamber, dining room, in short, whatever there is, is inside. Our guide even took us on a tour of one boat. But because there is very little room inside, we began to suffocate in just a short while and soon came outside. The extremely praiseworthy thing is that only Turks run such a magnificent factory. All the officers, artisans, and employees are Turks. Only a single European is an employee of ordinary rank, and even he has been retained with regard to seniority.[107] The engines, too, are prepared here, and the Turks state that they are no less than the engines built in Europe in any respect. One officer told me, “We have no dependency on Europe in any tasks of this kind.”

The Slain of the Yang Charīs. In the history of the Turks, the word *Yang Charī* [Janissary] is an extremely important word. [98] Sulṭān Ārkhān [Orhan], who was the second among the Sulṭāns of Turkey to sit on the throne, gave the order in 763 Hijrī [1361–62] that a particular number of the prisoners of war who arrived as captives in large numbers each year should be selected, and an army prepared from them. Ḥajī Baktāsh, who was the spiritual mentor of the sulṭān, named the army the Yang Charī, the meaning of which in the Turkish language is "new army." Considerable increases were made in the size of this army because of the large number of conquests. So much so that after two or three generations, the army became the hand and arm of the government. It is a strange thing that although these captives of war were generally Christian by descent, and even after entering the army stood firm in their old religion, they still had such genuine love for the Turkish government that the Turks themselves could not have had more. It was by virtue of these daring, self-sacrificing men that the Turks were able to make Europe their hunting ground for some time. In 1826, when Sulṭān Maḥmūd sought to organize the army on European principles, these people rebelled. The sulṭān had already prepared a modern army. The people of the city, too, stood by the royal modern army. In short, there was a harsh battle in Constantinople itself. The Yang Charī army was completely destroyed. In addition, the royal army, too, suffered a severe loss, and the Grand Wazīr and Shaikh al-Islām were killed.[108]

This space is an edifying monument to this battle. There are full-length statues of the Grand Wazīr, Shaikh al-Islām, and all the major, renowned officers of the Yangcharī army. The formidable form of the soldiers and generals, the garments and military weaponry of classical times, the scene of silence and tranquility—by all these things gathered together, such an awesome scene has been produced that one is afraid to go there even in the daytime. [99] I saw two warriors sunk from head to toe in iron, helmet on head, visor on face, iron gloves on hands, coat of mail and *chār-ā'īnah* armor on body, iron boots up to the knees. In sum, no part of the body was visible except for the eyes. By inquiry I learned that they are Kurdish youths who were appointed especially to the service of his majesty. In my estimation, there was no less than a burden of one maund of iron on their body. It is a wonder how they fought with such weight. The garments of officers are of a strange and wondrous kind. The turbans of some are a full forearm's length high each. There is an official guard at all times, and no person can go there without obtaining a ticket.

Museum. *Mūzah-khānah*. Meaning museum. The museums are two. One official, where there are extremely ancient stones and inscriptions, and monumental things of this kind. There is even a stone coffin of Alexander the Greek. Alas, I did not have a chance to visit it.

Some Christian businessman established the other. The building and all the other objects are ordinary. All that is worth seeing are the statues of people from different parts of the world. These statues have been made so well that they seem completely real. I saw a woman whose lips were extremely fat, and a pointed wooden peg had been pierced all the way through her bottom lip. I learned that it is an ornament in that place. At first I was extremely astonished. Then I thought that if in our country they pierce noses and ears and have people wear nose rings and earrings, then what fault did lips commit that they should be deprived of such adornment? [100]

A Painful Spectacle. Here, I saw a strange, painful spectacle, the effect of which remained on my heart for a while. In a separate room, there are several women who are afflicted with various kinds of torture. One is being pressed in a torture rack. On the back of another, they have set a burning slip of metal so that from the neck to the waist, four fingers' length of skin has peeled off. The others are similarly being tortured in a strange way. From their appearance and style of dress, these women seem wealthy and noble. Most are young, attractive, and of delicate figure. I was severely astonished to think which tyrannical hands had been so audacious as to raise a hand against these goddesses of beauty!! By inquiry, I learned that when the Islamic government was destroyed in Spain, and the sultanate of the Christians was established, Muslims were generally compelled to change their religion, and because the trace of Islam could not easily be erased from their hearts, they were tortured in various ways and manners, and, on account of their helplessness and weakness, even more tyranny was enacted upon women. These tyrannized women are memorials of this admonitory and morally instructive event. At that time I thought, "Aha! It is these very Christians who deride us that Islam was spread by the sword!!!"

I could not figure out to what end the founder of the museum, who is a Christian, has kept these images here. Does he desire to show this proud achievement of the Christians? And since the government of the Turks does not object and intervene, does it desire to offer proof of its impartiality? I extremely dislike and disapprove of the idea that the unpleasant events that have taken place at some time among different nations of the world should be brought once more into public view. [101]

Sights

In Constantinople and its outlying area and vicinity, wondrous, pleasant natural sights are in abundance, and it is a blessing that the people of the city appreciate the value of this boon. A particular day is fixed for each sight. On that day, there is a wondrous, pleasant gathering there. Alas, the people of our region are not aware of a taste for natural scenery. Otherwise, people would have travelled to Constantinople specifically to see these sights and to enjoy them, and this would not have been considered strange. I visited two or three of them, and I shall write brief accounts of them.

Khūnkar Ṣūī. Khūnkar Ṣūī [Hünkar Suyu] is the most pleasant and enchanting of all the sights in Constantinople. On this basis, it has been associated with the name of the Great Sulṭān. Khūnkar is an alteration of the Persian word *khūngar*. In Turkish, they call the Emperor *khūn kā mālik* [the lord of blood] or *khūn-rez* [blood-spiller] and the meanings of *sū'ī* are water and spring.[109] On this basis, the literal translation of *Khūngar Ṣūī* is "royal spring." This place is located at a distance of twenty to twenty-five miles from the city. A range of mountains stretches far into the distance, and it is extremely lush and verdant. In it, one area, which is located on the upper surface of the mountain, appears extremely attractive. The place where the spectators gather in particular is extremely pleasant. There are lines of shady trees on both sides. As far as the eye can see, one sees nothing but verdure. There is a waterfall on one side whose water gathers in a pool. All around, beneath the trees, there are parties of two to four people each. A round of tea and coffee is served. Music is played at the pool, [102] and there is French and Turkish singing. Jesters put on shows.

Five or six steps above is the actual summit of the mountain, and it is extremely open, level, and shady. This place is reserved for women to sit, and many Turkish ladies are always gathered. Covering a distance of twenty or thirty miles, climbing the mountain, and riding a horse or mule is a matter of no little discomfort for delicate-figured women, but this place is so alluring that all discomforts can be endured for it.

Maqrī Kūī [Makrıköy].[110] This is a coffeehouse that is exactly on the edge of the sea and is a place of extremely pleasant ambiance. Waves repeatedly come and crash against the steep banks, and one feels a wondrous sense of joy. One special thing about this place is that six or seven Jewish women sit on a high platform and sing Arabic songs. Because I had never heard Arabic music before, it left a special impression on me. Everyone sang together as they played a kind of frame drum.

Muḥarram

The Muḥarram of this place is also something worth mentioning.[111] The number of people of ʿAjam, who reside here by reason of different connections, is no less than fifty or sixty thousand.[112] A great many are employees in government offices. Many are traders, professionals, and laborers. Although these people are spread throughout all parts of the city, where they live in abundance is a neighborhood by the name of Wālidah Khānah [Valide Hanı].[113] At Muharram time, assemblies of great pomp and parade, and the massive gathering of lamentation and weeping, mostly take place right here. [103] In the assemblies here, there is no tradition of *soz* and *taḥt al-lafẓ*; only narration takes place.[114] And in truth this alone is the purpose of the assembly of mourning. The general practice of this place is that, first, a person, standing near the minbar, recites poems related to the virtues and accomplishments of Janāb-i Amīr (ʿa) and Imām Ḥusain, peace be upon him.[115] Then a learned scholar sits on the minbar and describes the circumstances of Karbala extremely finely and clearly in the form of a sermon. I was very happy at the fact that Turks generally participate in these assemblies with decorum and sincerity. So much so that the sermon that takes place, except for one or two occasions, in all other assemblies, takes place in Turkish in consideration of the Turks.[116]

The Strange and Wondrous Methods of Mourning. There are a few methods of mourning, and some are extremely wondrous and impressive. The mourning of the lowest order is that they beat the chest with extreme force, so much so that the flesh there swells up. The second method is to mourn with chains. There is a circle of thirty to forty people, and they beat chains on their chest or back with such force that the sound carries some distance. The third method is to mourn with swords, and this is exclusive to the *shab-i shahādat.*[117] The mourners, standing in ranks holding bare swords in their hands, repeat "Yā Ḥusain!" in a complete state of wondrous passion and rapture as they go on striking themselves with swords on their heads, foreheads, and shoulders. Sprays of blood fly up from the wounds and fall upon and cover the entire body, and it is as if the circle of mourning turns into a field of battle. There is an extremely dense crowd of people to see this edifying and admonishing spectacle, and it is difficult to reach there.[118] [104]

Salāmlaq or Sulṭān's Guard and Eid al-Z̤uḥā

There is nothing more impressive or interesting in Constantinople than the Salāmlaq. *Salāmlaq* is a Turkish word whose literal translation is "to make salaam." Because on this occasion the army and the army commanders come to make salaam to the sulṭān, they designate this ceremony Salāmlaq. The sulṭān generally never leaves the royal palace. He only graces the congregational masjid to read Friday namāz, and that is where, after prayers, this ceremony is performed. The reality is that it is difficult, severely difficult, to draw a picture of the grandeur and magnificence that appears at that time by means of language or pen. Despite the fact that this occasion takes place four times in a month and forty-eight times in a year, and for this reason it can be considered an ordinary thing, there is always such a crowd of spectators that people climb into trees and onto men's shoulders to watch the spectacle. European dignitaries and travelers who come to tour Constantinople never let this occasion slip from their hand. There is a gallery above the thoroughfare of the royal guard. Having bought tickets, esteemed people are given permission to sit there. Thus, a sizable assembly of these esteemed spectators is found every Friday. During my stay, many chief members of the sultanate of Hungary had come to tour Constantinople and had joined this assembly. [105]

I had already heard of these states of affairs in Hindustan. For this reason, immediately upon arriving at Constantinople, I made plans to see it. I took along a Syrian Arab, whom I had recently met, and reached the Ḥamīdiyah Congregational Mosque [Hamidiye Camii]. Having reached there, I looked to find that ranks of soldiers had formed stretching far off into the distance, and it was difficult for the eye to reach the royal guard. I had no choice but to turn back. Ḥusain Ḥasīb Āfandī was once the Turkish Consul at Bombay and now is police commissioner in Constantinople. He knew me by means of the fact that in the Russian War, I had sent three thousand rupees through him to Constantinople as the secretary of a society.[119] On the basis of this means of introduction, I appeared in his service. He treated me with extreme kindness and said, "Come on Friday to the Ḥamīdiyah Congregational Mosque. I shall hold a ticket for you." But unfortunately (and, if you ask the truth, then, fortunately), when I arrived there, he was nowhere to be found. I waited for him at the door of the masjid for a while. At nearly one o'clock, when the roar of the sulṭān's approach began, the armies, spreading far into the distance, formed ranks in the shape of a crescent, and all the roads stopped. Disappointed, I entered the masjid and regretted that this Friday, too, had been a miss. A little while had passed when there came a sound like that of thunder, and the entire area erupted with echoing roars. I learned that the sulṭān's cavalcade had drawn near, and the cry was "*Pādshāhim choq yashā*,"* which is the national cry of the Turks. These cries were raised three times in

* The literal translation of this is, "May our emperor live long."

succession. The sulṭān's guard arrived at the masjid, and the roar of the cries had not yet quieted when the muezzin, who was waiting for the beautiful appearance of the sulṭān, raised the cry of *Allāhu akbar*. Both sounds mixed together left a wondrous impression on the heart. The sulṭān was riding in an open carriage. Because the courtyard of the masjid is not a part of the masjid, meaning they do not perform namāz there and they can go there wearing shoes, the carriage entered the courtyard and came to a stop near the door. [106] The masjid is two stories, and on the upper story is a gallery, which is the place reserved exclusively for the sulṭān's namāz. Having stepped down from the carriage, the sulṭān went to the upper story and, as he went inside, satin curtains were released over the windows to the gallery so that no one could see him.

When people were calmly seated, the preacher began the sermon. Regrettably, the preacher was a Turk. He was not an Arab. Thus, there was not that quality and effect in his tone and accent which is exclusive to the Arab. Still, when the second sermon began, and when he, gesturing toward the sulṭān, recited the following words in a passionate voice, "*Allāhuma unṣur hāżā al-sulṭān al-sulṭān ibn al-sulṭān al-khāqān ibn al-khāqān al-sulṭān ʿAbd al-Ḥamīd Khān*,"[120] it produced a strange, wondrous feeling. My state was such that tears continuously flowed from my eyes, and for a while prayerful words poured from my lips. At exactly that moment, fifteen or twenty people stood up at once in whose hands were petitions and appeals. These people raised their hands in the sulṭān's direction and offered prayers for him as they presented their petitions. The petition officer collected and submitted their papers. I saw several as they, gesturing toward the sulṭān, bowed to the ground and, touching the ground with their hand, kissed the hand. Although all these matters went against the custom and tranquility of the sermon, they did not lack their own an appealing quality. I learned by inquiry that people for whom it is otherwise impossible to access the Great Sulṭān express their concerns in this way, [107] and because the temperament of the sulṭān is naturally beneficent and generous, the custom is not stopped.

After namāz, Ḥusain Ḥasīb Āfandī happened to run into me and complained, "I was looking all over for you. Where did you disappear to? You will not get a ticket for the upper gallery now, but I will find an even better opportunity for you." Having performed namāz, when all the people went outside, the sulṭān came down from the gallery and stopped on a stairway wherefrom the Salāmlaq could be seen well, and no one could see the sulṭān. The army officers and the pāshās, having formed a line, stood on the right side of the courtyard. Ḥusain Ḥasīb brought me to stand in the line and told the people, "He is our guest." An esteemed officer (because of fine moral character) stepped back and cleared a space for me.

The Arrival of the Troops. After a little while, the troops began to arrive. From the royal palace to the masjid, there is a wide and sloping road. The troops stood in ranks in the form of a crescent stretching far into the distance. Passing by the front of the royal palace, they entered the main gate of the masjid and left by the other gate. The orderliness of the ranks, the different divisions of cavalry, foot soldiers, naval, ground troops, artillery, riflemen, Turks, Kurds, and Arabs, the elegant and regimented pace, splendid glittering weapons, uniforms of different and attractive styles, the coming of armies in succession and passing in front of their emperor with loyal passion; it was a strange and wondrous scene that can in no way be described. [108] There were turbans on the heads of the Arab regiment, which is the imperial guard, and the green ends of their turbans, flying in the breeze, exhibited a wondrous pleasure. For three continuous hours this military sea continued to billow, and about ten thousand troops passed by. In the end, both of the sulṭān's princes came, and came with wondrous glory. They were in military dress, and swords were bound at their waists. Although they were around ten or twelve years old, the manner in which they rode on horseback and the boldness and glory that was expressed by their faces cannot be put into words. When the princes, too, had gone, the sulṭān came down the stairs, and the ranks of army officers and pāshās, which included me, too, immediately bowed for salaam. I was rapt with wonder from the beginning, and my eyes were fixed in a gaze. It had always been my intention that if I had occasion to have an audience with the sulṭān, I would pay my respects with extreme supplication, but I was in such a state of rapture that the entire rank remained bowed for a while and I, eyes fixed in a gaze, stood there just as before. Of course, prayerful words flowed from my tongue and not intentionally, either; rather, I had lost all control.

Having taken five or six steps on foot, the sulṭān mounted his carriage. The officers made salaam once again, and the strange and wondrous scene suddenly became hidden from the eyes: *dīdah-i man bāz o ba-khwābam hanūz*.[121] At the moment when the sulṭān, having come down from the staircase, moved toward the carriage, there was a distance of only three or four arm's lengths from our rank to him, and for this reason I could see him very well. The appearance of the sulṭān is as follows: of medium stature, rather, a bit taller; lean body; oblong face; dignity and intentness drip from his appearance—rather, it seems that he is thinking about something. [109] Completely simple clothing, that is, a coat of black broadcloth and an ordinary Turkish cap.

The Practice of Salāmlaq. The practice of Salāmlaq has existed for some time among the Turks and has become a part of the ceremonies of the sultanate. Royal majesty and magnificence alone are not intended by it. Rather, a great benefit is that a large part of the army is checked each week, and in this way all the troops that reside in the capital and its environs pass through the inspection of the sulṭān several times each year. The Sulṭān of the Age can make a sufficient estimate of the state of the army, and thoughts of passion and loyalty to the emperor become refreshed in the hearts of the army.

When I returned to my residence having seen this spectacle, my heart was filled with passion and effect. By the incitement of poetic emotions, a few lines spontaneously came and went across my tongue. Taking up pen and paper, I sat down and penned a few couplets. Then the idea occurred to me that there would be even more material on the day of Eid. When I had seen that, too, I should write. Thus, all the couplets of the introduction that had been composed at that time, I wrote down and set aside. By these couplets at the end of the introduction:

> And this you ask—that from that place of beautiful sites,
> What have your eyes obtained?

to this couplet:

> Because the gathering is full of beautiful visions,
> The garment hem of my eye is filled with spectacle.[122]

this impressive and passionate scene is meant. [110]

Eid Procession. There was no Salāmlaq on the day of Eid, and for this reason the number of troops was low, but the glory and grandeur, majesty and magnificence, passion and effect, were a bit greater than even the Salāmlaq. The troops began to arrive at around eight o'clock and the unbroken series continued for an hour to an hour and a half. After that, a great number of empty carriages came. People wondered, "What is meant by them?" Then all at once, ranks of foot soldiers appeared in the distance. It became known that all the wazīrs, pāshās, army officers, and major regional officers were coming on foot in the sulṭān's procession. These ranks continued for half a mile on both sides of the street, and a strange and wondrous glory and grandeur was expressed by their fashion and dress. Golden flowers [epaulets] on their shoulders; writing in gold and silver thread on their garment hems and sleeves; chests covered in bejeweled and golden medals; the reflection of the sun on all this; the entire field sparkled. When this rank had gone, then the world-adorning beauty of the sulṭān appeared. The lauded gentleman was mounted on horseback. His dress was entirely simple. A few great, renowned military officers were in stirrups to accompany him. The horse slowly and gently raised its step, and at each step the cry "*Bādshāhim choq yashā*" was raised such that the entire area echoed with thunderous roars.

When I returned after seeing this scene, I sat down with ink and pen so that I could show others what I had seen myself. But alas, extreme alas, the pen fell entirely short. The image that I have drawn is an entirely incomplete image. [111]

Eid Maśnawī[123]

June 1892[124]

Location: Constantinople

O happy messenger of mine, yes, come!
Allah has furnished you with a good end.[125]

An unavoidable journey has come before you.
With ardor, rise from your place and take the path to India.
Go quickly and do not think of the two worlds.
And do not pause to take a breath.
The dear ones of India gaze expectantly at your path, awaiting your return;
All precious gems of the mine of India.
When you begin to sing in that gathering,
All will form a circle around you.
In order to benefit from your account,[126]
Everyone will jump up like the wild rue,
All with these words, "O good-natured one,
Say a few words about that traveled friend.
What is his state? And how is he? And
What good and bad has he seen?
Does he live in the manner of those with eyes to see?
Or does he live like a so-and-so and such and such?
After this toil and great anguish,
What advantage has he borne from this journey to Turkey?
Was it a gathering of joy? What did he see?
There was much to be done. What of it did he manage?
When he sat in the rank of those who seek knowledge,
What from that fresh garden did he wrap in the skirt of his garment?" [112]
When the stage of question and inquiry is covered,
Say of my vagrant self to friends,
"O all you treasure-keepers of the field of learning,
O heads of the table of the field of learning,[127]
By the mercy of the lord of high and low,
My state is as it should be.
I live in the same style and manner as before,
I am alive and I live happily and free from care.
Although I am not with wealth and wares,
Neither am I beholden to doorkeepers and porters.
I have no mind to adorn the assembly.
It is just me and this corner of solitude.
And this you ask—that from that place of beautiful sites,

What have your eyes obtained?
Alas! What can be said? When a relish for expression
Pulls me from myself at every breath!
Although I do not wish to sit silently,
Where is a chance that I may come to my senses?
Although I am ready to offer a few words,
I am drunk with the quality of this wine.
Move past these words and do not ask again.
I saw a pleasant dream. And do not ask any more.
If I did not set the table of words myself,
Please pardon me. I am enchanted by the spectacle.
It was strong wine. I am still wrecked.
My eye is open, and I am still dreaming.
How shall I tell you what things I saw?
I have collected magic and sorcery before my eyes
    Because the gathering is full of beautiful visions,
    The garment hem of my eye is filled with spectacle."

As the sun pulled its head from the pocket of the horizon,
The cry of Eid arose from every quarter.[128] [113]
When they arose, eyes full of sleep,
Young and old all adorned their bodies.
A child, who does not know the way correctly,
His mother kindly washed his body and face.
The style and way of mirth was revived,
Alley and market filled with sounds and voices.
The good news came that the kind and beneficent shāh
Would soon come to perform namāz.
In order to bring provisions from the table of mercy,[129]
The people poured outside from every corner.
They so raised the reins of desire that
Children and youth fell upon each other.
The courier of sight could not find a way to reach the spectacle.
Nor could the footprint find a place to step on the ground.
All with a hundred desires and a hundred yearnings

Turned their faces toward Bashikṭāsh.
They desired the collyrium of the dust of the path of the shāh.
They desired a place on the thoroughfare.
On both sides of the road, to have the honor of visitation,
The people formed ranks, observing every civility.
As the sun shone light in every direction,
The shining star of the shāh's entourage appeared from afar.
One by one the cavalry and army flowed.
You might say that wave was breaking upon wave.
The manner of each was different from the other,
Each and every one had its own flag and banner.
The light rays of those shining weapons and armor,
Light poured into the skirt of the dust.
As this group passed with total grandeur,
At once the ground became filled with majesty.
There arose a shout, What glad tidings!
The world-illuminating sun, filled with the breath of the caliphate,
Who leaves marks on the forehead of the sun and moon,[130]
Honored emperor, guardian of the caliphate, [114]
Rule of the regime and basis of the creed,[131]
Reflection of the mercy of the Lord Protector,
Image of the grace and favor of great ones,
Shadow of God, country-conquering shāh,
Army-defeating and fortress-seizing king,
Shāh of the threshold of the heavens and throne of the celestial sphere,
Fātiḥah[132] of worldly power and royal heading of religion,
Adorner of diadem and crest and signet ring,
Shāh of the heavens, shining star ʿAbd al-Ḥamīd,
Ayyaduh Allāh bi-naṣr mazīd.[133]
Royal glory manifest on his brow.
Kissers of his garment hem on the left and right.
As the carriage of the Shāh stood before them,
The people immediately stepped forth from their place.
As the countenance of the Shāh cast its rays again,
Prayerful cries arose from every direction.

A roar erupted that as long as the world remains,
May the world and time be in accordance with your desire.
As long as the celestial wheel turns,
Live long, for the world lives because of you.
You are the beauty and ornament of the entire world.
You are also the shadow of God in the world.
Everyone knows that in the East and West,
The crown of the caliphate rests on your head.
Today you are that in the world
On which rests the stability of worldly power and religion.
The freshness of Badr and Ḥunain are because of you.[134]
Because of you, the sacred sites of Mecca and Medina remain beautiful
and ornamented.
O Shāh, whose army is the stars but yours?[135]
Who protects the shar' of the Prophet?[136]
The glory of the religion of the Prophet exists because of you.
The arm of Islam is strong because of you.
Since the sharia has had the honor of your magnificence,
May the high heavens be at your command. [115]
May the coin of prosperity be cast in your name.
May everything in the world be in accordance with your desire.

The Moral Character, Habits, and Social Manner of the Turks

Although I stayed in Constantinople continuously for three months, because of my unfamiliarity with the language, I had very little association with Turks. All the companions and friends that I did have were Arabs from Syria. For this reason, my acquaintance with the ethics and habits of the Turks is superficial and cursory. I saw many colleges and schools, and some factories of industry, and so on. I met several esteemed regional officers and ate in parties at their places. Sometimes I happened to meet someone at a coffeehouse. Sometimes I became acquainted with someone on the tramway or rail. In short, it was occasions of this kind on which I experienced the moral character and habits of the Turks, and whatever I write in this chapter will be on the basis of these occasions alone.

The Hospitality and Fine Moral Character of the Turks. Although my means of familiarity were so limited, I am completely certain in relation to several matters that the opinion that I have formed about them is absolutely sound and there is no possibility of even the slightest error. The foremost among them is the hospitality and general fine moral character of the Turks. There is no doubt that the moral character of the Turks is extremely capacious and generous. There is no sign of arrogance, haughtiness, supremacy, or narrow-mindedness in them. Rich and poor, worker and officer, plebian and noble, [116] unlettered and intellectual—I came into contact with people of every class. But in terms of fine moral character and generosity of spirit, you might say that all were students of a single school and cast from the same mold. Ghāzī ʻUṡmān Pāshā, whom the event at Plevna made known throughout the entire world, and Darwesh Pāshā, whose paternal grandson has the honor of being the son-in-law of the sulṭān, are people of the same rank as governor general or commander in chief in Hindustan. I have met both, and the impression of the hospitality and kind moral character with which they treated me remains on my heart even now.

It is a common thing that whomever you ask for directions while walking in the market, even if he is a person of some considerable rank, will turn his attention toward you with extreme kindness and tell you the way. On several occasions, I happened to pass through extremely narrow and winding alleyways; and because of losing the way, remained bewildered for a time. When a Turk happened to turn up, he did not content himself with telling me the way. Rather, he came along with me, and only tuned back once he had brought me to where I had to go.

Generosity and hospitality are the general characteristics of the Turks, and even people of extremely low status are extremely generous and beneficent. It is a common practice that if a few acquaintances happen to meet in a restaurant or coffeehouse, one person will pay the cost of the coffee, and so on, on behalf of all. One might say that all the people are the person's guests and he is the host. When I went to visit Khūngarsūī, which has already been discussed above, Khūjī Āfandī was with me. Because this location is twenty or twenty-five miles from Constantinople, and some other friends were with me, sixteen rupees were spent on the rate of the ship and carriage as well as amusement, and so on. [117] Khūjī Āfandī paid the entire amount. My Syrian friends, who were themselves of high status and generous, found it unbearable to be under the burden of the aforementioned Āfandī ṣāḥib's favor, but because of the general convention of the region, they could not insist much.

One time I had gone to Darwesh Pāshā's house. Several other gentlemen were there. I was introduced to everyone and kept company and conversed with them for a while. Because at that time I had not begun to use Turkish boots, and it is improper here to go inside houses wearing English boots, I removed my boots at the door. As far as the Turks are concerned, it is unseemly not to have a boot on the foot. Thus, some people took notice. Among those present, one gentleman, who was a schoolmaster and esteemed person, quietly got up, brought a pair of slippers, and placed them in front of me. The name of this gentleman was Kāẓim Āfandī. He is a young man. A writing of his on mathematics has already been presented before the sulṭān. While taking leave, he said to me, "After reaching Hindustan, remember that Kāẓim, too, was your humble servant."

Ḥusain Ḥasīb Āfandī, who is police commissioner and a man of esteemed rank, treated me with such favor and kindness that I cannot describe it. He insistently fed me. He took me on a tour of his mansion and rear garden. Having made arrangements for purdah, he showed me all the rooms of his house. When I turned to leave, he said, "I, too, have to go to the court. We shall go together." Thus, he sat me in his carriage and brought me along for a great distance. The best part is that at that time I had no other means of introduction except [118] that I was from Hindustan and was a Muslim. From incidents of this kind it is definitively proven that Turkish morals are extremely widespread, and for this reason there is no need for the recommendation of esteem and glory nor means and introduction.

The Society of the Turks. The manner of Turkish society is extremely recommendable and worthy of imitation. Not to speak of wealthy and esteemed officers, the cleanliness and fine moral character with which even people of ordinary status live their lives does not fall to the lot of the very wealthy in our country. I have seen the houses of people whose incomes range from ten thousand to twenty rupees per month. Although there was extreme disparity between both, as there should have been, they were still equal to each other in terms of good taste, order, and cleanliness.

The Form and Arrangement of Houses. The old manner of the drawing room was—and continues to be so among those of the middle class—that platforms nearly two arm spans wide are built along the wall, and a cushion is spread out on them. Although, now, table and chairs are more prevalent, because scholars and dervishes often come and go at the homes of esteemed Turks, one room or so necessarily remains arranged in this manner, too. I saw numerous rooms of this fashion even in the magnificent houses of 'Us̈mān Pāshā and Darwesh Pāshā. In the present age, the European manner is more prevalent. The Turks have made some of their own reforms and improvements to it, and they are truly praiseworthy reforms and improvements. In the drawing room (which is often decorated with excellent Turkish rugs), full arms'-width strips of carpet, and so on, are spread from this end to that end like a path. [119] The people who come and go from the room pass over it. They cannot set foot this way or that. Although the boots of the Turks are not soiled, by this practice the floor remains even cleaner.

The Way of Eating. Dining takes place in the European manner, meaning they eat at table and chairs. Of course, there is a difference in some matters, and to my thinking they require reform and improvement. The common practice is that when all the people sit down on chairs around the table, a servant comes and sets empty plates in front of each person. After that, plates filled with different dishes come one at a time and are set in the center of the table. All the people eat from a single plate. There are forks and knives, too, but they (mostly) eat with their hands. I ate at the homes of Police Commissioner Ḥusain Ḥasīb Āfandī and Darwesh Pāshā. Darwesh Pāshā's son Aḥmad Pāshā, who is the father-in-law[137] of the child of the Great Sulṭān, was at the table with us and ate in this way.

People recounted that this practice is now slowly being abandoned, and the present-educated eat in an entirely European manner.

The Doors of Houses Always Remain Closed. In contrast to Hindustan, the common practice is that the doors of houses always remain shut. Inside, there is a catch that automatically fastens when the door is closed. On the outside there is a ring. When a person goes to meet someone, he knocks on the door with the ring. Having heard the sound, the servant or the owner of the house opens the door. At the houses of the wealthy, a brass flower is attached to the external face of the door. By pressing it, a bell rings inside and the servant is alerted. This practice is extremely common. So much so that even the doors of the poorest of the poor do not remain open. [120] Although this practice has basically been adopted in order to avoid the cold, by means of it, extreme cultural refinement and reform has automatically been produced in the manner of social life. Every person is compelled to put *lā tadkhulū buyūtan ghair buyūtikum ḥattā tasta'nisū* into practice.[138]

Dress. The dress of the Turks, as I have already written above, is entirely European. Of course, an invention has been made in the boot, and it is truly praiseworthy. The boot is a combination of leather leggings and a slipper. The legging is entirely of the form of a boot, but there is no heel. There is a catch attached near the heel inside the slipper. Having put on the legging, when they attach it, the legging sticks in it, and both come together to form a boot. They wear both as they walk around the marketplace, but on floors and carpets they remove the slipper and only the legging remains, and because it remains pure from dust and dirt, no stains appear on the floors and carpets.

The Way of Meeting. The method of visitation is extremely cultured and choice. When you go to meet someone and knock on the door, a servant will come and open the door right away. A special room in the house remains appointed with carpets for this very purpose. The servant will seat you there and offer coffee or tea. After that, the owner of the house will be informed. He will sit in the meeting room, and that is where he will call you. This is the manner of visiting great, esteemed officers. One does not have to pace about the veranda outside the grounds and wait a long time like the English.

The Way of Making Salaam. There is a strange, wondrous manner of making salaam. They set their hand first on their chest, then lips, and then forehead. [121] It is not necessary to touch these parts with the hand. Just being in line with them is sufficient. Although the hand must cover three stages in doing salaam in this manner, because of extensive practice, all three stages are covered so quickly that it does not take much longer than an ordinary salaam. This invention has the benefit that one neither has to lower oneself to bow, nor is Asian reverence and etiquette abandoned. The manner of doing salaam in an assembly involves more formality. That is, once seated, one of those present must do salaam addressing each person separately, just like the custom in Lucknow. Who knows who taught soldiers like the Turks this Lucknowi formality?

The Lack of Unnecessary Pomp and Show. The thing that I like most in the social life of the Turks is that, despite their refinement and high-mindedness, there is no sign of needless pomp and show. When major wazīrs and wealthy amīrs go out into the market, they do so in an ordinary manner. I have seen the carriage of the Grand Wazīr many times.[139] Only one or two riders accompany him. There are no more than four or five riders with Sipah-sālār-i kul ʿAlī Rižā Pāshā.[140] Simplicity is found in the houses as well as in all matters of social life. With respect to the status of people such as ʿUṡmān Pāshā, Darwesh Pāshā, and Zakī Pāshā, their houses should be at least the Falaknumā and Bashīr Bāgh of Hyderabad,[141] but they are not even equal to the mansion of our Maulawī Mahdī ʿAlī Khān ṣāḥib.[142] Servants and stewards, too, are not in abundance, as is the standard at the places of our nawābs and supposed princes. [122] The truth is that the Turks are entitled to whatever pride they take in the fact that they have not abandoned their soldiership after spending six hundred years nurtured in the shadow of the sulṭanate. Otherwise, the Abbasids, Fatimids, Umayyads (the Andalusians), and Timurids, in just one or two hundred years, had become quite pleasure-seeking.[143]

The Education and Training of Women. The thing in the refinement and development of the Turks that is most valuable and worthy of imitation is the education, training, and social custom of women. The two great nations of the world, meaning European and Asiatic, are situated on two extreme sides of excessiveness, and for this reason the state of both is objectionable. The Turks have adopted an equitable, moderate practice that is a collection of both and is devoid of the flaws of both. Turkish women are educated, but they have not been educated in immodesty, impudence, inappropriate freedom, or dancing (and with strange men at that). They observe purdah but they are not unlettered, unaware of the world, shut in the cage of their home, or human-looking animals.[144]

Women's Madrasas [Schools]. Education in Music. There are many official and private madrasas for the education of girls, and there is such excellent arrangement for purdah and protection that the noble[145] have no hesitation in sending their girls. Along with intellectual-scientific subjects, the French language, too, is included in the course of study, and in some madrasas, instruction in music also takes place. There is a special madrasa for the education of women teachers whose director is Rafīqah Khānam.[146] She is a woman educated at the highest level, and a *tamghah* medal of the second order has been bestowed upon her by the sulṭān. Among the industrial madrasas, one madrasa is of an extremely high order and can be called a college.[147] [123] Its director is ʿAzīz Āfandī.[148] Attached to the madrasa there is also a boarding house, whose director is a French lady, Madame Hanly.[149] The secretary of the boarding house is an educated Turk whose name is Ḥasan Āfandī. There is another large industrial madrasa[150] in Iskīdār whose head instructor is Khairiyah Khānam.[151]

Women Writers. Because of these madrasas, education has become so common that in the present age it is difficult to find a woman who has not acquired an education up to an appropriate degree. Many women are essayists, and their articles are published in renowned newspapers. Jaudat Pāshā's daughter, Fāṭimah Khānam, is a famous author. Recently, an extremely excellent novel of hers has been published whose name is

Zanān-i Islām [The Women of Islam].* It has also been translated into Arabic and has been published at Beirut.[152] There are some more women authors, too.

Women Have the Freedom to Go Out. Women have general freedom to walk and stroll around. Women of every class and every rank go out into the marketplace. They visit the sights. They participate in assemblies and intellectual gatherings. This freedom notwithstanding, there is not a hair's worth of transgression from the circle of vigilance and caution. In every gathering, the society of women remains separate from men, and a woman cannot so much as say a word to an unfamiliar man, except in special circumstances.

Women's Clothing. Their clothing is entirely European. But when they go out, they wear an extremely loose-fitting silken gown, which extends from neck to foot, and there are buttons attached from top to bottom. By this, the entire body except for the face is covered in such a way that not even the shape of the body is apparent.[153] [124] There is a cloth tied around the head, and they hide their faces with a handkerchief, which extends from the bridge of the nose to the chin. Both eyes, the bridge of the nose, and to some extent the surface below the eyes remains open. These handkerchiefs are made of fine muslin.[154] If one peers from up close, the color of the face is apparent. But who would dare act so shamelessly?

One time I was seated in the library of ʿĀshir Āfandī. A Turk gentleman with whom I had become acquainted was also seated there. His two young daughters, one of whom had already been married, happened to come there to meet him. He introduced me to both. Because of the respect, firmness of character, and humility with which those innocent ladies

* Now this book has been translated into Urdu and published at the Muhammadan Press, Aligarh. [This footnote first appears in the second edition (1901). The book was published as Fāṭimāh Khānam, *Nisā al-muslimīn*, trans. Saʿīd Aḥmad (Aligarh: Muhammadan Press, n.d.).]

stood before me, it seemed to me that they were not women, but goddesses of decency and chastity.

Hindustanis in Constantinople

No one in Hindustan will even suspect that Hindustani gentlemen, too, reside in Constantinople. I myself did not suspect as much.

The main center of Hindustanis is the Indian hostel, which I have already mentioned above. Hindustanis often turn up there, but they are generally professional beggars. Apart from them, there are three or four people who reside there permanently, and their condition and status are not bad, either. I write their names and brief circumstances.

Nuṣrat ʿAlī Khān. This elder says that he is from Delhi. He had published a newspaper, too, from Constantinople. [125] But because its articles were against the British government, the British consul made an inquiry, and the newspaper was closed. Now he is an employee in the Department of Education. His salary is 250 per month. He has married a Turkish woman. They have two small girls. He himself is dark complexioned, but his daughters are fair and pretty.[155]

Mirzā Muḥammad Beg. This elder is from the region of Awadh. He held an esteemed office in the royal army. He left for Glorious Mecca before the mutiny. He has lived in Constantinople for fifteen years now. The sulṭān has allotted him a stipend of 150 per month. He is of fine character and noble nature.[156]

Ḥasan Āfandī. He is the cousin by the paternal uncle of Badr al-Dīn Ṭayyibjī, barrister at law and resident of Bombay.[157] He trades in Hindustani goods. Previously, his place of business was thriving. Thus, in addition to other expenses, the rent of the shop alone was eight hundred per month. But now, because the fashion has changed, these things no longer have any value, and his workshop is slow and weak. Still, he lives in prosperity. His house and furniture are amīr-like with respect to Constantinople. He has also had a garden built. All the people respect him. He has even received a medal from the sulṭān. He knows English well. He is an extremely moral, generous, enlightened, and kind person. He has a wondrous affection and love for Hindustanis, and it was this love of homeland that became the means of our introduction. One time, I was strolling in the market. The aforementioned Āfandī passed in front of me. Upon seeing me, he spontaneously came up to me and asked, [126] "Are you by chance Hindustani?" At that time, my attire was Arabic. The funny thing is that, as it happened, the word *na'am* came out in response instead of *hān*.[158] Still, how could my being Hindi have stayed hidden? He wrapped his arms around me said, "You belong to us. Where were you going, hiding from us?" As long as I stayed there, he often visited me at my place. He invited me to dinner several times and took me to his home. I do not know if this hospitality is the leaven of his nature or a particular feature of the environment at Constantinople. His address is this: Constantinople. In the Mujauhar Badastān.[159] Ḥājī Ḥasan 'Alī Āfandī Hindī.

I have written the address with the intention that if some ṣāḥib should plan to travel to Constantinople, he should certainly meet him. A friendlier, more compassionate person cannot be found.

Friends in Constantinople

It would be extreme ingratitude if I should conclude the delightful story of Constantinople and not mention the names of the affectionate friends who became my compassionate companions during this stay of a few days, and who remained my confidants and intimates in public and private. Thus, apart from Shaikh 'Abd al-Fattāḥ and Shaikh 'Alī Ẓabyān, whom I have mentioned above, I write the names and brief circumstances of the remaining friends.

Fawād Bey. He is a distinguished student at the Civil College. Ḥaṣbāyah is a district near Damascus where a family from the lineage of Ḥaẓrat Khālid bin al-Walīd is settled.[160] These people are wealthy and, along with that, have regional influence.[161] That is why, until recently, the ruler of those districts who was appointed on behalf of the Turkish government used to be selected from this very family. My association with Fawād reached the point of a close relationship. [127] A brother of his, Sāmī Bey, came to Constantinople in those days and stayed in a room in the house that I had taken on rent. He was preparing to enter the Maktab al-Ḥuqūq, and because the entrance examination also includes an examination in logic, he requested that I briefly help him cover all the points of logic. Although it was an interruption to my schedule, for his sake I taught *Īsāghūjī* to him and to two or three students with him.[162] By a fine coincidence, they passed the admission examination. Thus, the connection of friendship and affection became even stronger. In the evening, the three or four of us always sat together in a coffeehouse that was right on the edge of the water and kept wondrously pleasant and enjoyable company. Sometimes after evening prayers, we would rent a boat and roam about on the sea. Fawād knows how to sing. He would always get in the mood and sing Arabic songs. One day, they demanded that I recite something Hindī. I said over and over, "Brother, I am a maulawī. What do I have to do with singing?" But would they have let it go? In the end, left with no choice, making my voice rise and fall, I recited a few Urdu couplets and said, "This is how they sing in Hindī."

'Abd al-Salam Āfandī. There is a famous family of sayyids in Jerusalem. He is an esteemed member of it. The muftī of Jerusalem, mention of whom will come later, is from this family. Earlier, he was a joint magistrate. He was removed for some reason, and it is in this concern that he has come here. He is an extremely capable, well-educated, and lively person. He and I lived in the same house for a while, and for this reason we ended up having more interaction. We often had intellectual discussions. [128] He is familiar with contemporary philosophy and acknowledges its value. He thinks that no issue in the Quran opposes contemporary philosophy. We often used to converse about this matter. I am exceedingly grateful for his kindness toward travelers and his Islamic compassion. The astonishing compassion that he showed me on one difficult occasion will be mentioned at the appropriate occasion.

Khwājah Āfandī. He is an esteemed man. The daughter of Darwesh Pāshā's brother is married to him, and the aforementioned pāshā holds him very dear. He, too, lives in his house. I met him several times. He is able to speak Persian with some difficulty. He is a person of extremely fine character and humble temperament. He always used to serve me tea made by his own hand. One time he even came to visit me at my place and stayed until late. He is the one who took me to visit Khūngarsūī.

Mullā Muḥammad Āfandī. He is a resident of Mosul. He has acquired a basic knowledge of Arabic. He can speak Persian well. He has no means of livelihood. With no other choice, he lives in a takyah and spends his life in poverty and hunger. Despite all this, he maintains his honor extremely fervently and has a strong sense of dignity. A friend mentioned him when I decided to learn Turkish. Up to that time, I was entirely unacquainted with him. For this reason, I tried to engage him at ten rupees per month. This amount was a gift from the hidden realm for him. But when he learned that I have come here only for intellectual-scientific research, he refused to take compensation and taught me for free. He often came to my residence to teach. The broken Turkish that I learned, I learned from him. Alas, that, too, is now no longer preserved in my memory! [129]

Apart from these friends, a great many other acquaintances were made, mention of whom is not so necessary.

Visiting Ghāzī ʻUṡmān Pāshā and the Bestowal of the Majīdī Medal[163]

This is the same renowned general who wounded twenty-four thousand Russians and put eight thousand to the sword at Plevna; in confrontation with whom the Emperor of Russia spent his entire military force and appeared in person as a general; who, despite a lack of troops and dearth of provisions, confronted the collective power of Russia for a time; and when, having been wounded on the battlefield, he was captured, and the tsar of Russia himself tied a sword at his waist and kept him as his guest for months. These events became famous throughout Hindustan at that time by means of newspapers, and every child became familiar with the name of this renowned, brave hero. Although I did not meet any military officials in Constantinople, nor did I try to meet them, how could my heart not have desired to see this rare wonder of the age?

Although the aforementioned pāshā is a man of such rank that no one in Turkey is above, rather, even equal to him, and in this regard there could have been very little hope of reaching him, still, the eager restlessness of my interest would not yield, and I took a translator and went to his house. Upon ringing the bell, the door opened, and the doorman gave us permission to go inside. In accordance with the custom, I went and sat in the visitors' room. An esteemed Turk was seated there. He treated me with extreme kindness and after greetings and formalities, called for coffee. After a little while, we were informed that the aforementioned pāshā was in the women's quarters. He sent word, [130] "I shall come in a little while." After about ten minutes, an employee came and took me to the upper chamber. There was a beautifully appointed room. We sat there. After a short while, the aforementioned pāshā came. The ṣāḥib whom I had brought along for translation was an officer in the Department of Education. Stepping forward, he kissed the hem of the aforementioned pāshā's garment in accordance with the rule and stepped back in reverence. I made salaam in accordance with orthodox practice.[164] The aforementioned pāshā responded to the salaam and extended his hand for a handshake. After standard greetings, he asked my name and place. The translator told him, "He is from among the ʿulamā of Hindustan and has come for intellectual-scientific research." Having heard this, he showed me extreme kindness and favor and asked about the state of the Muslims of Hindustan for a while.[165] When I took leave and stood up, he also stood up and said, "I would be pleased if you came again."

The aforementioned pāshā is of short stature. He has a heavyset body and his color is fair and shining. Awesomeness and bravery drip from his face. His age is between sixty and seventy, but he shows absolutely no sign of old age. He knows Persian to the extent necessary, and because he lived as governor in Yemen for some time, he can speak effortlessly in Arabic. After the event at Plevna, the sulṭān made him commander in chief and the wazīr of the War Department, but because in that office he could not always remain present in the service of the sulṭān, the sulṭān appointed Fawād Pāshā to that office and gave him the officership of *mābain* [*mabeyn*],[166] because of which he mostly remains in the service of the sulṭān. The sulṭān does not have more confidence in any other friend or dear one or servant or officer than in the aforementioned pāshā, and for this reason he does not separate him from himself. [131] When he goes to the masjid on Friday and Eid, there is no one else in the carriage with him except ʿUṡmān Pāshā.

When I went to visit him for the second time, he had already come and sat in the room. When I entered, he rose from his seat, took a couple of steps forward, and met my hand just like the first day. Whenever I met him after that, he met me in the same way. The aforementioned pāshā treated me extremely kindly. When the time of my departure drew near, I said to him, "Now I am a guest of just a few days more." He said, "Come and meet me a day or two before you leave." In the meantime, he requested that the sulṭān bestow the Majīdī Medal on me, and it was accepted. But I was not informed of this at all. One day in the afternoon I was sleeping at my house when a friend of mine came running and, waking me up, said, "*Yā Shiblī*! *Wa-Allāh la-qad ṭuliʿa laka al-nīshān*.[167] I felt something like astonishment and said, "You're just saying that. Anyway, how do you know?" He said, "It is printed in all the papers." At that moment I got up and when, having gone to a reading room, I looked at the papers, the news was in fact true. The thought immediately occurred to me that I was a British subject, and therefore it was necessary to inform the British consul.[168] The next day, I went to the consul. As it happened, he was not there. I left my card.

The next day, all my friends came to congratulate me. I organized a small gathering for dinner. Shaikh ʿAlī Ẓabyān, ʿAbd al-Salām Āfandī, Fawād, Sāmī, Sharīf, and other friends participated in the gathering. On the morning of the dinner, I went for a farewell visit with ʿUṡmān Pāshā. News of the medal had become so widespread [132] that when I arrived at the aforementioned pāshā's house, the doorman first said, "Congratulations on the Tamghah-i Majīdiyah." I was astonished. How did he hear about it? I learned that the servants and attendants of the amīrs and pāshās here are generally educated and read newspapers in their free time. The aforementioned pāshā congratulated me on the medal when we met. The medal was set on the table in front of us. Removing it from the box, he first touched it to his eyes. (Turkish people show this degree of respect to even the smallest of small things of the sulṭān.) Then he gave it to me. I stood tall like a cypress and offered a prayer for the sulṭān. After a while, when I arose with the intention to leave, the aforementioned pāshā said, "Sit a while longer." Having said this, he sent for coffee again and continued speaking of this and that. In the end he said, "I am grateful that you came." As we walked together, he said, "Upon reaching Hindustan, give my greetings to all Muslims and especially the intellectuals and scholars,[169] and tell them that 'Uṡmān feels heartfelt affection for you." I thanked him with extreme sincerity and passion. The aforementioned pāshā gave me a photograph of himself and wrote these words on it: *Ish bū fotoghrāfam Shiblī al-Nu'mānī Āfandīyah hadiyah almishdir.* Muḥarram al-Ḥarām 1310 Hijrī [August 8, 1892].[170] [133] Meaning, "I gifted this photograph of myself to Shiblī Nu'mānī." This picture is with me at this time, and I consider it a great blessing and a mark of pride that will remain a memorial in my family and my lineage forever. The decree that was bestowed along with the medal is copied below.

Copy of the Farmān in Persian Script

Hindūstānin ʿAlīkadh nām maḥallindah kāyin dār al-muʿallimīn muʿallim-i ūlā Shiblī Nuʿmānī Āfandī nin shāyān-i talaṭṭufāt-i saniyah-i shāhānah-m oldīghīnah binā'an sharaf-afzā-ī sunūḥ o ṣudūr olān amr o farmān-i muʿālī-ʿunwān-i bādshāhānah-m mūjib-i ʿālīsī ūzrah kandūsinah majīdī nishān-i żīshānik durdunjī rutbah-sindan bir qiṭʿah-sī ʿināyat o iḥsān qilinmish oldīghinī mutażammin ishbū barāt-i ʿālīshānim taṣdīr oldinī ḥurrir fī al-yaum al-rābiʿ ʿashar min shahr Muḥarram al-Ḥarām sana ʿashar o śalaś māya.[171]

Translation

Because Shiblī Nuʿmānī Āfandī, who is a first instructor of the House of Educators at Aligarh located in Hindustan, was thought to deserve royal favor, the grand decree was issued to bestow upon him the Majīdī Medal of the fourth order, and, for documentation of it, this exalted *farmān* was issued. Recorded 14 Muḥarram al-ḥarām 1310 Hijrī [August 8, 1892].[172] [134]

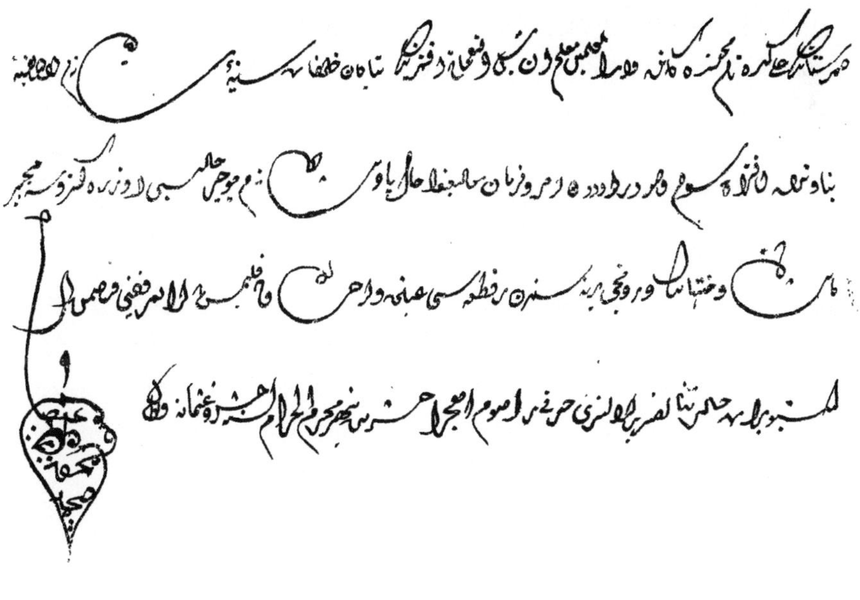

Government Resolution Concerning Foreign Medals. It was a strange coincidence that I did not put the medal to use anywhere—not at Constantinople, Beirut, or Egypt. Having arrived in Hindustan, the thought occurred to me that I should obtain permission from the government to put it to use. Thus, Mr. Harrison, magistrate at Aligarh, made a recommendation to the government by means of a formal letter.[173] The response came from there that the resolution dated May 2, 1886 requires consideration. The sum and substance of this resolution is that "No citizen of the English Government can put into use or accept any designation or medal of any other sultanate until permission is first obtained from Her Highness the Queen." In accordance with the execution of this order, I do not use the medal.

Departure from Constantinople—26 Muḥarram 1309 Hijrī [September 1, 1891][174]

The Celebration of the Enthronement of the Sulṭān. I resided at Constantinople for three full months. By the end, I had grown weary and restless. So much so that I could not even wait for the celebration of the enthronement of the sulṭān. In Constantinople, on the eighth night of Ṣafar of each year, which is the night of the enthronement of the sulṭān, a celebration takes place with great pomp and show. Lights are lit throughout the entire city. All the residents of the city illuminate their homes with great ceremony and care, and because this custom is evidence of sincerity and affection for the sulṭān, exceptional care is taken at the places of amīrs and pāshās. Shaikh ʿAlī Ẓabyān told me that last year at Darwesh Pāshā's house, fourteen thousand wax candles in glass were lit. On the doors of all the houses along the street, [135] *bādshāhim choq yashā*, that is, "May our emperor live very long!" is written in illuminated letters. This practice is not exclusive to Muslims. Rather, this phrase is also written in illuminated letters on the doors of the French, German, English, and European communities that reside or are either newly or temporarily settled here.

I extremely regret that I could not see this pleasing and exciting spectacle. Along with the weariness of my temperament, several reasons came together in such a way that it was not possible for me to wait any longer. People also said, "This celebration takes place everywhere in the Turkish realm. You will be able to see it wherever you go." But, clearly, how could the pomp, show, and care that take place in the capital take place in other locations? To crown all, it was unfortunately not in my lot to see this celebration even in an ordinary form because on that date I was in the world of water. That is, I was aboard the ship and had already come far from the inhabited area.

The Accompaniment of Friends at the Time of Departure. You will recall that when I entered Constantinople, I was alone. But upon my return, a group of friends is with me. All my loved ones have come to the harbor with me. At the time of my departure, they passionately embraced me and with prayerful words made me promise to maintain correspondence and friendly customs.

An Unpleasant Incident on the Ship. When I arrived on the ship, Ḥasan-i Hindī was already there waiting for me. I was very happy to see him. Pleasant and loving words were spoken for a while. Near evening, the ship raised anchor. Shaikh ʿAlī Ẓabyān, who was going home to Damascus on the same ship, was my traveling companion and intimate friend. [136] The ship arrived at Beirut via Rhodes, Izmir, and Cyprus. One day a strange disturbance and distressing unpleasantness occurred on the ship. There are two cities in Cyprus: Larnaca and Limassol.[175] The ship anchors at both places. Among the people who boarded the ship at Larnaca was a nobleman from Cyprus, and because he only had to go to Limassol, he came and sat near the bed of our friend Shaikh ʿAlī Ẓabyān on the deck of third class.[176] The aforementioned shaikh, despite his virtue and achievement, is a short-tempered man. The aforementioned nobleman set something down on his bed. At such a small matter, he became upset and enraged. The poor fellow stayed silent, but his servant, who by his appearance seemed powerful and physically fit, could not restrain himself. Things quickly escalated. So much so that other travelers on the ship, who were mostly Syrian Arabs, came over from all around and gathered around. Finding the support of the Arabs, our friend became sharper. The servant said, "Why are you so angry? We are no subjects of yours. Our city is connected with the British government."

As soon as these words came out of his mouth, all the Arabs became enraged. So much so that one Arab grabbed him by the waist, lifted him up, and said, "You wretch! I am going to toss you into the sea!" Because of the crowd, there was an extreme amount of back-and-forth struggle, and some people tried to stop him, but, pushing people out of his way, he came to the edge of the ship and gave him two or three shoves with such force that the poor fellow nearly fell into the sea. Just then, several people forcibly freed the servant from his grasp and directed, "Wretch! Go disappear in some corner of the ship!" Still, all the Arabs continued to shout and use inappropriate words in respect of the English government for a while. I was astonished that the ship's officers saw this whole ordeal with their own eyes and did absolutely nothing to intervene. [137]

Reason for Staying in Beirut. On the seventh day, our ship reached Beirut.[177] Shaikh 'Alī Ẓabyān disembarked the ship. I, too, disembarked with him, intending to return before the ship's departure. Upon reaching the city, it became known that Shaikh Ṭāhir Maghribī happened to be there in those days. The aforementioned shaikh is a teacher in Damascus, and his virtue and achievement are quite famous in these environs. I had heard his praises in Constantinople. Shaikh 'Alī Ẓabyān said, "You are not going to come to these regions again. You should not allow the chance to meet Shaikh Ṭāhir to fall from your hand." In sum, on his good advice, I had my things removed from the ship and stayed in Beirut for one week. Because this city is the station of the Damascus province and is considered the center of cultural refinement and civilization in the districts of Syria, I shall now write information about it in some detail.

Beirut

This is an extremely ancient city. Historians cannot precisely determine the time of its construction, but it is certain that it existed before the birth of Ḥaẑrat ʿĪsā [Jesus]. In AD 222, when Iskandar Safīrūs [Severus Alexander] sat on the throne of the government of Great Rome, he laid the foundation of a great university for legal education here, which stood at the zenith of prosperity for several hundred years. In 13 Hijrī [634–35], it came under the control of Islam. But in the subsequent period, having fallen out of the hands of the Muslims several times, it came into the possession of the Christians. Eventually, in AD 1517, Sulṭān Salīm I conquered it. From that time until today, it has been under the rule of the Turks. [138]

The Present Progress of Beirut. The beginning of its present progress is AD 1842, and from that time until today, its commerce and population has made daily progress. Twenty years ago, its census counted forty thousand people. In AD 1875, it became seventy thousand. And now it has become one lākh, seven thousand four hundred [107,400], among which 33,000 are Muslim. The remainder are Christians and some Jews and Druze. The ancient part of the city is extremely run-down. The roads and alleys are narrow and uneven, and the buildings are low and cramped. But the modern part is extremely lively and attractive. Hotels, serais, and coffeehouses are in abundance. One coffeehouse is right in the middle of the sea and is a place of wondrous atmosphere.

Clothing and Fashion. The language of this place is generally Arabic. Christians and Jews, and so on, all speak Arabic. The dress and fashion is very close to Arabia, but the style of their pajamas is that of Kābulīs. The gusset hangs to the ground like an elephant's trunk, and this is considered very beautiful. One pair of pajama trousers cannot be prepared with less than ten or twelve *yards*. Muslims, Christians, and Druze all dress this way. Of course, modern-educated people have begun to wear coats and pants. The climate is somewhat humid. Still, it is famously beneficial for bodily health. So much so that people come here from many other locations for a change of air. This may be so, but my experience is the opposite. As long as I stayed there, my constitution remained out of sorts. I came down with a fever for two or three days and had to seek treatment. Of course, Lubnān [Lebanon], which is a famous mountain and is three or four miles from here, is a famous place with regard to its climate. [139] Mutanabbī said of it:

> And the steep mountains of Lebanon. How shall they be crossed?
> For it is winter. And their summer is winter.[1]

The Scientific Progress of Beirut and Madrasas and So On

The Scientific Progress of Beirut. Although Beirut's intellectual-scientific progress began only a short while ago, with respect to the speed with which this city is progressing and the extent of the progress which it has already achieved, with the exception of Constantinople, no city in all the Islamic regions is equal to it, and in some particular qualities it even surpasses Constantinople.

Attention to the Arabic Language. A group of Christians has paid extreme attention and favor to the Arabic language and deserve our thanks in every way. These people have, with extreme effort, collected the classical dīwāns of Arabia from far and wide and have printed and published them. It is because of these people that the dīwāns of Khansā', 'Antarah bin Shaddād al-'Absī, Isma'īl Abū al-'Atāhiyah, Ibn-i Hānī, Abū Firās, and so on, have come to us.[2] Otherwise, neither their names nor even a trace of them was known to people. They have paid even more regard to the poetry of the Christian poets of Arabia (because of religious unity). They have collected the poems of all these poets in one place and have begun to publish a series of them. Three or four volumes have been printed, and the remainder are being prepared. Poets of both periods, Jāhiliyah and Islam, are included in it.[3] With extreme effort and care, they have properly and separately printed the dīwān of Akhṭal Naṣrānī, who was a contemporary of Farazdaq and Jarīr and a famous poet of the Umayyid government.[4] [140] This dīwān was extremely rare. So much so that even the libraries of Constantinople and Egypt were devoid of it. Only in the library of the Russian Emperor was there a copy of it. Thus, arrangements were made for it to be copied, and the Arabic professor in Saint Petersburg corrected it.[5] This penned copy, which the aforementioned professor corrected with his own hand, was shown to me, and I acknowledged heartily the ambitiousness and intellectual-scientific taste of these Christians. O Muslims! Do you, too, have a sense of honor?

These people themselves, too, have composed beneficial works related to the art of literature. Thus, *Rauẓat al-adab fī ṭabaqāt shuʿarāʾ al-ʿArab*, *Majānī al-adab*, and *Sharḥ-i Majānī al-adab* have already become famous and been published.[6] The astonishing, seriously astonishing, thing is that even the beneficial books in literature that the Muslim intellectuals of this place have written owe themselves to these very Christians. That is, the Christians have given them patronage and recompense and had them compose these books, and at their own expense have printed them and published them. The commentaries on *Maqāmāt-i Badīʿī* and *Rasāʾil-i Badīʿī* that have recently been printed and published with extreme care have been prepared in this way.[7] I asked people, "Why do these people care so much for Arabic?" People said, "These people consider themselves of Arab descent and they take pride in this lineage."

A taste for literature is so common that each and every child has a relish for poetry. A great many people are authors of dīwāns, and there are hundreds, no, thousands of people who have written five or ten odes. I met a famous poet at a coffeehouse. [141] I learned that he has been busily involved in the practice of poetry for forty years. Of course, it is regrettable that this taste is not sound.[8] Apart from ghazal and foolish encomium, they are unfamiliar with other genres of poetry. Concerning themes and poetic style, they do not like the work of anyone except the later poets. I often recited poems by Jāhiliyah and early-Islamic poets in conversation, and they thought that I had bad taste.

Modern Arts and Science. Modern sciences and the new taste are making a great deal of progress. Many books of modern philosophy, technologies, and arts have been translated. The curriculum of instruction in the large and important colleges and schools, and which is equivalent to the entrance, FA, and BA here, generally takes place Arabic.[9] Only education in the medical profession takes place in French, the reason for which, these people described to me, is that experience progresses so much every day with respect to this subject, and new books are written in such abundance, that translation cannot keep pace with them. A great author and master of modern philosophy and sciences is Professor Van Dyck, who is from America and has lived in Beirut for some time.[10] He has prepared an ordered series on modern sciences in Arabic whose name is *Naqsh fī al-ḥijar.*[11] Apart from that, he has written a great many separate books.[12] There was absolutely no encyclopedia in Arabic. Professor Buṭrus fulfilled this need. He began it in 1875 AD and wrote the first few volumes. But because he died, his son Salīm Āfandī planned to complete it. As it happened, he also died. Now another son of the aforementioned professor, Najīb Āfandī, is preparing the remaining volumes. [142] To date, ten thick volumes have been published.[13]

Historical Writings. Extremely beneficial books have been written on history and things related to history, and because these people are quite familiar with European languages along with Arabic, their writings contain the comprehensiveness that is not found in the writings of Europeans. Thus, the comprehensiveness and painstaking discernment with which *Āsār al-adhār* has been written equitably testifies to this claim.[14] Of course, it is regrettable that the hue of religious prejudice is found in the writings of these Christians. Thus, inequities of this kind are clearly felt in *Ṣannājat al-ṭarab* and *Uṣūl al-maʿārif*, and so on[15]

These authors are mostly residents of Lebanon [Lubnān], a great many of whom have come and settled in Beirut. These people have spread a wonderful intellectual-scientific taste throughout this land of mountains (Lebanon). Although these people are generally landowners or farmers and when necessary remain occupied with their business, whenever they have even a bit of time away from these necessary tasks, they occupy themselves with scientific pursuits. The result of this is that, although knowledge is not a means of wealth here, men of knowledge and authors have been produced in abundance and are still found in this area. A separate book has been written on the scholars and poets of Lebanon alone, but it is regrettable, severely regrettable, that all the scientific progress, composition, and writing, the whole of it, is exclusive to the Christians. Muslims do not so much as touch these things.

Madrasas. Madrasas are in abundance here, among which a chart of the famous madrasas is included below. [143]

NAME OF THE MADRASA	RELIGION	ANNUAL COST OF BOARDING AND FEES	NUMBER OF STUDENTS	DATE OF THE OPENING OF THE MADRASA
Isrā'īliyah	Israeli [Isrā'īliyah]	20 pounds	97	1875
Aʿdādiyah	Islam	20 pounds	150	1882
Iklīrīkiyah	Roman Orthodox [Rom ārthodaks]	free		
Baṭrīrkiyah	Roman Catholic [Roman kaitholik]	25 pounds	137	1866
al-Ḥikmah	Maronite [mārūniyah]		225	1876
al-Kulliyat al-Sūriyat al-ʿilmiyah, meaning the Scientific University of Syria	Evangelical [Injīliyah]	17 pounds	A detailed description will come later	1875
al-Kulliyat al-Sūriyat al-ṭibbiyah, meaning the Medical University of Shām	Evangelical [Injīliyah]	22 pounds		
Qaddīs Yūsuf	Latin	30 pounds		
WOMEN'S MADRASAS. THERE ARE A GREAT MANY MADRASAS FOR WOMEN'S EDUCATION, TOO, AMONG WHICH THE FAMOUS MADRASAS ARE THESE:				
Bākūrat al-iḥsān	Roman Orthodox [Rom ārthodaks]	15 pounds		
Rāhibāt-i Prātistant [Protestant Monks]	Evangelical [Injīliyah]	30 pounds	250	
Rāhibāt-i Prātistant [Protestant Monks]	Evangelical [Injīliyah]	free	500	

NAME OF THE MADRASA	RELIGION	ANNUAL COST OF BOARDING AND FEES	NUMBER OF STUDENTS	DATE OF THE OPENING OF THE MADRASA
ʿĀrzyāt Tayāmī	Latin	free		
ʿĀwariyāt Muḥabbah	Latin	25 pounds		
ʿĀrzyāt Nāṣiriyah	Latin	30 pounds	115	
Sūriyah Amīrikāniyah	Evangelical [Injīliyah]	12 pounds		

[144] The educational situation of Muslims relative to the educational progress of other communities will be known by the following chart.

NUMBER OF MALE MADRASAS	NUMBER OF FEMALE MADRASAS	NUMBER OF PROFESSORS AND TEACHERS	NUMBER OF WOMEN TEACHERS	NUMBER OF MALE STUDENTS	NUMBER OF FEMALE STUDENTS	COMMUNITY
21	3	50	20	2,000	500	Muslim
46	33	337	150	6,730	5,665	Christian, and so on

The Educational State of the Muslims. Although this number of Muslim students is small in its own right, it is even more regrettable that this number includes mostly people who are educated to a low degree. Otherwise, their number is so small with regard to higher education that one might say it is nothing at all. How regrettable is the fact that this city is a center of an Islamic government, the relationship between Muslims and Christians here is the relationship of governor and governed, yet Muslims are not even close to Christians in terms of cultural refinement and civilization. The state of education will have been made clear by the preceding chart. The state of writing and composition has already been covered above. In newspapers, printing houses, and commerce, the state of affairs is even worse. *Fa-ʿtabirū yā ūlī al-abṣār.*[16]

The Scientific University of Syria

University. Although (as mentioned above) there are many schools and colleges in Beirut, this college is a university, and for this reason its name is Kulliyah Sūriyah [The University of Syria]. The word *kulliyah*[17] has been applied here in the meaning of "university," and they call the country of Syria [Shām] "Sūriyah." Thus, "The University of Shām (Syria)." I toured this college in detail, and for this reason I shall write information about it in some detail.[18] [145] Roman Catholic priests established this college in AD 1875. There are nearly sixty teachers and professors, most of whom reside on the grounds of the college.

Printing House. When I went to the college, Shaikh 'Alī Ẓabyān and 'Abd al-Bāsiṭ Āfandī were with me.[19] When we arrived at the gate of the college, 'Abd al-Bāsiṭ Āfandī told us to wait there and went inside alone. After a little while, he returned. A man of stately appearance was with him. He welcomed us and took us along with him. The college building is two stories. There is a printing house on the lower level, and it is this very printing house that, because of the excellence of its print, has made Beirut known throughout the entire world. The name of the person who welcomed us is Ilyās, and the entire administration of the printshop is dependent on him.[20] Ilyās first took us on a tour of the press. All the work is done by means of a machine. The roller pulls the paper automatically. Ink is applied to the letter. The paper is printed on both sides and falls to the floor. The letters, too, are cast right here. Thus, Ilyās cast a few letters in front of us. The letters produced in the workshop here have attained such fame that orders come from far and wide, but the astonishing thing is that the clarity and fine script found in the books printed here is not found anywhere else. I asked Ilyās the reason for this. He said that in addition to the fine quality of the letters, a great deal of other care is taken here. After the form is removed, it is moistened and pressed with a tool in such a way that the letters no longer stick out at all and the paper becomes smooth and even. Thus, he showed us both kinds of forms. The corrected form seemed exactly like one printed on lithograph. [146] I praised the clarity of the print and the elegant balance of the letters. Ilyās said, "Actually, the person deserving of the praise is a Turk, Abū al-Żiyā, who has invented these letters. Of course, we have further refined and polished them."[21]

Book-Binding. In the printing-house itself there is also a binding shop. Extremely excellent gilded and gilt bindings are prepared. So much so that orders come from Syria and Egypt. I saw ivory book covers here, which I had never seen before.

College. Having finished at the printshop, we wanted to see the college. Because it was necessary for a professor from the college to be our guide for this, Ilyās first took us to meet Professor Anṭūn.[22]

There is an extremely sensible practice here, and it is worthy enough that it be imitated in our country. A small board hangs on the main door of the rooms of the employees and professors, and so on, who reside at the college. On this board, a detailed schedule of tasks spanning from morning until evening is written on separate lines, from which it is clear where the person who lives in the room is at what time and what he is doing. For example, on the first line is written "lecture room," on the second, "dining room," on the third, "leisure and recreation," and so forth. At the top of the board hangs a needle. The resident sticks the needle on the board in front of the line on which the activity and the activity's location are mentioned. The eye of whoever comes to visit him first falls on the board, and it therefore becomes known where the resident is at that time and what he is doing. [147] I do not know if this practice is exclusive to colleges or if it is customary in every class. In any case, this excellent practice is so worthy that it should be imitated everywhere.

Professor Anṭūn, the Fineness of the Building, and the Number of Instructors. In sum, Ilyās introduced us to Professor Anṭūn. The aforementioned professor is an extremely capable and qualified person. He knows French well. He is a master and professor of the Arabic literary sciences. The dīwān of Akhṭal that has recently been printed has been printed with his editing and care. The marginal notes that he has added to the aforementioned dīwān amount to a commentary in their own right, and from them one can gain an estimation of his breadth of vision. The college's weekly newspaper, which is issued in Arabic, and which is called *al-Bashīr*, is issued under his editorship.[23] Because of him, we saw every building and all the instruments, and so on, at the college. The fact is that this college is a source of pride for the Christians of this place and a cause of envy for all Muslims. Not to speak of Egypt and the Levant, even in Constantinople no college can claim to be its equal. The building is so magnificent, elegant, and beautiful that description is impossible. The floor on the upper story is made entirely of marble, and there is inlaid work in black stone. There is an extreme abundance of rooms. There are separate rooms for all the teachers and professors, who number more than sixty and remain in the college day and night. There is a magnificent room that is reserved for professors and ustāds, which is appointed with extremely excellent furniture and effects, and in the middle of which sits a rectangular table surrounded by a great many attractive chairs. In their free time, they come and sit here and keep friendly company. [148] There is also a smallish library in it. Whoever so desires picks up a book and amuses himself with it. At that time, the thought occurred to me that it is a great shortcoming in our college that there is no building of this kind where all the ustāds can sit for an hour or two even though this kind of company, in addition to enjoyment and entertainment, is also extremely beneficial for the national taste.

Instruction in science and modern subjects takes place at an extremely high level in the college, and to this end extremely expensive instruments and rare things have been gathered and made available. There are a great many cabinets in which there are many wondrous pieces of gems, stones, minerals, and soil of different colors and shapes. These rare things have been gathered and made available from faraway places for instruction in geology. There is a separate room for botany and it is very large. Professor Anṭūn told me that they have had to take extreme care in protecting and preserving these botanical specimens. The aforementioned professor showed me some kind of grass and said, "This is not found anywhere except in Hindustan, and it has been ordered from there."

College Library. Along with the college is a boarding house, and it is of the same fashion as the boarding houses of the large colleges at Constantinople. Although the college library is not very large, the books that have been collected are rare and uncommon.

They have arranged to have books, which have not been printed and old copies of which cannot be obtained, copied and reproduced from the famous libraries of Europe and Asia. I saw *Kitāb al-ʿumdah* by Ibn-i Rashīq Qairawānī, which is peerless in its subject, in this very library.[24]

In this college, the Arabic language and education in French are compulsory. [149] The remaining languages are elective. Thus, one Turkish, one German, five English, five Latin, and seven Latin and Greek classes are offered. It is a wondrous thing that although the founders of the university are generally Christians, and Roman Catholic Christians at that, among whom there is greater prejudice relative to other sects, there is still a selection of the Glorious Quran in the curriculum of literature, which proves that they, too, acknowledge the incomparability of the Glorious Quran in eloquence and rhetorical elegance. The subjects that are taught here, in addition to modern philosophy and the physical sciences, include the art of painting and music. The number of students is between five hundred and six hundred, of whom only eight or ten are Muslim.

The college building, despite the fact that everything in Beirut is extremely inexpensive, was built for under ten lākh francs, and a group of priests provided the entire amount.

Medical College. Along with the college, there is also a medical college, but its building is at some distance.[25] Professor Anṭūn took us on a tour of it, too. The building is extremely wide and tall, and the instruments are extremely expensive and abundant. In the room for anatomical dissection, which is very long and spacious, there is a wax image of every part of a human being, and they have made each one so finely and clearly that one does not even suspect that it is a replica. There are specimens of each organ in accordance with the number of diseases associated with each organ. Thus, in one space there are approximately two hundred eyes. In one there is leukoma, in another is an unguis, and in another the lashes have fallen out. I have never visited a Hindustani medical college, but I am fairly certain that there is not even one college [150] in all of Hindustan greater than, rather, even equal to it.

It would be extreme ingratitude if at this point I did not offer heartfelt thanks for the trouble that Professor Anṭūn took on our account and for the attention and fine manners with which he showed us all the rooms and instruments. It seems that the aforementioned professor enjoyed meeting me. Thus, in the issue of *al-Bashīr* that came out that week there was an editorial notice about me, the text of which is this: “We met in recent days with the gentleman scholar al-Shaikh Shiblī al-Nuʿmānī, head instructor of the Arabic sciences in the town of Aligarh in the country of Hind, and so we found him to be a man of many sciences [great learning]. And he received a Majīdiyah medal of the fourth order. He resided in the royal capital for a period of three months before coming to Beirut. And he set out today to visit Jerusalem, then from there to Egypt, then from there to the country of Hind."[26]

Societies and Newspapers

Societies, Newspapers, and Journals. Corresponding to the meaning in which the word *anjuman* [society] is spoken in our language, here there is the word *jamʿiyah* [society].[27] In Egypt, and so on, too, this same word is used. Societies are in abundance here, and their objectives are extremely beneficial. But it is astonishing, indeed quite astonishing, that not even one is of Muslims. A chart of some famous societies is included below, from which their objectives, too, will be known. [151]

NAME OF THE SOCIETY	RELIGION	PURPOSE	FOUNDER OF THE SOCIETY
Majlis-i millī [communal assembly]	Roman Orthodox	Public welfare	Maẓrān Ghafrāʾīl
Taʿlīm-i masīḥī	Roman Orthodox	Religious	Maẓrān Ghafrāʾīl
Qaddīs polis paighambar rasūl	Roman Orthodox	Religious	Maẓrān Ghafrāʾīl
Khairiyah	Roman Orthodox	The assistance of the poor	Khwājah Salīm
Maržā	Roman Orthodox	Medical treatment for the poor	Khwājah Najīb
Dafn al-mautī	Roman Orthodox	The funeral and burial of heirless and poor people	Khūrī Yaʿqūb
Zahrat al-iḥsān	Roman Orthodox	Literature	Sayyidah Ṭarīqah
Khairiyah	Maronite	The assistance of the poor	Khwājah Ḥināyah
Dāyirah ʿilmiyah	Roman Orthodox	Promotion of the sciences	Maẓrān Yūsuf

NAME OF THE SOCIETY	RELIGION	PURPOSE	FOUNDER OF THE SOCIETY
Akhwiyah Mārmārūn	Roman Orthodox	Literature	Salīm Āfandī
Yūḥannā mārūn	Marionite	Public welfare	Khwājah Khalīl
Khairiyah	Roman Catholic	The assistance of the poor	Yashārah Khūrī
Dair al-qamar	Roman Orthodox	The assistance of the poor	Khwājah Nakhlah
Shams al-Birr	Christian [Masīḥī]	Literature	Salīm Āfandī Kassāb
Bākūrat al-Sūriyah (meaning the dawn of Shām [Syria])		Literature	Sayyidah Ḥinah ʻAtīq
Injīliyah	Evangelical [Injīliyah]	Public welfare	Khalīl Āfandī Sarkis

[152] It will be evident from this list that all the branches of the Christian religion that exist there have separate societies. But Muslims have not touched this ridiculous business at all.

Among the newspapers and journals published from here, the most famous are *al-Bashīr, Bairūt, Taqaddum, Ṡamarāt al-funūn, al-Subḥ al-Munīr, al-Ṣafā, Lisān al-ḥāl, al-Miṣbāh, al-Hadiyah, al-Nashrat al-asbūʻiyah*, and *Ḥadīqat al-akhbār.*[28] Except for *Bairūt* and *Ṡamarāt al-funūn*, the owners and editors of all other newspapers are Christian. Because the press does not have freedom here, there is nothing in these papers except for ordinary news. Of course, intellectual-scientific journals come out with great splendor, and *al-Ṣafā* and *al-Muqtaṭaf* in particular were papers of such glory that they were equal to the magazines of Europe. It is regrettable that *al-Ṣafā* has ceased, and *al-Muqtaṭaf* has changed its location, that is, it now comes out of Cairo.

Observatory

There is also a small observatory here, which Professor Van Dyck Amrīkānī established in AD 1874. Many necessary instruments related to observation are present. Every day, the announcement of the things that are learned by observation is sent to Constantinople by wire, and from there it is published in Europe, and so on. Its direction is now in the hands of Mr. Robert, who is professor of mathematics at the American madrasa.[29] [153]

General Circumstances and Friends in Beirut

Scholars in Beirut. Shaikh Ṭāhir Maghribī. I have already written above that the main reason for my stay in Beirut was to meet Shaikh Ṭāhir Maghribī. Thus, I met him through ʿAbd al-Bāsiṭ al-Unsī and we spoke about intellectual-scientific things for a while. We met two or three other times. One time he even came to my rooms. The aforementioned shaikh is still young, but people respect him on account of his learning and virtue. The thing that I considered the substance of his perfection, and which I experienced myself, was that the aforementioned shaikh is not a man of limited thought like other scholars. He is acquainted with new ideas, even knows French in some measure, and has visited France. He is built of the material for national sympathy and is not unaware of the decline of the Muslims. Should this sensibility be produced in the common scholars of these regions, then there can be hope for real progress. The aforementioned shaikh is an instructor in the madrasa in Damascus. He is also the author of original writings, and several of his works on the subject of mathematics have been printed and published.[30]

I had the honor of meeting other scholars and people of achievement of Beirut. I usually sat at ʿAbd al-Bāsiṭ al-Unsī's shop.[31] Many intellectuals and people of rank used to turn up there, and I would meet and be introduced to them. So much so that when word spread throughout the city, several gentlemen even visited me where I was staying. Among them, Shaikh ʿUmar Jailī and one more gentleman whose name I no longer recall showed me great favor and regard.[32] Shaikh ʿUmar Jailī is the owner of the famous journal *al-Ṣafā* and is extremely generous and of fine moral character. [154] The other gentleman, who is a student, came with the intention to study logic. I excused myself for lack of time. Still, he would often come, and we would discuss literature. One day he asked me, "What is your view on Mutanabbī?" I said, "*lahu ḥasanāt wa sayyāt.*"[33] He said, *wa-l-ḥasanāt yużhibna al-sayyāt.*[34] I was extremely pleased by his delightful response.

One day, ʿAbd al-Bāsiṭ al-Unsī invited me and many famous scholars of Beirut to a party. The fraternal nephew of Shaikh ʿAbd al-Qādir al-Jazāyirī, who was the king of Algeria and fought against France for a time, Shaikh ʿAbd al-Raḥmān al-Jazāyirī, has lived here for a time and receives a stipend from the sulṭān.[35] He, too, graced the occasion. He is extremely aged and possessed of intellect. There is a small, beautiful rear garden in ʿAbd al-Bāsiṭ al-Unsī's house. Everyone sat there. The seating was of benches and chairs.

After a little while, everyone went into the dining room. Dinner was in the English style, meaning there were table and chairs, and when one course was finished, another was brought. After one dish, another came. I said to Shaikh Ṭāhir Maghribī that if such had been the case in Hindustan, a fatwā of *man tashabbaha bi-qaum* would have been issued.[36] He said, "This is appropriate in those regions because Islamic governance no longer remains there. For this reason, it is necessary to maintain traditions and religious prejudices (even if they are not correct) [155] to guard against the lessening of the general influence of religion. But in Islamic regions, there is no need for such ridiculous things." This company and conversation lasted a while and passed with great delight. The dishes were also extremely delicious.

Ill Health. Because the climate here is humid, my constitution remained out of sorts the entire time. One day I even ran a fever. The paternal cousin of ʿAbd al-Bāsiṭ Āfandī, ʿAbd al-Raḥmān al-Unsī, is among the famous doctors of this place and has acquired the highest degree of education in the medical college of Egypt.[37] I went to him for treatment. He was extremely kind and said, "After you return to where you are staying, the medicine will be delivered there." Accordingly, after two hours, a man came carrying a small bottle of medicine and said, "If this does not provide relief, then inform the doctor." The medicine not only acted quickly, but also tasted pleasant. The fever went away that same day. Although the doctor was educated in the European method, the effect of Asian, rather, Islamic hospitality remains in him to such an extent that, never mind the fees, he refused to take even the cost of the medicine.

This fever caused the great harm that I missed my chance to visit Tripoli. As it happened, a few scholars from Tripoli had come there in those days, and I happened to meet them at a social gathering.[38] These people were extremely insistent, "Come with us to Tripoli." Tripoli is a famous Islamic city and is considered an historic location on account of several Islamic characteristics. It is only two days from Beirut. There was enough time for me to go there and return before the departure of the ship. [156] I had even made preparations of every kind. But I came down with fever at the last moment and this heart's desire went unfulfilled.

Even more unfortunate was the fact that friends, too, left my side. Shaikh 'Alī Ẓabyān, who had been my intimate friend and companion for several months, had only remained in Beirut for my sake. A letter from his noble father[39] came from Damascus, and he had no choice but to leave. The time of his departure was eight o'clock at night. When he left, he kissed my shoulders as he embraced me (this is a common practice here), and recited this poem:

> Enjoy the scent of the flowers of Nejd,
> Since after this evening, there will be no more flowers.[40]

That is, if you aim to take delight in the *'arār* of Nejd (the name of a flower), take delight. Otherwise, after tonight, the 'arār will never fall to your lot again.

The Obscene Practice of the Cabaret. The thing in Beirut that I found extremely displeasing was a house that they call *maghnā* [cabaret].[41] This is an extremely unrefined and morally destructive thing, and I do not know how an Islamic government has allowed it. Right in the middle of the street there is a magnificent two-story building. On the upper story, there is a large room in which a great many chairs are set in order. At the front, there is a high, rectangular platform. Many European ladies sit on it and sing and play instruments. When one round ends, the ladies step down from the platform, stroll around the room, and pass by the spectators in the flirtatious manner of a beloved. Whoever so desires calls to them with a gesture, and they playfully and flirtatiously come and sit by his side. [157] Intimate relations begin with extreme immodesty and shamelessness. Wine is served, they wrap their arms around each other, and stroll around, embracing, kissing, and hugging. In sum, they do not neglect any fine point of immodesty. *Naʿūżu billāh min shurūri anfusinā wa min sayyāti aʿmālinā.*[42]

Departure from Beirut

As it was, my constitution was out of sorts in Beirut. After Shaikh ʿAlī Ẓabyān and Shaikh Ṭāhir Maghribī left, I became even lonelier. However, I had no choice but to stay for a few days to wait for the ship. On the evening of 8 Ṣafar 1310 Hijrī [September 1, 1892], I departed from Beirut. Shaikh ʿAbd al-Bāsiṭ and Shaikh ʿUmar Jailī came along to the harbor, and through them, it was easy to make arrangements for my luggage and so on. The next day, the ship arrived at Jaffa. With the anchoring of the ship, there was an onslaught of boatmen and coolies, and there was so much noise, shouting, and disorder that I lost my senses. Although I did not have much luggage, it was divided in pieces, and whatever a boatman could get his hands on, he took and loaded into his boat. I did not know where to go myself. Finally, trusting myself to fate, I sat in one of the boats. Having arrived on shore, I had to wait awhile for the boat, which held the remainder of my luggage. Once this was settled, I had to face the ordeal of passport and luggage inspection. At last, by afternoon, with a thousand difficulties, I was delivered from these quarrels and arrived at the city around the time of midday prayers. [158]

Jaffa [Yāfah]. Yāfah, which in English they call Jāfā, is an extremely ancient city. It is mentioned in the Torah, and the historian Bliny [Pliny] states that it existed before Noah's flood.[43] In 13 Hijri [634–35], which was the period of ʿUmar's caliphate, it came under the control of Islam. Because this city is a station of Jerusalem, that is, people go from here to Jerusalem, people of every nation and region are always coming and going in large numbers. The part of the city that can be called the European settlement is beautiful and full of atmosphere and ambiance.

Fruits are in abundance here. The pomegranate is extremely excellent and very inexpensive. A great feature of the city is that there is a series of gardens outside the city that runs continuously for two or three miles. Jerusalem is forty miles from here. A railway is now in place, but at that time horse carts ran.[44] I boarded around sunset. Along the way, we passed through several famous places (Ramla and so on), but I could not see anything because it was nighttime.

As dawn was breaking, I caught sight of a series of mountains that steadily became taller and taller. Although the road wound back and forth with great curves and twists, it was extremely level and smooth. The skirt of the mountain is entirely lush and green, and is a site of wondrous delight and atmosphere. All over, there are small settlements of Arab bedouins. Although the houses are cramped and small, they are made entirely of white stone. This whiteness looks extremely beautiful against the green landscape. The series went on for ten or twelve miles, then ended, [159] and the settlement of Jerusalem appeared.

Jerusalem and the Hostel for Indians. Jerusalem is settled on a mountain. I stayed here for one week and toured the Aqṣā Masjid and the Church of the Holy Sepulchre [Qumāmah]. Having stepped down from the coach, I went straight to the house of ʻAbd al-Razzāq Āfandī. He was indifferent (this incident will be covered in detail at the end of the book), so I decided to go to a hotel. Along the way, there was a hostel for Indians. I thought that it would be beneficial to meet the people there. Thus, when I entered the hostel, I first came face to face with the shaikh of the hostel. This shaikh is originally from Rampur and has lived here for some time. The poor fellow is not lettered, but he is an extremely intelligent and orderly person. He has fixed up the hostel in an extremely fine manner. One room, which is reserved especially for visitors, is reasonably appointed. There are flowerbeds in the courtyard. After the usual greetings, when he learned as we spoke that I wanted to stay in a hotel, he said, "You want to meet the muftī and other learned people. They consider it disgraceful to stay in a hotel." So I stayed there in the hostel. But I did not eat the food at the hostel, thinking that it was exclusively for faqīrs and the needy.

Jerusalem—The Aqsa Masjid—Church of the Holy Sepulchre

Early History of Jerusalem. Jerusalem is not the name of a particular building. Rather, it is the name of the city. But here people mostly call it Quds. Although this auspicious city is famous for its association with David and Solomon, and one might say the history of its existence begins from the time of these prophets, it in fact existed long before that time. [160] David seized it from the Madsī[1] 1,048 years before Jesus and established it as the seat of his throne. Since then, it has been the center of many major historical events. At the beginning of Islam, it was the qiblah of the Muslims, and it remains that of the Christians even today.

Present Circumstances. The population of the present city is not more than fifty or sixty thousand. The houses and buildings are of an ordinary grade. The streets are also not very broad, and because in many places there are covered markets, it is quite cramped and dark. Around the city is a stone fortification that Sulṭān Sulaimān the Magnificent had prepared in AD 1543. This is the state of the old city. But the modern settlement is extremely spacious and flourishing. The street is extremely broad, and there are magnificent buildings on both sides. Bungalows and mansions are in large numbers, and their grounds are generally extensive and decorated with plants and gardens. The language, fashion, and dress of the entire city are Arabic. Like Constantinople, there are many hostels and takyah here, too. There are separate hostels for every community and every region, and travelers receive food and coffee free of charge.

Fruits. The climate is extremely excellent. I arrived at the beginning of August.[2] Still, there was the mild cool of early springtime during the day, and at night it became quite cold. The fruits are in abundance and extremely sweet and delicious. At that time, it was the beginning of grape season. Just as they bring baskets full of corn, carrots, and so on, to the market in the morning in our area, and piles of them stretch far into the distance, the same is true of grapes here. [161] It was my habit to nibble on grapes all day.

The Aqṣā Masjid

This is that auspicious masjid whose foundation David laid and Solomon brought to completion. The grounds of the masjid, which they call ḥaram [harem], are extremely extensive, but mostly uneven and not level, and in many places are wild grass and bushes. I asked people the reason for this. I learned that the sulṭān has several times sent a substantial sum for repair and renovation, but the agents and caretakers of the masjid spent only a small portion of it. The amusing thing is, when I asked the caretakers, one gentleman said, "Yes, some amount of money also falls under the discretionary use of the caretakers. And why should it not? When a chef cooks food, he inevitably tastes the salt."

The masjid's building, which is 1,000 yards long and 700 yards wide, is extremely beautiful, elaborate, and magnificent. The ceiling rests on columns, and seven hundred are columns of pure white marble. There is mosaic and gold work all over. The building as it stands was built by 'Abd al-Malik bin Marwān.[3] Of course, it is said that the foundations are from the time of David. On the left side, at some distance from the building, is an extensive underground chamber. After walking down ten or twelve stairs, one comes to level ground. Here, there are seven rows of extremely magnificent arches. The columns of the arches are extremely broad and tall. The caretakers [162] say that these arches were constructed in the time of Solomon, and at the very least it is certain that they predate Islam.

The Dome of the Rock [Ṣakhrah]. Inside the sanctuary of the masjid, there are a great many other auspicious places. For example, the Qubbat al-Silsilah [Dome of the Chain], the Qubbat al-Miʿrāj [Dome of the Ascension], and the Qubbat al-Nabī [Dome of the Prophet] (saas), but the most magnificent is the Qubbat al-Ṣakhrah [Dome of the Rock]. Here lies the stone about which it is widespread among common people that it is suspended between heaven and Earth, and on the day of judgment the Glorious Throne will be set upon it. The people of Arabia call it *Ṣakhrah*, and the common people in our country call it *Takht-i rabb al-ʿālamīn* [throne of the lord of the worlds]. There is no doubt that this stone belongs to an extremely ancient period and has been extremely revered in every era. The Christians believe that Jesus, peace be upon him, had set foot on it. Thus, when it had come under the control of the Christians before the time of Sulṭān Ṣalāḥ al-Dīn,[4] they built a golden dome over this site in accordance with their belief. Muslims, too, afford it extreme respect, but I do not know if any excellent quality of it is mentioned in any authentic hadith.

In any case, the form of the dome is that on a high platform there is an octagonal tower, the height of which is around 100 feet. On the ceiling and walls there is extremely fine lapis lazuli and goldwork, and although it was made a long time ago, it is so brilliant and shiny that the eye cannot come to rest on it. In brief, with regard to its beauty and attractiveness, the claim of the great scholar Bashshārī that "I never saw such a beautiful and ornate building in all the Islamic regions" is not so inappropriate.[5] Stepping down a few stairs, you enter the cave where the sacred stone is set. The cave is so extensive that there is easily enough room [163] for sixty or seventy people. The rock is the height of two men from the ground. It is said that it used to be suspended entirely in the air. Perhaps at that time it was. But the present condition is that there is a circular wall, and the rock sits on it in such a way that it has become the ceiling of the wall. The caretakers say that, seeing the rock suspended in air, people used to be afraid while passing underneath it. So much so that one time a woman had a miscarriage. This event occurred during the time of Shaikh Muḥyī al-Dīn Akbar.[6] The aforementioned shaikh had a wall wrapped around it so that it would not appear to be suspended. The caretakers also say that the wall is so weak and hollow inside that it cannot in any way bear the weight of the rock. Thus, one caretaker rapped on the wall with his finger in front of me, and it made the hollow sound *khan khan*.

Whether or not this is true, there is no doubt that this place has been the residence of prophets and a place where prophetic revelation and divine inspiration have come down.[7] For this reason, no matter how many traces of divine signs and manifestations are found here, it is no occasion for wonder. In Jerusalem and its environs, there are also a great many other sites of pilgrimage. For example, Bethlehem, where Jesus (peace be upon him) was born; Maqām-i Khalīl [Hebron], where the graves of Abraham, Jacob, and Isaac are; Wādī-i Jahannam [Valley of Hinnom; lit., Valley of Hell], where Mary is buried. But unfortunately, on account of several chance occurrences, I did not have the honor of making pilgrimage to these places. I tried continuously for two or three whole days to go to Hebron, which is fifteen or twenty miles from Jerusalem, but there was a Jewish holiday at the time. [164] For this reason, transportation was completely nonexistent, and, even if found, cost four times the rate.

The Church of the Holy Sepulchre

The Large Church of the Christians. This is the same calamitous site for which all of Europe had once surged and burst forth, and this flood raged for a time. It is an extremely extensive church, and according to the belief of the Christians, Jesus (peace be upon him) was crucified and buried on this very site and went to heaven from here. Although the care and administration of this place is in the hands of Christians, because it is located within the Turkish government and is a relic of Ṣalāḥ al-Dīn's battles against six lakh Europeans, its gatekeeper that is, its key bearer, is Muslim. Accordingly, when I visited this church, I toured all the places with his guidance.

The Image of Jesus (Peace Be upon Him). When I entered the space, I saw that great monks and priests were humbly and reverently engaged in prayer all around. The gatekeeper first took me to the place where Jesus (peace be upon him) went to heaven (according to the belief of the Christians). This is a small room. Toward the front, there is an image of Jesus (peace be upon him) on a platform. The entire body except for the privates is nude. Neither holiness nor dignity of prophethood of any kind is expressed. When I went into the room, a candle was burning, and there was a very stately priest engaged in meditative contemplation, staring at an image. When he finished the meditation, the caretaker sprinkled a bit of water onto his head, which he rubbed on his face and beard with great humility and reverence. [165]

The place of crucifixion is very glorious and grand. But having seen it, one severely regrets the simplemindedness of the Christians.[8]

On a tall, rectangular platform, which is made of marble stone from end to end, stands a crucifix. Iron nails are stuck in Jesus' palms. His feet have been set one atop the other on the wood, and a spike has been driven through them such that it has broken through the foot and exited into the wood. Just near it, to one side, Mary stands, extremely sorrowful. The *mujassamah* [statue], meaning *isṫechū* [statue] of Mary is extremely glorious. It is a golden figure and has been made with clothing. Her dress is similar to a *peshwāz*.[9] There was a crowd of monks and priests at this site. Nuns were standing, humbly and reverently staring at the crucifix, hands folded. What a strange thing religious ideas are!!!

Meeting Scholars and a Few Other Circumstances

The Muftī of Jerusalem. The famous and renowned scholar in Jerusalem is Sayyid Ṭāhir, who is the muftī of the city and is known by the name Muftī alone.[10] Because I had heard his praises in Constantinople I first went to meet him upon reaching Jerusalem. As soon as I entered the room, Muftī ṣāḥib and everyone present rose out of respect. (This practice is common here and is used for everyone.) After standard greetings and brief introductions, one gentleman said, "*La-'alla ḥażratukum min al-'ulamā*,"[11] that is, "You are probably from among the scholars." I said, "*Lā, wa lākin min ṭullāb al-'ilm*,"[12] [166] that is, "No, I am not a scholar—rather, I am a seeker of knowledge."[13] They had been talking about an issue related to knowledge, and their conversation had been disrupted by my arrival. When they learned that I, too, was somewhat lettered, one gentleman said with extreme refinement and propriety, "We were just conversing about an issue. If you wish, let the issue be presented before you, too." His exact words were, "*Yā ḥażrat al-shaikh qadd kunnā qabl żālik fī baḥṡ fa-law aḥbabtum 'arażnā 'alaikum*."[14] He described the point in question.

It was that in the āyat of the Glorious Quran, "*A lam tara kaifa fa'ala rabbuka bi-Iram żāt al-'imād*,"[15] when God addressed the Prophet, he said, "Did you not see the event?" even though this event had occurred hundreds of years before the Prophet was born. I said, *rūyat* [seeing][16] is used for certain knowledge, too. It is in the Quran itself, "*A lam tara kaifa fa'ala rabbuka bi-aṣḥāb al-fīl*."[17] This use is also found throughout the poems of the Jāhiliyah [pre-Islamic] Arabs. One gentleman tried to object to my words, but Muftī ṣāḥib said, "This response is absolutely correct, and there is no room for debate." As long as I stayed in Jerusalem, I continued to take part in that pleasing company.

Mufti ṣāḥib is an embodied image of sanctity and noble character, and the effect of this is that the entire city extremely respects him. His salary is in total three hundred qurush [kuruş], that is, thirty or thirty-five rupees, but not even the ruler of the city has the influence in the city that he has. [167] One great virtue is that although he is a man of old times and is extremely sacred,[18] he is still free-thinking and acquainted with modern sensibility.

A Pleasant Anecdote. In these regions, it is necessary for the 'ulamā to wrap a white strip of cloth, which they call *laffah*, around their turban or cap. On the day that I went to tour the Church of the Holy Sepulchre, there was only a cap on my head, no turban. I was on my way when a gentleman who had become acquainted with me saw me and mentioned this at Muftī sāhib's session. Because this was an entirely new thing with regard to the practice there, the people were talking about it. So much so that when I went to Mufti sāhib's court the next day, one gentleman asked with great astonishment and wonder, "*Sami'nā anna hażrat al-shaikh kharaja min ghair laffah*,"[19] meaning, "We heard that our good sir went out in public without his turban and laffah." I said, "Yes, I had gone into a Christian church, and a scholar's clothing is not suitable in such places." Everyone exclaimed, "*Wa-Allāh qadd aṣabtum*,"[20] meaning, "You acted entirely appropriately."

One day I went to the hostel for the people of Bukhara. As it happened, several notables and esteemed people of Bukhara had come to Jerusalem for pilgrimage, having completed the ḥajj. The shaikh of the hostel introduced me to them. By their appearance and dress, they seemed wealthy, honorable, and dignified. Several were jurisprudents and men of knowledge. Because these people live under Russian rule, I spoke with them for a while about the Russian government. They made many complaints [168] and were mostly complaining about the fact that Muslims are compelled to enter the army, and when there is war with an Islamic country, the Muslims have to confront their own coreligionists.

Departure from Jerusalem

Alexandria [Iskandariyah]. Having departed from Jerusalem, I came to Jaffa, and having boarded a ship, reached Alexandria three days later. As soon as the ship anchored, I was faced with the trouble of the coolies and boatmen. Although it is true that this calamity is found everywhere, Alexandria surpasses all other locations in this particularity. With a thousand difficulties, I arrived on shore. There was a throng of coolies there, and four at a time descended upon each traveler. One coolie took my luggage by force. Compelled, I went along with him. Alexandria is a remnant of an extremely ancient period, and in this regard it was necessary to visit it. But I was in a hurry to go to Cairo, and therefore I rented a coach and arrived at the station. The best part is that the coolie sāhib, too, climbed into the coach and sat beside me. What power did I have to object to this audacity of his?

From the seashore to the station, the part of the city that passed before my eyes was extremely populous and full of life. The streets were wide and on both sides there were extremely tall houses and shops. Having reached the station, I learned that it would be another two or three hours. I thought, "All right, let me wander around till then." Just nearby there was a congregational masjid. I went there. It is extremely glorious and beautiful. [169] The pool for ablution is extensive and attractive. There are lavatories and toilets on all sides, but there is such care for cleanliness that there is not even a hint of smell or odor.

The Makeup of the Railway Cars. The train departed at ten o'clock. In the cars here, there are metal seats instead of benches, and they are connected in pairs in such a way that the backs of both meet. Eight people sit in each class: four on one side and four on the other side. There is no provision for sleeping, nor is there any arrangement for relieving oneself. By inquiry, I learned that there are cars of this kind in Europe, too. Of course, one thing is new and is not without comfort, which is that tray bearers, who sell biscuits, bread, cheese, and fruits, are at hand at all times right in the car. And because people can come and go from this end to that end in all cars, a tray bearer constantly makes rounds in all the cars.

In his travelogue, Sayyid Sāhib has severely ridiculed the railways, streets, stations, lanterns, in sum, every single thing of this place for its crudeness and filthiness.[21] Perhaps this was the state of affairs then, but now this complaint cannot be made. I traveled by rail from Alexandria to Cairo and from Cairo to Ismailia. As far as I am concerned, nothing was objectionable.

As much of Egypt as passed before my eyes on this trip was wondrously green and lush. Extremely verdant fields appeared as far as the eye could see. [170] I had never seen in even fifty acres in Hindustan excellent crops of the kind that were visible from Alexandria to Cairo. The rail reached Cairo around evening, and I stayed at a *lokāndah* (hotel) near al-Azhar.

Reaching Cairo and Staying in the Azhar Congregational Mosque. In Beirut, ʿAbd al-Bāsiṭ Āfandī had given me a letter to send to ʿAbd al-Ḥalīm after arriving at Cairo. Shaikh ʿAbd al-Ḥalīm is the paternal cousin of ʿAbd al-Bāsiṭ Āfandī and studies at al-Azhar. I sent the letter to him. He came to the hotel the next day and said, "If you plan to inquire about the conditions related to knowledge here and meet ʿulamā and shaikhs, then it is not appropriate to stay in a hotel. The ʿulamā here consider it very shameful." Thus, in accordance with his direction, I went into the Azhar Congregational Masjid, and he had a spacious room in the Riwāq al-Shāmi'īn [Hostel for Syrians] emptied for me. I resided here for more than one month. Shaikh ʿAbd al-Ḥalīm was with me nearly all the time and attended to my every need. He was my guide, intimate, means of introduction, and, if it isn't rude to say so, he was also both my attendant and servant—and that, too, free of charge and free of self-interest.

Summary Circumstances of Cairo

The Early History of Cairo. The Fashion of the People of the City. This city is the capital of Egypt [Miṣr]. Rather, when the word Miṣr is used in present-day idiom, it refers to this city. Jauhar, the Fatimid general, settled it in 358 Hijrī [968–69], and, from that time to today, it has seen daily progress.[1] The current population census is 374,838. [171] The roads are wide and the houses are generally tall and of pleasant ambience. Whenever I walked around its extensive and lively markets, I was deceived into thinking that it was Bombay. Coffeehouses are in extreme abundance, and they are a thing of great amusement and comfort. The clothing and fashion of this place are extremely ugly and inelegant. Common people wear a long blue kurta, the slit of whose collar remains open. They do not wear pajamas or sarongs, and so on, at all. Elites wear kaftans and cloaks, but because the cloak does not include a collar, the neck remains open and looks unattractive. The modern-educated wear coats and trousers, and this practice is becoming more and more accepted each day. Women's fashion and dress are so absurd and unattractive that one cannot imagine their being more so. Common women wear the same long blue kurta, but even wealthy begums and those of the new fashion, whose dress is entirely European, turn themselves into monsters or ogres by covering themselves with an unattractive blue burqa. On the burqa, a black strip of cloth hangs down from the bridge of the nose to the chest like an elephant's trunk. To attach this strip of cloth, there is a gold or brass bar that hangs on the forehead and is used in place of a piece of jewelry.

The Moral Character of the Common People. In the moral character of common people, lassitude is found in excess. In negotiating the cost of the most ordinary of things, the intermediation of Imām Ḥusain (peace be upon him) or ʿAbd al-Qādir Jīlānī is invoked.[2] A great deal of men and women beg, and they stick to you like affliction.

With regard to the weather, this region resembles our Hindustan; rather, it is worse. [172] The heat is of a strange kind. One feels fatigued and lethargic at all times, and does not desire to do any work. I thought that I would be able to get a lot of work done here, and I stayed only briefly at Beirut and Jerusalem so that I could spend more days here, but the heat upset all those plans. I worked for an hour or two in the morning. I spent the entire rest of the day lying idly in my room.

The State of Education in Egypt

The places in the Islamic regions that are thought to be centers of education these days are Constantinople and Cairo. In consideration of this, I made a great effort to learn about the state of education in both of these places. Like Constantinople, here, too, I met the officers of the Department of Education. I read yearly reports. I saw the programs of numerous colleges. I went to major colleges myself and saw the teachers' method of instruction. I offer to readers the things that I learned from these investigations. It is also necessary to say at this point that although Egypt and Cairo are nowhere near the breadth and progress that education has obtained in Constantinople, Cairo is nevertheless superior in that the official documents of the education department, which are widely published here, are more organized and detailed, and for this reason I shall be able to describe the state of education here in more detail and with more critical research than Constantinople. [173]

Classical Education. Like Constantinople, there are two methods of education here, too: modern and classical. Both methods are entirely different, and this difference has done extremely serious harm to both. Classical education, which is a degraded caricature of the style of education of a thousand years ago, has contaminated the climate of the country, and because it appears in the form of religion, even the influence of the sultanate cannot compete with it. The result of this is that although the foundation of modern education has been laid in Egypt for some time, and the government itself has taken it under its shadow of benevolence, and many boys are given a scholarship, and fees are not taken from 41 percent, and all the top offices are given only to the modern-educated—all this is the case—still, the state of the extent of education is that, putting all the large and small schools and colleges of the city and its environs together, the number of students is not even ten thousand, whereas the number of students under instruction in the classical method at the Azhar Congregational Mosque alone is in excess of ten thousand. It is certainly the case that modern education is ahead at every step, and the power of the classical method is growing weaker day by day. An estimation of the number of students of every kind in official madrasas, which is growing larger and larger each year, can be gained from the fact that in 1887 the number of boarders was 47 percent and in 1888 it became 56 percent. Similarly, non-boarders were 71 percent in 1887 and became 79 percent in 1888.

List of Colleges and Schools and Their Expenses and So On. At this point, we offer a summary chart that has been compiled from the 1888 report [174] and from which the details of all the schools and colleges, their annual expenses, the number of students, and other information will be known.

NAME OF THE MADRASA	ANNUAL EXPENSES, JUNE 1888	NUMBER OF PRESENT STUDENTS, JUNE 1888	NUMBER OF STUDENTS WHO PAY FEES	NUMBER OF FEES	WITHOUT FEES	WHO RECEIVE A SCHOLARSHIP	STATUS
Madrasat al-Ṭibb [School of Medicine]	8,412 pounds	182	79	6 pounds, annually	74	22	The pound is worth at least 15 rupees
Madrasat al-Wilādah [School of Childbirth]	816	11	—	—	11	—	
Muhandis-khānah [Engineer House]	4,140	33	7	15 pounds	12	18	

NAME OF THE MADRASA	ANNUAL EXPENSES, JUNE 1888	NUMBER OF PRESENT STUDENTS, JUNE 1888	NUMBER OF STUDENTS WHO PAY FEES	NUMBER OF FEES	WITHOUT FEES	WHO RECEIVE A SCHOLARSHIP	STATUS
Madrasat al-Ḥuqūq, meaning the school of law	4,142	62	27	15	15	11	
Dār al-ʿUlūm [House of Sciences]	1,526	31	—	—	1	37	When I saw this college, there were 54 students.
Madrasat al-Tarjumah [School of Translation]	1,435	30	3	6	23	2	
Madrasat al-ṣanāyiʿ [School of Industry, Craft]	7,819	270	12	6	260	—	
al-Taufīqiyah	6,418	288	Internal: 25; external: 221	Internal: 20; external: 12	37	15	By internal is meant a boarder; by external, a non-boarder.
al-Tajhīziyah	7,754	330	Internal: 52; external: 90	Internal: 16; external: 8	185	—	
Mubtadiyān [Elementary schools]	4,383	258	Internal: 69; external: 81	Internal: 14; external: 6	118	—	
Iskandariyah	1,368	214	109	1	79	—	
al-Manṣūrah	1,294	143	80	1	71	—	

[175]

Private Schools. Apart from these official madrasas, there are twenty private schools whose method of instruction and course of studies accord entirely with the official madrasas, and the examinations and so on, too, take place under the supervision of the Department of Education. In 1889, the annual expense of those schools was 8,233 pounds, which is more or less equal to one lakh, twenty-five thousand rupees. The number of students in 1888 was 2,363.

The Number of Students. The number of schools and students is progressing every year. Thus, in 1891, the number of private schools went from 20 to 120, in which ten thousand thirteen hundred [11,300] students are receiving education. Similarly, in that same year the number of students in official schools became 7,307, and the income from fees was more than two and a half lakhs.* [176]

In the terminology of Egypt, three levels of education have been established:

> *Ibtidā'ī* [elementary], in which there are four grades and the total course of reading and instruction is equal to our middle class.

* The present Khedive pays extreme attention to the progress of education. Thus, several phrases of the speech that the aforementioned Khedive made specifically regarding the Department of Education in this year's (meaning 1894) assembly in which the budget of the sultanate was presented, were as follows:

> There is an extreme need for extension and progress in the Department of Education. Thus, this year I approved an increase of twelve thousand pounds (nearly two lakh rupees) over the previous amount. People's inclination toward education is increasing day by day. This year, 1,500 boys more than other years have entered the colleges and schools.
>
> I gave the order to reinstitute the industrial [*ṣan'atī*] madrasas that had been closed.
>
> I have turned my attention to 'Alī Pāshā's memorandum, in which he proposed that five hundred elementary schools be opened in villages and towns, and I seek to fulfill this proposal entirely.
>
> In any case, rest assured with respect to education. I will give this office a great deal of support and power.

Tajhīzī [preparatory] begins after elementary. There are five classes in it, and its course of reading and instruction is equal to our entrance.

Khuṣūṣī [special or specialist]. That is, law class and the Dār al-ʿUlūm Academy, and so on.

In preparatory madrasas, education in French or English also takes place, and since 1888 the rule has been in place that history, geography, and the physical sciences necessarily be taught in French or English in these madrasas. For the promotion of these languages, the Department of Education issued the order that instruction in them be given only by means of European professors. Previously, because the influence of French was greater, the number of students studying French was greater. Thus, in 1889, their number was 2,500, and those studying English were only 800. But now the number of students studying English is more than two thousand and the number of those studying French is nearly the same as it was in 1889.

Now we mention the major colleges and several schools in some degree of detail.

The Dār al-ʿUlūm Academy

In Egypt, and not only in Egypt, but in all the Islamic regions, this was the college that pleased me most [177] and which I considered the sufficient cure for what ails Muslims. My thought has always been, and I stand extremely firmly upon this, that even if Muslims attain some degree of progress in the Western sciences, as long as the element of Eastern education is not within them, their progress cannot be called the progress of Muslims. No doubt, the present system of Eastern education is extremely inferior and unnecessary, but there are also things in that same education that are the spirit of the nationhood of Muslims, and any education in which there is absolutely no trace of that spirituality cannot keep alive the religion, nationhood, history, or anything at all of Muslims.

The same problem that is rued over in Hindustan is also found in Constantinople, Beirut, and Egypt. That is, the effect of nationhood and religious adherence is lacking in the new education, and the old education is not capable of keeping up with the present necessities of the world. It is this Dār al-ʿUlūm Academy that seeks to merge both domains. However, regrettably, it has not yet been entirely successful. The person who first thought of this college is ʿAlī Pāshā Mubārak, a famous and enlightened Egyptian.[3] He himself has received both Eastern and Western education and knows numerous European languages. He has several times been officer of the Egyptian Department of Education. His historical writings are spread throughout all the Islamic regions and are really quite beneficial. He also tried to reform the style of education at Azhar, but the shaikhs of Azhar would not consent. He probably laid the foundation of this college after that. [178]

Initially, it was decided that the external objective of this college would be for its graduates to be selected for teaching positions in official madrasas. But in 1888, in accordance with the permission of the government, the Department of Education approved the policy that its graduates could be appointed as judges, qāẓīs, and muftīs. Along with that, numerous other sciences were added to the course, and a committee, whose president was the Shaikh al-Shuyūkh [lead shaikh] at Azhar, selected the books for the course.[4]

The necessary requirement for admission to this college is that the student possess, among the Eastern sciences, appropriate preparation in hadith, Quranic exegesis, the principles of jurisprudence, jurisprudence, morphology, and syntax.[5]

The total period of instruction is four years, and details of the sciences that are taught, and the way in which lessons in them have been arranged each week, will be known by means of the following chart:

SCIENCES THAT ARE TAUGHT	FIRST YEAR	SECOND YEAR	THIRD YEAR	FOURTH YEAR
fiqh [jurisprudence]	5 lessons per week	5 lessons per week	5 lessons per week	5 lessons per week
tafsīr [exegesis (of the Quran)]	—	—	2	2
tārīkh-i tabīʿī [natural history]	2	2	—	—

SCIENCES THAT ARE TAUGHT	FIRST YEAR	SECOND YEAR	THIRD YEAR	FOURTH YEAR
'ulūm-i balāghat [science of rhetoric]	2	2	—	—
uṣūl-i fiqh [principles of jurisprudence]	—	—	2	2
ḥikmat-i 'amaliyah [practical wisdom]	1	—	—	—
jabr o muqābalah o ḥisāb [arithmetic]	4	4	4	4
jughrāfiyah [geography]	2 lessons per week	2 lessons per week	2 lessons per week	2 lessons per week
tārīkh-i 'umūmī [general history]	1	1	1	1
fann-i inshā'-i 'arabī [the art of Arabic writing (style)]	3	3	4	4
mukhtalif khuṭūṭ [various letters, scripts]	4	4	4	4
taṣwīr kashī [drawing, painting]	1	1	—	—
adabiyāt-i lughat-i 'arabiyah [literary studies in Arabic]	—	—	3	3
qasmūghrāfī [cosmography]	—	—	1	1
ṭab'iyāt o kīmiyā [physics and chemistry]	—	—	2	2
ḥadīṡ - kalām - manṭiq [hadith - theology - logic]	—	2	1	—
naḥw ṣarf - rasm-i khaṭṭ - 'urūż - qawāfī [syntax, morphology - script - prosody - rhyme]	3	2	—	—

Because only students who are familiar with the Arabic sciences, jurisprudence, and hadith can be admitted to this college, and only those who have obtained education in the classical method can be students of this kind, the number of students in this college is very small. Even though the Department of Education has not set any fees in this college in consideration of this—rather, instead, each student receives a scholarship of fifteen rupees per month and also receives one meal per day from the college, and the dress that has been set for the students is also the same classical maulvi-like dress, and the people who study and graduate from here also hold distinguished, high offices—[180] all this is the case, but the people whom the old education has touched even once remain afraid of modern sciences for their entire lives, even though these sciences are taught in Arabic. When I visited the college, there were fifty-four students in it, most of whom were educated at Azhar.

The Method of Education. The method of education, too, is special here. There is no book in anyone's hand, neither the professor's nor any student's. The professor lectures from memory and gives his speech with such breadth and eloquence that it impresses itself upon the heart. In consideration of this, the extremely renowned ʻulamā of Egypt have been selected for professorships: for example, Shaikh Ḥamzah Fatḥullāh, professor of literature; Shaikh Ḥasan al-Ṭawīl, instructor of hadith; and Dr. ʻUṡmān Bey, professor of natural history.[6] These are all famous Egyptian ʻulamā, and their scholarly writings are considered extremely valuable. Most of the people who are renowned prose stylists of Arabic in Egypt today have been educated at this college. The course in literature that has been established is neither any special book nor a selection of a few books. Instead, it is all those rare parts of Arabic literature that should be called the life of the art of literature. Similarly, in Quranic exegesis, instruction takes place only in the *āyats* that, with respect to rhetoric, elegance, ethics, or theological issues, are especially important. Thus, details of all these areas have been given in the curriculum of instruction that was established in 1890 and has been printed at the official state printing house and published.

One Student's Extemporaneous Poetry. I also attended lessons on literature and jurisprudence myself. The eloquence and excellence with which both professors spoke are still impressed on my heart. [181] If only the 'ulamā in our area, too, would follow this practice! The state of the talent of the students will be made evident by the fact that when we were touring the college, Aḥmad Bey Naẓīm, who is the secretary of the college, called a student whose name was Aḥmad Qūṣī,[7] and said, "Bring a pen and ink-stand, sit down, and write some verses in praise of him (gesturing toward me) at once." He sat in front of us on a bench and, having written these couplets, recited them:

> You are Muḥammad Shiblī, the exalted;
> You have surpassed mankind and are higher in value.
> And you have honored and graced us
> With your visit to the land of Egypt.
> We shall always look upon you in friendship;
> You offer grace and we offer gratitude.[8]

Although the construction "Shiblī al-ma'ālā" is disjointed and there is *iqwā'*[9] in the second couplet, considering the excellence of its language and the extemporaneousness of its presentation, I praised it highly.

The Law School [Madrasat al-Ḥuqūq]

Conditions of Admission. Legal education takes place in this college, and graduates of this place are appointed to civil offices. The necessary requirements for admission to this college are that the age of the student be greater than sixteen years, that he have a diploma in preparatory education (entrance class), that his conduct be good, that he have received the smallpox vaccination in childhood, and that his physical fitness be good. At the time of admission, a special oral and written examination is given. In the written, questions related to the knowledge of French and Arabic are asked, [182] and the oral includes, in addition to the above, history and geography. After successfully passing this examination, he has to present a letter from his father or some guardian in which there are the words, "I am responsible for the conduct of this boy outside of college hours." After all these things, one must deposit fifteen pounds, meaning more or less two hundred rupees, as fees, and then at last the student is admitted to the college. The period of instruction is four years, and the subjects that are included in the instruction are as follows:

Subjects Taught. First Year. Arabic, French, translation, bookkeeping (meaning spelling and writing), Islamic *shar'*, law, judgeship and court procedure, common law, and the general principles of politics.

Second Year. In addition to the subjects above, Roman law, criminal law.

Third Year. Ditto. In addition to the above, political economy, the penal code, and civil and commercial settlements and appeals.

Fourth Year. Islamic sharia, political economy, settlement, commerce law, court law, special sultanate law.

Each year, examinations are given in different subjects, and all these examinations and the final examination take place in French. Only the examination on Islamic sharia is in Arabic. When the students acquire some degree of legal proficiency, they are sent to the high court and other courts to become familiar with proceedings, and they are ordered to write summaries of the cases. [183] Court files are also ordered for the college, and students are made to practice writing claims, written statements, testimony, interrogation, objection and rebuttal, and case ruling. I toured this college thoroughly. The secretary of the college is a Frenchman and is entirely unacquainted with Arabic, but his assistant is a young Muslim who is an extremely competent person and knows numerous languages. He is also a professor at the college and can give lectures in French with the utmost spontaneity. He took me into his class and said, "Today was the day for giving the lecture in French, but I shall lecture in Arabic for your sake." Thus, he stood and gave a lecture on the principles of sentencing, and he spoke with extreme eloquence and breadth. All the boys in all the classes had clean faces and were neatly dressed. Resoluteness of character and dignity dripped from their faces.

School of Translation [Madrasat al-Tarjumah]

Because the French and the English are very influential in Egypt, and all the major state offices are in the hands of these two nations, Egyptians must study French and English in order to maintain relations with them and work underneath them. This was the principle aim of founding this college, and for this reason, at the beginning, it was limited to language study and could have been called an ordinary school. But in 1888, its program was greatly expanded and four more professors were added, among whom one is French. In addition to the Arabic, Turkish, French, and English languages, instruction in the following subjects has also been deemed necessary: [184] geography, history, arithmetic and accounting, geometry, algebra, physical sciences, chemistry, jurisprudence, tauḥīd.[10] All these subjects, except for jurisprudence and tauḥīd, are taught in French, and some subjects are taught in English, too. Just as this college has benefited Egypt with respect to national necessities, it has also proven extremely beneficial for scientific progress. The scientific language of Egypt is still Arabic, and it probably will always remain so. The books that are taught in the colleges have generally been translated from French. A special department has been established with the aim that excellent writings in medicine, and so on, published in French be translated immediately and included in college courses. Thus, to date, hundreds of books have been translated, and continue to be so. This college has fulfilled all these needs.

School of Medicine [Madrasat al-Ṭibb]

Science of Animals and Plants. This is a very large college, and its annual expense is more than one lakh. The college building is extremely extensive, and many separate, large rooms are designated for instruction in different subjects. The dissection room is extremely extensive, and in it can be found at all times many cadavers on which experiments in dissection are performed. In 1888, a separate work space adjacent to them was opened for education in micrography.[11] Instruction in biology takes place in an extensive building in which animals of different kinds are found in extreme abundance. On the premises of the college is a garden that has been prepared for the purpose of the science of botany, [185] and in it are plants of hundreds of different kinds that are maintained with extreme care and supervision. Chemistry, too, is a necessary part of its instruction. Until 1888, instruction in it only took place in a theoretical way. In 1887, numerous large rooms were added to the college building for practical experiments, and in 1888, gas and whatever was required for practical experiment were made available in it. Each year, a large group graduates from this college, some of whom are sent to Europe to complete their education.

Translation of European Medical Books. All the books that are included in the curriculum of instruction in this college are in Arabic and have been translated from French and so on. Because the medical sciences, like other sciences in Europe, progress every day, and each year there is an increase of a great deal of new information in many fields, a committee has been set up especially so that whenever a book of this kind is published in French, etc., it be translated immediately into Arabic and included in the course at this college. In this way, a large treasury of translated books related to the medical sciences has been prepared, the number of which can be learned from the catalogue of the Khedive Library. Egyptian scholars, too, have themselves composed a great many books in this field and have also comparatively studied Greek and present-day medicine. If only the physicians in our country, who, by not knowing English, are deprived of European research, would collect these modern writings and avail themselves of them! But where can one find such courage in our nation? Although, if you ask the truth, this is not even a matter of courage. [186]

There are fifteen professors total at this college, among whom three are European and the rest are Egyptian.

The Remaining Colleges and Schools

Engineering College. Apart from these colleges, there are numerous other engineering, industrial, etc., colleges, and they are in a state of progress. The arts and sciences that are taught in the engineering college, and the rules that are related to its admissions and examinations, have been printed in a separate treatise fifty-one pages long. Looking at it, it seems that the scheme of education is of an extremely high order. When I visited this college, the principal complained to me that the present director of public instruction has caused severe harm to the college. Previously, the course here was the same as that of the engineering college in France, and to this end all subjects were taught in French. But the present director has issued the order that all subjects be taught in English, and that Hindustan's Roorkee College be imitated.[12] The principle sāhib said, "The books used at Roorkee College have been ordered here and I have seen them. They are books of an extremely inferior quality compared to the present course here, but unfortunately we are compelled to teach them."

School of Industries [Madrasat al-Ṣanāyi'], in which education in industry and crafts takes place, and whose annual expense is more than one lakh, is in a state of extreme progress. The crafts of carpentry, blacksmithing, and so on, which [187] are taught are taught in a scientific way, and on this basis, until a student has acquired an elementary education (which is equivalent to middle school), he cannot be admitted. In addition to the Arabic, French, and English languages, elementary parts of the mathematical sciences, machines, chemistry, and physics are taught. Each day, education in these theoretical sciences takes place for three hours, and applied practice in different industries is given for seven hours. The Department of Education has reported that this madrasa enjoys extreme progress, and the things that are produced there are marvelous.

General Schools.[13] General schools, too, are in abundance. The preparatory madrasas are two: the Taufīqiyah[14] and the Tajhīziyah. The annual expense of the Taufīqiyah is more than one lakh, and nearly four hundred students acquire an education there. This includes the elementary levels, too. The madrasa building is extremely beautiful and spacious. The Khedive of Egypt granted an extensive building from among the royal buildings, the name of which is Qaṣr al-Nuzhah, and because its structure was not suited to educational purposes, he granted fifty thousand rupees so that additions and improvements could be made to it as needed. Thus, in accordance with the direction of the secretary of the madrasa, additions and expansions were made to its building. Because there are three levels of education in the madrasa, *qism-i khāṣṣ* [special or specialized section], ibtidā'ī [elementary], and tajhīzī [preparatory], separate buildings were built for all three and boarding rooms for 350 students were made. Adjacent to the madrasa are two large rooms for practice in chemistry and drawing, and they are extremely attractive. [188]

The Tajhīziyah School. Its annual expense is around two lakh, and four hundred boys acquire an education in it. An annual fee of 25 pounds, meaning 450 rupees, is taken from the boarders. Although the boarding house is not extensive, nor are there separate rooms for the students, all the boys live extremely decently and cleanly. When I visited this madrasa, it was time to eat. The secretary of the madrasa, whose name is Aḥmad Bey Naẓīm, said to me, "First, please see the dining room." The room was extremely extensive and attractive, and there were two or three tables and lots of chairs set in order. Although the manner of eating was in accordance with Constantinople and Syria, meaning there was one plate in front of each group of four people, and there were absolutely no forks or knives, I was surprised, rather, astonished, that the boys ate with such fineness and tidiness that neither were their hands stained with food nor did a stain appear anywhere on the tablecloth. They chatted among themselves, but there was not so much as a hum or echo, let alone noise and shouting. By inquiry, I learned that one or two of the officers of the madrasa always eat with the students, and each week a lecture is given on the etiquette and proper manner of eating.

People Educated in Europe

Students Who Acquire an Education in Europe. The practice has been in place in Egypt for some time that, each year, some students were sent by the sultanate to Europe to complete their education. This number was kept in proportion so that at all times thirty students were present in Europe. The government of Egypt had to bear the entire expense of travel and residence there. Although the government bore these expenses extremely generously, unfortunately, neither the government nor the country profited for a while. [189] Just like our Hindustan, very few of the people who returned having acquired an education turned out to be accomplished in any given subject, nor could the country derive benefit of any kind from them. In the end, the head of the Department of Education turned his attention to it and, after much investigation, discovered the reasons for the loss, among which a major reason was that there used to be an error in the selection of the boys. Mostly older boys were sent, and because their elementary education and training were not excellent, European education and training had very little effect on them. From that time, it was made compulsory that, in the future, the age of the boys sent not be more than twelve years. One problem with this was that arrangements for education in religion and the Arabic language could not be made. Thus, the rule was made that a few ʿulamā should go with the students to continue instructing them in Arabic and religion. This method proved extremely useful, and because the country saw the excellent examples of these students, people began to send their children at their own expense. So much so that in 1888, of all the students who acquired education in Europe, twenty-five acquired education paid for by the government and fifty-two by their own expense. The details of all the students who were present in Europe in 1888, and the sciences in which they were educated, are as follows.

BY THE GOVERNMENT'S EXPENSE	BY THEIR OWN PRIVATE EXPENSE	THE FIELDS IN WHICH THEY RECEIVED AN EDUCATION
5	17	The barrister profession
4	12	The medical profession
1		Economic matters
3		Teaching or professorship
	2	Agriculture
1	2	Preparation for the barrister profession
	1	Preparation for technical college

Among these, thirteen students, who received scholarships from the sultanate, obtained degrees of an extremely high level. One of them was Rushdī Ṭapūzādah, who received a doctoral degree in barristership. One boy, whose name was Isma'īl Āfandī, and who used to study professorship at a college in France, ranked tenth in the entire college on the physics examination, while the total number of candidates who participated in the examination were 351 and all were from France. Another boy, whose name was ʿAbdullāh, acquired an award for the highest grade in political economy. Apart from these students, some other students acquire education in England, Italy, and Germany. Some of them learn the trade of making machines, and the government of Egypt pays for all of them.

In the 1888 report, the director of education[15] has written an extremely useful and evidence-based speech concerning the acquisition of education in Europe. In it, he has addressed the people of the country to say that if they do not pay attention to a few special things, then no benefit can be obtained from education in Europe, as has been proven by longstanding experience. [191] He writes that either extremely young boys should be sent to be educated in Europe alone from start to finish, or, if they are older, then it is necessary for them to have already obtained an FA degree before going to Europe. In our Hindustan, too, a general complaint is that sufficient compensation is not received for the great expenses that are borne in a European education. This complaint is entirely correct, and the reason for it is likely the same reason that the Egyptian director of education has described.

Classical Education and the Azhar Congregational Mosque

The Early History of Azhar. The Number of Students. The System of Student Boarding. Classical education here is, in other words, education at the Azhar Congregational Mosque. For this reason, in order to describe the state of classical education, it is sufficient to describe the circumstances at Azhar. This is the congregational masjid about which it is said that no university in the entire world is older than it. This is a congregational masjid, and the first masjid to be built in Cairo. One of the slaves of Caliph al-Muʿizz li-Dīnillāh of the Fatimids of Egypt, who was from Sicily and by his God-given ability had become the hand and arm of the Fatimid government, laid the foundation of this masjid in 359 Hijrī [969–70], and it was completed in 361 Hijrī [971–72].[16] In 378 Hijrī [988–89], the Caliph ʿAzīz Billāh had some houses for students built adjacent to the masjid, and established a scholarship for thirty-five students.[17] [192] Ḥākim bi-Amrillāh renovated the masjid structure in 400 Hijrī [1009–10] and endowed property with annual proceeds of 167 dinars for its expenditures.[18] In 761 Hijrī [1359–60], Amīr Ṭawāshī established a special school for orphans and, along with that, endowed many properties for the common students at the masjid. Gradually, it became a great academy. So much so that in 818 Hijrī [1415–16], the number of its students exceeded seven hundred, including people of every nation and every region. And today its state is such that, with regard to the abundance of students, no university in the world can equal it. Around four or five thousand students reside in the masjid. A great many live in nearby masjids, but receive food from here. In sum, the number of students of every kind who are connected to Azhar exceeds twelve thousand. There are separate galleries, which they call *riwāq* here, for the students of each region. There is neither place nor room for a great many, rather, most students. Hundreds, rather, thousands of small cabinets are set one atop the other in the courtyard of the masjid. These are their storage spaces, in which they keep their clothes and necessary belongings. The entire courtyard of the masjid lies there for sleeping and sitting. The first time I went to the masjid, I heard the sound of rumbling from far away. When I entered inside, I saw students and nothing but students in every direction. Teachers were giving lessons all around, and surrounding each of them were crowds of thirty or forty students. There were no less than thirty or forty of these circles, and because they were close together, [193] there was so much noise that one could not even hear the sound in one's ears. I thought, "Today is some special day, and for this reason most of the students have gathered." But after staying there for a few days, I learned that this is the ordinary state of affairs. I thought, "In this chaos, not to speak of mental composure, does the voice of the instructors even reach the ears of the student?"

Food. People from the regions for which the riwāq have been built, such as Syria, Morocco, Algeria, Iraq, Bukhara, Khurasan, Afghanistan, Hindustan, and so on, always send some amount annually by means of merchants, which is given to the students as pocket money for expenses. Ordinary food is received from Azhar itself, but because only bread is provided, they have to make arrangements for main dishes themselves. A great many students, who receive four or five pieces of bread each, give two or three to a baker in exchange for main dishes, and in this way no burden falls upon their pocket money. The system for distributing bread is that, at a scheduled time, a group of students forms and stands in a double line in the market (which is in front of the masjid), and the bread begins to be distributed. After one group, another group comes, and this process continues for several hours. There is no towel or handkerchief in the hands of the students. Just as beggars hold out their hands and take whatever they are given, so too is the condition of these students.

Number of Instructors. The number of instructors is more than forty. The principal instructor, who is called Shaikh-i Azhar, [194] and whose salary is no less than six or seven hundred per month, is extremely revered.[19] So much so that the government itself takes him into consideration. The collective expense of this madrasa is not less than two or three lakh rupees per year. In 1894, in addition to this amount, the Department of Education approved the amount of two lakh per year more.

Moral Character of the Students. Nothing on my entire journey made me more certain of the misfortune of the Muslims than the conditions at Azhar. An academy in which the Muslims of every part of the world are gathered, whose yearly expense is no less than two or three lakh, the number of whose students is in excess of twelve thousand; what hope could one not have had from the education and training there? But, unfortunately, instead of benefitting lakhs of Muslims, it has already ruined them, and goes on doing so. Because of the method of training and social life there—which I have just mentioned—ambition, lofty aspiration, passion, courage, in short, all noble characteristics are destroyed. I have seen students here whose relatives, and extremely close relatives (paternal and maternal uncle, and so on), themselves hold highly esteemed offices in this very city and provide for their every need. Still, because these students live at Azhar, they do not feel a modicum of shame in stretching out their hands and taking bread in the public market. The state of the baseness and low-spiritedness of the students is such that when they buy a paisa's worth of vegetables in the market, they make the vegetable-seller swear, *Birās sayyidnā al-Ḥusain*, meaning, "Upon the head of Imām Ḥusain, tell the right price!" Can it be hoped that people trained in this way will increase the glory and majesty of Islam? Azhar is even farther gone than the madrasas of this kind in our region. [195]

Even more regrettable is the wretched state of education. Only education in jurisprudence and syntax takes place in a proper and true manner here, and eight years each are scheduled for both. One might say that logic, philosophy, mathematics, and other rational sciences are nearly absent from the course of instruction entirely. There is instruction in the principles of jurisprudence, Quranic exegesis, the traditions of the Prophet, literature, semantics, and rhetoric, but it is so meager that it is not worthy of such a large academy. Even the education in syntax and jurisprudence, upon which a lifetime is spent, is not scholarly and innovative. Commentaries on *Kāfiyah*, and so on, marginal notes on those commentaries, and marginal notes on the marginal notes are taught and made to be memorized.[20] Shaikh Ṣabbān is an elder who recently passed away.[21] He has a commentary. This commentary has been considered of such great significance that commentaries on it, and marginal notes on those commentaries, are included in the course of studies, and it is thought to be a great achievement to memorize the entire series. Because I resided at Azhar, I often kept company with the students. I would see them engaged in extremely ordinary, trivial discussions unworthy of attention and feel regret. The result of this absurd method of education is that Azhar has not produced any valuable scholars or authors. I asked the students, "Does the Shaikh-i Azhar, who is considered *ustād al-kull* [teacher or master of all], even have one original writing?" They said with great pride, "Yes he has written some very important marginal notes on Ṣabbān."

More regrettable is the fact that the education is not based on any principle. Neither are there grade levels, nor is there a particular curriculum, nor is there an examination, nor has a rule for progressing been put in place. It is even more regrettable that there is no plan for reforming these wretched conditions. ʿAlī Pāshā Mubārak, who at one time was the head officer of the Department of Education, tried to reform it. [196] All the ʿulamā at Azhar became his enemies, and because the influence of the Shaikh-i Azhar is not confined to the students, but rather the entire country accepts him as its religious leader, the aforementioned pāshā was compelled to shut his eyes to it. Azhar is in reality a regional power, and the sultanate itself cannot easily dare to confront it.

The Khedival Library

The System for Checking Out Books. This is an extremely magnificent library, and in terms of organization and arrangement, beauty and attractiveness, excellence of administration, and the fineness of its building, it is better than all the libraries in Constantinople. The building is extremely glorious and expansive, and is divided into different parts. One part is especially reserved for browsing and study. There are three large rooms in it. In one room, there is a very large, long table on which the volumes of the register and catalogue are set. One room is reserved for study, and one for copying and writing. The head officer of the library gives a printed card to anyone who wants to take out a book. The following headings are on the card: the name of the person taking the book, along with the clarification of place of residence and occupation; the name of his surety (an unknown person cannot be given books without suretyship); the name and subject of the book, and the clarification of whether he takes the book for study or for copying; the number of days. Having filled out this card, it is turned over to an employee of the library, and, after a little while, the book arrives in the study or copy room. Although this method is evidence of fine organization and management, it is not without inconvenience.

The place where the books are kept is an entirely separate section in which there are numerous rooms. In one room, which is extremely expansive, there is an extremely ornate Turkish carpet. [197] There are glass cupboards along the walls on all four sides. In the middle, there are transparent glass tables, inside of which manuscripts and rare books are open. Among them is a Quran that is written on deer leather and about which it is said that it was written by the hand of Imām Jaʿfar-i Ṣādiq.[22] Apart from that, there are other rare copies of the Quran that the sultāns of Egypt had endowed in the eighth and ninth centuries.

The History of the Library. This library was established in 1286 Hijrī [1869–70]. Its brief history is that there were previously a great many small endowed libraries in Cairo and Alexandria, and so on, and because there was not sufficient arrangement for their preservation, the books were becoming ruined and wasting away. Taking this into consideration, the library was established upon the report of ʿAlī Pāshā, director of the Department of Education, and the books of all the classical libraries were deposited into this library. By order of the Khedive, an assembly of ʿulamā was established, the task of which was to seek out excellent and rare books so that they could be copied and deposited in the library. When a considerable treasury of books had been collected, the Khedive ordered the preparation of a catalogue. Thus, the catalogue began in 1300 Hijrī [1882–83] and reached completion in 1309 Hijrī [1891–92]. The catalogue is in eight volumes and only includes the Arabic books. Turkish, French, and English books have separate catalogues.[23]

Summary information related to the Arabic books will be obtained from the following chart: [198]

NAME OF THE SUBJECT	NUMBER OF BOOKS	NAME OF THE SUBJECT	NUMBER OF BOOKS
Maṣāḥif-i majīd [glorious copies (of the Quran)]	161	hadith	1,503
ʿilm-i qirʾat [science of recitation (of the Quran)]	85	*tauḥīd* [declaring God's unity]	563
tafsīr [exegesis (of the Quran)]	647	*taṣawwuf* [Ṣūfism]	705
mawāʿiẓ [sermons]	377	*al-fawāʾid wal-adʿiyah* [benefits and sayings (of prophets and spiritual elders)]	644
uṣūl-i fiqh [principles of jurisprudence]	225	*ādāb al-baḥṡ* [protocols of argument]	108
fiqh-i Ḥanafī [Ḥanafi jurisprudence]	1,451	fiqh-i Mālikī [Mālikī jurisprudence]	237
fiqh-i Shāfiʿī [Shāfiʿī jurisprudence]	520	fiqh-i Ḥanbalī [Ḥanbalī jurisprudence]	26
ʿilm al-farāyiż [science of duties]	138	*ʿilm-i ṣarf* [morphology]	238
naḥw [syntax]	1,029	*balāghah* [rhetoric]	285
ʿilm al-ważʿ [science of formation (of words)]	18	*ʿilm al-lughah* [linguistics, lexicography]	160
ʿurūż wal-qawāfī [prosody and rhyme]	68	*ʿilm-i adab* [the science of literature]	1,249
tārīkh [history]	1184	*riyāżī* [mathematics]	188

NAME OF THE SUBJECT	NUMBER OF BOOKS	NAME OF THE SUBJECT	NUMBER OF BOOKS
'ilm al-hai'ah [the science of (astral) forms]	19	*'ilm al-mīqāt* [the science of appointments, dates]	554
'ilm al-ḥarf wal-usmā' [science of letters and names]	185	*ikīmīyā' wal-ṭabī'ah* [chemistry and physics]	98
ṭibb [medicine]	464	*manṭiq* [logic]	256
ḥikmat o falsafah [practical wisdom and philosophy]	124	*funūn-i mutanawwi'* [various sciences]	1,096
Total	14,705		

[199] At this time, I record the names of several rare books that are found in this library.[24]

***Tafsīr* [Quranic Exegesis]**. *Aḥkām al-Qur'ān* by Abū Bakr al-Jaṣṣāṣ (d. 305 Hijrī) [917–18]; *Aḥkām al-Qur'ān* by Ibn al-'Arabī; *Aḥkām al-Qur'ān* by Kiyā al-Harāsī (d. 504 Hijrī) [1110–11]; *A'rāb al-Qur'ān* by Naḥās al-Naḥwī (d. 338) [949–50]; *I'jāz al-Qur'ān* by Bāqillānī;[25] *al-Baḥr al-muḥīṭ* by Ibn-i Ḥayyān al-Andalusī; *al-Burhān* by Shaikh Abu al-Ḥasan al-Auḥadī (d. 435 Hijrī) [1043–44] *Fī 'ashr al-mujallidāt* [in ten volumes]; *al-Basīṭ* by al-Wāḥidī; *Tanzīh al-Qur'ān* by al-Qāẓī 'Abd al-Jabbār al-Mu'tazilī;[26] *Jāmi' al-bayān fī tāwīl al-Qur'ān* by Muḥammad Jarīr al-Ṭabarī, 21 volumes; *Tafsīr* by Ibn-i Jauzī, 4 volumes; *Tafsīr* by Ḥāfiẓ 'Abd al-Razzāq bin Hammām (d. 211 Hijrī) [826–27]; *Gharīb al-Qur'ān* by al-Sijistānī (d. 330 Hijrī) [941–42]; *Gharīb al-Qur'ān* by Aḥmad bin Muḥammad al-Harawī (d. 401 Hijrī) [1010–11]; *Gharīb al-Qur'ān* by Ibn al-Shiḥnah; *Qānūn al-tāwīl* by Qāẓī Abū Bakr ibn al-Maghribī al-Andalusī (d. 543) [1148–49]; *al-Kafīl bi-ma'nī al-tanzīl* by 'Imād al-Kindī Qāẓī of Alexandria (d. 710) [1310–11].

Hadith. *al-Aḥkām al-kubrā* by 'Abd al-Ḥaqq al-Ishīlī;[27] *Ikhtilāf al-ḥadīṡ* by Imām Shāfi'ī. *Ādāb al-ḥāfiẓ* by Baihaqi; *Jāmi' al-masānīd wal-alqāb* by Ibn al-Jauzī; *al-Jawāhir al-taqī. al-Ḥāwī fī bayān āṡār al-ṭaḥāwī*; *Sunan-i kubrā* by Baihaqī; *Sharḥ-i ma'ānī al-āṡār* by al-'Ainī; *Musnad* by Imām Ḥanbal; *Musnad* by Imām Rāhwiyah; *Musnad* by Ḥāfiẓ Abū 'Awānah; *Musnad* by Ḥāfiẓ Abū 'Abd-allāh al-Marżarī; *Musnad* by Ḥāfiẓ Abū Na'īm.

History. *Iḥāṭah fī akhbār Gharnāṭah*; *Akhbār Abī Nuwās* (number of pages, 120); *Akhbār of Sibawaihi al-Naḥwī*[28] (36 pages); *al-Imāmah wal-siyāsah* by Ibn-i Qutaibah, incomplete; *Tārīkh-i Dimashq* by Ibn-i 'Asākir, imperfect; *Tārīkh-i Baghdād* by Khaṭīb, incomplete; *Tārīkh al-ḥukamā* by Jamāl al-Dīn al-Qiftī; *Ṭabaqāt al-umam* by Ṣā'id al-Andalusī; *Sullam al-wuṣūl ilā ṭabaqāt al-fuḥūl* by the author of *Kashf al-ẓunūn*;[29] *al-Saham al-maṣīb fī al-radd 'alā al-khaṭīb*; *Ṭabaqāt al-ḥuffāẓ* by al-Żahabī; *Ṭabaqāt al-kubrā* by Subkī; [200] *Ṭabaqāt al-Shāfi'yah*; *Ṭabaqāt al-shu'arā'* by Ibn-i Qutaibah; *Ṭabaqāt al-fuqahā'* by Imām Abū Isḥāq Shīrāzī; *Ṭabaqāt* by Ibn-i Sa'd; *Tārīkh* by 'Ainī; *Ṭabaqāt ḥamalat al-mażhab* by Ibn al-Mulaqqin; *Fażāyil Abī Bakr al-Ṣiddīq* by Ibn al-'Ushārī min aṣḥāb al-qarn al-khāmis;[30] *Fażāyil Abī Ḥanīfah al-Nu'mān* by Ibn al-'Awwām; *Fażāyil-i Miṣr* by Ibn-i Yūsuf al-Kindī (d. 350) [961–62] manqūlah min nuskhat al-aṣl al-kutbitah li-Kāfūr al-Akhshīdī;[31] *al-Lubāb fī al-ansāb* by Ibn al-Aṡīr; Manāqib al-Shāfi'ī; *Mukhtaṣar al-muntaẓim* by Ibn-i Jauzī and a summary of it likewise by him; *Masālik al-amṣār* by Ibn-i Fażlallāh; *Manāqib al-Imām al-Shāfi'ī* by al-Rāzī; *Manāqib-i Imām Aḥmad Ḥanbal* by Ibn al-Jauzī; *Sīrat al-Fārūq* by Ibn-i Jauzī; *al-Muntaẓim* by Ibn al-Jauzī; *Nihāyat al-arab* by al-Nuwairī, incomplete.

Literature. *al-Ishtibāh wal-naẓayir*; *al-Bayān wal-tabyīn* by al-Jāḥiẓ; *Jamharat al-ash'ār al-'arab* by Ibn-i Warīd; *Ḥamāsat al-Baṣra'īn*; the *Dīwān* of Ḥāfiẓ ibn-i Ḥajar; the *Dīwān* of Ibn al-Rūmī; the *Dīwān* of Ibn al-Mu'tazz; the *Dīwān* of Abū Nuwās; the *Dīwān* of al-A'shā; Żū al-rammah; the *Dīwān* of Quṭāmī; the *Dīwān* of Qais ibn al-Khaṭīm; the *Dīwan* of Labīd; the *Dīwān* of al-Mutalammis; *Raużat al-balāghah*; *al-Zāhir* by al-Zajjājī; *Sharḥ* [commentary] on al-Mutanabbī by Ibn-i Jinnī; *Sharḥ* of the *Dīwān* Abū Tammām by al-Ṣūlī (d. 335 Hijrī) [946–47]; Sharḥ of the *Dīwān* of Jirān al-'Aud by al-Imām al-Sakrī (d. 275 Hijrī) [888–89]; *Sharḥ* of the *Dīwān* of Ḥaṭiyah; *Sḥarh al-Ḥamāsah* by Marzūqī; *Sharḥ al-Ḥamāsah* by Abū al-'Alā' al-Ma'arrī; *Sharḥ-i Dīwān al-Ḥamāsah* by Ibn-i Jinnī; *Sharḥ-i Dīwān* by Kharīq Dahabī, Jāhiliyah [pre-Islamic] poetess; *Sharḥ-i Dīwān-i Zuhair bin Abī Sulmā* by Imām Ṡa'lab; *Sharḥ-i Dīwān-i Zuhair* by al-A'lam al-Shantamarī; *Sharḥ-i Dīwān-i 'Ubaidullah bin Qais wal-Ruqayyāt* by al-Sakrī; *Sharḥ-i Dīwān al-Muṡaqqib al-'Abdī*, and he is Jāhilī; *Sharḥ al-Mu'allaqāt* by Ibn al-Naḥḥās; *Sharḥ al-mufażżalāt* by Ibn al-Anbāri;

the *Dīwān* of Surāqah bin Mirdās; the *Dīwān* of Shammākh; the *Dīwān* of ʿUmar ibn Abī Rabīʿah; *Sharḥ-i Dīwān-i Rūbah; Sharḥ-i Dīwān al-ʿAjjāj*; the *Dīwān* of Wāwā al-Dimashqī. [201]

Ancient Monuments and Sites Worth Visiting

With regard to ancient monuments [archaeology], no city can match this city. The truth is that each and every potsherd here is a history of antiquity. In the deserted areas around the city, hundreds of pieces of pottery are found, even now, on which letters and engravings of several thousand years ago are carved. Where could I have found the time—rather, the truth is, the resolve—to tour all of the ancient monuments? Of course, I did see a few famous places, and I shall consider information about them sufficient.

Pyramids. These are the ancient towers which are generally reported to have existed before the flood of Noah. At the very least it is absolutely proven that they predate the scientific progress of the Greeks, since Galen has mentioned them in his writing. These towers were in extreme abundance, meaning they were spread out over a distance of two days' journey. Most were razed in the time of Ṣalāḥ al-Dīn. Those that have remained, and to which the word *ahrām* [pyramids] is applied specifically, are only three. The height of the largest is 480 feet, meaning twice that of the pillar of Quṭb sāḥib.[32] Each side of the bottom platform is 764 feet. The volume of the tower is eight crore, ninety lakh feet, and the weight is 68 lakh, 40,000 tons. One lakh people worked on its construction for twenty years. At the base are blocks of stone each 30 feet long and 5 feet wide, and the smallest at the top are of 8 feet. Its appearance is as follows. [202]

There is an extremely extensive, square platform. Another platform rests on that, leaving some amount of the surface on all sides. There are platforms one atop the other like this all the way up to the top, and with the platforms' gradually becoming smaller, the shape of stairs has been produced. The wondrous thing is that the stones have been joined in such a way that, not to speak of the appearance of joints or cracks, there does not seem to be even a trace of lime or mortar. On top of that, it is so firmly built that a thousand years have passed and not even a hair's worth of separation has been produced in its joints. Having seen these towers, one has no choice but to accept that the art of mechanics and levers existed in the ancient period, since such large stones cannot be raised onto to such a height without mechanics, and if we consider this invention exclusive to the present time, then we shall have to acknowledge some wondrous industry or technique even greater than mechanics.

Smallest Pyramid. Among these towers, one, which is the smallest, has been ruined to some extent, the circumstance of which is that in 593 Hijrī [1196–97] Malik al-ʿAzīz (son of Ṣalāḥ al-Dīn), persuaded by some fools, tried to demolish it.[33] Thus, some esteemed officers of the court and a great many miners, stone carvers, and laborers were appointed to the task. The work went on continuously for eight months, and extremely serious attempts were made. Thousands, lakhs of rupees were squandered. But except for the fact that the upper plastering was ruined, or here and there a stone or so was torn out, there was no result. Left with no other choice, Malik al-ʿAzīz abandoned this plan.* [203]

The Sphinx [Abū al-Haul]. There is a very large idol near the pyramids, which the people here call Abū al-Haul. Its entire body is inside the ground. Its neck, head, and both its hands are exposed. There is some kind of red paint rubbed onto the face, the luster of which remains to this day. Proportionate to these parts, it is estimated that its entire height is no less than sixty or seventy gaz.[34] Despite the extraordinary length, all the body parts—nose, ears, and so on—have been made with such order and proportion that there is not a hair's worth of difference in the mutual proportionality of the body parts. Someone asked ʿAbd al-Laṭīf Baghdādī,[35] "What is the most wondrous thing that you have seen in the world?" He said, "The proportion of Abū al-Haul's members." Because to maintain such proportionality in something of which no example exists in all of creation is not the work of man.

*ʿAbd al-Laṭīf Baghdādī has with regret recorded this event in *Miṣr kī tārīkh* (*The History of Egypt*).

Fort. The Well of Joseph. This fort is from the time of Ṣalāḥ al-Dīn. I was not able to see the actual structure of the fort. Still, I did see the masjid of Muḥammad ʿAlī Pāshā. It is of great glory and grandeur. There is gilt ornamentation on the ceiling and doors. An extremely excellent Turkish carpet is spread across the floor throughout the masjid. Near the masjid is a strange and wondrous well, which the common people have called and made famous as the Well of Joseph and the Prison of Joseph, and people go to it for pilgrimage. Because the real name of Sulṭān Ṣalāḥ al-Dīn was Yūsuf [Joseph], the caretakers got hold of a good means of misleading the common people. What's amusing is that they have dug a grave in it and they say that it is the grave of Joseph, peace be upon him. The caretaker tried to deceive me, too, and when I asked, "Joseph? Here?" He promptly responded, "I was mistaken, this is the grave of the prisoner who had entered the prison with Joseph [204] and had asked him to interpret his dream."[36]

This well is truly wondrous. An estimate of its depth can be made from the fact that, after descending three hundred steps, one finds its rim. They have made the steps very crooked and twisted, and the path is so dark that nothing can be seen without a candle. Thus, the caretaker, taking a candle, accompanies the people who go to visit it. After reaching the rim, when I tossed in a pebble, it took a while to make a sound, from which it became known that the water was at a great distance.

Museum. **Ancient Corpses**. Antīk-khānah [antique house], meaning museum.[37] Khedive Muḥammad ʿAlī Pāshā established this museum in 1835. At a distance of ten or twelve miles from the city, there is an official garden, which is several miles long and wide. In it is where the museum is located. There are countless rooms in it, and they are extremely beautifully arranged. Relics from long before Jesus are found here. There are plates, cups, jars, and hundreds of vessels of this kind which are all several thousand years old. The strangest and most wondrous are the corpses that, despite being thousands of years old, still remain in their original form. They call them *mūmiyāī* in Arabic and *mammī* [mummy] in English. It was the custom of the ancient Egyptians to carve wood or stone in the form of a boat and put the corpses of the dead into them. And, filling the empty space with slaked lime, and so on, they would make an image of the dead person on the upper surface. A special kind of paste was applied to the corpses because of which the body remained preserved from rot and decay. A great many coffins of this kind exist here, and they are what they call mūmiyāī or mammī. Among them, two or three coffins have opened up, [205] meaning the paste and slated lime on top have moved out of the way, and for this reason the entire body is clearly visible. I looked at these corpses very carefully. Despite the passing of thousands of years, there is not even the slightest trace of decay on the body. The hair on the head and the fingernails remain as before. Seeing them, a strange impression is left on the heart, and, in truth, what would be a more edifying and admonishing display?

The Prison of Joseph [Sijn-i Yūsuf]. Meaning the prison of Joseph. This is that very prison which is mentioned in the Glorious Quran, and which was the envy of Iram because of the beauty of Joseph. Couplet:

> Zulaikhā was in the garden and longingly recounted
> Memories of the prison in which the one who adorns the assembly resides.[38]

The great scholar Maqrīzī has written, "It is proven by sound narratives and reasoned inferences that the prison in which Joseph was imprisoned is this very location."[39] I severely regret that I could not tour this edifying and auspicious site. I have only mentioned it so that if God should bring one of our fellow countrymen to this place, he should not, like me, be deprived of a visit to it.

Masjids. Ancient Islamic monuments are also in abundance here. There is no end to the masjids. There are hundreds, rather, thousands. The oldest among them is the ʻAmr bin al-ʻĀṣ Congregational Mosque, which is a monument to the time of the caliphate of Fārūq.[40] The Mashhad-i Ḥusain [Tomb (lit., site of martyrdom) of Ḥusain] is a masjid in which the auspicious head of Imām Ḥusain is famously said to be buried. I do not know to what extent this narrative is authentic. [206] But on this basis, the common people here hold the masjid in extreme reverence. It is also cared for by the government. It is a glorious, spacious, and beautiful masjid. Ornamentation and appointments have increased its splendor even more. A Turkish carpet is spread throughout the masjid, and it is probably changed frequently because, when I saw it, there was absolutely no trace of age or wear.

The strangest and most wondrous masjid is the masjid of Sultān Ḥasan, which is near the fort.[41] In constructing this masjid, twenty thousand dirhams (five lakh rupees) were spent every day for three continuous years. Its construction began in 757 Hijrī [1356–57] and reached completion in 760 Hijrī [1358–59]. They call it the Madrasa of Sultān Ḥasan because there are four large halls on its four sides, in which jurisprudents of the four imāms used to give lessons in fiqh and hadith.[42] The historian Maqrīzī has written, "No religious building like it has been constructed in all the regions of Islam." Although I do not accept this claim, there is no doubt that no masjid in the world is as tall and lofty. It is regrettable, seriously regrettable, that such a wondrous monument is becoming entirely deserted. Not even a lamp burns in it at night. And the door always remains closed. After having the door opened, when I went inside, desertion rained down all around. Such a lack of appreciation for such a magnificent masjid in an Islamic sultanate is extremely surprising.

Burial Sites or Shrines [Mazārāt]. Burial sites and tombs are also in abundance, and there are a great many endowments for their expenses.[43] [207] The grave sites of Zainab (as) (the sister of Imām Ḥusain, peace be upon him), Kulṡūm (as), Imām Shāfiʿī (ra), and Imām Laiṡ (ra) are of great grandeur and magnificence. I made pilgrimage to the burial site of Imām Shāfiʿī. I intended to visit other burial sites, too, but I became distraught by the situation that I saw upon arriving there and returned full of sorrow and regret. The people of Egypt have scheduled certain days of the week on which, according to their belief, the souls of Zainab and Imām Shāfiʿī, and so on, turn their attention toward their burial sites from the world above. They call these special days *ḥażrah* [presence], and there is a large crowd at the burial site of whoever's day of ḥażrah it is. People come for pilgrimage in large numbers, and, kissing the grave, ask for their needs and desires. If there is any difference between the state of the people at that time and polytheism and idol worship, then it is so subtle that it is not apparent to a person like me who only sees the external.[44] I used to cry about grave-worship in Hindustan, but, having come to Egypt, the following couplet came to mind in relation to the entire Islamic world:

> From his foot to his head, every place I look,
> Miracle tugs on the garment hem of the heart, saying, "this is the place."[45]

Classical Madrasas. Madrasas of the classical age, of which I have made summary mention in *Guzishtah Taʿlīm*, are still extant, but they are becoming more and more deserted.[46] I happened to visit a madrasa while walking along. Although it was just an ordinary madrasa, the building was attractive and very tall. There were rooms for the students to live in on all sides, an extensive courtyard in the middle, a flower bed or two in the courtyard, and a few date palms. In sum, one could estimate from its condition [208] that if this was the state of a very small madrasa upon being deserted, then the great madrasas must have been even more glorious, elegant, and beautiful.

Printing Houses and Newspapers

Printing Houses. Because the books printed in Egypt are spread throughout all of Hindustan, and Egypt has gained popular renown in printing and spreading Arabic books, it is also necessary to discuss these printing houses and the booksellers of this place.

The printing houses are in extreme abundance here, and a few of them are praiseworthy. In particular, the official printing house at Bulaq is a magnificent printing house and, with regard to accuracy, clarity, fineness of paper, and excellence of printing, is one of a kind. This printing house was established in 1827 by the order of Muḥammad ʿAlī Pāshā, and at that time four hundred people worked in it. It is still extremely active, but, regretfully, and severely regretfully, because the taste of the region is bad, few excellent books on rare subjects are printed. If even one or two hundred books among the rare manuscripts that are found in the Khedival Library were printed, the world would be rich with beneficial information.

I discussed this with several enlightened printing-house people. They responded that books of this kind are not commonly favored. Of course, commonly favored books are printed and sold over and over again. For example, they said that the volumes of the book *al-Kharāj* by Qāżī Abū Yūsuf, which was printed more than eight years ago, still have not sold out.[47] It is a matter of regret and shame that [209] the rare books in the Khedival Library go to Europe to be printed and are published from there. Sayyid ʿAbd al-Wāḥid Ṭūbī is a famous merchant.[48] The Europeans have made a business deal with him. He has books copied in accordance with their order and sends them to Europe. Accordingly, Sayyid ʿAbd al-Wāḥid showed me the manuscripts of three or four books that he had had copied to send to Europe.

Of course, Egypt has done us the favor of making books extremely inexpensive, because of which it is common to benefit from them. I bought a great many books that cost even less than Naval Kishore publications. Everyone who seeks Egyptian books should order them directly from Egypt and not from Bombay, whose merchants are not content with even quadruple profit. For Egyptian books, they should correspond with Sayyid ʿAbd al-Wāḥid Ṭūbī. His address is this: Miṣr. Cairo. Near al-Azhar. Rupees can be sent easily by money order.

Newspapers. The newspapers that are issued in Arabic are more than thirty. Among them, *al-Muwayyad*, *al-Muqaṭṭim*, *al-Taqaddum*, and *Ahrām* are the most renowned. In addition, twenty-five to thirty newspapers are issued in French and English.

By virtue of the English government, the newspapers here enjoy freedom. For this reason, these newspapers write extremely freely about regional affairs of all kinds, and write finely. Because very few books have been written in Arabic about politics, and the ʿulamā of Hindustan cannot write even four lines on subjects of this kind, several eminent gentlemen thought that [210] the ideas of politics could not be presented fully in this language, but the newspapers of Egypt have absolutely disproved this idea.

Monthly journals, too, are numerous, and several of them are published quite capably. Among them, the most successful are *al-Muqtaṭaf* and *al-Hilāl. Al-Hilāl* comes to our Lajnat al-Adab.*[49] Eight rupees is the annual cost. I recommend that other people of taste purchase it and benefit from it.

Theaters

There are two or three theaters here. One is state owned and was built in the time of Khedive Isma'īl Pāshā.[50] It is of great elaborateness, magnificence, and grandeur. But it was closed at that time, so I could not visit it. There is another theater, which belongs to a Christian company. I visited it once. The curtains, stage, equipment, and appointments are nice. The show was about a dispute between the Queen of Nubia (or) Greece (I do not recall the location) and the Caesar over the borders of the realm. The Caesar requested several new regions from the queen. The queen refused. They argued back and forth two or three times about it. So much so that war broke out, [211] and a great conflict ensued. The dress of the woman who played the queen was entirely European. There was a bare sword at her waist and it looked extremely attractive on her. She also acted well. The way she leapt up in agitation upon hearing the Caesar's message from the messenger, wielded the sword, and spoke these words in a wrathful tone, "*Kaifa narżā bi-hāżā al-żullin wa-l-hawān,*"[51] and, along with them, recited a few prideful poems of pre-Islamic Arabia, truly produced a wondrous effect. She did not sing the poems—rather, she presented them in a tone of wrath and assertiveness. During the fight, both armies fought hand to hand holding swords. One could clearly see the blows of the swords and the writhing of the people who were wounded and fell. And from their falling powerlessly to the ground, it seemed that they were falling after being wounded for real. The thing that I liked best was that, in the end, everyone sang a song for the well-being of the Khedive. I do not recall

* This is a society that has been in place for the last year and a half in our academy. It meets three times per month to debate issues, and all the lectures and speeches, rather, all its activities, take place in Arabic. This is probably the first such meeting in all of Hindustan. Our classical Arabic madrasas should imitate this society.

the entire song, but there were definitely these words: "*al-ʿaish tamm wa-l-nafʿ ʿamm min al-khadīw al-muḥtaram.*"[52] There were numerous other rhyming words like this. The rising and falling of voices at each phrase, the singing in an Arabic tone, the regard for musical principles, and, most of all, the thought that all the people singing the raga for the Khedive's well-being with such passion were Christian, left a wondrous impression on my heart.

Whether the theater is Hindustani or Arabian and Egyptian, it is opposed to dignity and propriety to participate in it in my view. But everything of the Islamic sultanate seemed honorable and dear.

> How prostrating to that footprint debased me;
> I entered the lane of my rival standing on my head.[53] [212]

Clubs and Societies

Societies. Societies are in abundance here, and they have different purposes. Nine are charitable ones whose purpose is the aid and assistance of the poor, but it is surprising that not one of them belongs to Muslims. Intellectual societies, too, are numerous, among which Jamʿiyat al-ʿulamāʾ al-Miṣriyah [Society of Egyptian Scholars], which was founded in 1859, and al-Majmaʿ al-Jughrāfī [the Geographical Society], which Khedive Ismāʿīl Pāshā founded in 1875,* are the most renowned and useful. Ḋibeṫing klab (debating clubs), meaning assemblies for debate, are in extreme abundance, and because of them, the Egyptians have made great progress in the art of lecturing and public speaking. I myself took part in one assembly. Toward the front, there was a high platform on which the chairs of the president of the society and the secretary were set. The general attendees were seated on benches. Four or five people spoke in front of me. Their speeches were so apropos, powerful, and eloquent that something like wonderment spread over me. The amazing thing is that

* This society has collected extremely rare research and information related to geography, which have been printed and published as a proper journal. This society has a special building and library, and other necessary things.

the common speech of the Egyptians is absolutely erroneous—rather, meaningless—with respect to syntax, but on occasions of this kind, they speak extremely polished Arabic, and there is no sign of ostentation or affectation. Not even a shadow of the general live-heartedness, freedom of thought, boldness, and ambitiousness that have been produced in the Egyptians because of such assemblies and the freedom of the newspapers exists in the Turkish regions or in fact in any of the present Islamic states. [213]

The Birthday of the Prophet

The Egyptians really should pride themselves on the fact that if anyone has understood the basic meaning of *maulid* [(the Prophet's) birthday] they have. The way that the birthday is celebrated here is that there is an extensive plot of land outside of the city which an esteemed lady has endowed for this very function. Tents and pavilions are set up on three sides of the field with extreme order and good taste, and the land in the middle is reserved as a courtyard. The courtyard is entirely in the shape of a circle, and small red flags are erected in all four directions around it. Because the tents and pavilions generally belong to pāshās and amīrs, they are decorated with extreme elaborateness and refinement. Each pāshā and amīr decorates his tent in a different style. The light comes from chandeliers and is plentiful. Sherbet or chai, or something else of this kind, is available at all times in each tent. Whenever a person, even if he be a common spectator, enters a tent, he is immediately offered chai or sherbet.

The tent of the Khedive, in which a deputy participates on his behalf, is red and extremely glorious and lustrous. Special groups of Sūfīs and faqīrs gather in each tent and perform żikr in accordance with their respective practices.[54] The method of żikr is entirely different from that of the faqīrs of Hindustan. All the people stand in a circle and continue repeating the particular words of the żikr all together in a loud voice. [214] Along with these words, lowering their heads to almost a deep bow, they move their waist and neck strangely. If someone were to see it from afar, he might mistake it for exercise. The method of the dancing dervishes is even stranger, and the truth is that it is a debasement and insult to *faqr* and Sufism.[55]

The garments of these people are of a special fashion. I do not entirely recall the shape, but, as far as I do remember, there is a low-hanging garment and a green sash at their waist. They sit in rows, and whoever among them wants to do żikr goes into the middle of the gathering and begins to dance. People say that all the principles of dance are observed. But what I saw was only that the person, standing in one place, spun around like a pinwheel. He continued to dance like this for nearly an hour. But neither his hand nor any other part of his body moved. There was another group whose method differed somewhat. Their garments were shorter and fuller, almost like a skirted battalion. While dancing, these people danced with both hands extended.

I was filled with extreme regret that these people consider this foolish practice to be worship, and that it is the belief of a great many people that these people attain to the rank of *ghauṡ*, *quṭb*, *abdāl*, and *autād*.[56] *Wa li l-nās fī-mā ya'shaqūn mażāhib.*[57]

Mention of the dancing dervishes had come only in passing. Now I turn to the actual event, meaning the particulars of the birthday. This gathering begins on the first day of the month and grows larger and larger each day. So much so that on the night of the twelfth, there is such a massive crowd of people that one cannot find a place because of all the coming and going. In the morning, everyone, [215] especially the government deputy, qāżī, muftī, and Shaikh al-Azhar, gather in Mashhad-i Ḥusain, and a scholar recites the details of the birth of His Majesty [the Prophet]. At the exact moment of the mention of the birth, everyone stands up in accordance with the usual practice, and a short while later the assembly ends, with which the series of events for the birthday celebration ends.

This method of celebrating the birthday pleased me with respect to the fact that the expression of passion and joy that should be expressed upon the birth of His Majesty should take place in this way. Where will one find such large gatherings, such glory and grandeur, and such arrangements in small assemblies? But two or three things are objectionable. The first is that there are fireworks on the eleventh and twelfth, and this does not befit such a sacred custom. The second is that, theaters, and so on, seeing the large gathering of people, are set up on the streets near the site of the gathering. The government should absolutely stop them.

People of Achievement and Useful Writings

People of Achievement. Like Constantinople, here, too, there are two groups of ʿulamā and writers, and the sensibilities of both are entirely separate. Several of the shaikhs and disciples of Azhar are thought to be accomplished masters in their subjects, meaning syntax and jurisprudence, but the entire foundation of their accomplishment rests on the memorization of minutiae, in which there is not even a suspicion of critical research and innovative thinking. The Shaikh of Azhar himself, who is called the leader of the field, does not have an original scholarly work in any field. Although new education still has not produced anyone of great achievement, [216] one does find glimpses of scholarly research and innovative reason in it, and its writings are in the style of Europe. I record information about several famous people from both groups.

ʿAlī Pāshā Mubārak. Whatever reform and progress has taken place in Egypt's Department of Education has done so because of him. He was sixteen years old when in 1255 Hijrī [1839–40], he entered the Muhandis Khānah [Engineering House] madrasa. In 1260 Hijrī [1844–45], he traveled to France with the sons of Muhammad ʿAlī Pāshā, and, having lived there for a few years, obtained numerous degrees. In 1285 Hijrī [1868–69], he was entrusted with the service of the Office of Madrasas and Department of Endowments. During that time, he accomplished a number of tasks related to knowledge. He (1) reformed domestic schools, (2) established head madrasas in the districts, (3) laid the foundation of the Dār al-ʿUlūm Academy, and (4) established the Khedivial Library. In 1285 Hijrī [1868–69], he was appointed director of education. He promoted education in the extreme. He also authored scholarly writings and compositions. He has written an extremely excellent appendix to *Khiṭaṭ o āṡār* by Maqrīzī.[58] The Emperor of France and the King of Austria have sent him honorary medals. I was quite keen to meet him, but unfortunately he had gone to Alexandria with the Khedive at that time. He passed away three or four months ago.[59] All the greats of the sultanate participated in his funeral procession. A biography about him was recently written and published.[60]

'Alī Pāshā Ibrāhīm. He is an extremely enlightened and educated person. In 1260 Hijrī [1844–45], he went to France for education, and, [217] having stayed five years there, obtained a degree of an extremely high level. In 1296 Hijrī [1878–79], he was appointed director of education. It was he who first established schools for teachers. The sultanate of France sent him a medal of the rank of officer, which is not given to anyone except for famous men of achievement.

Amīn Bey Fikrī. He is a Judge in the High Court. He acquired education in France. He attended the Oriental Conference that was held in Sweden as a delegate of the sultanate of Egypt. Accordingly, he has written a book on the circumstances of the journey that gives readers an estimate of his abilities as a writer. The cost of the book is eight rupees, and it really is a book worth visiting.[61]

Aḥmad Zakī. He is the secretary of the Department of Translation. He knows French extremely well. He had written a treatise in French on the issue of slavery that was extremely well received, and famous French newspapers and authors wrote articles on and reviews of it. Thus, the original treatise along with the reviews, and so on, has been translated into Arabic and printed, the name of which is *al-Riqq fī al-Islām* [Slavery in Islam].[62] He has other useful writings, too. He went as a delegate to the last Oriental Conference that was held in London.[63]

Shaikh Muḥammad 'Abduh. He is classically educated. Egypt and Syria acknowledge him a master in the field of literature. He has extremely capably written a commentary on the *Maqāmāt-i Badī'*.[64] Along with his enlightenment, he is acquainted with the new sensibility [218] because of the company of Sayyid Jamāl al-Dīn Afghānī.[65] He has translated a tract by the aforementioned sayyid into Arabic, and has briefly written a biography of him in its introduction. I will write several select phrases and sentences from it here, from which one can gain an estimate of the aforementioned shaikh's mastery of the subject and the power of his writing. The people in our region who have taken up the subject of literature should imitate this practice and should adopt this style of writing events. Where mention has been made of the appearance, morals, and qualities of the aforementioned sayyid (Jamāl al-Dīn Afghānī), he writes:[66]

> As for his physical constitution, it appears to the observer as purely Arab. Medium in height and moderate in build. Wheaten in his color. Nervous and sanguine in temperament. Great-headed in moderation. Broad-browed in proportion. Wide eyes. Full cheeks. Broad-chested. Cheerful upon meeting someone. As for his character, an integrity of heart stands out among his attributes. And he has great patience, accommodating what God wills be accommodated until someone comes to insult his honor or his piety. Then his patience turns to anger. So while he is patient and pious, in this case he becomes a lion and ferocious. And he gives generously what he has in his hand. Strong in his faith in God. He does not care what adversities of the world come to him. Gentle with whoever treats him with kindness. Harsh to anyone who is uncivil to him. And he has command over the subtleties of meaning and the definition and presentation of them in their proper form, as if every meaning had been created for him. He enters into discussion of every topic that is set before him, and it is as if he created it by his own hand, and he comes to it from all its sides and encompasses all its aspects.[67]

I met him. We had a long, pleasing conversation. He lamented the miserable state of education at Azhar, but along with that, he also complained about the new education, and would say, *hā'ulā ażall sabīlan.*[68] [219] Alas, the government of Egypt has appointed him to the office of judgeship in Islamic courts. He was better suited for the Department of Education. Thus, he, too, lamented this.

Shaikh Ḥamzah Fatḥullāh. He is classically educated and a man of old ideas. He is a great master in the field of literature. The curriculum in literature that is taught at the Dār al-'Ulūm is his selection. He is the inspector of the Department of Education. He was appointed as a member of, and attended, the Oriental Conference in Sweden along with the Egyptian delegation, and presented a treatise related to the rights of women at the conference, the name of which is *Ḥuqūq al-nisā' fī al-Islām* [The Rights of Women in Islam].[69] This treatise has been printed at the official state press.[70] He has written very little on the actual topic, and even what he has written is *maulawī*-like.[71] Still, the writing is extremely masterful, elevated, and powerful.[72]

I met him in the office of the Ministry of Education.[73] We spoke about scientific matters for a while. He kindly bestowed upon me five copies of the aforementioned treatise as a gift. After leaving the office, he had me brought to his home and insisted on feeding me. The food was extremely simple, meaning there was dry bread and dates. Because he is a master of the Arabic language and has special love and affection for Arabia, his simple Arab food left a unique impression.

Anecdote. The aforementioned shaikh and I were eating when the sound *hīchūn hīchūn* came from nearby. [220] I wondered, "Where is this most detestable of sounds coming from?"[74] When I looked, I saw that there was a donkey tied up in a room. I learned that it is not considered shameful here to keep a donkey in the home. Although I had already seen many people, even Englishmen, going around on donkeys in the market (rather, I myself had the honor once or twice), I still did not expect there to be stables for donkeys like those for horses in the homes of respectable men.

The End of the Journey and the Generous Moral Character of the Arabs

The Generous Moral Character of the Arabs. With my departure from Egypt, one might say, my journey, too, came to an end, since after that I neither saw any new populated places nor experienced any new incidents. I spent the entire duration of the journey (against expectation) in extreme pleasure, ease, interest, and satisfaction. But it is my duty at this point to say why this pleasure and ease befell my lot and because of whom they did so. There is only one answer to these questions. That is, the generous moral character of the Arabs* and the Turks. The reality is that if I had not encountered the generous moral character of the Arabs, life would have been unbearable; forget about the interesting things that happened on the journey. Obviously, to go and live, socialize, shop, tour, seek out and discern information, and search for matters worthy of discovery in a city—in short, all this depends on knowing the language, and I am totally unfamiliar with Turkish. [221] Whatever Arabic I knew was also useless, or very nearly useless. Nor was I so wealthy that I could compensate for this shortcoming by spending money carelessly. In such circumstances, to spend a period of six months with such pleasure and ease that it was as if I were in my own homeland was the grace of the Turks, and most especially the Arabs, alone. They were the ones who interpreted for me. They were

* Most Muslims of Syria and Egypt are of Arab descent. For this reason, I designate all Syrians and Egyptians as Arabs for the sake of brevity.

the ones who brought me things from the market. They were the ones who introduced me to people. They were the ones who acted as my guide in places worth visiting. They were the ones who joined me in amusing conversations. In sum, there was no task or need in which they did not act as my surety, and, what's more, they did so without self-interest and without selfish motive, simply out of regard for hospitality and kindness toward poor strangers far from home. It is impossible to give an account of each and every particular instance on which I experienced the generous morals of these people. I write two or three events as examples. At this point, you should read once more the instances of the generosity of Shaikh ʻAbd al-Fattāḥ, Shaikh ʻAlī Ẓabyān, Khūjī Āfandī, ʻAbd al-Bāsiṭ Āfandī, Shaikh ʻAbd al-Ḥalīm Āfandī, and ʻAbd al-Salām Āfandī, which I have already written.

During the period in which I resided in Constantinople, the paternal cousin of ʻAbd al-Salām Āfandī, Shākir Āfandī, came to Constantinople for a case in court. ʻAbd al-Salām Āfandī tried to have Shākir Āfandī stay with him, but there was no space in ʻAbd al-Salām Āfandī's room. He said to me, "Let him stay with you." I agreed for his sake. When the time of my departure drew near, he said, "I, too, am ready to travel. It would have been nice to go together, but at this time I do not have the money. I have sent for some money from home. [222] I am waiting for it to arrive." Since he was from Jerusalem, the thought occurred to me that, in addition to ease and comfort, in Jerusalem I would also receive a lot of help in seeking out and finding information about everything because of him. I told him, "Take the money from me. Come along and repay me there." He refused, and, despite my insistence, was in no way willing to do so. But I so compelled him that he could not refuse, and I handed over two hundred rupees to him. At that time, ʻAbd al-Salām Āfandī was not at the house. When he returned in the evening, I mentioned this to him in passing as we spoke. Hearing what had taken place, he struck himself on the head and became extremely distressed. Over and over he said, "*Shū faʻalta, shū faʻalta*?"[1] meaning "What the hell have you done?" "Shākir is my cousin, but he is an extreme swindler and he has deceived you and taken your money." The amusing thing is that it was my money that was in danger, but ʻAbd al-Salām Āfandī was even more upset than I was. When Shākir

Āfandī came home, ʿAbd al-Salām Āfandī harshly rebuked him and had him draft a document, which he himself and another person witnessed. He took me aside and said, "This is a matter of national disgrace. That is why I have had to expose my brother. This boy (Shākir) is a swindler and dishonest. He does not even have any personal property. His paternal uncle, ʿAbd al-Razzāq, is responsible for him. Turn this document over to him. He will give you the money."

In short, Shākir and I boarded the ship together the next day. When we reached Smyrna, a wire in Shākir's name came from his lawyer telling him to return immediately. Shākir said to me, "How can I leave you and go?" [223] I did not think it appropriate to stop him and happily—or rather, insistently—sent him back. Having arrived at Jerusalem, I went straight to see ʿAbd al-Razzāq, and I must say of necessity and with regret at this point that he treated me with bad moral character. I have no complaint that he did not give me the money. The shocking thing is that he treated me with such crooked moral character. The next day, I went to Mufī ṣāḥib (whom I have mentioned above) and told him the whole story and showed him the document. Muftī ṣāḥib sent someone to ʿAbd al-Razzāq. He sent word, "At this time, I do not have the money. Of course, I can pay you in a few days." Because Muftī ṣāḥib was sure that he could trust him, he simply said, "You will certainly receive the money," and said no more. But the other people who were there and were members of the family of ʿAbd al-Razzāq became very angry and said, "*Wa-Allāh yabīʿu līḥyatahu wa yuwaddī*,"[2] meaning, "He should sell his beard and pay the money back."

The next day, when I went to Muftī ṣāḥib, he gave me the full amount, meaning two hundred rupees of his own. I said, "If you are giving this to me from your own pocket, then I do not want to take it." He said, "No, ʿAbd al-Razzāq has consigned it to me.[3] But even if he had given it to me and I had not had the money, I still would have sold this scholar's robe of mine and given you the money."[4] Despite this, Muftī ṣāḥib and all those present were severely embarrassed. The people beseeched my forgiveness, saying over and over, "We cannot look you in the eyes." As I was leaving, Mufti ṣāḥib walked with me for some distance and said, "*Al-marjjuww minkum an tasturū ʿuyūbanā fa-innahu min shiyam al-kirām*,"[5] [224] meaning, "My hope is that you will cover our faults because the task of the noble is to cover things." I still find in my heart the impression of the embarrassment that Mufti ṣāḥib and his companions felt for the behavior of ʿAbd al-Razzāq and the way in which they asked me over and over for forgiveness.

The second occurrence is as follows. Having arrived in Alexandria (as I have written above), I became severely distraught on account of a lack of familiarity. Because it would be awhile before the train departed, I went and sat in a coffeehouse, which was attached to the station. A Syrian Arab was seated there. Understanding me to be a man from a foreign country, or who knows why, he treated me very warmly. He was going to Cairo. I told him, "I am traveling with you, and, on account of my lack of familiarity, I must endure loss and difficulty at every occasion. I want us to remain together as far as Cairo." He said, "*Bi-l-ra's wal-ʿain*."[6] Because of him, I did not experience any discomfort during the entire journey. When we arrived at Cairo, I said to him, "Please tell me the name of a hotel that is near Azhar and whose fees are not too expensive." I had only said this so that he would tell me an address. He stayed with me at the hotel for two days. On the third day, he said, "I have come to Cairo on pressing business and must return in two or three days. With your permission, I must leave." Having said this, he gave the rate for two days and the fees for food to the manager of the hotel. Although I protested, "Why are you paying my fees?" he refused to yield, saying, "Till now you have been my guest." Having said this, he departed, [225] and I continued to regret severely that I did not meet him again.

The Arabic Language of the Present Day

Because one of the necessities of a travelogue is also that the current language of the region about which information is written be discussed, it is necessary to write something about the Arabic language, which is the language of all the districts of Syria and Egypt. Our fellow countrymen will also benefit from this—those who are extremely interested in the newspapers of Egypt and Syria, but who cannot avail themselves of them on account of not knowing the Arabic language of the present day. The Arabic of the present day is so different from classical Arabic that if a great scholar from our country traveled to Egypt and Syria, he would have nearly the same difficulty understanding the language there as a commoner. The characteristics of the present language, because of which it has become different from the classical language, are briefly recorded below.

(1) A great many words have been so abbreviated that, until someone explains, the mind does not turn toward the original words. These are some words of this kind: [226]

CHANGED WORD	ORIGINAL	MEANING
shū	*ayyu shai'in*	*kalimah-i istifhām* [interrogative word]
mūsh	*mā huwa shai'un*	*ḥarf-i nafī ke ma'nī men isti'māl hotā hai* [it is used in the meaning of a particle of negation]
mā 'alaish	*mā 'alaihi shai'un*	*kuchh harj nahīn, kuchh mużāyaqah nahīn* [there is no harm; it is no problem]
bilāsh	*bi-lā shai'in*	*muft* [free]; and it is used in the meaning of the word before, meaning, *kuchh harj nahīn* [there is no harm].
hīk	*hākażā*	*is-ṭaraḥ* [thus]

CHANGED WORD	ORIGINAL	MEANING
hādūl	*hāżihi hā'ulā'*	*yih log* [these people]
qaddaish	*qadr ayyi shai'in*	*kis qadr* [how much]

(2) They have added some letters to the beginning or end of words, because of which the form of the word completely changes. For example, in Syria they add *b* to the beginning of all present-tense verbs. They say the words *mā aqūlu*[1] *mā a'rifu*[2] like this: *mā bi-aqūl, mā bi-a'rif.* In Egypt, they add *sh* to the end of words. For example, *ya'khużush* instead of *ya'khuż.*[3]

(3) The pronunciation of letters has become utterly ruined. Rather, one should say that all the characteristics of Arabic pronunciation have died. They say *hamzah* instead of *qāf*, *gāf* instead of *jīm*, *dāl* instead of *żāl*, and *hamzah* instead of *'ain.*[4] And this is not only the pronunciation of the ignorant and commoners. Rather, scholars and the noble, too, pronounce letters this way. In Egypt, I once asked a student, "Where are you coming from?" He said, "*Gā'i min gum'ah*" (*jā'a min jum'a*),[5] meaning, I am coming from the *jum'ah* [Friday] masjid. [227]

(4) There are many classical words whose manner of use has changed. For example, when a person is praised or thanked, he will say in response, *astaghfirullāh*, meaning, "Of what am I worthy?"[6] Or if an astonishing thing is described to someone, he will say *amān.*[7] Or, for example, if one wishes to say, "What concern is it of yours?" one will say, *shū biddak.*[8] *Shū* is the abbreviation of *ai sha'in,* and *budd* is the same word that we use with *lā-budd* [inevitably].[9]

(5) European words have entered into usage in abundance, and because changes have been made to them to some degree, those who know Arabic and those who know English both have difficulty understanding them. Several words of this kind are listed by way of example:

CHANGED WORD	ORIGINAL	MEANING
shū	*ayyu shai'in*	*kalimah-i istifhām* [interrogative word]
mūsh	*mā huwa shai'un*	*ḥarf-i nafī ke ma'nī men isti'māl hotā hai* [it is used in the meaning of a particle of negation]

CHANGED WORD	ORIGINAL	MEANING
mā ʻalaish	*mā ʻalaihi shaiʼun*	*kuchh harj nahīn, kuchh mużāyaqah nahīn* [there is no harm; it is no problem]
bilāsh	*bi-lā shaiʼin*	*muft* [free]; and it is used in the meaning of the word before, meaning, *kuchh̉ h̉arj nahīṅ* [there is no harm].
hīk	*hākażā*	*is-ṭaraḥ* [thus]
hādūl	*hāżihi hāʼulāʼ*	*yih log* [these people]
qaddaish	*qadr ayyi shaiʼin*	*kis qadr* [how much]

[228]

Now we include a brief lexicon of the words of the present language. In it, most are also words that had already come into existence five or six hundred years ago, but because they did not acquire common currency in writings, and so on, they, too, are thought to be new words. Specifically on words of this kind, I will write the symbol *q*, which means that they are old [*qadīm*] words.

WORD	MEANING	WORD	MEANING
	(a)	*imtiyāz*	*lāysins* [license]
imžā'	*dast-khaṭṭ* [signature]	*aghrāž*	*asbāb* [objects; things]
almān (German)	*salṭanat-i jarman* [the sultanate of Germany]	*adab-khānah*	*pā-khānah* [lavatory]
ajzā-khānah (Turkish)	*dawā-khānah* [pharmacy]	*antīkah-khānah*	*qadīm ashiyā kā 'ajā'ib-gḣar* [house of wonders for old objects]
(q) *usṭūl*	*jangī jahāz yā jahāzoṅ ka beṙā* [a warship or a fleet of warships]	*ishtirāk al-jarīdah*	purchasing a newspaper; and the cost of a newspaper *badal-i ishtirāk* [exchange of share]
ūžah or ūdah	*kamrah (makān kā)* [room (of a house)]		
āghā; pl. *aghwāt*	*khwājah-sarā* [eunuch]		

WORD	MEANING
	(b)
batātah	*ālū* [potato]
(q) *baraṭlah*; pl. *barāṭīl*	*rishwat* [bribe]
baladiyyah	*miyūnisipalṫī* [municipality]
bākhirah	*dukhānī jahāz* [steamship]
(q) *barnāmaj* (Persian)	*fihrist* [list, catalogue]
barrād	*chāydān* [tea box]
bait al-mā'	*pā-khānah* [lavatory]
(q) *badrī*	*sawerā* [early morning]
(q) *bakīr*	*aiżan* [early morning]
bāsh-kātib (Turkish)	*mīr munshī* [chief clerk]
	(t)
takkah	*azār-band* [waistband]
tur'ah	*baṙā tālāb* [large pond]
tamrīnāt 'askariyah	*qawā'id* (*fauj kī*) [drills (of the military)]
tashkhīṣ	*ṫheṫar meṅ aikṫ karnā* [to act in the theater]
tażkirah	*parwānah. ṫikaṫ. sanad.* [passport. ticket. license.]
taṭ'īm al-judarī	*chīchak ka ṫīkā* [smallpox vaccination]
tamrīnāt jasadiyah	*warzish* [exercise]
	(ṡ)
ṡaurah	*baghāwat* [rebellion]
(q) *ṡurayyā*	*jḣāṙ* (*raushnī kā*) [chandelier (of light)]
ṡaub	*lambā kurtā* [long kurta]
	(j)
(q) *jubn*	*panīr* [paneer]
(q) *jarīdah**; pl. *jarāyid*	*akhbār* [newspaper]
(q) *jūkh*	*bānāt* [broadcloth]
jam'iyya	*anjuman* [society; club]
jamrak or *gamrak* (Turkish)	*chungī* [tariff]
junaina	*bāgh* [garden]

**phalī*. It is what they used to call a register of military salary.

WORD	MEANING
	(ḥ)
ḥawāyij	*maile kapṙe jo dhone ko diye jāte hain* [dirty clothes which are given to be washed]
(q) *ḥarrāqah*	*tārpīḋo kī kashtī* [torpedo boat]
(q) *ḥalīb*	*dūdh* [milk]
ḥizb al-aḥrār	*libral pārṫī* [liberal party]
	(kh)
kharīṭah	*naqshah* (jughrāfiyah kā) [map (geographical)]
khān	*sarāe yā hoṫal* [serai or hotel]
	(d)
dalījāns (not Arabic)	*shikram* [horse-cart]
dā'irah	*maḥkamah, ṣīghah* [office, bureau]
daqīqah	*minaṫ* [minute]
	(r)
rubbān	*kaptān-i jahāz* [the captain of a ship]
riwāyah	*nāwal, qiṣṣah* [novel, story]
Rūmān (English)	*aižan* [novel, story]
rīsh	*nib, angrezī qalam kī zabān* [nib, the tip of an English pen]
rabṭat al-raqabah	*nikṫā'ī* [necktie]
raṣāṣ	*bandūq kī golī* [rifle bullet]
rasm	*taṣwīr, naqshah* [image, sketch]
	(z)
zunnār	*peṫī* [belt]
	(s)
sā'a	*ghaṙī jis se waqt ma'lūm hotā hai* [a clock/hour, by which the time is known]
sikkat al-ḥadīd	*relwe* [railway]
sikūrtah (derived from English)	*bīmah karnā* [to insure]
sajjādah	*qālīn, darī* [carpet]
siyāsiyya	*pālīṫiks* [politics]
sarīr	*chārpā'ī* [charpai, bed]

WORD	MEANING
	(sh)
shirka	*kampnī* [company]
shaukah	*kānṫā (jis se angrez khānā khāte hain)* [a prong (with which the English eat food)]
shamsiyyah	*cȟatrī* [umbrella]
shamindūfar (French)	*rel* [rail]
shanṭah	*porṫ manṫo, baṙā ṣandūq* [portmanteau, a large trunk]
(q) *shakhṭūrah*	*chȟoṫī kashtī* [small boat]
	(ṣ)
ṣaidaliyyah	*'aṭṭārī kī dūkān* [an apothecary/perfumist's shop]
ṣihrīj	*tālāb* [pond]
ṣaut	*woṫ* [vote]
	(ż)
żau	*charāgh, lamp* [lamp, lamp]
(q) *żarībah*	*ṫiks* [tax]
żabṭiyyah	*polis* [police]
żābiṭ; pl. *żubbāṭ*	*afsar-i fauj* [army officer]
	(ṭ)
ṭarbūsh	*ṫurkī ṫopī* [Turkish cap]
ṭabsī	*sīnī* [tray]
	(ẓ)
ẓarf	*lifāfah* [envelope]
	(')
'ulbah	*ḋibiyah* [a small box]
(q) *'aish*	*roṫī* [bread, sustenance]
'aish afranjī	*pā'o roṫī* [European-style leavened bread]
'amārah	*beṙah jahāzāt* [a fleet of ships]
(q) *'arabah*	*gāḋī* [carriage, coach]
'ajalah	*aižan* [carriage, coach]
'amd	*akhbār kā kālam* [newspaper column]
'użwl pl. *a'żā'*	*mimbar* (kamītī) [member (committee)]

WORD	MEANING
	(gh)
ghasīl	*kapṙe kī dhulā'ī* [the cost of having clothes washed]
	(f)
funduq	*hoṫal* [hotel]
funjān; pl. *fanājīn**	pyālī [cup]
falūkah	*ḋongī, chhoṫī kashtī* [dinghy, small boat]
faṭrah, faṭūr	*nāshtah, ṣubḥ kā khānā* [breakfast, the morning meal]
fābrīqah (English)	*kal waghairah ka kār-khānah* [a machine, and so on, workshop/factory]
furjah	*sair o tafrīḥ* [touring and amusement, fun]
farājah	*ṫurkish 'auraton kā burqa'* [Turkish women's burqa]
furātah	*rezgārī, rūpiyah kā khurdah* [spare change, small amount of money]
	(q)
(q) *qāyimah*	*fahrist-i kutub* [catalogue of books]
qarār	*rizolūshan, ḥukm* [resolution, order]
qāyim maqām	[It is the name of an office (*'uhdah*) that is close to a deputy collector (*ḋipṫī kalakṫar*) in our area]
qarīnah	*zaujah, begam* [wife, begum]
	(k)
kufiyah	*ṫopī* [hat]
kundurah (Turkish, probably)	*būṫ* [boot]
karrūsah	*shikram* [horse-cart]
(q) *kāk* or *ka'k*	*biskiṫ* [biscuit, cookie]
kibrīt	*diyā salā'ī* [matches]
	(l)
lāyiḥah	*fahrist* [list]
laffah	[A turban (*'ammāmah*) tjat they tie over the cap (*ṫopī*)]
līrah	*ponḋ*, ashrafī [pound, ashrafi gold coin]
lūkāndah (it is not Arabic)	*hoṫal* [hotel, restaurant]

* A poet says: *qum hātihā qahwa ka-l-misk ṣāfiyah taḥyī al-nufūs wa shannifa lī al-fanājīnā*. Arabic: "Arise and bring it; coffee is like pure musk / It enlivens souls, and cups delight me."

WORD	MEANING
lajnah	*kamīṫī* [committee]
laḥẓah	*sikanḋ*...[second (a sixtieth part of a minute)]
lailī	*borḋar*...[boarder (on the condition that the word be used for a student)]
libās	*pā-jāmah* [trousers; pajama]
laban	*daḣī* [yogurt]
	(m)
maṣārī	*fulūs, paise* [coins, money]
mustashfā	*aspatāl* [hospital]
marfa'	*ghāṫ, bandar-gāh* [wharf, port]
mūmisāt	*ranḋiyān, kasbiyān* [prostitutes, harlots]
miqaṣṣ	*qainchī* [scissors]
(q) *muzayyin*	*ḥajjām* [barber]
mu'tamir	*kānfarins* [conference]
mandūb	*ḋilīgeṫ, safīr, wakīl* [delegate, ambassador, counsel]

WORD	MEANING
maḥjar	*qaranṭīnah* [quarantine]
māmūriyyah	*naukrī* [service]
midfa'	*top* [cannon]
mažbaṭah	*mimoriyal, 'arž-dāsht* [memorial, memorandum]
ma'mal	*kār-khānah* [workshop, factory]
ma'mal	*ma'raž*
mutaṣarrif	[the name of an office ('uhdah)]
mufattish	*inspikṫar* [inspector]
maḥfaẓah	*noṫ buk, yād-dāsht kī kitāb* [notebook, a book of memoranda]
matḥaf	*'ajā'ib-khānah* [museum, "house of wonders"]
mushamma'	*mom jāmah* [waxcloth]
maskūb	*sulṭanat-i Rūs* [the sultanate of Russia]
markan	*gul-dān* [flower vase]
mikhaddah	*takiyah* [pillow]

WORD	MEANING	WORD	MEANING
miqlamah	*qalam-tarāsh, chāqū* [pen carver, knife]	*maḥkamat al-ḥuqūq*	*'adālat-i dīwānī* [civil court]
mil'aqah	*chamchah* [spoon]	*maḥkamat al-jazā'*	*'adālat-i fauj-dārī* [criminal court]
(q) *miẓallah*	*chḣatrī* [umbrella, parasol]	*maḥkamat al-istīnāf*	*'adālat-i apīl* [court of appeal]
maḥramah	*rūmāl* [handkerchief]	*maḥkamat al- tam'īz*	*hā'īkorṫ* [high court]
(q) *mandīl*	*aiżan* [ditto]	*muḥāmī*	*wakīl* [counsel]
minshaf	*tauliyah* [towel]	(q) *mīnā*	*ghāṫ* [wharf]
markūb	*jūtā* [shoe]	(q) *markab*	*jahāz* [ship]
madāsah	*silīpar, gḣar men pahanne ke jūte* [slipper, shoes worn at home]	*mumaśśil*	*aikṫar* [actor]
miḥaṭṭah	*rel kā isṫeshan* [rail station]	*musaukarah* (derived from English)	*rajisṫrī-shudah khaṭṭ yā pārsal waghairah* [registered letter or parcel, and so on]
(q) *majallah**	*megzīn, 'ilmī risālah* [magazine, scientific journal]	*mīzāniyyah*	*bajaṫ* [budget]
mudarra'ah	*āhan-posh jahāz* [iron-clad ship]	*makkārah*	*charkhī* [spinningwheel]
maḥkamah	*'adālat* [court]	*maṣlaḥah*	*maḥkamah, sīghah, jaise maṣlaḥat al-būsṭah ba-ma'nī-i ḋāk-khānah* [office, bureau; as in *maṣlaḥat al-būsṭah*, meaning post office]
		ma'āsh	*pinshan* [pension]
		mujāwir	*qadīm madāris ke ṭalib-i 'ilm* [students of old (classical) madrasas]
		maḥall al-adab	*pā-khānah* [lavatory]

* In the Jāhiliyah [pre-Islamic period], they used this word for a book in which there were essays on practical wisdom and advice. Nābighah has a couplet: *majallatuhum żāt al-ilāh wa dīnuhum qadīm fa-mā yarjūna ghair al-'awāqib*. Arabic: "Their book is the essence of God and their religion / is ancient, so they fear nothing but the consequences [of their actions]."

WORD	MEANING
māddah	daf'ah (qānūn waghairah kī kitāb kā) [item (of a book of law, and so on)]
ma'ārif	sar-rishtah-i ta'līm [department of education]
mujassamah	isṫechū, pūrī qadd kī mūrat [statue, an image (mūrat) of full height]
muzāyadah	nīlām [auction]
	(n)
nahārī	*ghair borḋar ṭālib al-'ilm. is ko khārijiyah bḣī kahte hain* [non-boarding student; they also call him a *khārijiyah* (external)]
nīshān; pl. *nishānāt*	*tamghah* [medal]
(q) nāmūsiyyah	*palang* [bed]
nimsā	*sulṭanat-i āsṫriyā* [The Sultanate of Austria]
nāriyyah	*ātish-bāzī* [fireworks]
naẓẓārah	*dūr-bīn* [telescope]
(q) *niẓārah*	*sar-rishtah, sīghah* [ministry, bureau]
nāẓir	*sikriṫarī* [secretary]
nārgīlah (it is Persian)	*ḥuqqah*
	(w)
wisām	*tamghah* [medal]
wābūr or *fābūr* (not Arabic)	*jahāz* [ship]
waraqah	*ṫikaṫ* [ticket]
warqat al-ziyārah	*mulāqāt kā kārḋ* [a calling card]
(q) *wuṣūl*	*rasīd* [receipt]
wīrkū (not Arabic)	*ṫaks* [tax]
waraq	*kāghaż* [paper]

IT ENDED WELL

Translator's Afterword

The Author

Shiblī Nuʿmānī was born in Bindwal, a small village in the Northwest Provinces of British India, around the time of the Rebellion of 1857, and died at his family's estate in the nearby town of Azamgarh on November 18, 1914. His father, Ḥabībullāh, was a landowner, deputy agent (*wakīl*), and entrepreneur who dealt in indigo. Ḥabībullāh also established a local madrasa, mostly for the education of his son. Shiblī was privately educated in Arabic and Persian at home, then in nearby Jaunpur, and, eventually, Lahore and Saharanpur. Shiblī's teachers included respectable local tutors as well as some of the brightest and most respected educators in British India in the subjects of Arabic, Islamic studies, and Persian. Among those who had the most influence on Shiblī was Fārūq Chirayyākoṫī (d. 1909), who was renowned in his time, and later remembered for his mastery of the Arabic-Islamic rational sciences and his taste for literature. Perhaps the most widely published of Shiblī's teachers was Faiẓ al-Ḥasan Sahāranpūrī, who taught Arabic under Gottlieb Leitner (1840–99) at the Oriental College in Lahore. Faiẓ al-Ḥasan wrote Arabic treatises on classical Arabic literature. He also wrote in Urdu on disputation and logic.

After completing his studies, Shiblī returned home and soon discovered he had no taste for his father's business. He studied for and passed (on the second try) the government law examinations, only to find that he had no desire to practice law. In 1882, he accepted a professorship in Arabic and Persian at the British-administered Mohammedan Anglo-Oriental (MAO) College in Aligarh. Ḥabībullāh had been an early supporter of the college and its founder, the reformer and Islamic scholar Sayyid Aḥmad Khān. Ḥabībullāh and Shiblī had visited the college along with Shiblī's younger brother, who had enrolled there, shortly before Shiblī was offered the position.

In his early intellectual life, that is, before coming to Aligarh, Shiblī had occupied himself primarily with the study of Arabic and Persian literature, as well as the study of Islam. His earliest extant writing, a short, polemical tract on an issue of Islamic jurisprudence argued from a Ḥanafī sectarian perspective, is in Arabic, and he wrote his early letters to friends and family in Persian. In Urdu, he seems to have written only a few lines of verse, which he recited in literary salons.[1] Soon after coming to the MAO College, and likely encouraged by Sayyid Aḥmad Khān, he began to write essays, letters, and reformist verse in Urdu in a register of language inflected by the Arabic and Persian traditions in which he was trained.

Encouraged by Sayyid Aḥmad Khān, Shiblī's career as an Urdu writer began in the 1880s with a series of works on the history of Islam. Shiblī lived in a small bungalow on the grounds of Sayyid Aḥmad Khān's home at the college and had access to his sizeable library of Egyptian publications of Arabic literature and his privately commissioned Urdu translations of European literature, including Edward Gibbon's *The Decline and Fall of the Roman Empire*. He also had limited access to European literature in translation both through his connections with the British faculty at the college and his English-educated students. His earliest work, *Musalmānoṅ kī Guẕishtah Ta'līm* (The Past Education of the Muslims)—*Guẕishtah Ta'līm* for short—is an intellectual and social history of translation at the Abbasid court in which Shiblī relied on classical Arabic sources and Gibbon. *Guẕishtah Ta'līm* was soon followed by the first two of many book-length biographies on major figures in Islam. The series was initially called Heroes of Islam (Urdu: Hīroz āf Islām) or Rulers of Islam (Urdu: Farmān-rawānān-i Islām). The first installment was *al-Māmūn* (1887; second edition 1889), which studies the eponymous Abbasid Caliph (786–833). The next was *Sīrat al-Nu'mān* (1889), which examines the life, ideas, and influence of Nu'mān bin Ṡābit (b. ca. 699; d. 767), known as Abū Ḥanīfah, the eponym of both the Ḥanafī tradition of Islamic jurisprudence and Shiblī's adopted epithet, Nu'mānī. As he had done in *Guẕishtah Ta'līm*, Shiblī drew extensively on his training in Arabic and Persian, and to a smaller extent on his limited access to European literature, in composing the biographies, both of which cemented his position among Urdu's foremost historians and most celebrated prose stylists.

In April 1892, following a period of illness, Shiblī took six months leave from his teaching duties at the college to travel to the Ottoman Empire and British-controlled Egypt. The *Aligarh Institute Gazette* (the Urdu organ of the college) announced that he had been asked to collect information about educational institutions and boarding houses and to purchase books for the college's library. The travelogue itself, as well as Shiblī's letters and later writings, tell us that he also planned to acquire materials for his own research projects. Outstanding among them was a planned biography of 'Umar ibn al-Khaṭṭāb (d. 644; the second caliph of Sunnī Islam), which Shiblī eventually published as *al-Fārūq* (1898). Shiblī's letters suggest that Sayyid Aḥmad Khān had also asked him to collect works by the theologian Abū Ḥamīd (al-)Ghazālī (b. ca. 1058; d. 1111) and by writers associated with the Mu'tazilah movement. Sayyid Aḥmad Khān had already sponsored a translation of Ghazālī's autobiography into Urdu (completed by Sayyid Mumtāz 'Alī, a correspondent of Shiblī's) and eventually published a series of essays on his work. Shiblī eventually published his own lengthy biographical and critical study of Ghazālī, *al-Ghazālī* (1902). He also later wrote in detail about the Mu'tazilah movement in his theological works *'Ilm al-kalām* (1902) and *al-Kalām* (1904).[2]

Turkey, Egypt, and Syria: A Travelogue

In July 1894, Shiblī published *Safarnāmah-i Rūm o Miṣr o Shām* (*Turkey, Egypt, and Syria: A Travelogue*). Writing mostly in the early months of 1894, Shiblī paints a vivid, critical, and sometimes humorous picture of the social, political, and intellectual life of the Ottoman Empire and Egypt in the nineteenth century. Shiblī's account is remarkable in that it draws not only on his personal recollections and experiences, but also on the kind of archive that appealed to him as a historian inspired by the Enlightenment and by the classical Arabic tradition: government and institutional records (which he collected on his travels) and classical and contemporary Turkish and Arabic literature. The narrative records first-hand accounts and secondary-source information about educational institutions, including colleges, printing houses, manuscript archives, libraries, literary societies, and debate clubs, complete with charts detailing student enrollment, school curricula, and library catalogues, to which Shiblī often adds historical context through broad discussions of regional history and contemporary politics.

Against the backdrop of educational institutions, Shiblī records sketches and anecdotes that offer rare glimpses of intellectual networks, religious festivals, visual and literary culture, and everyday life in the Ottoman Empire and Egypt: the community of Damascene Ṣūfīs in Istanbul with ties to Ottoman statesmen and Ṣūfīs in India; literary and intellectual salons in Beirut, Jerusalem, and Izmir; manuscript archives in Istanbul and Cairo; the Jesuit college (Université Saint-Josef) in Beirut; descriptions of restaurants, hotels, mosques, colleges, and lodges in Istanbul; the office of the muftī of Jerusalem; Hindu merchants in Aden; the community of Indians merchants in Istanbul; museums, theaters, and staged dramas in Cairo; the Muḥarram mourning rituals in Istanbul; and a brothel in Beirut. Most of the accounts favor description over analysis or reflection, but several anecdotes are specifically crafted for the purposes of edification and reform. These anecdotes reflect something of the cosmopolitanism of the Ottoman Empire and Egypt in the late nineteenth century. They also reflect, and sometimes directly address, the effects of colonialism on local economies and politics and shed important light on the formative role that new forms of print media, literature, and education played in shaping the intellectual culture of the day, giving us microcosmic glimpses of broader processes of historical change.

The travelogue is mostly in Urdu, but is interwoven with long poems in Persian, quotations of classical and modern Arabic, and some Ottoman Turkish. In the case of Turkish and Modern Arabic passages, Shiblī typically provides an Urdu translation. However, in the case of classical Arabic poetry and proverbs, quotations from the Quran and hadith, Persian poetry, and a paragraph-long excerpt from a modern Arabic biography, he provides no such translation. Thus, it would seem that Shiblī imagined his audience capable of reading these languages and understanding the cultural significance of the literature quoted, or at least imagined that the travelogue might inspire them to learn to do so. The narrative unfolds in a conversational style, but ranges in tone and register from the highly erudite to the colloquial. In this way, the language of the travelogue is distinguished from some contemporary Urdu works, which mimicked aspects of Persian grammar and relied heavily on long technical phrases borrowed from Arabic. Yet it does reflect Shiblī's background as a scholar of Arabic and Persian as Shiblī weaves the technical language of logic and fiqh, as well as new vocabulary borrowed from contemporary Arabic, into Urdu without remark.

The travelogue is also rather less polished than many of Shiblī's works. Extant manuscripts of Shiblī's notes and draft copies of his other works testify to his thoroughness as an editor, but the published version of the travelogue does not. He repeats words like *nihāyat* (extremely), *ʿajīb* (wondrous; strange), and *taʿajjub* (wonder). This is likely due to the haste in which Shiblī was writing. I have attempted, therefore, to preserve the stylistic aspects of the original. This was not possible in most cases, but in the case of the word *nihāyat*, I have rendered it either as "extreme" or "extremely" throughout the text, even when other English words may have seemed more idiomatic.

Shiblī intended the work to be a fair account of the Ottoman Empire, Egypt, Turks, and Arabs in his time. Introducing the text to a considerable number of English-educated (or English-influenced) Urdu readers, Shiblī writes that one of the main purposes of the book is to depict Turks and Arabs in a way that differs from the prejudice that, in his view, characterized depictions of them in European literature. In many ways, this fits squarely with the aims and methods of Shiblī's historical oeuvre. In his earlier writings, Shiblī had imagined the purpose of history to be to engage not merely in discussions of political dynasties but also in broader discussions of social and intellectual life. In practice, this led him to draw not only on political chronicles but also on other genres of literature, including travelogues. Shiblī also sought to be objective and impartial. In the foreword to *al-Māmūn*, Sayyid Aḥmad Khān judged that Shiblī did not exaggerate the beautiful or ugly, but rather sought to "leave them as they are."[3] The narrative of the travelogue, too, while clearly informed by a concern with social reform, education, and the Muslim community, still seems to align with Shiblī's agenda to achieve impartiality. If Shiblī praises 'Abd al-Ḥamīd II in verse and admires the intellectual culture of Turkish society in Istanbul, he flies into a rage at the censorship of Arabic literature that he witnesses at an Ottoman printing press and criticizes (albeit with an apology) the lack of freedom of the press in the Ottoman Empire. He criticizes European literature for failing to recognize recent developments in the Ottoman Empire, particularly in education, but writes that he is largely unimpressed with the state of Muslim education in Turkey and is frustrated by the paucity of information in government publications (albeit, again, with apology). He criticizes the deceptive means by which the British gained colonial and imperial power, but praises the relative freedom of information in British-controlled Egypt.

Throughout the travelogue, Shiblī contextualizes what he observes in the light of classical Arabic historiography and modern Arabic publications. In one passage, he uses the travelogue of Ibn Baṭṭūṭah to compare the state of Istanbul in the fourteenth century with that of his own time. This leads him to make broad comparisons of the economic state and moral character of Muslims and Europeans, civilizational comparisons being an important trope in the kind of historical writing that inspired Shiblī, be it Gibbon or Ibn Khaldūn. The use of Ibn Baṭṭūṭah is especially interesting and may shed light on the nature of Shiblī's collaboration with colleagues at the MAO College. Shiblī returned to Ibn Baṭṭūṭah as a source in his biographical study of the Persian poet Rumi, but context suggests that he may also have read and discussed the work with his colleague at Aligarh (and traveling companion as far as Port Said), the British Orientalist Thomas Arnold. Arnold's *The Preaching of Islam*, which acknowledges collaboration with Shiblī, includes in its bibliography a bilingual French-Arabic edition of Ibn Baṭṭūṭah. Shiblī mentions in the travelogue that he had studied some French with Arnold, whom he names as his teacher. There is a passage in the travelogue in which a Spanish passenger sees Arnold reading Arabic and mocks the language, sending Shiblī into a silent rage. It is likely that Shiblī and Arnold were reading the bilingual French-Arabic edition of Ibn Baṭṭūṭah's travelogue together at the time.

Community and Language in the Travelogue

Shiblī wrote the travelogue during a period of intense literary production in Urdu. He also wrote it as a member of a group of Muslim social reformers. The Urdu essays, novels, and poetry of his contemporaries and interlocutors, from Sayyid Aḥmad Khān, to Nażīr Aḥmad, to Alṭāf Ḥusain Ḥālī, were largely concerned with reforming the moral character and historical consciousness of their coreligionists in British India. The objective of Shiblī's first major biographical writing, *al-Māmūn*, was not only to inform the Muslim community about its history beyond the borders of India but also to use history, and biography in particular, as a means of cultural education. In the introduction, Shiblī tells us that his aim is to acquaint readers with the works of Arabic literature on which he bases his study (which he calls the languages in which their communal or national history is recorded), but also with the new methods of historical scholarship, which he attributes to innovations by European historians.[4] The travelogue, too, can be read as a part of this broader project, since it is concerned with the economic and intellectual state of Muslims in the Ottoman Empire and Egypt, the curriculum of Islamic education, the Arabic language, and Islamic culture and history in general.

At the center of contemporary reformist debates among Indian Muslim thinkers was the role of education. In 1886, Sayyid Aḥmad Khān and his supporters established the Mohammedan Educational Congress (later Conference), separating the Muslim community from the project of the Indian National Congress, formed in 1885 to represent Indian interests to the British. In his view, the path to social reform and the improvement of the status of the Muslim community lay not in the politics of a representative parliament, which he felt could not speak for the interests of both the Hindu and Muslim community, but in the reform of character and the attainment of government offices through education. Shiblī played a leading role in the first meeting of the Educational Congress, held in Aligarh in December 1886, proposing that the Muslim community should support education in European sciences and literature. He also argued relevant points that aligned with Sayyid Aḥmad Khān's self-help agenda: that the community should not rely on the British government to support education in "Oriental languages" (Arabic and Persian), that existing British support for these languages in official colonial colleges and schools was enough as far as government support was concerned, and that it was, in fact, the duty of the community, not the government, to encourage the study of these subjects among interested students. The reason, he continued, was that the study of these languages was inextricably tied to religious education, which the British could not patronize. Moreover, the Muslim community would not support the separation of religious texts from the study of such languages, nor could scholars trained exclusively in the British system earn the respect and trust of the community. The resolution was seconded by Sayyid Aḥmad Khān and passed with unanimous support.

In the broad program to reform the Muslim community through education, Arabic held the unique and often precarious position of being both a classical and a modern language. In the colonial university system, it was among the classical languages required to pass examinations. Students were expected to read and translate poetry by Mutanabbī and excerpts from the compendium *Ḥamāsah* by Abū Tammām. In the eyes of Sayyid Aḥmad Khān, Arabic (and Persian) were inseparable parts of Muslims' intellectual and cultural heritage. Shiblī's historical writing supported the program of the Educational Congress by acquainting Urdu readers with the overlapping histories of the Muslim community and Arabic literature.

For scholars like Shiblī who did not know European languages, Arabic was also a means of access to information about the contemporary world. Sayyid Aḥmad Khān, who did not know English well, wrote about the Ottoman Empire and the experiences of Muslims inside and outside British India by means of contemporary Arabic literature. In his reformist magazine, *Tahẕīb al-akhālaq*, he published the Arabic introduction, along with an Urdu translation, of *Aqwām al-masālik fī ma'rifat aḥwāl al-mamālik* (1868) (which Shiblī mentions in the travelogue) by the Tunisian statesman and eventual Ottoman official Khair al-Dīn Pāshā (b. 1822–23; d. 1890), which argues that Muslims should adopt what is good in Europe in pursuit of progress. The *Aligarh Institute Gazette* also carried articles concerning global affairs translated from Arabic newspapers. Altāf Ḥusain Ḥālī, while an employee of the British at the British Book

Depot in Lahore, produced an Urdu translation of *al-Aqwāl al-marḍiyya fī ʿilm binyāt al-kura al-arḍiya* (Sufficient Discourses on the Structure of the Globe and the Earth) (1841) by the Egyptian scholar Aḥmad Fā'ẓ, itself a translation of *Géologie Élémentaire Appliquée à L'agriculture et à L'industrie* (Elementary Geology Applied to Agriculture and Industry) (1833) by the French entomologist Nérée Boubée. Shiblī relied heavily on contemporary Arabic publications in his research. He used Egyptian editions of classical Arabic literature in his studies of Islamic history. Such editions were cheap and readily available in India.

Shiblī returned to India with information about Arabic manuscript archives and the contact information of Arabic publishers. He also returned with books, some by the scholars whom he had met, and information about Arabic journals and newspapers. For the remainder of his life, Arabic (and especially Egyptian) newspapers, journals, and books remained for him important sources information about contemporary politics, Islamic reform, and European science. In his theological writing, he relied on the Arabic works of Farīd Wajdī (1878–1954; Arabic journalist and theologian) on European spiritualism. He corresponded with Jurjī Zaidān (1861–1914; journalist and novelist), whom he eventually criticized in the pages of the Egyptian journal *al-Manār*.

In the travelogue, Shiblī presents Arabic as the language of both traditional learning and contemporary scholarship. It is the language of classical education in the Quran, hadith, jurisprudence, logic, philosophy, and poetry. It is also the language that ties Muslims like Shiblī to the cosmopolitanism of the contemporary Muslim world. Shiblī's friendship with the Syrian Arabs in Istanbul, "the preface to all his successes" on the journey, as he puts it, stems from his classical training in Ḥanafī jurisprudence and a treatise on the subject that he had written in Arabic. Shiblī is surprised to learn that the treatise had traveled from India to Damascus. Arabic is also the language in which he converses with them about subjects as varied as contemporary politics, Muslim reform, and the pleasures of everyday life. The travelogue reflects all these registers.

The travelogue also offers unique insight into the use of Arabic by the diasporic communities he encounters during his travels. For example, Shiblī uses the word *injās* (pear)—which he spells incorrectly with a sīn *(s)* instead of ṣwād *(ṣ)* (Urdu does not distinguish phonetically between *s* and *ṣ*; was Shiblī unable to distinguish between them?)—to describe a fruit that he encountered for the first time in Istanbul. Arabic linguists record that this word is unique to the Syrian dialect. As both the travelogue and Shiblī's letters emphasize, Shiblī did not understand Turkish and therefore only occasionally communicated with Turks. Thus, Shiblī's use of the word *injās*, which he does not identify as an Arabic word, hints at the mediating role that the community of Damascene Arabs with whom he lived and socialized in Istanbul played in his experiences there. In Beirut and Egypt, too, Arabic is the language by which he communicates with people from various communal and professional backgrounds, from professors and printers to doctors and merchants. Even in Aden, it is the language he speaks, much to his surprise, with the Hindu merchants there.

The travelogue sustains the significance of Arabic as a language of classical learning as it attempts to introduce Modern Arabic (*ḥāl kī 'Arabī zabān*, as Shiblī calls it) to Arabic schools in India. This may explain why Shiblī quotes from the Quran, hadith, rational tradition, and classical literature in the travelogue. It is also why he quotes from the people he meets and from modern Arabic literature, including a Jesuit journal in Beirut and the work of Egyptian reformer Muḥammad 'Abduh. (Shiblī met Muḥammad 'Abduh in Cairo and praised the style of his biography of the anti-imperialist reformer-activist Jamāl al-Dīn Afghānī.) It may also explain why he includes a brief linguistic study of Modern Arabic dialects that compares the pronunciation of spoken and standard Arabic and why the text concludes with a brief Arabic-Urdu lexicon to aid in the study of contemporary Arabic newspapers.

In positioning Arabic as a language of not only Islam and classical literature, but also of modern learning and the European sciences, the travelogue can be read as a bridge between the classicism of traditional 'ulamā (scholars of Islam trained in Arabic) and the reformers associated with Aligarh. Indeed, Shiblī advocated a similar position as administrator of the Nadwat al-'Ulamā (Congress of Scholars), which was initially conceived as a reforming congress of Islamic scholars and later became an academy. Nadwat al-'Ulamā held its first annual conference in 1894, the same year the travelogue was published. Among the agendas initially adopted by the academy was the promotion of modern sciences in Arabic. At the first meeting of the Nadwat al-ʿUlamā, Shiblī spoke about the need to promote new ways of engaging with the classical canon of Islamic learning, taking an example from the contemporary jurisprudential scholar Ḥusain al-Jisr (1845–1910) and his book *Ḥamīdiyah*, in which al-Jisr had famously argued that the basic ideas about the universe found in the Quran were compatible with Darwinism. (Sayyid Aḥmad Khān had made a similar argument in his Urdu exegesis of the Quran.) Shiblī judged that *Ḥamīdiyah* had laid the foundation of a series of new works that could "breathe new life" into the souls of the great Islamic theologians of the past, Ghazālī and Rāzī.

The Ottoman Empire through Indian Eyes

A few words remain to be said about the reception of the text, both in its immediate context as well as later in the twentieth century. The Ottoman Empire had considerable symbolic significance in the decades preceding Shiblī's travels and took on new political significance in the decades following the publication of the travelogue.

Like many Muslims in British India, Shiblī had collected funds to send in support of Turks during the Russo-Turkish War (1877–78). In a Persian letter, Shiblī wrote admiringly about (Ghāzī) ʿUsmān Pāshā (meetings with whom Shiblī discusses in the travelogue) and his heroic defense of Plevna against the Russian forces. During and shortly after the war, Sayyid Aḥmad Khān's *Aligarh Institute Gazette* carried pro-Ottoman letters in Urdu written by the Turkish Consul to British India, Ḥusain Ḥasīb (whom Shiblī discusses in the travelogue), in which the Ottoman Sulṭān is depicted as the heart of the global Muslim community. Urdu newspapers called for the British to defend the Turkish Empire against Russian aggression. One editorial predicted that if Russia defeated the Turkish Empire, it would next try to invade India, and the British might not be able to protect Indians.[5] Another, fearing such an invasion, wrote that if England and Russia were to go to war, Turkey should side with England, implying that the defeat of Russia would amount to a victory for Islam.[6] The

Aligarh Institute Gazette itself described the Anglo-Turkish Convention of 1878, which "secures the Asiatic provinces of Turkey from further Russian 'encroachments' as a 'perfect godsend to Turkey.'"[7] To be sure, some Urdu newspapers severely criticized the British for failing to come to Turkey's defense, but in the minds of people who thought like Sayyid Aḥmad Khān, there was no contradiction between support for Turkey and support for the British. The safety and security of India depended on British support for the security of the Ottoman Empire.

Nearly half a century after its initial publication, the Ottoman Empire and the travelogue had assumed new political significance. Indo-Muslim political mobilization during the Khilāfat Movement eventually aligned the community for a time with Gandhi's noncooperation movement. The Khilāfat Movement, spearheaded by a handful of students closely connected to Shiblī, emerged partly as a response to Britain's lack of support for the Ottoman Empire against Russia and political uprisings in the Balkans in the first decades of the twentieth century. At the level of discourse, the movement argued for the legitimacy of the caliphate of the Ottoman sulṭān in order to distance themselves from the kinds of arguments made by loyalists like Sayyid Aḥmad Khān. After World War I, the movement gained widespread support, aligning itself with Congress in opposition to British support for the punitive actions taken against the Ottoman Empire. The movement marked a watershed moment not only in the anticolonial history of Indian Muslims, but also in the significance of the Ottoman Empire and the sulṭān (as caliph) in Urdu literature.[8] Shiblī, who died in 1914, did not live to see the emergence of the movement, and it is difficult to know how he might have responded to it. However, in the decade prior to his death, he published a clear theological stance on the politics of the Ottoman caliphate. "Khilāfat" (caliphate), a short article included in his essays, Shiblī argues on canonical authority that only a member of the Quraish, that is, the tribe of the Prophet, could rightly lay claim to *khilāfat*. In the article, he claims that the Turks were not members of the Quraish, that Muslims had at no point in history regarded anyone as caliph who was not from the family of the Quraish, and that the Turkish claim to khilāfat began with Bayazid II, the eighth Ottoman sulṭān. In the same article, he also points readers to a passage in the travelogue in which he expresses outrage at the censorship of the line "The imāms [caliphs] are from the Quraish" from a standard work of Islamic theology.

In 1940, Sayyid Sulaimān Nadwī, who had been a student of, and later worked as an assistant to, Shiblī, and who had been a leading figure in the Khilāfat Movement, published *Ḥayāt-i Shiblī* (The Life of Shiblī), a six-hundred-page Urdu biography of his former teacher. In the text, Nadwī claimed that the travelogue marked a major point in Shiblī's intellectual and political departure from the authoritarianism ideas of Sayyid Aḥmad Khān, evinced by the fact that Shiblī published the book not from the college press, but from the Mufīd-i ʿĀm Press in Agra. Nadwī pointed to passages in the text praising ʿAbd al-Ḥamīd II as evidence of Shiblī's political loyalty to the Ottoman Empire, which, he claims, angered the loyalist Sayyid Aḥmad Khān, who sought to weaken the movement of *Ittiḥād-i Islāmī* (Islamic Unity; Pan-Islamism) through his writings. Nadwī wrote that the travelogue was incomplete, and that Shiblī was forced to censor himself for fear of negative repercussions on the college. Writing in Pakistan in the 1980s, another critic echoes Nadwī's reading, arguing that if Shiblī had written the travelogue in detail, the book would have "inspired feelings of affection and love for the Turks, by which waves of freedom would have run and the occasions for bricks to strike against the bricks [that is, the complete destruction] of the English government would have been illuminated."[9]

Writing against Nadwī in this interpretive battle was Muḥammad Amīn Zubairī, with whom Shiblī had corresponded in the 1900s, when Zubairī worked as secretary to the begum of Bhopal. Zubairī, a staunch supporter of Sayyid Aḥmad Khān and Aligarh, argues against Nadwī's claims with reference to history and context, taking pains to defend Sayyid Aḥmad Khān and to show that Nadwī exaggerates, misunderstands, and misrepresents both the content and context of the travelogue. He cites articles in which Sayyid Aḥmad Khān advocated for friendship and sympathy between Muslims in the Ottoman Empire and British India. He challenges Nadwī's characterization of Sayyid Aḥmad Khān as anti-Ottoman, explaining his position by citing a famous article in which he had argued that the Ottoman sulṭān was not to be considered the caliph of the Muslim community in India because Indian Muslims were bound by their religion to be loyal to the British, in whose country they lived in safety and freedom to practice their religion. (Shiblī later made a similar point in his own writing on the caliphate.) One by one, Zubairī addresses and dismisses Nadwī's claims as figments of his imagination, from his inference about the travelogue's publication in Agra, through the political significance of the text, to the supposed conflict with Sayyid Aḥmad Khān.[10] The publication history of the travelogue casts further doubt on the reliability of Nadwī's claims about censorship and conflict. The second edition of the travelogue was published in 1901, three years after Sayyid Aḥmad Khān's death and after Shiblī's departure from the college. It contained a number of small changes to the text, presumably made by Shiblī, but no major revisions or additions. At the same time, and over the course of the following decade, Shiblī criticized the British and disagreed with Sayyid Aḥmad Khān in print. This history, along with Zubairī's arguments, suggest that Nadwī and later critics have interpolated their own political attitudes about the Ottoman Empire into the travelogue. As has been suggested here, it was possible for someone in Shiblī's position to feel fellowship with his Muslim coreligionists in the Ottoman Empire, to admire the Ottoman sulṭān as a symbol of Islamic political power, to criticize British policy, and to advocate loyalty to the British in Islamic terms, while not advocating the kind of pan-Islamism that Nadwī attributes to him.

The World of the Travelogue

As a historical document, the travelogue offers rare glimpses into the workings of intellectual networks, educational institutions, and literary culture in the Ottoman Empire and Egypt of the late nineteenth century. Shiblī visited Istanbul at the height of the networks established by Sulṭān 'Abd al-Ḥamīd II to create strong bonds between Ottoman administrators at the center of the empire and Arabs at its margins. Shiblī's discussion of his social milieu in Istanbul is a fascinating eyewitness account of the informal and formal networks created by this broad political program. Particularly fascinating is the network that comes into focus through close study of his relationship with 'Alī Żabyān, the son of a prominent leader of the Qādirī Ṣūfī community in Damascus. Shiblī and Żabyān met at the apartment that Shiblī shared with another Damascene Ṣūfī, 'Abd al-Fattāḥ. 'Abd al-Fattāḥ was the nephew of Khālid Naqshbandī, who had been initiated into the Naqshbandī order of Ṣūfism in Delhi in the early nineteenth century before returning to the Ottoman Empire, where he promoted Naqshbandism and eventually gained widespread religious, social, and political influence. Shiblī never claimed to be part of the Naqshbandī order, but Sayyid Aḥmad Khān had close familial ties to some of its most prominent leaders in Delhi. When Shiblī and Żabyān met, the latter was living at the home of retired Ottoman statesman and military commander Darwesh Ibrāhīm Pāshā, who was a follower of the Khālidī Naqshbandī order and owned property in Syria. Żabyān seems to have taken Shiblī to Darwesh Pāshā's home, where Shiblī met Ottoman historian and retired statesman Aḥmad Jaudat (Ahmet Cevdet) Pāshā, who had attended the same school as Darwesh Ibrāhīm. The two statesmen had also led Ottoman military campaigns together in the 1860s. Shiblī praises the writings of Aḥmad Jaudat's daughter, Fāṭimah Khānam (Fatma Aliye [Hanım]) in the travelogue. Aḥmad Jaudat spoke with Shiblī at some length in Arabic and, one imagines, may have introduced him to the writings of his daughter. In turn, Shiblī not only seems to draw inspiration from her work in the travelogue but also appears to have been involved in bringing the Arabic translation of her work to India and having it translated into Urdu and published by the press in Aligarh.

The travelogue offers a fascinating perspective on the circulation of texts, scholars, and ideas between the Ottoman Empire and South Asia. In addition to personal networks, Shiblī also records information on modern language, scientific journals, and literary culture in Arabic and Turkish. In Beirut and Cairo, Shiblī encounters an Arabic literary culture replete with translations of European scientific works, critical editions of rare texts, original compositions in a variety of genres, and journalism. He writes that he was surprised to discover that the authors and patrons of these works of literature were Christians who considered themselves members of the Arab community. This great discovery leads him not only to admonish Muslims in India for their indifference to the enrichment of Arabic literature (especially to rare works of history, literary criticism, poetry, and contemporary journalism), but also to imagine British India and the princely state of Hyderabad as possible centers for the excavation and publication of rare works of Arabic literature through distributors in the Ottoman Empire and Egypt. In the travelogue, Shiblī mentions the Hyderabad-based Dā'irat al-Ma'ārif (Circle of Sciences), which was an organization founded by, inter alios, administrator Sayyid Ḥusain Bilgramī to collect and publish rare works of Arabic literature. After returning from his travels, Shiblī was asked to join the advisory board of the organization and wrote to its director, Iqbāl Yār Jang, advising that the organization order copies of rare manuscripts from the archives in Istanbul and Cairo, print them in Hyderabad, and distribute them through two of the booksellers that Shiblī had met in Beirut and Cairo, 'Abd al-Bāsiṭ al-Unsī and Wāḥid al-Ṭūbī. The plans appear to have stalled, initially, but the Dā'irat al-Ma'ārif eventually developed into a major center of Arabic research and publication.

Shiblī also returned to India with subscriptions to Arabic newspapers and journals, which he taught to students at the MAO College and used as sources for thinking and writing about relevant issues of the day. Shiblī advises in the travelogue that Arabic schools in India should begin training students in Modern Arabic newspapers and journals. Shiblī later attempted to implement a curriculum of studies at Nadwat al-'Ulamā that included contemporary Arabic journalism and scholarship. Through the Department of Education in Cairo, Shiblī met a handful of scholars writing about contemporary issues from an Islamic perspective. Among them was Hamzah Fatḥullāh, whose book on women's rights in Islam (mentioned in the travelogue) Shiblī sent to Sayyid Mumtāz 'Alī, who soon published his own feminist Urdu treatise, *Ḥuqūq-i niswān* (The Rights of Women).

The travelogue also offers remarkable, on-the-ground glimpses of Arabic intellectual networks and culture in Beirut and Cairo. In Beirut, Shiblī's friendship with bookseller 'Abd al-Bāsiṭ al-Unsī leads him to encounters with Jesuit institutions of Arabic literary scholarship and publication as well as the Damascene Islamic reformer Ṭāhir al-Maghribī (also named al-Jazā'irī). Shiblī's broad discussion of Arabic intellectual culture includes some of the most famous and well-studied scholars and institutions of the time, such as the lexicographer Buṭrus al-Bustānī, the American missionary and professor Cornelius Van Dyck, and the Protestant College (later American University of Beirut). The travelogue adds detailed information about debate clubs, intellectual societies, charitable organizations, and women's institutions that enrich our understanding of the vibrancy of the intellectual environment in Beirut. It also records Shiblī's experiences in conversation with scholars and institutions that have not received significant scholarly attention. For example, his discussion of printing techniques at the Jesuit college (Université Saint-Josef) gesture toward the local and transregional histories of the print culture and textual production in the Ottoman Empire. Similarly, his discussion of the Jesuit priest, Arabic professor and critical editor of Arabic literature, Anṭūn Ṣāliḥānī, offers glimpses of the collaborations between Orientalists in Europe and the Middle East in the production of texts and knowledge in Arabic at the end of the nineteenth century. In addition, his discussions of *al-Ṣafā*, the short-lived journal in Beirut, and of the students at Azhar and the Dār al-'Ulūm in Cairo draw attention to lesser-known figures whose roles in the history of Arabic letters have been largely overlooked by scholars.

In addition to scholarly networks and cultural environments, the travelogue also includes a wealth of information about, and rare first-hand accounts of, contemporary educational institutions. Especially rich is Shiblī's comparative discussion of two major institutions in Cairo. His eyewitness accounts of the classical madrasa al-Azhar, where he stayed, include descriptions of instructional methods, boarding arrangements, and the attitudes of students about their teachers and education. Shiblī's criticisms of the intellectual culture at the academy echo those of the Egyptian reformer Muḥammad 'Abduh, whom Shiblī met, and hint at the kinds of discussions taking place among students, teachers, administrators, and reformers both inside and outside the academy. Similarly, his description of the Dār al-'Ulūm (House of Sciences) and its hybridized curriculum, which drew from the classical curriculum taught at al-Azhar and introduced both the study of European sciences as well as a broader curriculum of Arabic literature, not only includes interesting details of his visit to the academy, but also anticipates the vision that he would eventually develop for the reformed curriculum of Arabic-Islamic studies through the Nadwat al-ʿUlamā in India. Indeed, in the early life of the institution, Shiblī tried unsuccessfully to arrange for some of its students to study at the Dār al-ʿUlūm.

The value of the travelogue as a historical source is not limited to its discussions of intellectual culture and educational institutions. Shiblī was a scholar with specific research interests, but he was also a tourist, and an intellectually curious and open-minded one at that. His descriptions of museums and coffeehouses in Istanbul; Khungar Sūī (Hünkar Suyu), the idyllic retreat for the city's elites; and the city's various forms of public transportation and infrastructure not only convey his sense of wonderment at the cultural landscape of the city (the ubiquity of the words *ʿajīb* [strange, wondrous], *taʿajjub* [wonderment], and *ḥairat* [amazement] in the travelogue give us an indication of Shiblī's attitude overall) but also include details related to day-to-day life, from the cost of crossing the Galata Bridge to the types of lodging available to travelers. His account of the Indian travelers' lodge and its corrupt administrator is perhaps unique in the literature, as is the information that he includes about the community of Indian merchants there.

The travelogue also offers perspective on emergent technologies and forms of tourism. Shiblī and Thomas Arnold begin their journey on a ship run by the Cook Company sailing toward Brindisi, Italy. Thomas Cook & Son had begun establishing offices in India in 1880 when the Italian government offered the company commission on bookings between India and Brindisi to promote overseas travel in Europe through Italy. The program to establish Cook Company was supported by the British on the idea that it would encourage "wealthy Englishmen" to visit India and inspire a small number of "wealthy Indians" to see "who and what the people are . . . who govern them."[11] Shiblī's description of the company office at Port Said and the interpreter Samuel is historically interesting because although Port Said had been a major regional hub since the completion of the Suez Canal in 1869, the Cook Company, famous for its Grand Tours of the region, had only established its tourist office there less than a month before Shiblī arrived. Also interesting are Shiblī's descriptions of culture aboard the Cook Company vessel and the stark contrast between the Cook

Company ship and the ship that he takes from Port Said along the coast of the Eastern Mediterranean.

Travel Writing in Shiblī's World

In the opening section of the travelogue, Shiblī critiques the relationship of religion and politics to cultural representation with specific reference to travel literature, implicating the travelogue genre in a long and broad history of unjust representations of Turks and Arabs by European writers. Implying that his own travelogue takes inspiration for its interventionist project from the work of the Turkish feminist Fāṭimah Khānam (Fatma Aliye), Shiblī claims to offer Urdu readers a depiction of Turks and Arabs that runs counter to the irrational, prejudiced, and superficial one that he considers ubiquitous in European literature. The stated purpose of Shiblī's travelogue thus aligns with Shiblī's historical writing, one aim of which was to correct European depictions of Islam and Muslims by means of evidence-based reason. Shiblī's essay on the destruction of the Library at Alexandria, for example, deconstructs arguments made by some European writers that 'Umar ibn Khaṭṭāb (the second caliph of Sunnī Islam) ordered that the library be burned and its books destroyed. Through close, historicized readings of the Arabic sources, rational analyses of the claims, and references to European histories similarly arguing that 'Umar did not destroy the library, Shiblī not only seeks to correct a false historical narrative, but also to demonstrate a method of historical reason based on rational principles and close attention to Arabic primary sources. First published in Urdu in 1892, the essay was soon translated into English as "An Inquiry into the Destruction of the Alexandrian Library" and was submitted, along with the English translation of his methodologically similar essay "The Jizyah or Capitation Tax," to the meeting of the International Congress of Orientalists in Geneva in 1894. Thomas Arnold, Shiblī's colleague at the college, was among the Asian delegates to the conference. So was the Egyptian scholar Aḥmad Zakī, whom Shiblī mentions in the travelogue. Shiblī later reviewed Aḥmad Zakī's Arabic travelogue discussing his experiences in Europe while attending the 1892 conference in London.

Travel writing was an important part of Shiblī's literary-cultural background and his intellectual milieu. He relied on Arabic and Persian travel literature in his own historical studies, some of which he uses and discusses in the *Safarnāmah*. He also taught travel writing in Aligarh, specifically the Persian travelogue of Nāṣir Khusrau (b. 1004; d. 1072–78),[12] a selection from which he eventually included in the curriculum of Persian literature that he wrote for the University of Allahabad. The travelogue also had its own history in Urdu literature. Sayyid Aḥmad Khān had published fragments of a travelogue detailing his journey from India to London in 1869 in his reformist magazine *Tahzīb al-Akhlāq*. He later published *Safarnāmah-i Panjāb*, comprising materials gathered during a speaking tour in 1884, to which Shiblī wrote the introduction (in Persian). In the early 1880s, Shiblī had also read the Persian travelogue of the Shah of Iran, Nāṣir al-Dīn Shāh (r. 1848–96), which includes descriptions of Istanbul and Europe, inter alia, during his travels in 1873.

Travel writing in Urdu had been used as a means of reform by writers associated with Aligarh long before Shiblī wrote his travelogue. Shiblī had read an Urdu travelogue by Samī'ullāh Khān (who was among the founders of the MAO College), which detailed his experiences as part of a British deputation to examine the courts in Egypt. It was later published in the *Aligarh Institute Gazette*. Sayyid Aḥmad Khān's travel writing about his time in Britain included discussions of education and reform. In *Safarnāmah-i Panjāb*, Sayyid Aḥmad Khān had used the travelogue as a vehicle to promote the MAO College and advocate for educational reform among Indian Muslims. Shiblī wrote the preface (in Persian), in which he praises European efforts to publish the large body of valuable travel literature, now cheaply available, written by Muslims when "the reins of command were in [their] hands." He contrasts this with what he considers an utter lack of travel writing, even if travel itself were undertaken, in the regions of India. Shiblī describes *Safarnāmah-i Panjāb* not only as a text that revives a neglected yet important historical genre, but also one that is particularly well-suited to contemporary purposes of ethical reform and Muslim progress. Indeed, he writes that a "sensible man" can derive many lessons from it, and anyone who feels compassionate toward Islam can be roused to the assistance and aid of Muslims. In Shiblī's words, Sayyid

Aḥmad Khān's travelogue could direct the attention of the community to its infirmity, expose its weakness, awaken its sense of dignity, and inspire it to strive to rid itself of vice and attain virtue. If the community failed to do so, nothing less than the status of Islam was at stake.

Shiblī's remarks about *Safarnāmah-i Panjāb* and his comments in the introduction to *Turkey, Egypt, and Syria: A Travelogue* suggest that Shiblī knew relatively little about the history of travel writing in India in general and in Urdu in particular (assuming that he is not feigning ignorance, of course). Indeed, what we know about them make it impossible to agree with Shiblī's claim that the Muslim community had all but abandoned the practice. The Indo-Persian tradition includes a rich corpus of travel literature traversing genres and geographies.[13] Urdu literature, too, includes a diverse corpus of travel literature, and travel and journey had been important tropes and narrative strategies in Urdu literature in North India since the eighteenth century. The poet Mīr Ḥasan (d. 1786), for example, wrote an autobiographical account of his own travels in verse and used travel as narrative devices in his famous fantasy mathnawī. *Tārīkh-i Yūsufī* (published from Delhi College in 1847), also known as *Ajā'ib-i Firang* (The Wonders of Europe), by Yūsuf Khān Kambalposh, often cited by Urdu literary historians as Urdu's first prose travelogue, records the author's experiences while traveling from Calcutta to London in 1837–38.[14] From the 1870s to the 1890s, globetrotter Nawwāb Muḥammad 'Umar Khān wrote and published travelogues of his journeys in, inter alia, India, Arabia, Iraq, Persia, Egypt, Syria, Sri Lanka, Burma, China, Spain, Italy, Switzerland, Turkey, and Russia. The Urdu literary journals that Shiblī read, and in which he published, also included travel accounts. And, of course, travel diaries and other forms of autobiographical travel writing existed in manuscripts.[15]

Travel is also an important part of the literary and religious traditions in which Shiblī was educated. In the Arabic-Islamic tradition, and especially in the kind of Sufistic traditions that interested Shiblī's father, one often encounters the hadith of the Prophet commanding that one seek knowledge as far as China. Travel in the pursuit of knowledge also plays an important role in the Persian tradition. In addition to the many Persian travelogues, some of which Shiblī had read, one might also note the

Gulistān of Sa'dī, whose narrator speaks of his experiences in Damascus, Mecca, Jerusalem, Tripoli, Basra, Kufah, Kish, Kashgar, Diyarbakir, and Balkh, as well as unnamed places in the desert and on the sea, though their historical authenticity is contested.

The language of travel is also central to the language of Ṣūfism, in which the seeker-mystic is often called the *sālik* (traveler). Ḥabīb al-Raḥmān Khān Shirwānī, Shiblī's colleague and correspondent beginning in the mid-1890s, draws attention to this language in his review of Shiblī's travelogue. The term Shirwānī uses, *safar dar waṭan* (travel in the homeland), alludes to the mystical process of journeying within the self in order to draw closer to the divine. The same theme permeates Persian mystical poetry, such as *Manṭiq al-ṭair* (*The Speech of the Birds*) by Farīd al-Dīn 'Aṭṭār, in which a group of birds sets out on a quest to find the sīmurgh only to discover that they themselves (who number thirty) were the sīmurgh (*sī* = *thirty*; *murgh* = *bird*) all along. In his youth, Shiblī, too, associated travel with the pursuit of learning and left home, sometimes against his father's wishes, to study at the feet of respected teachers in Jaunpur and Lahore. This perhaps explains the reference in the first sentence of his travelogue to a "student's journey" (ṭālib al-'ilmānah safar; lit., seeker-of-knowledge-like journey [student-like journey]).

Shiblī was not the only late nineteenth-century traveler to the Ottoman Empire, and his travelogue invites comparison with contemporary travel writing about the region. Two recent anthologies in English offer glimpses of European perspectives on Beirut and Cairo and attest to the popularity of travelogues and their relationship to the history of tourism and colonialism in the nineteenth century.[16] Comparison with many of the travelogues excerpted in these collections reveals both similarities and differences in the content and style of Shiblī's own travel writing. Like the European travelers, Shiblī visited mosques, the pyramids, and colleges, witnessed the economic disparities among religious communities in Beirut, admired the city's beauty, and witnessed its flourishing intellectual culture. Also like European travelers, Shiblī was interested in describing the appearance and character of the communities he encountered. Yet it is hardly surprising that Shiblī's experience and narrative are distinguishable from his European contemporaries in many respects. For example,

Shiblī's *Safarnāmah* is deeply concerned with the state of education and letters in these regions, particularly with the state of Muslim and Arabic education, and he takes pains to investigate and record information about the educational institutions in the Ottoman Empire. Shiblī's travelogue also bears comparison with a recent English translation of an Arabic travelogue of Istanbul whose author was concerned with the political state of affairs in the Ottoman capital.[17]

Comparative studies of travel writing have emphasized the social and documentary importance of the genre and its role in the processes of defining the self and the other, both in individual and communal terms.[18] Nineteenth-century travelogues, in particular, reflect the influence of new technologies of transportation, increased affordability, and greater access to the means of travel. Some episodes in Shiblī's travelogue reflect this shared historical context, such as his experience of the Suez Canal and his discussion of transportation in Istanbul and the steamships operated by the Cook Company. Scholars also note that many nineteenth-century travelogues include acts of cultural defiance or exploration—the journey itself becoming a means of engaging in practices deemed illegal or culturally taboo at home. One might situate Shiblī's visit to a brothel in Beirut in this comparative context.

Mark Twain, who traveled to the Ottoman Empire in the mid-nineteenth century, writes about guides and travel literature in general, both of which he mocks and dismisses as unreliable. Shiblī also considers guides unreliable, but, unlike Twain, he views them as a major source of the kind of literary misrepresentation that he seeks to oppose in his travelogue. The stakes of their misrepresentations are much higher for Shiblī. Similarly, if Henry David Thoreau dismissed "shallow books of travel" in favor of an inner journey of self-reflection, Shiblī is much more concerned with aspects of Muslim communal identity. To be sure, Shiblī does engage in self-reflection in the travelogue. For example, he is acutely aware of the ways in which his clothing and appearance mark his identity and his judgments about food, social behavior, and literary taste, for example, indicate his individual and cultural perspective. Still, on the whole, he is more concerned with historical processes and external institutions than self-discovery or individual self-definition. One hesitates to reduce the difference between Shiblī's travelogue and the works of his European contemporaries to any one aspect of Shiblī's background. Indeed, if the institution of colonialism encouraged cultural differentiation and the reification of identities, it also circulated ideas across the porous borders of empire, culture, and language. Thoreau and Sayyid Aḥmad Khān both wrote about Carlyle and his notions of heroism and history. But one also cannot ignore the significant ways in which Shiblī's position as a colonized subject and his Indian and Muslim identities, which he foregrounds in the text, distinguish him from other writers of his day. Shiblī and other Muslim reformers in India responded to the experience of late nineteenth-century British colonialism by emphasizing self-help, education, and critical engagement with European writings about Islam. Thus, community or nation (qaum), whether conceived in terms of religion, education, language, or cultural heritage, remains a major focus of his travelogue.

Conclusion: The Travelogue in Translation

Shiblī wrote as someone deeply concerned with issues of representation, power, religion, and community, specifically with the effect of European literature on Indian Muslims. He saw himself as part of a group of Urdu writers who had the power to inform thinking about the past and thereby reform thinking about the present. As a scholar of Islam, Arabic, and Persian, and an accomplished stylist in Urdu, Shiblī found himself in a unique position to guide British-educated and traditionally educated Muslims in their thinking about their communal history—past and present—outside British India, and other issues that mattered to him and his colleagues.

Turkey, Egypt, and Syria: A Travelogue is an important aspect of this broader intellectual program. It has become a classic of Urdu literature, a means by which generations of Urdu readers have imagined the role of the Ottoman Empire and its relationship with the Muslims of South Asia since the nineteenth century. Though the text itself has undergone little change since its initial publication in 1894, its readership has changed significantly. From the nationalist readership influenced by anticolonial politics and the demands for independence from British rule that took hold after the First World War, through the formation of new Urdu communities in India and Pakistan, to the institutionalization of Urdu studies in academies inside and outside of South Asia, Urdu readers of the *Safarnāmah* have brought a wide range of cultural, linguistic, geopolitical, and communal perspectives to bear on it. Once a text for Muslim colonial subjects with an interest in Arabic newspapers and the Ottoman Empire, it is now, in English translation, a window into a world partly lost to historical memory, but whose legacies are nonetheless relevant today. It is hoped that, having made the journey into English, this text will encounter new communities of readers and inspire new discussions of colonialism, religion, social history, and literature.

Appendixes

Glossary

Notes

Index

APPENDIX 1

Biographies

Muḥammad ʿAbduh (1849–1905). Social reformer, jurist, journalist, educator, and muftī of Egypt. Born in Egypt, educated at al-Azhar in Cairo, and mentored by Jamāl al-Dīn Afghānī (q.v.). ʿAbduh eventually taught at al-Azhar and the Dār al-ʿUlūm (q.v.). He was exiled from Egypt in 1882, first living at Beirut and then in Paris, where he and Afghānī published the anti-imperialist *al-ʿUrwah al-Wuṡqā*, which carried articles criticizing Sayyid Aḥmad Khān (q.v.) and his colleagues and advocating for Muslim unity against European imperialism. **ʿAbduh** eventually returned to Beirut, where he translated a Persian work by Afghānī, severely critical of Sayyid Aḥmad Khan and his followers, into Arabic. In Beirut, ʿAbduh also lectured on theology, compiled critical editions of classical Arabic texts, and wrote editorials promoting unity among religious communities. He returned to Egypt in 1888 and was appointed as a judge and then as a consultant to the Court of Appeals. In 1892, he founded a charitable society (*jamʿiyah khairiyah*). Around this time, he edited critical editions of Arabic literature, including ʿAbd al-Qādir Jurjānī's *Asrār al-Balāghah* and *Dalāʾil al-Iʿjāz*, for a society dedicated to the revival of the Arabic sciences. In 1899, he was made muftī of Egypt, a position he held until his death.[1]

Zain al-ʿĀbidīn (d. 1905). Sub-judge, *raʾīs* of Machhlīpūr. A close associate of Sayyid Aḥmad Khān. He spent his last years in Rāmpūr.[2]

Jamāl al-Dīn Afghānī (1838–97). Muslim reformer, journalist, and anti-imperial activist. In his writings and speeches, he promoted Muslim revival, liberation from European influence (especially in Egypt, Persia, and India), and the unification of Muslims under a single caliphate. As a lecturer, he traveled to India, Egypt, and Istanbul. In Cairo, he taught future influential Egyptian thinkers Muḥammad ʿAbduh and Saʿd Zaghlūl and promoted journalism as a tool for political change. He was expelled from Egypt in 1882 and returned to India, where he lived under British surveillance in Hyderabad and Calcutta. In Hyderabad, he wrote a now-famous refutation of "naturist" (*necharī*) materialists, a term of abuse directed at Sayyid Aḥmad Khān and his followers in Aligarh. As Keddie has argued, his criticism of the school and its founder, though couched in theological language, was mainly political and directed at their policy of cooperation with the British. Around this time, he debated French intellectual Ernest Renan in print, though he agreed with Renan's assessment that Islam is antithetical to science. In 1884, he and Muḥammad 'Abduh published the journal *al-'Urwah al-Wuśqā* from Paris, the organ of a Muslim society that carried articles that attacked British involvement in Muslim countries. The journal also carried articles that specifically attacked Sayyid Aḥmad Khān and his followers (notably Samī'ullāh Khān) (q.v.). The British banned the journal in Egypt and India. Afghānī spent time in Persia, from which he was expelled, before moving to Constantinople at the request of 'Abd al-Ḥamīd II in 1892.[3]

Sayyid Mumtāz 'Alī (1860–1935). Scholar, Urdu journalist, feminist author. Educated in the Islamic sciences at the Deoband madrasa in India, he eventually found work as translator at the Lahore High Court. He corresponded with Sayyid Aḥmad Khān, who was impressed by him and invited him to spend time in Aligarh. Mumtāz 'Alī wrote religious pamphlets as well as longer tracts on religious subjects. Among his most famous works is *Huqūq al-niswān* (The Rights of Women), an Urdu treatise on women's rights in Islam, which he appears to have written partly in response to a work by Ḥamzah Faṭhullāh, which Shiblī brought to him from Egypt (see Appendix 2). He also translated the biography of the reformist theologian al-Ghazālī, *Munqiż min al-Żalāl*, into Urdu, ostensibly at Sayyid Aḥmad Khān's request.[4]

Nuṣrat 'Alī. Indian-born pro-Ottoman, anti-British journalist who lived in Istanbul. Like many Indians, he collected funds to support the Ottomans during the Russo-Turkish War (1877–78), and it is through these efforts that he likely came into contact with Ḥusain Ḥasīb (q.v.), who kept detailed records of contributions. Nuṣrat 'Alī published a newspaper in India, which was shut down by authorities. By 1880, he had moved to Istanbul, where he soon began to publish the periodical *Paik-i Islām* (The Messenger of Islam), in which he supported the pan-Islamic rhetoric of Sulṭān 'Abd al-Ḥamīd II by promoting him as the caliph of Islam. Although rhetoric of this kind was typical at the time and not necessarily tied to political allegiance, in this case it took on a markedly political character. Indeed, Nuṣrat ʿAlī's petition to the Sublime Porte promoted the paper as a tool to garner political allegiance to the sulṭān by Indian Muslims, since the British would eventually be forced out of India and Indian Muslims would need a new political ruler. The paper thus promised to promote ʿAbd al-Ḥamīd as the caliph of Islam in India. Two thousand kuruş were given to support the paper, which began publication in May 1880 in both Urdu and Turkish. The British viewed it as part of a broad, anti-British conspiracy and were outraged at the thought that the sulṭān was trying to incite Muslims against England. Jaudat Pāshā, whom Shiblī met in Istanbul, blamed the affair for heightened British-Ottoman discord and alienation. The historian Karpat says that the significance of the paper was exaggerated: only eighteen copies of the short-lived paper reached India, and a British secret investigation found that Nuṣrat ʿAlī had very little influence.[5]

Thomas Walker Arnold (1864–1930). Orientalist and educator. Born in Devonport, England, he studied Sanskrit at the City of London School, then entered Magdalene College in Cambridge, where, in addition to the classics, he studied French, German, Italian, Dutch, Spanish, Portuguese, and Russian. While in Cambridge, he also became interested in Arabic and Islam, in part due to the lectures of the Arabic professor William Robertson Smith (1846–94), whose lectures on early Islam (later published as *Kinship and Marriage in Early Arabia*) were given at the school in 1885. Arnold also studied Sanskrit, and perhaps Persian, with Edward Byles Cowell (1826–1903), who is perhaps most famous for encouraging Edward Fitzgerald to translate the Persian quatrains of ʿUmar Khayyām. In 1888, Arnold was hired to teach philosophy at the Mohammedan Anglo-Oriental College in Aligarh. It was there that Arnold met Shiblī, who had been teaching Arabic and Persian there since 1883. The two eventually became friends and collaborators. Shiblī seems to have taught Arnold some Arabic, and Arnold seems to have taught Shiblī some French (q.v.). Arnold also relied on Shiblī while preparing a series of lectures on the early spread of Islam, later published as *The Preaching of Islam* (1896). Arnold left the college in 1898 to teach philosophy at the Government College in Lahore and eventually became the first president of the Anjuman-i Taraqqī-i Urdu (Society for the Promotion of Urdu). He returned to England in 1904 as assistant librarian at the India Office Library, was later appointed to the chair of Arabic at University College, London, and eventually taught at the School of Oriental Studies. He also accepted the English editorship of the *Encyclopaedia of Islam*, and was educational advisor for Indian Studies in England at the India Office. He retired in 1920, was knighted in 1921, and spent the last years of his life writing broad studies of Islamic history, art, and culture.[6]

Madanī ʿAzīz Āfandī (Medeni Aziz Efendi) (1842–95). Musician, educator, and a master of Turkish and European instruments, including the piano. He taught music to the granddaughters of Ottoman Sulṭān Maḥmūd II (d. 1839), and performed both at the royal court in Istanbul and for the Khedive in Egypt. He spent the second half of his life as a teacher. He became director of the Kız Sanayi Mektebi (Women's Technical School) in 1881, taught music at a school for deaf and mute girls, and worked as inspector of women's schools.[7]

Theodore Beck (1859–99). Principal of the Muhammadan Anglo-Oriental College in Aligarh from 1883 until his death. Educated at a Quaker school, then London University, and eventually Trinity College in Cambridge.[8]

Friedrich Bohndorff (1848–94). German explorer, officer, translator, and zoologist. Bohndorff lived for a time in Savoy, Genoa, and Turin before moving to Cairo in 1876, where he studied Arabic. He spent most of the 1880s in Africa, returning to Europe briefly to sell zoological specimens to European museums. He joined the Wissmann expedition in 1889, during which he met fellow zoologist Franz Stuhlmann in Bagamayo. Stuhlmann had ties to the museum in Hamburg and an interest in primates. Indeed, a species of blue monkey bears his name. Bohndorff returned to Germany via Aden in 1892 and may have intended to bring the specimens mentioned here to Hamburg via Berlin.[9]

Buṭrus al-Bustānī (1819–83). Scholar of Arabic literature and encyclopedist. He was born in Dibbiyya and educated at a Maronite seminary in Lebanon and at the Maronite College in Rome. He learned English and eventually settled in Beirut, where he formed friendships with Protestant missionaries and scholars, notably the American physician and Arabic scholar Cornelius Van Dyck (q.v.). Busṭānī worked as a translator for the American consulate and assisted in the translation of the Bible into Arabic. He wrote Arabic manuals on mathematics and grammar, started a handful of Arabic periodicals, and founded the National School in Beirut. His two most famous works are his massive Arabic dictionary,

Muḥīṭ al-muḥīṭ and his encyclopedia, *Dā'irat al-ma'ārif*, of which he completed six volumes before his death.[10]

Najīb al-Bustānī (1862–1919). Wrote for Arabic journals and practiced law in Cairo.[11]

Salīm al-Bustānī (1846–84). Arabic novelist, journalist, encyclopedist, and the son of Buṭrus al-Bustānī (q.v.). He worked as an interpreter at the American consulate at Beirut and also helped his father run the National School. He participated in local intellectual societies and published articles in his father's Arabic journal, *al-Jinān*. He penned novels, short stories, history, biography, and translations of French and English literature in Arabic. His novels were especially innovative and inspired later Arabic novelists, notably Jurjī Zaidān. He eventually took over the project of completing his father's encyclopedia upon his death, adding two volumes to it before his own death.[12]

Cornelius van Dyke (1818–95). Physician, Christian missionary, Arabic scholar, and educator in Beirut. He was born in Kinderhook, New York, and studied medicine at Jefferson Medical College in Philadelphia. He moved to Syria as a medical missionary in 1840, where he studied Arabic with Buṭrus al-Bustānī (q.v.). In 1866, he helped establish the Syrian Protestant College (later the American University of Beirut), where he taught medicine and science. In 1882, van Dyck resigned after a colleague was fired for endorsing the ideas of Charles Darwin. The incident and van Dyck's resignation are seen as representing tensions among religious tradition, modern science, and intellectual freedom in Beirut in the late nineteenth century. Many of Van Dyck's students, including Shiblī's interlocutor Jurjī Zaidān, left the college in protest. Van Dyck spent the remaining years of his life working on the series of scientific textbooks in Arabic titled *al-Naqsh fī al-ḥajar*, which Shiblī mentions in the travelogue.[13]

Ḥamzah Fatḥullāh (1849–1918). Educator, Egyptian official, and Islamic scholar. He studied at al-Azhar in Cairo and spent his early career in journalism in Tunisia and Alexandria, and eventually became inspector of Arabic language instruction at the Ministry of Education and held the post for the remainder of his life. He traveled twice to the International Congress of Orientalists (1886 and 1889) as a representative of the Egyptian government. His work includes treatises on women's rights in Islam, Arab drawings of animals, and the Islamic calendar. He also published translations into Arabic.[14]

'Abd al-Fattāḥ. The third son of Maḥmūd al-Ṣāḥib (d. 1866), who was the brother of the immensely influential Naqshbandī Ṣufī and reformer Khālid (q.v.). Very little has been written about 'Abd al-Fattāḥ, but Maḥmūd al-Ṣāḥib was a leading Naqshbandi authority in Damascus, and the family was influential in the city in the nineteenth century, both because of its connection to Khālid and because of its relationship with the Ottoman state. Sulṭān 'Abd al-Majīd II (d. 1861) granted Maḥmūd authority over the Ottoman Takkiyah mosque in the Marjah area of the city. 'Abd al-Fattāḥ's brother, As'ad Ṣāḥib (d. 1927) inherited control of the mosque from Maḥmūd and promoted Khālid's ideas by editing and publishing his writings. At the end of the nineteenth century, As'ad and his family competed with other claimants to Naqshbandī authority in Damascus and ultimately used their network of supporters in Constantinople to secure support from 'Abd al-Ḥamīd II and weaken support for their rivals.[15]

Ḥasan 'Alī Faiżī (Hasanally Fyzee) (1838–1903). Merchant in Istanbul and Bombay. Ḥasan 'Alī's father, Fezhyder (Faiż Ḥaidar) and paternal uncle, Tyabjee (Ṭayyibjī) were wealthy brokers and merchants in Bombay in the mid-nineteenth century, and family wealth and business seems to have provided the capital and motivation for Ḥasan 'Alī to establish himself as a merchant of Indian wares in Istanbul. He had a large family, including three daughters, Zahrā (1866–1940), Nazlī (1874–1968), and 'Aṭiyah (Atiya Fyzee) (1877–1967). The daughters, though born in Constantinople and connected to Turkish cultural traditions, were raised mostly in Bombay. Shiblī first met Ḥasan 'Alī in Constantinople and later developed a close relationship with the family, often visiting them on trips to Bombay. Shiblī's letters to Zahrā and 'Atiyā, written in the 1900s, were published as *Khuṭūṭ-i Shiblī* (Shiblī's Letters) after his death.[16]

Muḥammad Amīn Bey Fikrī (1856–99). Jurist, Egyptian official, and traveler. Born in Cairo, the son of a leading Egyptian poet, intellectual, statesman, and educational reformer. He was educated in Cairo, then studied law in Aix-en-Provence in France. After returning to Egypt, he was made judge in the National Appeals Court, then governor of Minufiyya and Alexandria. His father was head of the Egyptian delegation to the Congress of Orientalists in Stockholm in 1889. Amīn Bey joined him and lectured on modern Arabic. His travelogue,

Irshād al-alibbā alā maḥāsin urūbbā, printed at the al-Muqtaṭaf press in Cairo, describes his experiences in Europe. He also wrote about Egyptian geography.[17]

Shaikh Ḥabībullāh (d. 1900). Legal advocate, entrepreneur, landowner, and educationalist in Azamgarh, and Shiblī's father. Ḥabībullāh's father worked in the collector's office in Azamgarh. Ḥabībullāh learned Arabic and Persian as a child, passed the *wakālat* (legal deputyship) examination, and obtained permission to work as a deputy for the British High Court in Allahabad. He was a prominent figure ih Azamgarh, worked to quell violence and maintain stability during the Rebellion of 1857, and eventually held the appointment of honorary secretary of the Azamgarh municipality. He owned several indigo warehouses and sugar factories, the profits from which he used to buy land around Azamgarh, which he divided among his brothers. He also opened a small Arabic madrasa there, where Shiblī studied, and was known to host gatherings of poets at his properties in the city. Ḥabībullāh was an early and long-time supporter of Sayyid Aḥmad Khān and the Muhammadan Anglo-Oriental College in Aligarh. Unlike Shiblī, Ḥabībullāh's other three brothers were educated in the British system (one in Aligarh and England) and were employed in the British legal administration.[18]

'Abd al-Ḥamīd II (1842–1918; r. 1876–1909). Ottoman sulṭān remembered for policies that favored centralized authority and his self-promotion as the *khalīfah* (caliph) of Islam both inside and outside the Ottoman Empire. As part of this "pan-Islamic" program, he enacted educational policies and built infrastructure to strengthen ties between Istanbul and regional Arab centers. He also enacted policies that favored Muslims with positions of political authority, fostered loyalty to the sulṭān among influential Arabs, and worked to garner sympathy and support from Muslims outside the Ottoman Empire, especially in India.[19] In doing so, he was encouraged by the Hungarian Orientalist Arminius Vámbéry (q.v.), whom he invited to as a guest of his court. He also admired the pan-Islamist and Sunnist ideas of Jamāl al-Dīn Afghānī (q.v.).[20]

'Abd al-Ḥaqq Ḥāmid (1852–1937). Turkish poet, dramatist, and Ottoman official. Born in Istanbul to a family of scholars, his father was a well-known historian and Ottoman ambassador. He studied in Istanbul, Paris, and Tehran, then held various official posts in Russia, Greece, Bombay, London, Brussels, and Vienna. According to critics, his poetry is characterized by experimentation with form, including new meters, new rhyme schemes, and blank verse, as well as the introduction of new themes related to history and nature. His dramas, which include the South Asia–related *Dukhtar-i Hindū* (The Hindu Girl), address themes of history, gender, religion, and philosophy.[21]

Annie Hanly (1857–1907). Educationist. Her father, John Laffan Hanly (1836–82), and uncle, Baron Henry Hanly (1848–95), were Irish-born brothers who moved to the Ottoman Empire and published English- and French-language journals. John Laffan Hanly moved to Istanbul in 1867, where he eventually edited and published *The Levant Times* (in English) and *Stamboul* (in French). Baron Henry Hanly took charge of *Stamboul* after his brother's death. Annie Hanly is remembered as being especially fearless. One anecdote records that she once used a revolver to ward off an angry mob. Another records that she once rescued her father from attack by a group of assailants armed with swords. She is reported to have received a medal from the Ottoman minister of education and to have spoken French, German, Greek, Turkish, Arabic, Armenian, and Bulgarian.[22]

Ḥusain Ḥasīb (1838–1912). Ottoman consul in Bombay and official in Istanbul. Born into a Bosnian family in Trebinje, he was brought to Constantinople at age eighteen by the Ottoman Ministry of Education. After graduating from the high school in Beşiktaş in 1861, he worked for the Correspondence and Recordkeeping Offices in Istanbul. Because of his competence in Slavic languages and his work as a translator, he was employed at the Sublime Porte Translation Office in 1863. In September 1870, he was appointed to the Ottoman consulate in Bombay. As consul, he promoted Ottoman agendas in the vernacular press and ran a fundraising campaign during the Russo-Turkish War (1877–78). He eventually left India and was appointed in 1884 as the vice secretary of the Foreign Correspondence Office in Constantinople. In 1890, he was appointed to the office of governor (*mutasarrıf*) in the Beyoğlu district of the city (it is this post that he likely held when Shiblī met him in the city), and then to the Postal and Telegraph Ministry in 1895. He was removed from office after the Young Turk Revolution in 1908 and eventually spent two years imprisoned in Rhodes. He returned to Constantinople after his release, where he died and was buried. He was a highly decorated officer: he was given the Silver Imtiyāz Medal in 1884–85, made an Osmani of the first order in 1885–86, and finally given the Gold Liyakat Medal in 1893–94. He is said to have known Turkish, Arabic, Farsi, Slavic, French, English, and Urdu.[23]

Ṭāhir al-Ḥusainī (1842–1908). Muftī of Jerusalem. Born and educated in Jerusalem, he inherited the office of muftī in the city from his father in 1865–66. The Ḥusainī family had risen to prominence in the late seventeenth century, lost influence, then regained authority in Jerusalem in the nineteenth century through repeated appeals to Ottoman authorities in Istanbul. Ṭāhir's father, Muṣṭafā al-Ḥusainī, became mutfī of the city in 1856, the same year as the Ottoman Imperial Reform Edict. After 1876, the family campaigned in Istanbul to secure positions of power there and in Jerusalem. One member of the family held office in the Ottoman Parliament in 1876. By 1886, members of the family occupied a large number of prominent administrative positions in Jerusalem as, inter alia, the head of the criminal court, the muftī, and the director of education. In the late 1890s, Ṭāhir al-Ḥusainī played a leading role in opposition to Zionist activities in city. His home was a gathering place for literary scholars and politicians, and he is remembered as a caretaker of cultural and literary affairs.[24]

Ilyās (1840–1901). Manager of the printing house at the Université Saint-Joseph in Beirut. He converted to Christianity following a miraculous survival from injury. He took over the administration of the Catholic printing press when it moved from Ghazīr to Beirut.[25]

Shams al-Dīn al-Inbābī (Shaikh al-Azhar) (d. 1895–96). In 1888, Inbābī and a committee of scholars were asked to design a program for the Dār al-ʿUlūm academy to train students in Ḥanafī law in preparation for positions in sharia courts as qāẕī, muftī, and other court officials. Few of these jobs existed, and were traditionally held by scholars educated at Azhar. This led to a series of tensions and reforms, with Dār al-ʿUlūm returning its focus to training Arabic teachers in 1895 and Azhar resolving to broaden its curriculum.[26]

ʿUmar Jubailī. Owner and director (*ṣāḥib idārah*) of the short-lived journal *al-Ṣafā* (1886–90) of Beirut. Very little has been written about Jubailī, and what little we do know about him comes mostly from the pages of *al-Ṣafā*, in which he identifies himself as ʿUmar al-Ḥisāmī al-Jubailī (or Jabīlī). The journal began under the directorship of the Druze intellectual ʿAlī Nāṣir al-Dīn and had the support of both the governor (*mutasarrif*) of Lebanon, Wasa Pāshā (1825–1892) and Naṣīb Bey Janbulāt (Junblat), who was an administrator in the district of al-Shūf (Chouf). Like the editors of the journal, the Janbulāt family was a Druze family of Kurdish origin that held considerable political authority in the Levant in the eighteenth and nineteenth centuries, and it is likely that Jubailī either belonged to the Druze community or had close ties to it.[27]

Mirzā Maẓhar Jān-i Jānān̈ (b. ca. 1700; d. 1781). Urdu poet, leading Ṣūfī of the Naqshbandī community in Delhi, and founder of the Shamsiyah order. Sources differ on his spiritual lineage, but all agree that he spent much of his youth deeply involved in spiritual practice, which he eventually taught to a large number of disciples. Among his closest disciples was Shāh Ghulām 'Alī (1745–1824), who wrote a definitive biography of Maẓhar and promoted his teachings in Delhi. Among the disciples of Shāh Ghulām 'Alī was the family of Sayyid Aḥmad Khān (q.v.).[28]

'Abd al-Qādir al-Jazā'irī (1807–83). Revolutionary, intellectual, and mystic. Ṭāhir Maghribī was closely tied to the family of 'Abd al-Qādir al-Jazā'irī. After fighting against the French, 'Abd al-Qādir eventually relocated to Damascus in the 1850s. There, he attracted a large following of scholars and Ṣūfīs. One of his close associates was 'Abd al-Ghanī al-Ghunaimī, the teacher of Ṭāhir Maghribī (q.v.). One of Ṭāhir Maghribī's most influential students, Muḥammad al-Mubārak (Arabic grammarian, literary scholar, and ascetic), was also among 'Abd al-Qādir's followers. Members of 'Abd al-Qādir's family became high-ranking officials in the Ottoman state. One received a stipend from the government for his involvement in military resistance against French forces in Algeria in the 1870s. Another branch of the family led a movement of scholars in Damascus. Also among the scholars in Ṭāhir's intellectual circle in Damascus was 'Abd al-Qādir's son, 'Umar al-Jazā'irī. In the travelogue, Shiblī mentions another relative, 'Abd al-Raḥmān, whose residence in Beirut may explain why a recent biographical entry on the Damascene branch of the al-Jazā'irī family does not list him among 'Abd al-Qādir's descendants (see al-Sawwāf).[29]

Sayyid Mu'īn al-Dīn Khān (Iqbāl Yār Jang) (d. 14 Muharram 1321 (April 13, 1903)). Statesman and educator in Hyderabad. Born in Aurangabad to a family with a scholarly background, he eventually tutored Fażl al-Dīn Khān, later Waqār al-Umarā (prime minister of Hyderabad). Around 1875, he was appointed tutor to the niẓām of Hyderabad, Mir Mahbub Ali Khan, and eventually tutored his son, future niẓām of Hyderabad Mīr 'Uṡmān 'Alī Khān. He is remembered for his work with the Dā'irat al-Ma'ārif (which he cofounded in the 1880s) and the educational institutions that he established in Hyderabad, notably his founding of kindergarten (*gulshan-i aṭfāl*) programs. He also wrote Persian and Urdu poetry.[30]

Aḥmad Jaudat Pāshā (Ahmet Cevdet Paşa) (1823–95). Ottoman statesman, jurist, and historian. Trained in Arabic, Persian, and the Islamic sciences, he worked as a qāẓī for the Ottoman government and was eventually made a wazīr. He drafted important legislation as part of the Tanẓīmāt legal reforms assembly, and edited its first collection of laws in 1863. He was founding chair of the Supreme Court of Appeals and Minister of Justice, and was involved in the foundation of the law school (q.v.) in 1880. This was appropriate given his intellectual and administrative interests, as he had codified Ḥanafī jurisprudential tradition into a civil legal code (the Mecelle) for the Ottoman state. Among his most important works are his history of the Ottoman Empire, 1774–1826, in twelve volumes, his work as official chronicler (1855–66), and his Turkish translation of the third section of Ibn Khaldūn's Muqaddimah. His daughter, Fāṭimah ʿAliyah (q.v.), was a novelist and feminist writer.[31]

Maḥmad Nāmiq Kamāl (Kamal Bey) (1840–88). Turkish writer. He was educated in Turkish, Persian, and Arabic literature, and also studied mystical traditions. He eventually worked in the Translation Bureau, taught writing at an Islamic school in Istanbul, and was part of a milieu that included poets, French scholars, and publishers. He wrote poetry, which impressed the publisher Abū al-Żiyā (q.v.), that was thematic, including verse about patriotism and love. He published some of his poetry in *Tarjumān-i ḥaqīqat* (q.v.) under pseudonyms. He also wrote articles on a variety of subjects, including contemporary politics, which he published in Turkish journals and newspapers, and edited the journal *ʿIbrat*. In 1886, he began to write a history of the Ottomans, but the introductory section was seized and banned when it was printed in 1887 because of its language.[32]

Samīʿullāh Khān (1834–1908). Judge, scholar, and early supporter of the Muhammadan Anglo-Oriental College in Aligarh. His grandfather was a respected Islamic scholar and Sūfī in Delhi, and his father worked for the British as a *munshī* (clerk). Samīʿullāh studied Persian and Arabic in Delhi, then law. He eventually became a wakīl (legal deputy) in 1856 and was admired by British officials and judges. In 1873, he was made a sub-judge, a position he held in Aligarh, Allahabad, Muradabad, and Fatahgarh. He traveled to London in 1880 to study educational reform and published a travelogue of his experiences, which was translated into English as *Jottings of a Six Months Trip to England* and published from Calcutta in 1882. In 1884, the Earl of Northbrook sent him to Egypt to inspect Egyptian courts. He prepared a memorandum of his findings, for which the British government made him a Companion of St. Michael and St. George (CMG). In 1885, he was promoted from sub-judge to district judge, then eventually to session judge. He retired in November 1892. In addition to law, he also worked in education. He ran an Arabic madrasa in Delhi from 1862 to 1868–69, helped found the Muhammadan Anglo-Oriental College in Aligarh, and initially oversaw its educational program and boarding house. He was also the first president of the Muhammadan Educational Congress (later, Conference), held in Aligarh in 1886. He and Sayyid Aḥmad Khān eventually had a bitter falling-out, and he spent his last years mostly involved with spiritual and religious pursuits, though he did remain engaged with educational and intellectual life in British India and Hyderabad. He was among those whom Jamāl al-Dīn Afghānī attacked for collaborating with the British.[33]

Sayyid Aḥmad Khān (1817–1898). Indian educational reformer and scholar. Born into an aristocratic family in Delhi with close ties to the Mughal court, the British, and Naqshbandī Sufism. In his early career, he wrote about and edited works pertaining to Islam, Mughal history, Persian literature, and the architecture and culture of Delhi. Following the uprising of 1857, he strove to build intellectual and institutional bridges between Indians and the British administration. To this end, he wrote comparative studies of Christianity and Islam, published moralist essays, and published a journal, *Tahẓīb al-akhlāq* (*The Refinement of Character*). He also founded an institute for the study of modern sciences in Aligarh, which developed into the Muhammadan Anglo-Oriental College (1875). (Shiblī was hired onto the faculty to teach Arabic and Persian in 1882 and began teaching in 1883.) In the 1880s and 1890s, Sayyid Aḥmad Khān wrote a controversial commentary on the Quran as well as a series of short works on the Islamic theologian and reformer al-Ghazālī (1058–1111). His interest in rational sciences, Islam, and Ghazālī are reflected in the letters that Shiblī sent to him from Istanbul.[34]

Sayyid Mahdī ʻAli Khān (Muḥsin al-Mulk) (1837–1907). Indian statesman, educational reformer, and leader in Aligarh. Born in Etawa, he studied Arabic and Persian and joined the British service, eventually becoming deputy collector (1867). In 1874, he joined state service in Hyderabad, eventually became secretary of finance, but ultimately resigned amid controversy in July 1893. He was an early supporter and colleague of Sayyid Aḥmad Khān and a major figure of the Muhammadan Anglo-Oriental College and the Muhammadan Educational Conference. Just before his death, he played a leading role in the Muslim League, organizing its first major deputation in 1906. He also wrote articles for journals (including that of Sayyid Aḥmad Khān) as well as a controversial work in refutation of Shīʿism, from which he had converted.[35]

Fāṭimah Khānum (Fatma Aliye Hanım) (1862–1936). Ottoman journalist, biographer, feminist, and novelist. Born in Istanbul to the Ottoman statesman and historian Jaudat Pāshā, she traveled and lived throughout the Ottoman Empire in her youth. She was educated in Arabic, history, and philosophy at home, and translated literature from French into Turkish, which she published under a pseudonym. From 1895 to 1908, she also wrote the editorial column for a women's newspaper. She corresponded with the modernist thinkers Aḥmad Midḥat Pāshā and Muʿallim Nājī (q.v.) and published her writings in their journal, *Tarjumān-i Ḥaqīqat* (q.v.). She and Aḥmad Midḥat collaborated on scholarly projects, and he wrote a biography of her in her own lifetime. In addition to biographies of famous philosophers and her own father, she also wrote works focused on women, particularly women in Islam. The most famous of these is *Niswān-i Islām* (q.v.). She founded the first women's association in the Ottoman Empire and worked for other charitable foundations, and her work is said to have been exhibited at the World's Columbian Exposition in Chicago in 1893.[36]

Khairiyah Khānam (Hayriye Hanım). Educator. She graduated from Darülmuallimat, taught at a number of girls' schools, and was eventually appointed as head teacher at the Kız Sanayi Mektebi (Industrial School for Girls) at Üsküdar in Istanbul in 1890.[37]

Rafīqah Khanum. Educator and musician in Istanbul. She taught at the women teacher's college Dār al-Muʿallimāt (Darülmuallimat). She also seems to have privately tutored Fatma Aliye Hanım on piano.[38]

Ṭāhir al-Maghribī (al-Jazāʾirī) (1852–1920). Educator, government official, and Arabic and Islamic scholar. Although he was born in Damascus, his father was a scholar of the astral and rational sciences from Algeria (hence the titles Maghribī (Western) and Jazāʾirī (Algerian). Ṭāhir studied at home and under an associate of the Algerian political leader ʻAbd al-Qādir al-Jazāʼirī (1807–83), and traveled extensively in the Middle East and France. A prolific writer, by the time he met Shiblī, he had published works on literary technique and rhetoric (1878), the art of riddles and puzzles in literature (1885–86), Arabic prosody (1886), and hadith criticism (1885). He had also translated a work on the lives of the prophets from Turkish into Arabic (1881) and written original works on poetry (1883) and geometry (1884) as well as an elementary textbook on mathematics (1885). When he met Shiblī, he was probably working on his extensive commentary on the discourses of the poet and scholar Ibn Nubātah (b. 946–47; d. 984–85). Ṭāhir's commentary was published from Beirut in 1894. Eventually, the Ottoman government appointed him as superintendent of schools in Damascus in 1879, and in 1881 he founded the first public library in Syria (later the Zāhiriyah Library). Like Shiblī, Ṭāhir looked to the Abbasids, particularly the caliph al-Maʼmūn, as exemplary patrons of learning and promoters of intellectual freedom. Also like Shiblī, he advocated for the use of *ijtihād* (reasoned innovation) in the training of Islamic intellectuals, whom he viewed as a major source for social reform.[39]

Aḥmad Midḥat (1844–1912). Ottoman writer, journalist, and publisher. He and ʻAbū al-Żiyā Taufīq (discussed throughout the travelogue) knew each other and spent time together in exile. Midḥat returned to Istanbul in 1876, shortly after which he found favor with Sulṭān ʻAbd al-Ḥamīd. From 1878, he edited the journal *Tarjumān-i Ḥaqīqat* (q.v.). Among his many books was a biography of Fāṭimah Khānam (Fāṭimah ʻAliyah Khānam), published in 1893–94.[40]

ʻAlī Pāshā Mubārak (1823–93). Egyptian statesman, scholar, and educationalist. Educated in military and engineering academies in Cairo and Paris, he rose through government ranks under Khedive Ismāʻil Pāshā (r. 1863–79) and was eventually appointed to a series of positions in education, public works, communications, railways, and endowments. As an institution builder, he is chiefly remembered for designing the Egyptian curriculum of education and founding both the Dār al-ʻUlūm teachers' college and the Khedival Library, both of which Shiblī visited. As a writer, he is remembered for his multivolume history of nineteenth-century Egypt, *al-Khiṭaṭ al-Taufīqiyah al-jadīdah* (The New Districts of Taufīq) ("Taufīq" is a reference to the Khedive Taufīq Pāshā [r. 1879–92]). The title alludes to *Khiṭaṭ wal-āṡār* by the Egyptian historian al-Maqrīzī (d. 1441), which Shiblī references both in the travelogue and in his work on the history of Islam.[41]

Salomon Munk (1808–67). Orientalist, critical editor, and historian, educated in France and Berlin. He studied Arabic, Hebrew, and Sanskrit; catalogued manuscripts at the Bibliothèque Nationale de Paris; critically edited, annotated, and translated into French *Dalālat al-ḥā'irīn* (Guide for the Perplexed) by the Jewish, Arabic-language philosopher Moses Maimonides (1135–1204); and worked for the French government in Egypt.[42] Munk had attended Hegel's lectures on the philosophy of history in 1825–26, but was disappointed by Hegel's ignorance of the influence of Jewish and Islamic thinkers on European philosophy. Munk's subsequent debates with German Orientalist Herman Ritter were instrumental in introducing Jewish and Islamic philosophy to discussions of the philosophical tradition in Europe. Shiblī refers to Munk's *Mélanges de Philosophie Juives et Arabe* (Paris: Franck, 1859), which Shiblī cited in his own analysis of the place of the Islamic theologian Abū Ḥāmid (al-)Ghazālī (d. 1111) in the history of European philosophy. Since Shiblī read little if any French, he likely relied either on Thomas W. Arnold or Sayyid 'Alī Bilgrāmī (a collaborator of Shiblī's in the 1890s and eventually his supervisor in Hyderabad) for help reading the text.[43]

Mu'allim Nājī (Muallim Naci) (1850–93). Ottoman teacher, journalist, official historian, and poet. Nājī's father-in-law, Aḥmad Midḥat, charged him with overseeing the literary section of the influential Turkish journal *Tarjumān-i ḥaqīqat* (q.v.), but eventually dismissed him following disagreements with other poets. Nājī wrote modern and classical Turkish poetry, essays, a memoir, a lexicon of literary terms, and an Ottoman dictionary, *Lughat-i Nājī*, which he did not finish. Scholars remember him as a neoclassicist.[44]

Khālid Naqshbandī (b. ca. 1780; d. 1827). Ṣūfī, traveler, Naqshbandī proselytizer, and founder of the Khālidī branch of the Naqshbandī order, which was highly influential in the Ottoman Empire in the nineteenth century. He was initiated into the order in Delhi in the late eighteenth century. Khālid and his followers gained influence throughout Kurdistan, the Caucuses, Baghdad, Damascus, and Istanbul in the middle of the nineteenth century, eventually ingratiating themselves with Islamic scholars and religious and state authorities in the Ottoman capital.[45]

Aḥmad Naẓīm (d. 1894). Egyptian author of mathematics and geometry textbooks and member of the Khedivial Ministry of Education. He was appointed in charge of the Dār al-'Ulūm in Cairo from November 1886 until December 1886, then served as director from January 1887 to October 1889.[46]

Darwesh Pāshā (Derviş İbrahim Paşa) (b. ca. 1811–12; d. 1896). Ottoman military commander. Born in Lofça, Bulgaria, he attended the same school as Jaudat Pāshā, then entered the military and was eventually promoted to general (1862). He commanded Ottoman forces at Mount Lebanon in the 1860s, led campaigns in Kozon along with Jaudat Pāshā, saw military success in the Russo-Turkish War (1877–78), then unsuccessfully fought to maintain control of Egypt in 1882. Thereafter, he held high-ranking positions in the Ottoman government, and was for a time a senior advisor to ʻAbd al-Ḥamīd II. He was also a close disciple of the Ṣūfī Shaikh Muṣṭafā Fahmī (d. 1881), leader of the Khālidī Naqshbandī order at Erzincan. As one historian has argued, his ties to the Naqshbandī community affected his political views, most apparently in his opposition to European interference in Ottoman affairs and to non-Muslim participation in Ottoman government. He lived in a luxurious palace surrounded by a garden and decorated with paintings depicting the battles in which he had fought. He also had a summer home on the Bosporus in Ortaköy, later made part of Istanbul, and it is likely here where Shiblī dined. His son, Khālid ʻAlī Pāshā (1860–1948), himself a disciple of a prominent Naqshbandī Ṣūfī in Istanbul) married Nazime Sulṭān (1866–1947), the daughter of Sulṭān ʻAbd al-ʻAzīz. This is likely the marriage to which Shiblī refers in the travelogue. Darwesh Pāshā had strong ties not only the Naqshbandī community in general, but to the community in Damascus in particular. His many properties (located in Bulgaria, Albania, and Syria) included a home in Damascus, and he employed at least one Naqshbandī Ṣūfī to administer his Syrian estate. This may explain why it seems that a steady stream of Damascene Naqsbandīs resided with him at intervals in Istanbul. Anecdotes suggest that Darwesh may have generated income by accepting bribes in exchange for securing licenses for European traders.[47]

(Ghāzī) ʻUśmān Pāshā (Osman Nuri Paşa) (1832–1900). Ottoman military commander. Although his career included campaigns in Crimea, Anatolia, Lebanon, and Crete, he is most famous for his extended and strategically significant, if ultimately unsuccessful, defense of Plevna against the combined army of Russian and Romanian forces during the Russo-Turkish War (1877–78). The defense earned him the title *ghāzī* (warrior, conqueror, or hero). After the war, he was put in charge of the armies of Sulṭān ʻAbd al-Ḥamīd II and remained close to him.[48]

Khair al-Dīn Pāshā (b. 1822–23; d. 1890). Tunisian politician and Islamic political thinker. Born in the Caucuses, orphaned at a young age, and raised in

Istanbul by an Ottoman statesman, he worked for a time as a military officer in Tunisia and a governmental representative in Paris. He also attempted to reform Tunisian economic policy with the goal of retaining Tunisia's political independence. At the same time, he supported close ties between the Ottoman sulṭān and Tunisia, which he felt would guard against excessive European influence and intrusion. He left office in 1877 amid controversy, but Sulṭān 'Abd al-Ḥamīd II brought him to Istanbul as grand wazīr. However, Khair al-Dīn's sympathy for the kind of constitutionalism that 'Abd al-Ḥamīd II had recently displaced led to his dismissal in 1879. He lived the rest of his life in retirement in Istanbul. The introduction to his *Aqwām al-masālik fī ma'rifat aḥwāl al-mamālik* (1868), an Urdu translation of which Sayyid Aḥmad Khān had published in his journal *Tahżīb al-akhlāq* in the 1870s, lays out strategies for the recovery of Muslim prosperity. Khair al-Dīn argues (1) that European strength resulted not from religion, but from the centralization of authority in parliamentary form; (2) that there were precedents for parliamentary institutions in Islamic jurisprudential traditions; and (3) that Islamic scholars had a key role to play in the process of enacting these reforms, since they not only held sway over the opinions of the public, but could also advise legislators on the compatibility of government policy and Islamic law.[49]

Zakī Pāshā (1849–1914). Ottoman military officer and director of the Military Academy in Istanbul. His father was an Armenian convert to Islam and administrator at Izmir. Born in Aydin, Zakī Pāshā eventually graduated from the Military College in Istanbul and joined military service. After the Russo-Turkish War (1877–78), he became a personal assistant to the sulṭān and tutor to the royal princes. He was transferred to the Ministry of Military Schools in 1883 and appointed administrator of the Tophane (military area) of Istanbul in 1891. He held these positions until the 1908 revolution, after which he was exiled to Buyukada and then to Rhodes. He was eventually released, spent time in Europe, and died in 1914 in Buyukada. He is said to have known English, French, German, Greek, Italian, and Turkish.[50]

Aḥmad Qūṣī (1864–1915). Literary scholar born in Qūṣ and educated at Asyut, then in al-Azhar and the Dār al-'Ulūm. He later worked as a teacher and published his writings in Arabic literary magazines and newspapers. A collection of his poems has been published. He is especially remembered for his work in the *zajal* genre.[51]

Muḥammad ibn ʻAlī al-Ṣabbān (d. 1791–92). Author of many marginal commentaries on earlier works. Ṣabbān's writings were regularly printed in Egypt in the nineteenth century, perhaps owing to his prominence in the curriculum at Azhar.

Anṭūn Sāliḥānī (1847–1941). Jesuit priest and Arabic scholar. Born in Damascus, he was orphaned in the communal violence of 1860 there and sent to study with the Jesuits, first in Ghazīr, then in Beirut, where he studied Arabic, French, Latin, and Greek. He traveled to France in 1868, taught at Valse and Avignon, and studied theology in Aix-en-Provene, where he was eventually ordained to the priesthood. He lived for a time in Alexandria and Cairo, then in Slough in England, before returning to Beirut in 1887 to take final vows. Here, he also began a professorship in Arabic at the Université Saint-Joseph. In addition to editing the school's organ, *al-Bashīr*, he produced critical editions of classical Arabic literature, including *Kitāb al-aghānī* (The Book of Songs) by Abū al-Faraj (d. 967), *Alf lailā wa lailā* (*The Thousand and One Nights*), *Tārīkh al-mukhtaṣar fī al-duwal* (A Brief History of Governments) by Abū al-Faraj (Bar Hebraeus) (b. 1225–26; d. 1286), and the *Dīwān (*Collected Poems*)* by the Umayyad poet al-Akhṭal (d. 710). He later participated in Catholic polemical debates and led religious societies in Beirut, in addition to continuing his work on Arabic literature.[52]

Muḥammad Amīn ibn ʻĀbidīn al-Shāmī (1784–1842). Ḥanafī jurisprudent and Naqshbandī Ṣūfī who lived in Damascus. He authored the famous rebuttal-commentary *Radd al-muḥtār ʻalā al-Durr al-mukhtār.* The book, which later became canonical among Ḥafanī jurisprudents, challenges the authoritative *Durr al-mukhtār* by al-Ḥaṣkafī (d. 1677). Al-Shāmī's book is celebrated for its innovation, contributing new categories of authority, such as convention, to jurisprudential reasoning. Al-Shāmī himself was also a Ṣūfī and both a follower and polemical defender of Khālid Naqshbandī. His son, ʻAlā al-Dīn (d. 1888), assisted Jaudat Pāshā (q.v.) in the compilation of the Ottoman Ḥanafī-aligned legal code, known as the Mecelle.[53]

Ḥasan al-Ṭawīl (d. 1899). Educated at Azhar, where he and his colleague Muḥammad ʻAbduh studied with two teachers who later became members of the first faculty at Dār al-ʻUlūm. After studying at Azhar, Ḥasan al-Ṭawīl worked for the Ministry of Education before joining the faculty at Dār al-ʻUlūm. According to one historian, all teachers at the Dār al-ʻUlūm had either been trained at Azhar or were closely associated with the reform movement of Muḥammad ʿAbduh (or both). In turn, Ḥasan al-Ṭawīl emphasized the study of literary history and criticism.[54]

Badr al-Dīn Ṭayyibjī (Badruddin Tyabji) (1844–1906). Judge and leading figure in the Indian National Congress. He was born in Bombay to a family of merchants from the Sulaimānī Bohrā-Ismā'ilī community. His father, Ṭayyib 'Alī, known as Ṭayyibjī (Tyabjee) and his paternal uncle, Faiż Ḥaidar (Fezhyder) amassed a small fortune as brokers and merchants in Bombay in the mid-nineteenth century. Badr al-Dīn studied law in London, then returned to practice in Bombay, where he eventually became chief justice in the Bombay High Court. He was also active in Indian politics and Muslim educational reform. He presided over the 1887 session of the Indian National Congress (a body of prominent Indians founded in 1885 to represent Indian interests to the British government) as well as the 1903 session of the All-India Muhammadan Educational Conference in Bombay, which Sayyid Aḥmad Khān founded in 1886 in part to distance the Muslim community from the politics of the National Congress. Ṭayyibjī corresponded with leading figures in Aligarh, including Principal Theodore Beck, Mahdī 'Alī Muḥsin al-Mulk, and the founder of the institution, Sayyid Aḥmad Khān, with whom he disagreed over the benefits of the National Congress for the Muslim community.[55]

Sayyid ʿAbd al-Wāḥid al-Ṭūbī (d. 1927). Book publisher in Cairo. He was a member of a family of merchants, officers, and educators in Cairo. In the course of his career, he owned at least two publishing houses near the al-Azhar mosque, which was the center of the private printing industry in the city. The first, Matbaʿat al-Khairiyah, published canonical works of Islamic scholarship: the authoritative hadith compendium, *al-Ṣaḥīḥ*, (pub. 1886–87) by Bukhārī (810–70); *Anwār al-tanzīl wa asrār al-taʿwīl* (pub. 4 vols., 1893), a widely read commentary on the Quran and discourse on interpretation by Baiżāwī (fl. thirteenth century); *Sirāj al-mulūk* (pub. 1888–89), a work on Islamic statecraft and legislation by Abu Bakr Turtushi (d. 1126) with *Kitāb al-tihr al-masbūk fī naṣīḥat al-mulūk* by the theologian al-Ghazālī (d. 1111) in the margins; and *Tadrīb al-rawī* (pub. 1889–90), a key work on hadith terminology by al-Suyūṭī (d. 1505). The second, Matbaʿat (ʿAbd al-Wāḥid) al-Ṭūbī, also published classical and contemporary works of literature and texts in Islamic studies: *Kitāb al-mustaṭraf fī kull fann mustaẓraf* (pub. 1902), a famous anthology of Arabic literature that also deals with epistemology, ethics, and aesthetics by Muḥammad ibn Aḥmad Ibshīhī (fl. 1388–1446); marginal notes (pub. 1885) by the former shaikh of al-Azhar Ibrāhīm Bājurī (d. 1860) on the canonical hadith compendium *al-Shamā'il al-Muḥammadiyah* by Tirmiżī (d. 892); multiple printings of the widely read exegesis of the Quran, *Tafsīr al-Jalālain* (pub. 2 vols., 1910–11) by Jalāl al-Dīn Maḥallī (d. 1459) and Jalāl al-Dīn al-Suyūṭī (d. 1505); a collection of sermons by Muṣṭafā Burullusi (d. 1846–47); *Kitāb akhbār al-nisā* (Biographies of Women) (pub. 1901) by Ibn Qayyim (d. 1350); marginal notes (pub. 1882) on the grammar manual *Mughnī al-labīb* by Ibn Hishām (d. 1360); a ninety-two-page commentary (pub. 1900) by Nawawi Baten (1813–98) on *Bidāyat al-hidāyah* by the theologian and philosopher Abū Ḥamīd al-Ghazālī (1058–1111); and an exegesis of the Quran (pub. 4 vols., 1899) by Khazin al-Baghdādī (d. 1341) that also commented on a work of interpretation by the theologian al-Nasafī (d. 1310). Sayyid 'Abdul Wāḥid's brother (Ibrāhīm al-Ṭūbī) and nephew ('Abd al-Ḥamīd al-Ṭūbī) also worked in the publishing industry. In addition to publishing, 'Abd al-Wāḥid also seems to have compiled critical editions of works of Arabic literature. These include *Mukhtaṣar tażkirat al-Imām al-Suwaidī fī al-ṭibb* (The Brief Discourse by Imam Suwaidī on Medicine) (published 1866) and *Kitāb al-rasa'il* (letters) by Muḥammad ibn al-'Abbās al-Khwārizmī (d. 993–94) (published 1894).[56]

'Abd al-Bāsiṭ al-Unsī (d. 1928 or 1940[57]). Bookseller, journalist, and linguist. Born in Beirut, he was educated there and in Jerusalem. His father was closely tied to religious scholars and officials in Beirut, and through him 'Abd al-Bāsiṭ maintained close connections with both the local scholarly community and state officials. After completing his education, he taught Arabic, then, in 1890–91, he opened a bookshop, which is said to have sold works in Arabic, Turkish, French, English, and German and to have distributed books to sellers in Cairo, Baghdad, and India. The catalogue of the shop lists Arabic texts on a wide range of subjects, including religious studies, history, and literature.[58] In 1902, 'Abd al-Bāsiṭ established the Arabic journal *al-Iqbāl*, which is remembered for opposing the French and the English during the Ottoman and Mandate periods in Palestine and for advancing the careers of a number of influential Arabic journalists. In addition to selling books, al-Unsī also critically edited volumes of Arabic poetry, wrote a guidebook to the city of Beirut (*Dalīl Bayrūt*, 1909–10), a Turkish grammar in Arabic (*Durūs al-lisān al-'Usmānī*, 1913–14), and published a handful of textbooks for students, including primers on epistolary style in Arabic.[59] In addition to scholarly activities, he also participated in state organizations and deputations, including the Red Crescent and an endowments committee. After returning to India, Shiblī developed a plan to print rare works of Arabic literature in India and distribute them from Beirut and Cairo. The plan names al-Ṭūbi and al-Unsī as potential distributors, and it is possible that they corresponded about the project.[60]

Arminius Vambéry (1832–1913). Turcologist, Orientalist, and traveler. He lived for a time in Istanbul and wrote several autobiographical works, including travelogues, about his experiences in West and Central Asia. He also spent time in London, notably to give a series of lectures on Turkey in London at the Royal Geographical Society in the 1860s. He was eventually employed as an informant by the British government and maintained close ties with Turkey and the sulṭān. Though a Turcologist by training, Vámbéry also wrote in support of British colonialism in India, citing Indian Muslims as proof that "Asiaticism" could be reformed. He argued that British policies in India had brought peace and security and that the British were therefore justified in collecting large revenues from their colonized subjects. He also saw India as a reason for England to continue to support Turkey, which he deemed an important force in the resistance against Russia. He articulated these positions in *The Coming Struggle for India* (1885), which he based partly on a series of lectures given on a speaking tour in England. In 1889, he sent a letter to the Mahommedan Literary Society at Calcutta, which was published in 1889 as *Professor Vambery to Islam in Hind Greeting*. In the travelogue, Shiblī mentions an Urdu translation of Vambéry's lecture, "The Progress of Culture in Turkey," which Vambéry delivered at Exeter Hall in 1889. The lecture was translated into Urdu and published from Hyderabad in the same year.[61]

Robert Haldane West (1862–1906). Professor at the Syrian Protestant College. He earned his AM from Princeton in 1884 and worked for a time at the Allegheny Observatory in Pittsburgh. The Syrian Protestant College hired him to teach English, but he soon became instructor in mathematics and astronomy as well as director of the Lee Observatory. He was made professor in 1887, principal in 1899, and was eventually appointed as the dean of the school.[62]

'Alī Ẓabyān. Little is known about his early life. His grandfather, Muḥammad Ẓabyān (1789–1871) was a leading Qādirī Ṣufī who worked closely with Ottoman authorities to promote charitable works in Damascus. 'Alī Ẓabyān's father, Muḥammad Sharīf (d. 1927), who succeeded his father as the leader of the

Qādirī community in Damascus, wrote poetry and worked to promote the Ṣūfī practice of żikr (ritual recitation) in the city. Ẓabyān later worked as a qażī under the Ottomans and as a qāżī and lawyer under the government of King Faisal in Syria. He took part in a deputation to French delegates in Syria in 1936 and was still actively involved in learned societies of 'ulamā in Damascus in July 1951, when 'Abd al-Ḥasan 'Alī Ḥasan Nadwī (1914–99) (the son of one of Shiblī's colleagues at the Muslim reformist organization and madrasa Nadwat al-'Ulamā) met him there.[63]

Zakā'ullāh (1832–1910). Historian, mathematician, translator, and professor of Urdu, Arabic, and Persian. He was born in Delhi to a family of scholars who had worked as tutors at the Mughal court. He studied Arabic and Persian at home, then English at the British-administered Delhi College. In his youth, he befriended Samī'ullāh Khān (q.v.), whose biography he later wrote. He published a treatise on mathematics at a young age, which led to his being introduced to Sayyid Aḥmad Khān. Zakā'ullāh continued to write about mathematics, and also wrote works on history. Shiblī refers in the travelogue to Zakā'ullah's Urdu translation of Arminius Vámbéry's "The Cultural Progress of the Turks," titled *Lakchar: Turkī kī 'ām taraqqī o shā'istagī par*, which was published from Hyderabad in the journal *Ḥasan* in August 1889.[64]

Aḥmad Zakī (1857–1934). Arabic scholar, philologist, and Egyptian official. He studied in Cairo, then taught Arabic at the French Archaelogical Institute there and worked as a translator in the Egyptian government's board of supervisors (al-Majlis al-nuẓẓār). By the time Shiblī traveled to Egypt in 1892, Aḥmad Żakī had translated works on Andalusia, the pre-Islamic astral sciences, and a tract on slavery in Islam. By the time Shiblī arrived in Cairo, Zakī had already left on August 13, 1892 to attend the Ninth International Congress of Orientalists in London (September 5–12, 1892) as a delegate of the Egyptian government.[65] At the conference, Zakī translated the speeches and poems of another Egyptian scholar in attendance from Arabic into French. He also spoke about his own scholarship on a panel on Arabic language and pedagogy, which included the German Orientalist Karl Vollers (1857–1909) (then director of the Khedival Library in Cairo) and Colonel George Tindall Plunkett (1842–1922) (the author of several English-Arabic vocabulary books and Urdu-Hindi-Persian-Pashtu phrasebooks). Plunkett took advantage of the occasion to pass a resolution to petition the British Secretary for Foreign Affairs to improve instruction in modern Arabic in Egypt.[66] When Shiblī was in Cairo, Aḥmad Zakī was probably working on his Arabic translation of *L'Egypte et la Géographie: Sommaire Historique des Travaux Géographiques Éxecutés en Égypte sous la Dynastie de Mohammed Aly* (1889) (Egypt and Geography: Historical Summary of the Geographical Work Performed in Egypt under the Muhammad 'Ali Dynasty) by the Italian Orientalist Frédéric Bonola. Zakī's translation was published in 1892–93. This appears to be the source of Shiblī's notes on the history of the museums and the archaeological society in Cairo.[67]

Abū al-Żiyā (Ebüzziya Tevfik) (1848–1913). Publisher, journalist, Turkish writer, Ottoman official, and an associate of the prominent Turkish writer Nāmiq Kamāl. Early in his career, he and Kamāl ran a small printing press, which published their writings. He also contributed to Kamāl's magazine *'Ibrat*. In 1872, he assumed editorship of the journal *Ḥadīqah*, but was soon exiled to Rhodes. He worked in the publishing industry in Vienna for a time, and eventually returned to Turkey. In 1880, he obtained the right to publish his own magazine, *Majmū'ah-i Abū al-Żiyā*, in the Ottoman Empire, which he published from his private printing press, Maṭba'ah-i Abū al-Żiyā. He also published a popular series of short biographies modeled on a French series, and about one hundred volumes (some of which he wrote) of a universal library in Turkish modeled on a similar series in German. Eventually, Ottoman authorities demanded that Abū al-Żiyā submit all publications for censorship, and he closed the press. Arrest, exile, and revolution interrupted his attempts to revive his publishing career, though he did enjoy periods of intermittent success, particularly when he held the office of minister of education. As a printer and publisher, he is especially remembered for producing the first illustrated printed texts in Turkey and the first works printed in the Kufic script.[68]

APPENDIX 2

Letters

Letters to Sayyid Aḥmad Khān

When I girded my loins . . . [1]

My Qiblah,[2]
Salutations!

I have already written one letter from Bombay. I am writing this letter from Aden. Because of the motion of the ship and the spinning of my head, I am excused from writing in detail about my situation. I write this letter lying down. For two days I suffered terribly. I remained lying here, half dead. I am fine now. But because of the horrible smell and motion of the ship, my health never recovers. One is given extremely excellent food. The Italian dishes are extremely tasty. What should I write? I am not able to write.

Shiblī Nuʿmānī
Saturday, 8 May 1892[3]

My Sayyid,

Greetings. I arrived here on 22 May, but owing to various concerns, I could not find time to write. This letter, too, is brief and private. If you select a few things to print, then it is possible. For the time being, I have taken a small room at the rate of eleven rupees per month, but the cost of food here is very high.

The most crucial thing is that you send two or three hundred rupees, or even more, so that whatever book comes to hand at whatever time be bought, or arrangements for copying and a copyist be made. The books here are many and rare, but to what extent can copies of them be made? Imām Ghazālī's writings are found here, and one can find perhaps all the writings of Bū ʿAlī Sīnā. Imām Ghazālī's letters, too, are extant. Whatever is possible will be done.

Meetings can happen with most people here, but the difficulty is that of language. I have seen several large colleges, but because of unfamiliarity with the language, it is extremely difficult to find out information about them. I have begun to study Turkish, and God willing, I shall learn enough to get by in it by the time I return. At that time, I shall be able to prepare a report of all the colleges and so on.

The circumstances are interesting, and much material will be acquired for a travelogue, but at this time, rather, for the duration of my stay, I will find absolutely no time. I have to travel three or four miles back and forth each day. It is a very large city and all the libraries and so on are located far away.

The easy way to send money is to request a note from the Cook Company and send it registered to my place. I, too, have brought along Cook notes, and they can be used effortlessly in the Cook office.

ʻAinī's commentary on Bukhārī is being printed here these days.[4] Nine volumes have already been printed. It is a very large book. The Ḥanafīs were looking for it. If it is useful to any strict Ḥanafī, then they can order it.

The scholars in Beirut have prepared and begun to publish a collection of the poems of all the Christians of Arabia, whether they are of the Jāhiliyah [pre-Islamic] period or Islamic. One volume has already been printed. It contains the *Dīwān* [collected poems] of Akhṭal, but that has been printed in three volumes. It could not be found anywhere until today. It was even being looked for in Europe.

There are no books by Muʻtazilah here, either.

Whatever you write of the state of affairs will bring great comfort to me. I have left the boys entrusted to your excellency. Please urge Ḥamīd to look after himself.[5]

This letter should be sent to my father (qiblah). Or a copy of it. I do not have time to write numerous letters. I have composed a qaṣīdah about the circumstances of the journey. It is included with the letter. If it were printed at the Mufīd-e ʻĀm press and published with the *Aligarh Gazette*, it would be appropriate. Please send a few copies of it to my father (qiblah).

I have ordered that the newspaper of this place, *Akhtar*,[6] which is in Persian, and whose publication is two thousand, be sent in your name. The cost of six months is six rupees. Please send this with the other rupees. It is possible for the information about our college to be published regularly in this newspaper, and it will certainly yield some benefit or another. Most people here are not familiar with so much as the name of Hindustan. Otherwise, if all the circumstances and necessities of Muslims were known, then certainly it would not be difficult for the college to receive assistance. The benefit of the endowments of this place reaches thousands of miles away.

Shiblī Nuʿmānī
25 May 1892
Constantinople.
Location: Takhtah Khān.
Near Khān Maḥmūd Pāshā.

My Sayyid and Maulā,

This is the third letter that I am writing from Istanbul. You and the elders of the homeland should not wait for my letters. That is, in case of silence, you should infer, rather, you should be certain, that I am well. That leaves the circumstances of the journey. I have already written about this, so I shall not write anything here.

I did not get manuscripts here. They can sometimes be gotten in Egypt. For this reason, only printed books can be purchased, but their number is numerous. All the books and treatises of Imām Ghazālī are found here. There is also a copy of his letters. You won't find so many writings by Bū ʿAlī Sīnā anywhere else. Original translations of books by Aristotle, and so on, in extremely old hand, are found, but what is the point? The rate of copying them is in no case less than four rupees per part. The books of the Muʿtazilah are completely nonexistent. The exegesis by ʿAbd al-Qādir Jurjānī exists, but there is nothing new in it.

The day before yesterday, I met ʿUs̱mān Pāshā. He received me extremely kindly. He can understand Arabic, and can make some ordinary conversation. I tried to kiss his hand, but he did not agree to it. Rather, he tried to imitate me in response.[7] As I was leaving, he said, "Please come whenever you wish. I would be happy to meet." One can even meet all the other, very big and important pāshās, too, but, first, there is the foreignness of the language, and, second, I have no interest in meeting anyone else.

The typeset here is excellent. It has no equal in the entire world. It should definitely be purchased for the *Aligarh Gazette* or for an independent press. Such fineness and subtlety is not found even in the letters of Beirut and Holland.

Alas, the scale of Arabic education here is very small, and there is not the slightest reflection of Europe in the classical method of education. Modern education exists with breadth, but the limits of both have been kept apart, and until both boundary lines are brought together, there can be no fundamental progress. The same shortcoming exists in our country, too, which is lamentable.

I saw the college results in *Akmal al-akhbār*[8] and was infinitely pleased. Rather, the truth is that I sat down to write the letter in this state. Otherwise, why should I write ordinary matters every day?

Send as many rupees as you plan to send for books immediately. After I leave from here, I will not be able to receive letters, and so on, or anything else. You know the things that are famous here. If you seek anything, please do write to me so that I can bring it for you. I want to purchase for the college some excellent books in Turkish from which an estimation of the scientific progress here can be made.

This letter should be sent to my father (qiblah). Insist that Ḥamīd write me a detailed letter, and also write the examination results of my dear ones [students].

When my writings are ready, I need a few copies here. But I will not receive them if they there is a delay. I will stay here until 15 August, God willing.

Yes, today I met Ḥusain Ḥasīb Āfandī, who was the consul in Bombay and is now police general here. He treated me infinitely kindly. He showed me all the rooms of his home. He invited me to dine with him. He bestowed a great many other kindnesses upon me. He speaks Urdu well. Please immediately send a copy of *Sīrat al-Nuʿmān,*[9] which I have seen there and on which the college seal has not been stamped. I will certainly present it to him as a gift. He is a man of just this taste.

Wal-salām
Shiblī
Constantinople
15 June 1892
Bāb-e ʿĀlī
Idārah-i Akhtar

Our Sayyid and Maulānā,

Ilqā bi-kum Allāh. Your last letter, along with *Sīrat al-Nuʿmān* and the *Aligarh* newsletters, arrived. I had been extremely distraught and broken hearted that letters did not come. In exactly this state, your exalted letter, you might say, did the work of the Messiah. I did not receive the letter sent to the Cook Company address. The mail here has a strange arrangement. The office of English mail is separate. The letters that come from Hindustan, and so on, go to this office, and they are not distributed from there. Rather, the addressee must go and retrieve them himself.

Before the arrival of your exalted letter, I had purchased three or four books. It's a good thing that I did not buy too many. You sent the rupees needlessly. There was a loss in the exchange, and so on, and the existing amount was sufficient for me. Had there been a need, I would have made the request myself. In the previous letter, I had enclosed the *Qaṣīdah-i safariyah* in its entirety, and had expressed my desire that it be printed in the newspaper, but I find no sign of it anywhere. Perhaps it did not arrive. Or it did not please my good sir.

The excellence of the climate in Constantinople is so fitting that a person should certainly dedicate a part of his lifetime to it. If I had been able to restrain myself, I could have profited from the excellence of the weather and returned well fit and fresh, but the flavorful fruits, which, along with their flavor, are also extremely inexpensive—cursed things!—in no way allow a person like me to stay within the boundaries of moderation. I saw this city well, and for this reason, despite the fineness of the climate, my heart does not desire to stay here any longer. Several tasks remain. If they are completed, then I shall depart by 15 August, God willing. Where shall I go? This is not absolutely certain yet.

I have now changed to another place, which is extremely attractive and well-appointed with furniture and so on. There are numerous rooms in it, and the rate of my room in particular is fifteen rupees. But it is not an extensive room. It is even smaller than my bungalow; rather, very small.[10]

I saw all the colleges, courts, sights, and scientific workplaces here, and I may be able to sit in peace and write a reasonable report related to them, but not now. Rather, even after I arrive there, I may not be able to write in detail. Praise be to God that Arnold changed his philosophy and got married. When he comes, he will probably bring the lady with him. I regard his esteemed wife as nearly equal to mothers and sisters.

I am very pleased by the progress of the college. Your request and the rivalrous debate between Mr. Horst[11] and the principal[12] gave me extreme pleasure. May God keep your exalted being safe and sound. After you (may God not bring that day for a long time), who will show these ways to the community?

I know that my loved ones forgot me, but the incidental mention of my beloved Khwushī Muḥammad Nāẓir[13] left a tender effect in my heart. Please be sure to call for him and express love and indebtedness on my behalf.

Yes, I am ashamed, severely ashamed, that I did not ask the state of my beloved and sincere friend Maulawī Sayyid Mumtāz 'Alī[14] in any of my writings.

Truly, there cannot be any greater faithlessness and dereliction of duty than this. Please do inform me of his well-being, health, and present activities. If I find a suitable book in Egypt, I shall bring it with me, God willing, to give to him as an offering, and this will be the penance for my sin.

I wrote two letters to my father (qiblah), but no writing came from there. I am worried. You, too, have not mentioned him. I hope to God that all is well. After writing this much, I received a letter from my father (qiblah) from which I learned all the important information and was also informed of the publication of the qaṣīdah.

I read in *Akmal al-akhbār* that Zain al-ʿĀbidīn was made a Khān Bahādur.[15] Although there were no further details in the newspaper, I have come to be certain that our own Maulawī Zain al-ʿĀbidīn Khān is meant. If this is so (and certainly it is so), then please give him a long and lengthy congrats on my behalf. I have not (God forbid!) forgotten him.

I learned from the letter from my father (qiblah) that he sent some rupees through you. Please send this letter of mine to him. I have no need of rupees at this time. He should not trouble himself. I never did anything to serve him. At the very least I should not cause him any trouble.

From now on, please do not send anything in my name to Constantinople. Rather, with the arrival of this letter, dispatch letters, newspapers, and so on, to the address of the Cook Company office in Cairo. Please be sure to send some copies of the qaṣīdah and pages of the *Aligarh Gazette*. I had begun to write a *maśnawī*, which remained incomplete. It came to seventy or seventy-two couplets, then my mind stopped. I copy several couplets. They should surely be printed:

Qāṣid-i farkhundah

. . . .

goshah-i tanhā'ī[16]

You will be pleased to hear the news that a *tamghah-i majīdī* of the fourth degree was bestowed upon me by the court of His Highness the Sulṭān. Now my hope is that, after I return, you will surely have the title of *Shams al-ʿulamā* given to me.[17] Otherwise, pardon my impertinence, the idiom *charāgh tale andherā* will truly apply.[18]

God willing, I shall depart for Jerusalem in a few days. Please send letters in my name to the Cook Company office in Cairo. By the time I arrive in Egypt, the response to this letter will have already arrived and be there waiting for me. If in this letter some of the text differs or varies more or less from other text, it is because this letter was written now and then over the course of five or six days. Thus, because of the change in some events, this difference was unavoidable. Regards.

Shiblī Nuʿmānī
5 Muḥarram al-Ḥarām 1310H
[29 July 1892][19]

Letters to Shaikh Ḥabībullāh[20]

My Qiblah. Salutations.

I am, by his grace, well. I have now shifted to another place, which is extremely attractive and includes all the necessities. The rent was higher, but there was no other choice. The details of this place cannot be contained in a letter. Thus, I shall set them aside. Alas, no language but Turkish is in use here. Trouble arises in everything, and meeting major figures is completely meaningless. They cannot understand me; nor I them.

The books here are rare and wonderful, but I can obtain nothing apart from unfulfilled desire. I can neither copy them, nor is my memory sufficient for them. I go on foot three miles each day because the libraries are located far away. This walk is very beneficial for my health. I have just begun to study Turkish. Let us see if I can complete it or not. There are a few Hindustanis here, too, and they are employed in state offices. But their salaries are meager. Salaries here are generally meager. Because I do not plan to reside here very long, you should not delay in sending letters. Otherwise, they will not be able to reach me. A letter arrives in twenty to twenty-two days.

Please tell Uncle [mother's brother] that ʿAinī's[21] commentary on Bukhārī, is being printed here these days. Nine volumes are already printed. It is being printed extremely excellently. I think that there is some research in it that is not found in *Fatḥ al-bārī*.[22] The cost is not fixed yet. There is a 150-lakh shared company that has established a magnificent printing house. This book is being printed in it. All the work in the printing house is done by means of the society and machines.

One thing about the colleges here has pleased me very much. Each college has a particular dress, and the name of each college is written on the coat near the collar. I was extremely pleased by this. Why not adopt this method in our college? It would be good if my Sayyid [lord] and qiblah fixed a special dress for the college without delay.

The Great Sulṭān visits the Masjid-i Ḥamīdiyah each Friday, and it is an extremely excellent scene. They say that there is a wondrous atmosphere on the day of Eid. I hope to God that I am able to see it. I do not want to stay here longer than two or three months. After that, God willing, I will tour Tripoli and Damascus, then go to Cairo and stay there for a few days.

Although my hopes with respect to the progress and power of Muslims have been completely dashed because the state of affairs here is not any better than there, still, the journey was no doubt necessary. The impression that was left on my heart by this journey could not have occurred by studying a thousand books. I learned that until a person sees the major parts of the world, he cannot truly be human. I feel sorry for those people whose entire life is spent in a single, small four-walled space.

You should send letters in my name to this address: Constantinople. Bāb-i ʿĀlī. Idārah-i Akhtar. But both English and Arabic should be on the envelope. Please give my salaam to all my loved and dear ones. I do not know if miyān Muḥammad Isḥāq's[23] name has been filed among the munṣif[24] candidates or not. Please be sure that the details of the college examination results are in your letter of response. Please send this letter, or a copy of it, to Sayyid ṣāḥib (qiblah). I humbly request that the aforementioned gentleman issue the *Aligarh Gazette* in my name. Wal-salām.

Constantinople.
Jādah-i Bāb-i ʿĀlī. Care of Idārah-i Akhtar.
5 June 1892
Shiblī Nuʿmānī[25]

My Qiblah,

I have already dispatched a letter in your eminent service. I have written a letter to Sayyid ṣāḥib in today's mail. You will receive it, too.

I was delighted to meet Ḥusain Āfandī, who was previously consul of Bombay and is now an officer in the police department here. His virtuous character left a heavy burden on me, and I wish to lighten the load from my shoulders to some degree. Thus, I request that you arrange to ship wares from Niẓāmābād with extreme propriety and extreme effort, painstakingness, and scrutiny. Please send a mindful person to Niẓāmābād who will have them built to specifications by means of a distinguished person. Indian wares are available on the streets here, but not good ones. If this is not possible, then a piece of *chikan* cloth from Lucknow, but extremely excellent; there should be individual flower-pattern stitches. It should be extremely fine and delicate work, and it should not cost less than thirty rupees. If it is purchased by means of Khwājah 'Azīz al-Dīn, then it will probably be good.[26] I shall remain here until the end of August. It must arrive by then. If this, too, is not possible, then a ware from Murādābād. But it should be extremely excellent. In sum, be sure to send some rare thing.

Regards,
Constantinople
Idārah-e Ma'ārif[27]
Bab-e 'Ālī
15 June 1892
Shiblī[28]

My Qiblah,

Today I dreamed a wondrous, enchanting dream. Wondrous because it was midday and my eyes were fully awake, and the feeling of enchantment was such that although I have been awake for some time, the scene continues to play out before my eyes. Listen to the detailed account. Today was Friday, and, in accordance with custom, it was the time for the show of the sulṭān's forces. I, too, went, a full embodiment of desire. I entered the Ḥamīdiyah Congregational Mosque. The Great Sulṭān came in great magnificence and glory, but I could not see anything because this only falls to the lot of people who are already present on the sulṭān thoroughfare, and who cannot move from their place until prayers have ended.

At a short distance from the sulṭān's palace is an extremely ornate congregational masjid, which is famously known by the name of the sulṭān, Ḥamīdiyah. On this thoroughfare there is a building, and esteemed travelers and officers visiting from faraway countries who wish to view the royal forces obtain permission by means of some esteemed person and watch this spectacle seated on the roof of the building. There is no other way apart from this because, at the time of the mounted carriage, the army forms a circle stretching out in all directions, and no one can enter it. Ḥusain Ḥasīb Āfandī, former consul of Bombay, had promised to have permission given to me, but, as it happened, he came late. The time of the carriage and entourage had come near on that side, and calls of "*Tarriqū*" [Make way!] and "*Dūr bāsh*" [Move aside!] began to be raised. With no choice, I entered the mosque and sat in the front row. The sulṭān's coach comes up to the stairs, and, stepping down from the carriage, he immediately moves into the upper part of the mosque, where no one can go except for those extremely close to him and special people. There is a *maqṣūrah*[29] there whose door is to the right of the minbar. This is the place for the sulṭān's prayers. When the sulṭān arrives, satin curtains are lowered, and no one can see him. When the preacher raised his eyes towards the sulṭān's maqṣūrah and said with great passion, "*Allāhuma unṣur maulānā al-sulṭān al-sulṭān al-ghāzī 'Abd al-Ḥamīd Khān*,"[30] tears spontaneously began to flow from my eyes and for a while the state of my heart was such that it continued to overflow. First the preacher read the names of the companions, and when the name of the sulṭān came, he stepped down by one so that it would be clear that although the sulṭān is the shadow of Allah today, his rank does not have any comparison to Hažrat-i Ṣiddīq and Hažrat 'Umar,[31] *ražīullāh 'anhumā*.[32] After prayers, Ḥusain Ḥasīb Āfandī happened to see me and took me into the courtyard of the masjid where pāshās and head army officers stand in a circle, and told the people, "Let no one obstruct him." The sulṭān came out of the maqṣūrah and sat behind the curtain near the stairs, and the armies began passing by. For a full two hours, a strange and wondrous spectacle continued to appear. It was an army of nearly ten thousand. There were different regiments, and each regiment had different equipment and weaponry. What can I say? The brave statue-like figures of Turkish youths, shining weapons, the measured and ordered pace, the rising and falling of the horses, the gold-embroidered dress of the pāshās, shining medals—it was a strange and wondrous atmosphere that cannot be described in any way. In the end, both princes came. The age of the elder son is nine or ten years, but the majesty and glory with which he rode his horse—great, brave men cannot have such style. When the armies had passed, the sulṭān sat in his carriage and passed in front of us. When the carriage procession came opposite, the entire circle bowed near a full bow and made salaam. The sulṭān responded with both hands. Most of the esteemed people from Europe come to watch this spectacle. Although it was an ordinary thing and it happens every Friday, they say that on the day of Eid there is an atmosphere like that of the day of resurrection. May God show me that day, too.

19 June 1892
Shiblī Nu'mānī
Constantinople[33]

Letter to Sayyid Mumtāz ʿAlī

Good sir! Salutations!

I arrived here yesterday. I received your exalted letter in Egypt on the evening before the morning I departed from Egypt for Hindustan. I could not do anything about the Arabic dictionary, though I did bring a copy of *Mukhtār al-siḥāḥ*.[34]

As for your questions regarding women, I hope to earn one hundred out of one hundred on the examination. Whenever you wish, send the examination papers.[35]

An esteemed member[36] of the delegation that went from Egypt to the Oriental Conference, which previously was organized in Stockholm located in Europe, presented a tract related to women at the conference. Although with respect to its contents and subjects, it is not too valuable, the text and writing is completely like that of the classical writers. In any case, I have brought a copy of it, too, for your exaltedness. I will dispatch both books into your service in a few days.

Connection in Turkey. Perhaps you have no need of it now, and doubtless there is no need. Still, if you want to converse about it, I can certainly do so. But the result is that this idea is without benefit.

Well, I wrote all this regarding you. Now hear my motives, too. You have become an employee. By God I felt unlimited happiness. I prayed for this from my heart. But tell me this. Will you remain of use to us or not? That is, does one have a break from government work or not? If not, and you, like others, have become merely a scrap of paper in government offices, then I am not so happy.

I am playing with the idea of a shared series of writings in which you were to play a purposive part, but I do not know if this can be expected or not given your situation. Please write your response, and write soon.

Regards,
Traveler of Egypt and Turkey[37]

APPENDIX 3

Contemporary Reviews of the Travelogue

Āzād, Kanpur. 17 August 1894

Turkey, Egypt, and Syria: A Travelogue

> O confidant, tell for the sake of a grieving heart
> The story of that night which was spent with the beloved!

Dear Editor,

"*Safar dar watan*"[1] is a well-known issue in the subject of Sufism. Of course, this is manifest to the esoterics, but we who see the exoteric are deficient in comprehending its meaning, and, after all, how can we understand that we are both restfully stretched out on our bed and also touring Constantinople? But thanks to the [31] abundance of favor of our lord 'Allāmah Shiblī, we, too, have witnessed this phenomenon and, without setting one foot outside our home, have seen the heart-captivating qualities of Constantinople, Jerusalem, Beirut, and Cairo, and so on. If you read the aforementioned learned scholar's travelogue, this state will be manifest to you, too. Ceremony aside, the travelogue, the desire for which had cast hearts into longing and engrossed them in yearning, has now been printed and published. And with regard to the conditions of Egypt, it would be entirely right and appropriate to say that a dear one of the Egypt of Meaning has come to be sold in the market.[2] 'Allāmah Shiblī's principle aim in this ambitious undertaking was to discover the educational state of affairs in Turkey, Syria, and Egypt, and to tour the rare libraries of the Asian sciences. He fulfilled his praiseworthy aim with extreme diligence and discernment, and has included in this travelogue with breadth and exposition whatever he saw. He has given an extremely reliable and documented account of the conditions of madrasas of different subjects, including yearly expenses, education, the number of students, the arrangement of the boarding house, and method of training—all these matters. Information about old libraries, and information about their valuable books, too, is discussed in detail. Along with that, discussion has also been made of the interesting sights and civilization of each city. Nearly seventy-seven headings are listed in the index of the travelogue. I assure my distinguished readers that upon reading each heading, the heart desires nothing but that this one should be read first. Here are a few as examples: "Constantinople's Present Condition and Civilization"; "The State of Education"; "Military College"; "The Intellectual-Scientific Condition of the Turks"; "Libraries"; "Sights"; "The Sulṭān Coming to Friday Prayers and the Inspection of the Armies"; "The Manners, Habits, and Style of Society of the Turks"; "The Education, Training, and Fashion of Women"; "Dress"; "Meeting Ghāzī 'Uṡmān Pāshā"; "A Copy of the Royal Medal and Decree"; "Beirut"; "Jerusalem"; "Cairo"; and so on.

The virtue that is particular to this travelogue is that these Islamic regions have been seen from a perspective that is suited to the situation. In this age, there are many travelers and many who write about the circumstances of travel, but they view Constantinople and Cairo with the same interest and eye that is the demand of the age. Thus, they derive conclusions from visiting the cities according to their own taste. [32] They remain utterly unaware of the impression that every single mote of those regions leaves on a Muslim heart. Our renowned traveler viewed those regions through the eyes of a discerning, scholarly Muslim, and has provided unending material of interest to Muslims in his travelogue. The second special quality of this travelogue is that the classical Islamic history of those Islamic cities is itself included throughout in accordance with the accounts of reliable Muslim historians. And who can do this task better than the laudable learned scholar? Having read this travelogue, you can discover that the places that are thought to be infinitely important in the political world, and upon which every single glorious sultanate looks with eyes of envy, have remained and did remain for centuries trodden beneath the feet of the courageous ones of Islam. This has been very finely printed on 235 pages of excellent paper and can be obtained from 'Allāmah Shiblī ṣāḥib for one rupee, five annas at the address of the Aligarh Muhammadan College.

Ḥabīb al-Raḥmān Shirwānī[3]

Aligarh Institute Gazette Vol. XXIX No. 61, pages 762–63
Tuesday, July 31st 1894

Turkey, Egypt, and Syria: A Travelogue
compiled by Maulānā Shiblī Nuʿmānī

Having set our eyes on the travelogue that Shams al-ʿUlamā Maulānā Shiblī Nuʿmānī, professor of Arabic, MAO College Aligarh and fellow of Allahabad University, recently published after visiting Turkey and Egypt in 1892, we aim to show what is in it and for whom what is in it is material of interest.

The lauded professor, having written the details of his arrival in Aden from Bombay and in Smyrna from Aden, has recorded a summary of the events that occurred during the voyage in the form of a qaṣīdah, which has already been published in newspapers before the travelogue. After that, having arrived at Constantinople, he has given a brief account of the classical and modern history of that place. Then he has begun to describe in an extremely interesting fashion the intellectual-scientific and practical progresses that have become manifest in the auspicious age of the sultanate of Sulṭān ʿAbd al-Ḥamīd II. In this way, he has described with soundness and breadth the moral conditions of students and professors, the administration of boarding houses, and educational programs of large schools and colleges connected with agriculture, maritime navigation, engineering, industry and manufacturing, law, civil administration, and the military.

Then he has begun to show us the form of the rich literary sciences of the Turkish language, in which he has written with extreme excellence an account of the intellectual writings of the Turks and their newspapers, journals, libraries, and printing houses. After that, he has given a description of the heart-enchanting and pleasant conditions of the capital city's magnificent masjids, charitable travelers' lodges, places of interest, and well-known locations worthy of seeing. After that, the writer's powerful pen, having drawn an image of the painful and edifying Muḥarram of Constantinople, has shown a magnificent scene of the Salāmlaq [the Sulṭān's Friday procession] and the Sulṭān's Eid procession, from which every Muslim in whose chest there is a heart and in whose heart there is aching, cannot help but burst into tears, affected by the glory and grandeur of this latest age of his community. At the end of this description, the praiseworthy *maulānā* has added a maśnawī of his own, too, in which he has drawn an impression of this magnificent scene in effective words. The reality is that the pleasure of prose is doubled by this poem. Then the manners and habits of the Turks, the style of their civilization, and Turkish women's education and training, their fashion, their dress, their modesty and virtue, and their domestic behavior is mentioned.

Having left Constantinople, he has penned the state of Beirut's colleges, societies, newspapers, and publishing houses, and has shown that the intellectual progress of Beirut is completely in the hands of Christians, which is enviable and a whip of edification for our community.

From Beirut, traveling to Jerusalem and the shore of the sea of Syria, the maulānā enters Egypt and gives information in breadth and detail with regard to the education in schools and colleges of all kinds there, their expenses, and the famous classical university Azhar. He has written an extremely excellent memorandum on Egypt's official libraries, printing presses, newspapers, ancient monuments, burial sites, clubs, societies, and theaters. Then, having described the pomp and glory with which celebration is made on the birthday of the Prophet in Egypt, he has briefly mentioned the writers and people of achievement there. At the end of the journey, he has expressed gratitude for the manners of the people of Arabia, whose sympathy has been a cause of attachment and friendship in the difficulties of the journey. At the end of the book, he has added a valuable note on the modern Arabic language, and, along with it, a lexicon in which he has written words of the current language and their meanings.

These are the gifts that our lord Maulānā Shiblī has brought for the people of our homeland from Turkey and Egypt. All the people of Islam who hold communal affection and religious sympathy for Turkey and the Sulṭān of Turkey, who are delighted by their progress and saddened by their decline, who turn the pages of hundreds of newspapers and books to read their true conditions, who fall silent upon seeing the one-sided picture of decline of Turkey in the writings of fair-minded English authors—for all these people, this satisfying book is an excellent means of familiarity. Thus, all together, this book is brimming with interesting information and pleasure-filled events.

It is unnecessary to write anything about the writing style of this book because all who have seen maulānā's previous writings will certainly be able to judge for themselves after seeing the book that the beauty of his description has day by day become more polished and approached its apogee, and will continue approaching it.

Writer
Waḥīd al-Dịn Salīm Pānīpatī[4]

Turkey, Egypt, and Syria: A Travelogue

When this travelogue first comes to hand, the heart is delighted to see the fineness of the paper and the elegance of the script and printing. Then, upon reading the following text on the title page, "*Turkey, Egypt, and Syria: A Travelogue*, in which, in addition to the minute, interesting incidents that have arisen in the course of the narrative, the following circumstances related to Constantinople, Beirut, Jerusalem, Cairo, and so on, have been written in detail, that is: summary circumstances of the city; sights worth visiting; famous buildings; the administration of the Department of Education; academies and madrasas; boarding houses and students; women's education; writers and their writings; libraries; newspapers and journals; encounters with famous pāshās and people of achievement; and the character and habits of the Turks and Arabs. In the end, there is a very brief lexicon of the newly fashioned terms that have come into use in Egypt and Syria today and, without knowing which, people cannot take advantage of Arabic newspapers," the heart is struck by the idea that this travelogue is a treasury of intelligence and knowledge. Then one reads on the title page that "the cost is one rupee, five annas," from which it appears that buyers are quite fortunate that they can get their hands on this treasury of intelligence and knowledge so inexpensively that they can pay the cost to the author himself and acquire the book. It is indeed the good fortune of the country that at a time when such poisonous knowledge and literature is being sold inexpensively in it, this antidote should be sold cheaper than that poison. Now if one sets aside the first page and looks at the entire book, then all the subjects and headings, which have been briefly described above, can be studied in detail. These subjects and headings are different and require different capacities to describe. From the way in which the author has described all of them, it is clear that his mind is a collection of a great many talents. He has written each subject in accordance with principles. The description is extremely interesting and effective. With respect to the text and writing, it is a book of Urdu literature of the highest order. There are generally different reasons for travel. Business, seeking livelihood, enjoyment, preservation of one's health, meeting dear ones and relatives, intelligence-gathering [*jāsūsī*], acquiring education and training, and many others. Of all these reasons, the best reason is that some good-natured lord of virtue and achievement travels to a foreign country with an eye to add to his experience, observations, knowledge, and intelligence with an aim to return to his homeland and add to the intelligence and knowledge of his community. The progress of a community is possible only insofar as such virtuous people are in abundance in it who reform their intellect, knowledge, and character purely in order to develop the intellect, knowledge, and character of others. The reasons for this journey by the maulawī ṣāḥib that I learned from this travelogue are so virtuous that if their equal is not absent in the history of Islam, then it is certainly rarely found. The reasons are as follows.

First, maulawī ṣāḥib is writing the Heroes of Islam series. Thus, two of the books, *al-Māmūn* and *Sīrat al-Nuʿmān*, have already been printed and published several times, and the remaining books are being written. In order to complete this writing, the thought occurred to him to travel to the Islamic regions of Turkey, Egypt, and Syria and visit the libraries of the royal academies and schools, collect materials for this writing of his from them, and select the books that are entirely unavailable in this region [India]. Thus, he did not leave any renowned library in Turkey, Egypt, and Syria through which he did not sift thoroughly. From the reviews that he has written about them, one learns what intellectual treasures our forebears have left behind in books. But alas, worms make more use of them than we do! As far as I am concerned, this journey that the maulawī has made in order to complete the writing of the Heroes of Islam is such a virtuous undertaking that it gives him the right to the Heroes of Islam title, and I am certain that the closing verse in the Heroes of Islam series will be *Sīrat al-Shiblī al-Nuʿmānī* [Biography of Shiblī Nuʿmānī].

Everyone who performed service became the served.

Secondly, the maulawī has acquired mastery in the French language. The amount of information about Muslims that has been written in this language has not been written in any other European language. By studying books in this language and the English books that are translated into our language, the maulawī has learned that, in European literature, descriptions of the flaws of Islamic governments and Islamic societies are taking place in an extremely wise and clever way, sometimes in religious guise, sometimes in the guise of history, stories, and drama. There is always great talk of it in newspapers and journals. Even capable European writers become of one eye and paint a one-sided portrait of the conditions of Muslims. That is, they close one eye in seeing virtues and they open the other eye in seeing vices, and in painting the picture they toss away the side of virtues. All Muslims in general, but especially the Turks, are a writing pad for the people of Europe. This European literature had a very bad effect on English-educated students. He considers it his duty to remove this also. Thus, he has written *al-Jiziyah* and *Kutub-khānah-i Iskandariyah* for this purpose.[5] But writings of this kind cannot have breadth until he himself observes the state of the Muslims in their own sultanate with his own eyes. Thus, he has mentioned these objections in many places in his travelogue and has made a sufficient response to them. Muslim students will gain much benefit by reading them.

Third, the Muslims of India do not know anything about the present state of their community. Where do they rule? What is their moral and civilizational state? What kind of administrative system does it have? For this reason, the maulawī ṣāḥib has sought to go there, see the state of affairs for himself, and on the basis of this, apprise the community. Thus, he has described these things with such sound and true virtue that even if some intelligent scholar went and saw them, no more information about the state of affairs would be known than from his account.

Fourth, the maulawī is Arabic professor at the Madrasat al-ʻUlūm, Aligarh. A very important goal of this college is that we produce in all the students of our college as many religious and worldly virtues as exist. The maulawī has also made the journey with an eye to examine the schools in the Islamic regions and tell which virtues there are in them that can be beneficially implemented in this college, too. Thus, more than anything else, he has paid attention to the education department, academies and schools, boarding houses, the training of students, and women's education, and has selected a few things among them for our college.

In brief, Maulawī Shiblī is that profound scholar upon whom the Sultanate of Turkey shone favor with its *tamghah-i majīdiyah* purely by reason of his intellectual ability, by means of which the coin of his knowledge has been minted throughout the Islamic regions. Here in Hindustan, the high government has bestowed upon him the title *shams al-ʻulamā*, from which he has obtained the honor of being seated in the durbar of the Qaisar-i Hind [Queen Victoria] after authorized rājās and nawābs. Thus, the Muslim who has any intellectual taste at all is quite unfortunate if he does not purchase such a travelogue by such an intellectual by sending the extremely inexpensive price of one rupee five annas to the author and does not become informed of the circumstances of his community at present by reading it.[6]

Zakāullāh

APPENDIX 4

Newspaper Reports

Aligarh Institute Gazette Vol. XXVII No. 32, page 438
Tuesday, April 19 1892

Maulawī Shiblī Nuʿmānī
Professor of Arabic and Persian, Madrasat al-ʿUlūm, Aligarh

Friends of Maulawī Shiblī will be surprised to hear the news that he suddenly took leave from the college and will soon depart for Constantinople.

For several years, his intention has been to go to Constantinople and Egypt to see the libraries of those places and meet the scholars of those places. In recent days, Mr. Arnold, professor at the Madrasat al-ʿUlūm, has taken six months' leave to go to Europe. This also ignited Maulawī Shiblī's desire, and he thought that he had found good company as far as Port Said. Thus, he, too, suddenly took leave and made plans to go along.

Our hope is that he will also see the colleges and boarding houses of Constantinople and Egypt, and will compose a report on them that will provide good insight for our college, too; also, that during this journey of his, several beneficial books will be purchased for the library of our college. We pray to God that he goes safe and sound and that he returns safe and sound. This journey of his will be beneficial to him, to our college, and to our communal education.

Aligarh Institute Gazette Vol. XXVII No. 38, page 486
Tuesday, May 3 1892

Maulawī Muḥammad Shiblī Nuʿmānī
Professor at the Madrasat al-ʿUlūm, Aligarh
On April 30, Saturday, twelve o'clock, our professor Maulānā Muḥammad Shiblī, along with Mr. Arnold, professor, boarded the ship. He will go straight to Italy and from there to Constantinople. He has sent this couplet in his letter:

Dar nawishtam cho rah-i koh o biyābān Shiblī
Hāliyā rah-sipar-i jādah-i daryā bāsham[1]

Aligarh Institute Gazette Vol. XXVII No. 38, page 497
Tuesday, May 3 1892

College News and Notes

Professor Maulawī Shiblī ṣāḥib and Professor T. W. Arnold departed from Bombay on 29 April. That is, Maulawī Muḥammad Shiblī ṣāḥib will go to Constantinople—his plan is to stay for six months—and Mr. Arnold, on leave for the same period of time, left for Europe. Both professors will travel together for some distance.

Aligarh Institute Gazette Vol. XXVII No. 37, page 510
Saturday, May 7 1892

Storm in the Arabian Sea

It has been learned by the newspaper that it was learned from the ships that have arrived in Bombay that the weather in the Arabian Sea is severe, meaning a strong and stormy wind is blowing. The ship *Saint Florence* was blown 150 miles off course by the force of the wind. On one of the stranded ships, a Hindustani traveler fell with such force from the shock of a gust of wind that he died as soon as he fell.

On 4 May, the special correspondent sent a special wire to the editor of the *Aligarh Institute Gazette* from Bombay that the Indian traveler who fell and died on the ship was coming from Aden.

We have made a request of a special correspondent by means of electronic wire that, when Mr. Arnold and Maulawī Shiblī arrive in Aden, he inform us of their safe arrival in Aden by means of electronic wire.

Aligarh Institute Gazette Vol. XXVII No. 41, page 558
Saturday May 21 1892

Letter from Professor Maulawī Muhammad Shiblī
From Aden

Chūn kamar bastam . . . [2]
My qiblah.

I have already written one letter from Bombay. I am writing this letter from Aden. Because of the movement of the ship and the dizziness in my head, I am excused from writing of my state in detail. I write this letter lying down. I suffered terribly for two days. I remained lying here, half dead. I am fine now. But because of the foul smell and motion of the ship, I never fully recover. The food is extremely excellent. The Italian dishes are extremely tasty. What shall I write? I am not able to write.

Shiblī Nuʿmānī
Saturday, 8 May 1892[3]

Aligarh Institute Gazette Vol. XXVII No. 48, page 639
Tuesday June 14 1892

Professor Maulawī Shiblī Nuʿmānī

A brief postcard from Maulawī Shiblī came to us from Port Said; it is copied below. And we expect that by now he will have arrived at Constantinople and from there a detailed letter will come.

Copy of the Postcard

I arrived at Port Said on 14 May in the year 1892 and I will not add more to that. I expect that today I will travel to Constantinople. Regards.[4]
Shiblī Nuʿmānī
From Port Said

Most probably this postcard was written on 22 May 1892.

Aligarh Institute Gazette Vol. XXVII No. 52, page 693
June 28 1892

Maulawī Shiblī Nuʿmānī, Professor, Madrasat al-ʿUlūm

We are happy to learn that Maulawī Shiblī has arrived safe and sound at Constantinople. For the time being, he is residing in Tākhtah Khān, which is near Khān Maḥmūd Pāshā. He is busy meeting people and seeing libraries. He has written a qaṣīdah in Persian about the circumstances of his journey. We publish it along with this paper, by reading which his friends and loved ones, who are asking about him, will acquire some information.

Aligarh Institute Gazette **Vol. XXVII No. 53, page 706**
Saturday July 2 1892

Professor Maulawī Shiblī Nuʿmānī

Another letter from Maulawī Shiblī Nuʿmānī dated 5 June 1892 has come from Constantinople. He has left the location at which he lived before and has now taken up residence in a spacious place adjacent to the Bāb-i ʿĀlī [Sublime Porte]. And letters can reach him care of the *Idārah-i Akhtar*, which is a Persian newspaper there.

His plan is that, after staying there for two or three months, he will leave to see Tripoli and Damascus, and from there he will come to Egypt and spend a few days there, and then from there return to Hindustan.

In Hindustan, he had never seen a case in which the students of every single college had a special dress and all the students of that college wore that special dress. He was extremely pleased to see this practice in the colleges of the Islamic sultanate. And he extremely regrets that this practice was never adopted in the College at Aligarh and desires that a special dress be set for the students at the College.

Aligarh Institute Gazette **Vol. XXVII No. 71, page 936**
September 3, 1892

Maulawī Shiblī ṣāḥib Nuʿmānī
Professor, Madrasat al-ʿUlūm Aligarh

We have learned that the professor at our college Maulawī Shiblī Nuʿmānī has begun to write a maṡnawī in Constantinople. He will probably write about the circumstances of his journey in it. He has sent us couplets, which are the *bahār* [springtime] section of the preface, and which we copy here.

Qāṣid-i farkhandah . . . [5]

Aligarh Institute Gazette Vol. XXVII No. 83, page 1090
Friday, October 14 1892

Maulawī Shiblī Nuʿmānī, Professor, Madrasat al-ʿUlūm

We have received a letter from Maulawī Shiblī from Egypt. He will depart from Port Said on 18 October and arrive at Bombay on 20 October. He will probably stay there for one day and then depart for Aligarh.

In Egypt, he stayed in the Riwāq al-Shāmiyīn [The Hostel of the Syrians] at the Azhar Congregational Mosque, where there is a group of scholars. Fifteen thousand students are receiving an education at the Azhar Congregational Mosque, among whom nearly ten thousand live as boarders in the rooms and courtyard of the Azhar Congregational Mosque. Their education is in accordance with the classical method, but the thoughts of some, who have received an education in European sciences, have become broader. Among them, one person has written a highly praised tract in French on slavery and has published it all over Europe.[6]

Aligarh Institute Gazette Vol. XXVII No. 85, page 1114
Friday, October 21 1892

Maulawī Muḥammad Shiblī Nuʿmānī

We are delighted that Maulānā Maulawī Muḥammad Shiblī Nuʿmānī reached Aligarh safe and sound on 20 October 1892 after a journey to Constantinople, Syria, and Egypt. All friends were extremely delighted to see him. This journey of the maulawī reached its conclusion with extreme pleasure and pleasantness. And praise be to God for that.

Aligarh Institute Gazette Vol. XXIX No. 60, page 751
Friday, July 27 1894

Travelogue of Turkey
By Shiblī Nuʿmānī

In this travelogue, the extremely interesting circumstances of Constantinople, Egypt, the Levant, and detailed accounts of the intellectual and practical progress of these places, have been written by means of his personal experiences and familiarity.

Publisher: Mufīd-i ʿĀm. Paper: Excellent. Thickness of pages: 254. Cost: One rupee, five annas. Purchasers of more copies receive a twenty percent commission.

Advertiser,
Shiblī Nuʿmānī, Aligarh

APPENDIX 5

Transliterations of Persian Poems

[6]

Chūṅ kamar bastam ba-ʿazm-i īṅ safar az rūyi ʿazm
Dushman o ham dost rā dar pech o tāb andākhtam
Har kase rā bas shaguft āmad kih ḥāṣil chīst az-īṅ
Tā chirā khwud rā badīṅ sāṅ dar ʿażāb andākhtam
Har yake pandam hame dād o hame gufte kih man
Zīṅ sukhan az ʿāriż-i maʿnī naqāb andākhtam
Chūṅ lajājat rā zi ḥadd burdand guftam bas kunīd
Har chih bādābād man kashtī dar āb andākhtam[1]

[29]
Qaṣīdah[2]

Bahr-i takmīl-i fan o ham pay-i taḥṣīl-i ʿibar
Rozgār-īst kih mī-dāshtam āhang-i safar
Fārigh az ḥajj o ziyārat cho mirā kard khudāe
Khwāstam tā ba-sūy-i Rūm shawam rāh-sipar
Garchih man garm-i ṭalab būdam o bas mustaʿjal
Lek tākhīr hamī-raft ba-farmān-i qadar
Der ān māyah shud ākhir kih ḥasūdān guftand
Kih fulān juz hawas-i khām na-dārad dar sar
Rūm go'ī do sih gām-ast kih īn khām ṭamaʿ
Bī-takalluf ba-safar chust ba-bast-ast kamar
Rah chunīn dūr o darāz o safar īn māyah khaṭīr
Chūn muyassar shawad ān-rā kih nah zor-ast o nah zar
Man darīn ghuṣṣah o gham khūn-i jigar mī-khordam
Nā-gahān shāhid-i maqṣūd dar-āmad az dar
Ittifāqī ʿajabī gasht marā ʿuqdah-kushāe

Kih az-ū wahm o gumān nez namī-dāsht khabar
Yak-do mah peshtarak z-ān-kih zanam kos-i raḥīl
Būdam az zaḥmat-i tap khastah-dil o taftah-jigar
Chūn sutūh āmad-am az tap ba-dil āmad kih marā
Chārah juz naql-i makān hech na-bāshad īdar
ʿazr-i derīnah ba-yād āmad o guftam chih khwush-ast
kih ba-yak ḥīlah do tā kār bar-ārad Dāwar
Ārnalḋ ān-kih rafīq-ast o ham ustād marā
Ham darīn ʿarṣah ba-Inglanḋ hamī-khwāst safar
Guftam īn ṣiḥḥat o īn wāqiʿah nadir uftad
Pas ba-ʿazm-i safar az jāy ba-jastam mużṭar
Chūn az-īn dāʿiyah mardum hamah āgah gashtand
Ham ba-yārān o ʿazīzān-i waṭan raft khabar
Hamah rā mihr ba-junbīd o ba-dard āmad dil
Jumlah guftand kih īn zaḥmat-i be-ṣarfah ma-bar [30]

Dil ba-hijrān ma-nih o rasm-i wafā ra ma-guzār
War na-khwāhī kih kashī pāe az-īn rāh-guzar
Rozkī chand ba-yāsāy o sipas sāz ba-dah
Sāz o barg-i safar ān gūnah kih bāshad dar khwar
Bā khwud az naqd o ham az amtaʿah-ān māyah ba-gīr
Kih agar der ba-mānī na-buwad ḣech khaṭar
Maṣlaḥat nīst kih īn marḥalah tanhā sipare
Lā-jaram khādimake nez ba-hamrāh ba-bar
Guftam īn jumlah kih guftīd buwad ʿain-i ṣalāḥ
Lek ṭālib na-buwad dar giraw-i nafʿ o żarar
Mard īn marḥalah gāmī kih farā pesh nihād
Bāz pas mī-nah-kashad gar hamah marg ārad bar
Al-gharaż az ramażān bist o shashum būd kih man
Garm bar khāstam az jāy o shudam rāh-sipar
Ūftādam ba-rah-i koh o biyābān yak chand
Pas ba-kashtī ba-nishastam man o yārān-i digar
Zaḥmatī ṣaʿb kashīdīm ba-kashtī do sih roz
Bas-kih az mauj ba-har laḥẓah shudī zer o zabar
Kas na-yār-ast sar-ash bāz girift az bālīn
Kas na-yār-ast judā kard tan-ash az bistar
Na-buwad māyah-i āzār ba-kashtī chīzī
Ghair az-īn miḥnat-i sih-rozah k-az-ū nīst mafar

Nān-khwurish būd zi-har gūnah muhayyā mā rā
Az kabāb-i barah o murgh o may o nuql o shakar
Garchih man z-ān may-i pālūdah na-yālūdam lab
Dīgarān lek ʿalā al-raghm zadandī sāghar
Haftum-i māh-i Maʾī chūn ba-rasīdīm ʿAdan
Kashtī āsūd o ba-yandākht zamāne langar
Man farod āmadam o rūy ba-shahr āwurdam
Tā khabar jūyam az-īn mamlikat az badw o ḥażar
Kohsārī-st kih har chand buland-ast o farākh
Lek az sabzah o gul nīst dar-o hech aṡar
Har kujā mī-guzarī reg-i rawān-ast o khazaf
Har ṭaraf mī-nigarī khāk siyāh-ast o ḥajar [31]

Gabr o tarsā kih nazīl-and dar-īn buqʿah hamah
Ba-zabān-i ʿArabī ḥarf zadande yak-sar
Mardum-i shahr kih khwud rā bah Sumālī nāmand
Ḥayawān-and nah bal az ḥayawān ham bad-tar
Khwār o bad-bakht o tabah-kār o siyah-chardah o zisht
Suflah o mumtahan o kaj-rawish o bad-gauhar
Khweshtan rā bah ʿArab bastah o ḥāshā kih ʿArab
Īn chunīn khwār o zabūn-shān ba-pasandad Dāwar
Chūn zabān-i hamah Tāzī buwad o ham cho ʿArab
Nām-shān bastah buwad bā laqab-i jadd o pidar
ʿĀmiyān dar ghalaṭ uftand o gumān bāz barand
kih magar dar nasab o nasl zi Maʿd and o Mażar
Tukhm o ham reshah-i īn nakhl zi khāk-i Ḥabash-ast
Kih dar-īn jāe ba-bār āmad o afshānd ṡamar
Shām-gah kashtī-i mā bāz ba-raftār āmad
Tā ba-yak haftah guzar kard zi Baḥr al-Aḥmar
Bah Suez āmad o istād o chunān zūd guzasht
Kih zi kaifiyyat-i ḥālash nashudam hech khabar
Īn hamān nahr-i ʿajībī-st kih z-īn-sān kārī
Juz dar afsānah-i pārīn nah shanīdīm digar
Bist farsang darāz-ast o bah pahnā chandān
Kih do wābūr tawānand az-ū kard guzar
Mardī az ahl-i Firansā kih Lasaps-ash nām-ast
Zadah īn naqsh o dar aqṣāy-i jahān gasht samar
Ān khirad-war cho dar āghāz ba-daʿwā bar-khāst

Kih tawān āmadan az ʿuhdah-i īn kār ba-dar
Mardumān sukhrah giriftand-ash o guftand kih īn
Harzah-ī hast kih farzānah na-dārad bāwar
Az Maʾī chārdahum būd kih dar Poṙt Saʿīd
Ba-rasīdīm o nishastīm bah wābūr-i digar
Darmiyān-i man o Arnalḋ ba-yuftād firāq
z-ān-kih rāh-i man o ū gasht judā z-īn maʿbar
Poṙt jāʾī-st kih tā chashm o nigah kār kunad
Zauraq o kashtī o wābūr buwad sar tā sar [32]

Ṣad bah-bīnī kih bar-afrāshtah īn-jā rāyat
Ṣad bah-bīnī kih dar-andākhtah ān-jā langar
Shām-gah kashtī-i mā bāz rawān gasht o guzasht
Az rah-i Yāfah o pas kard ba-Bairūt maqar
Man ba-sāḥil shudam o mardī az abnāy-i Ḥalab
Ham-rah-am gasht o ba-har nāḥiyah-am shud rah-bar
Khūb jāʾīst kih nā-khwāstah dar bāzad dil
Har kih sozī ba-dil-ash dārad o dardī ba-jigar
Mauẓʿī khurram o sairī khwush o jāy-i dil-kash
Rāh ham-wār o zamīn pāk o makān khwush-manẓar
Gabr o Muslim hamah khwush-jāmah o mauzūn-andām
Khāṣ o ʿāmī hamah gulgūn-tan o zebā-paikar
Jama-hā-shān ba-ʿArab mānad o darzī o libās
Hech farqī zi Musalmān na-buwad tā kāfir
Chūn birūn raftam az-īn jāy o az-ān chārah na-būd
Pesh mī-raftam o bāzam ba-qażā būd naẓar
Az Maʾī shānzdahum būd kih gashtīm rawān
Pas bah Qubrus ba-rasīdīm ba-hangām-i saḥar
Īn hamān jāy qadīmī-st kih dar ʿahd-i Amīr (yaʿnī Amīr Muʿāwiyah)
Sipahī raft ba-taskhīr-ash o zad fāl-i ẓafar
Ḥāliyā daulat-i Inglanḋ girift-ash az Turk
Lek bā ṣulḥ nah az yāware-yi tegh o tabar
Masjid-i jāmiʿ o aiwān-gah-i Qubrus dīdam
Sair-i īn buqʿah marā bas ʿajab afzūd ʿibar
Rūḋas o Sakz ba-rah āmad o z-ān pas Izmīr
Kashtī ustād bah Izmīr o shabī burd ba-sar
Man suy-i shahr rawān gashtam o yak yak dīdam
Masjid o maktab o bāzār o rah o kūchah o dar

Farż-i ādīnah adā kardam o az ba'd-i namāz
Dar kutub khānah-i sulṭānī-am uftād guzar
Majlisī az fuqahā būd darān jāe ba-ham
Baḥṡ az mut'ah hamī-raft o ham az qaul-i 'Umar
Z-ān yakī rū ba-man āwurd kih chūnī chih kasī
Tā chirā bar zadah-ī dāman-i miḥnat ba-kamar [33]

Guftam az Hind-am o az khwān-i adab zallah rubāe
Ṭurfe me-baram az har jihat o har kishwar
Guft ḥālā sukhan az mut'ah hamī-raft o to ham
Gar tawānī sukhanī goe o miṡālī āwar
Man ba-pāsukh dar-i ma'ne zadam o mustami'ān
Lab ba-taḥsīn ba-kushādand pas az baḥṡ o naẓar
Pas zi Izmīr rawān gashtam o dar 'arż-i do roz
Ṭai shud īn rāh o ba-pāyān ba-rasīd īn daftar
Mukhtaṣar guftah-am īn ḥarf o to ham mī-dānī
Kih dar-īn bādiyah bas tang buwad rāh-guzar
    Har kih joyā buwad az ḥāl-i man o riḥlah-i man
    Bāyad-ash guft kih īn naẓm ba-khwānad yak-sar

[111]
Maṡnawī-i 'Īdiyah
June 1892[3]
Constantinople

qāṣid-i farkhundah-i man hān ta'āl
matta'ak Allāh ba-ḥusn al-ma'āl
pesh rasīdat safare nā-guzīr
garm zi-jā khez o rah-i Hind gīr
zūd raw o fikr-i do 'ālam ma-kun
war nafasī rāst kunī ham ma-kun
dīdah ba-rāh-and 'azīzān-i Hind
jumlah girāmī guhar-i kān-i Hind
chūn to dar ān bazm kashe zamzamah
dāyirah gardand ba-gird-at hamah
tā zi-ḥadīṡ-i to shawad buhrah-mand
har yake az jāe jahad chūn sipand
jumlah badīn ḥarf kih ae nek-khūe

ḥarfe az ān yār-i safar-kardah gūe
tā ba-chih ḥāl-ast o chisān-ast o khwad
raft chihā bar sar-ash az nek o bad
bar rawish-i dīdah-warān mī-ziyad
yā kih cho bahmān o falān mī-ziyad
az pas-i īn miḥnat o ranj-i shigarf
az safar-i Rūm chih bardāsht tarf
bazm-i khwushī būd tamāshā chih kard
kār base būd az ān-hā chih kard
dar saf-i dānish-ṭalabān chūn nishast
z-ān chaman-i tāzah ba-dāman chih bast [112]

ṭai cho shawad marḥalah-i purs o joe
az man-i āwārah ba-yārān ba-goe
k-ae hamah ganjīnah-kashāyān-i fann
ṣadr-nishīnān-i sar-i khwān-i fann
az karam-i Dāwar-i bālā o past
ḥāl-i man ān gūnah kih bāyast hast
ham ba-hamān ṭarz o rawish mī-ziyam
zindah-am o fārigh o khwush mī-ziyam
garchih khwud-am bā sar o sāmān niyam
nāz-kash-i ḥājib o dar-bān niyam
nīst sar-i anjuman ārāi'e
īn man-am o goshah-i tanhāi'e
w-īn-kih ba-pursīd kih z-ān jalwah-gāh
tā chih buwad ḥāṣil-i chashm o nigāh
hī chih tawān guft kih żauq-i sukhan
har nafas-am me-barad az khweshtan
garchih na-khwāham kih nishīnam khamosh
furṣat-i ān kū kih bayābam ba-hosh
garchih ba-'arż-i sukhan āmādah-am
mast zi-kaifiyyat-i īn bādah-am
bugżar az-īn ḥarf o mukarrar ma-purs
khwāb-i khwushī dīdam o dīgar ma-purs
khwān-i sukhan gar nah khwud ārāstam
'użr ba-nih maḥw-i tamāshāstam
tund ma'ī būd kharābam hanūz

dīdah-i man bāz o ba-khwābam hanūz
bā to chi-gūyam kih chihā dīdah-am
shuʿbadah-hā pesh-i naẓar chīdah-am
 bazm cho az jalwah-i zebā pur ast
 dāman-i chashm-am zi tamāshā pur ast

mihr cho az jīb-i ufuq sar kashīd
khāst zi har nāḥiyah gulbāng-i ʿīd [113]
dīdah pur az khwāb cho bar khāstand
pīr o jawān jumlah tan ārāstand
ṭifl kih īn shewah na-dānad durust
mādar-ash az mihr tan o rūy shust
shewah o āʾīn-i ṭarab tāzah gasht
kūchah o bāzār pur-āwāzah gasht
muzhdah rasīd īn kih Shah-i chārah sāz
zūd bar-āyad ba-adā-e namāz
tā barad az khwān-i karam toshah-i
khalq birūn rekht zi har goshah-i
bas-kih ʿinān-i ṭalab angekhtand
ṭifl o jawān bar sar-i ham rekhtand
pek-i naẓar rāh-i tamāshā na-yāft
naqsh-i qadam ham ba-zamīn jā na-yāft
jumlah ba-ṣad shauq o ba-ṣad ārzūe
sūy-i Bashikṭāsh nihādand o rūe
surmah-i khāk-i rah-i shah khwāstand
jā ba-guẓar-gāh-i sipah khwāstand
az do sū-e rāh ba-kasb-i sharaf
khalq ba-āʾīn-i adab bast ṣaf
mihr cho dar har jihat afshānd nūr
kaukabah-i Shāh ʿayān shud zi dūr
gasht rawān az pay-i ham khail o fauj
mauj to gūī kih shikastī ba-mauj
būd shiʿār-i hamah az ham judā
har hamah rā rāyat o parcham judā
partaw-i ān asliḥah-i tāb-nāk
nūr hamī rekht ba-dāmān-i khāk
bā hamah tamkīn cho guẓasht īn giroh

gasht bah yak-bār zamīn pur shikoh
ghalghalah bar-khāst kih bādā nawīd
mihr-i jahān-tāb-i khilāfat damīd
dāgh-nih-i jabhah-i khwurshīd o māh
ḥażrat-i khāqān-i khilāfat-panāh [114]

qā'idah-i daulat o dīn rā madār
ā'īnah-i raḥmat-i Parwardagār
paikar-i luṭf o karam-i kibriyāe
sāyah-i Yazdān shah-i kishwar-kushāe
khusraw-i lashkar-shikan o qil'ah-gīr
shāh-i falak-'atbah o gardūn-sarīr
fātiḥah-i daulat o tughrā-e dīn
zeb-dah-i afsar o tāj o nagīn
shāh-i falak kaukabah 'Abd al-Ḥamīd
Ayyaduhu Allāh ba-naṣrin mazīd
Farrah-i shāhī zi jabīn āshkār
Ḥāshiyah-bosān bah yamīn o yasār
Markab-i shah pesh cho bugżasht pāe
Khalq bah yak-bār dar-āmad zi jāe
Ṭal'at-i shah-bāz cho partaw figand
Bāng-i du'ā gasht zi har sū buland
Shor bar-āmad kih buwad tā jahān
Bād ba-kām-i to zamīn o zamān
Charkh badān māyah kih gardindah ast
Zindah ba-mān k-az to jahān zindah ast
Zeb o ṭarāz-i hamah 'ālam to'e
Sāyah-i Yazdān ba-jahān ham to'e
Jumlah ba-dānand kih dar gharb o sharq
Hast turā tāj khilāfat ba-farq
Ān to-e amroz kih dar roz-gār
Hast bar-o daulat o dīn rā qarār
Tāzagī-i Badr o Ḥunain az to hast
Zeb o ṭarāz-i ḥaramain az to hast
Juz to kih hast ay shah-i anjum-sipāh
Ān-kih buwad shar'-i Nabī rā panāh
Farrah-i dīn-i Nabawī az to hast
Bāzūy-i Islām qawī az to hast

shar' ba-jāh-i to cho shud arj-mand
bād ba-farmān-i to charkh-i buland [115]

sikkah-i iqbāl ba-nām-i to bād
har chih ba-gītī ast ba-kām-i to bād

Glossary

This section provides readers with glosses of the Arabic, Persian, Turkish, and Urdu words found in the translation of the travelogue that are either absent from or inadequately glossed in the *New Oxford American Dictionary* (*NOAD*). The glosses that follow draw from *The Encyclopaedia of Islam* (Brill Online); John T. Platts, *A Dictionary of Urdu, Classical Hindi, and English* (London: W.H. Allen & Co., 1884); J. W. Redhouse, *Redhouse's Turkish Dictionary in Two Parts* (London: Bernard Quaritch 15 Piccadilly, 1880); and Francis Joseph Steingass, *A Comprehensive Persian-English Dictionary* (London: Routledge & K. Paul, 1892).

annī Adjective related to anna, a monetary unit in British India, now obsolete (*NOAD*). For example, *do-annī* is a two-anna piece, and so on.

āyat Lit., a sign. A verse of the Quran.

beg (*bey* in *NOAD*). A courtesy title used in Ottoman Turkey and Egypt. Also, the governor of a district or province in the Ottoman Empire.

dīwān The collected poems (typically lyrics or odes) of a single poet.

faqr Poverty, indigence; mendicancy, asceticism. Related to the word *faqīr* (*fakir* in *NOAD*).

gaz A yard of measure, varying formerly from about thirty-two English inches upward; now fixed by the government at thirty-three inches (Platts).

ḥaram (*harem* in *NOAD*). *NOAD* defines the term as "the separate part of a Muslim household, the women occupying the harem, and (derogatory) a group of women perceived as centering around a particular man." In Urdu (and in Islamicate languages in general), the term simply means a sanctuary or sacred space.

In Urdu and other languages, its dual form, *ḥaramain* (the two sanctuaries), refers to Mecca and Madina.

jāhiliyah Lit., ignorance. The time before the revelation of the Quran to the Prophet.

jāmiʿ masjid Congregational mosque. The word *jāmiʿ* was used in the early period of Islam to describe the Friday mosque (the word is related to the Arabic word for Friday, *jumʿah*). Later, *jāmiʿ* came to describe any mosque of considerable size.

maulawī (*Moulvi*, *maulvi*, *molvi* in *NOAD*.) *NOAD* defines the term as "a Muslim doctor of law; an imam." In Urdu, the word is used more broadly as a title for a scholar learned in the Arabic-Islamic sciences.

mażhab Lit., way of going, path; school (especially theological or jurisprudential school in Islam); religion.

Naskh The name of a style of writing typically associated in South Asia (in Shiblī's time and ours) with Arabic and the Quran, as opposed to Nastālīq, which is the style in which Persian and Urdu are typically written. All the classical and modern Arabic in the travelogue is written in Naskh, whereas the Persian and Urdu sections are written in Nastālīq.

peshwāz A full gown with a fitted bodice and a long skirt.

qażā The office or order of a judge or qāżī (*cadi*, *kadi*, or *qadi* in *NOAD*).

qormah (*korma* in *NOAD*). A spiced gravy dish.

takyah (*tekke* in *NOAD*). A site of repose, support, hostel. In Urdu, most commonly a pillow, though it also shares with Ottoman Turkish the sense of a monastery of dervishes.

żabḥ Lit., slaughter; the lawful slaughter of animals for consumption according to Islamic jurisprudential tradition.

żabīḥah An animal slaughtered in accordance with the rules for żabḥ.

Notes

Translator's Preface

1. For example, Karaca inserts the word *Shias* (*Şiiler*) into Shiblī's account of the Muḥarram rituals in Istanbul. Shiblī uses the word *'ajamī* (non-Arab; Persian) (109). Other examples include the insertion of a sentence into the closing section of the travelogue about the degradation of Arabic (197), the attribution of Muḥammad 'Abduh's description of Jamāl al-Dīn Afghānī to Shiblī (195), the omission of Shiblī's quotation of 'Abd al-Laṭīf Baghdādī saying that the proportion of the pyramids is not the work of human beings (183–84), and the omission of Turkey among the "other Islamic governments" that lack the qualities Shiblī finds admirable among Egyptians (191). Shiblī Nu'mānī, *Andolu, Suriye ve Misir Seyahatnamesi* (*Sefername-i Rum u Şam u Mısır*), trans. Yusuf Karaca (Fatih: Risale, 2002), 109, 183–84, 191, 195, 197.

2. Shiblī Nu'mānī, *Riḥlat Shiblī al-Nu'mānī ilā al-Qusṭanṭiniyah wa Bairūt wal-Quds wal-Qāhirah*, trans. Muḥammad Akram al-Nadwī (Damascus: Dar al-Qalam, 2011).

Preface

1. Arabic: Ḥāmidan wa-muṣalliyan.

2. Persian: dar mausam-i gul gar bah gulistān narasīdīm / az dast nadādīm tamāshā-e khizān rā.

3. *safarnāmah* (Urdu, Persian: travelogue); *kitāb al-riḥlat* (Arabic: travelogue; the name of the travelogue of Ibn-i Baṭṭūṭah, which Shiblī was reading at the time; the word is rare in Urdu).

4. Arabic: That which is not attained in its entirety should not be abandoned in its entirety.

5. It is likely that Shiblī refers to the novelist and essayist Aḥmad Rāsim (1865–1932), who wrote about Ottoman progress under similar titles, e.g., *Taraqqiyāt-i 'ilmiyah o madīniyah* (Terakkiyat-ı İlmiyye ve Medeniyye; Scientific and Civic Progress). *Taraqqiyāt* begins with a broad survey of world civiliations (China, Egypt, Iran, Greece, Rome, and so on), then focuses on European intellectuals (Locke, Rousseau, Darwin) and technological advancements such as the lithograph press and modern energy sources. *Taraqqiyāt*

was published as part of Kitāb-khānah-i Abū al-Z̈iyā (a series of works intended as a general library of modern Turkish writing) by the Ottoman writer Abū al-Z̈iyā, whose role in developing Turkish printing Shiblī discusses in the travelogue. Perhaps Shiblī had this work in mind. But bibliographies of works by and about Aḥmad Rāsim do not mention *Daur-i taraqqī*. Suat Hızarci, *Ahmet Rasim: Hayatı, Sanatı, Eserlerı* (Istanbul: Varlik Yayinevi, 1953), 1–23; Aḥmad Rāsim, "Taraqqiyāt-i ʿilmiyah o bashariyah," in *Kitāb-khānah-i Abū Z̈iyā*, vol. 5, ed. Abū Z̈iyā (Constantinople, 1886–87).

6. jāmiʿ (Friday masjid / congregational masjid). In the first centuries of Islam, this term was used to refer to the main masjid of a place, but it later came to refer to any large masjid. Here, the reference is to the Azhar mosque, which houses an academy known by the same name. Shiblī resided at Azhar while in Cairo and discusses it in detail in the travelogue. Huart and Massé, "Djāmiʿ" and Jomier, "al-Azhar." *Encyclopaedia of Islam*, 2nd ed., edited by P. Bearman T. Bianquis, C. E. Bosworth, E. van Donzel, and W. P. Heinrichs. BrillOnline. https://referenceworks.brillonline.com/browse/encyclopaedia-of-islam-2; Skovgaard-Peterson, "al-Azhar, modern period." *Encyclopaedia of Islam, Three*, edited by Kate Fleet, Gudrun Krämer, Denis Matringe, John Nawas, and Everett Rowson. BrillOnline. https://referenceworks.brillonline.com/browse/encyclopaedia-of-islam-3.

7. *Twelve Years' Reign of His Imperial Majesty Abdul Hamid II, Sulṭān of Turkey* by Princess Annie de Lusignan is a survey of contemporary Ottoman political and social culture. In the preface, Lusignan argues that political circumstances and "party polemics" in England have engendered foreign policies and attitudes toward Turkey that distort, misrepresent, and "throw out of focus" the words and actions of "all things Turkish," especially Turkish statesmen. Correspondents who speak the "whole truth" and whose words do not fit the political polemics of the day face censorship, inattention, or the loss of livelihood. The raison d'être of the book as described by Lusignan is strikingly similar to that of Shiblī's travelogue. Lusignan argues that "reliable information" about the Turkish Empire is impossible to obtain, and therefore undertakes to write a long account of her experiences living in Turkey under ʿAbd al-Ḥamīd II. Lusignan and Shiblī are similar in other respects, too. Both published poetry in praise of the sulṭān. In other respects, their approach to producing "reliable information" about the Turkish reforms differed. Lusignan praises Turkish governmental reforms following the Berlin Congress and Ottoman policies toward Egypt (pp. 134–244). By contrast, Shiblī wrote very little about Ottoman international politics and political relationship between the Ottoman Empire and European power. Instead, he focuses primarily on domestic reforms in civic and military infrastructure and education. Princess Annie de Lusignan, *Twelve Years' Reign of His Imperial Majesty Abdul Hamid II, Sulṭān of Turkey* (London: S. Low, Marston, Searle, & Rivington, 1889). For verse by Lusignan in praise of ʿAbd al-Ḥamīd II, see "Birthday Ode for His Majesty Le Sulṭān Abdul Hamid" in *Scraps* by Princess Annie de Lusignan (London: Chapman, 1887), 45–58.

8. Ármin(ius) Vámbéry (1832–1913) (see Appendix 1). Shiblī's use of the word *shā'istagī* (propriety, refinement; civility, urbanity, civilization) suggests that he refers to the Urdu translation of a speech by Vámbéry titled *Lakchar: Turkī ke 'ām taraqqī o shā'istagī par* (Lecture: The General Progress and Propriety of Turkey) (1889). The translation was made by the Aligarh affiliate by Zakā'ullāh (see Appendix 1) and appears to be a translation of "The Progress of Culture in Turkey," a lecture that Vámbéry gave at Exeter Hall in London in May, 1889, as part of a speaking tour. Ármin Vámbéry, *The Story of My Struggles* (London: T. Fisher Unwin, 1904), 486–87. The lectures on the tour were aimed at raising support for British control of India and opposition to Russian expansion into the Ottoman Empire. David Mandler, *Arminius Vambéry and the British Empire: Between East and West* (Lanham: Lexington Books, 2016), 82–85. Zakā'ullāh's translation was published from Hyderabad in the Urdu journal *Ḥasan* in August 1889 (Zakā'ullāh, "Lakchar," *Ḥasan* 2, no. 8 [1889]: 1–16). The same issue of *Ḥasan* included more travel writing: portions of a travelogue by Mahdī Ḥasan Fatḥ Nawāz Jang (1852–1904) (later published as *An Indian Passage to Europe*) and excerpts from a travelogue to the Nilgiri Mountains by Munīr al-Mulk Bahādur (revenue minister at Hyderabad and son of then-deceased Hyderabadi prime minister Sālār Jang). Shiblī read *Ḥasan*, published his work in the journal, and shared it with family members, and it is likely that he read Zakā'ullāh's translation in it. Shiblī may also have encountered Vámbéry's work through the Orientalist Thomas Walker Arnold (see Appendix 1). Arnold, in his *The Preaching of Islam* (1896), on which he and Shiblī collaborated, referenced *Sketches of Central Asia* (1868) and *Geschichte Bocharas* (History of Bukhara) (1872) by Vámbéry. Thomas W. Arnold, *The Preaching of Islam: A History of the Propagation of the Muslim Faith* (Westminster: Archibald Constable & Co., 1896), 382. Vámbéry had previously published writings on Turkish history and language, for example, his *Ueber die reformfähigkeit der Türkei* (On the Reformability of Turkey), originally published in 1877 and then in French translation in 1878.

9. Beyoğlu and Galata, two neighborhoods on the eastern side of Istanbul.

10. Shiblī uses the English *gāyaḋ* (guide), which he glosses in Urdu as *rah-numā* (lit., path shower; leader; guide).

11. Arabic: "Perhaps God will bring about something after that" (Quran 65:1).

The Beginning of the Journey

1. *Hīroz āf Islām*. The Heroes of Islam was initially designed as a series of biographies of Islamic statesmen, one from each of a list of major Muslim political dynasties, to be written by Shiblī. Shiblī conceived of the project in collaboration with Sayyid Aḥmad Khān (see Appendix 1), his boss, landlord, and founder of the Muhammadan Anglo-Oriental College. The first entry in the series was *al-Māmūn* (1888), a life of the Abbasid caliph Māmūn (786–833). The second, *Sīrat al-Nu'mān* (1889) focused not on a statesman,

but on the founder of the Ḥanafī school of Islamic jurisprudence, Nu'mān ibn S̈ābit (d. 767), whose name Shiblī adopted in his youth (Nu'mānī). In 1899, Shiblī published *al-Fārūq*, his biography of 'Umar ibn Khaṭṭāb, the second caliph of Sunnī Islam. Although by this time Shiblī was no longer publishing as part of the Heroes series, he continued to produce biographies of major figures in Islam until his death. The title of the series, Heroes of Islam, recalls the writings on heroism and history by the British philosopher Thomas Carlyle. Sayyid Aḥmad Khān admired Carlyle, whom he praised in the introduction to his essays on the life of the Prophet as among a handful of Christian historians who not only approached the biography of the Prophet with justice (*inṣāf*) and without prejudice, but defended Islam against its opponents. As evidence, he quoted from Carlyle's *On Heroes, Hero, Worship, and the Heroic in History*, in which Carlyle argued that the accusations of madness and mendacity made against the Prophet were matters of disgrace for Europe. Shiblī did not know English well enough to read scholarship on his own, and it is likely that his exposure to Carlyle, as to other English authors, was mediated by Sayyid Aḥmad Khān, Thomas Walker Arnold, and the students at the MAO College. Sayyid Aḥmad Khān, *al-Khuṭbāt al-Aḥmadiyah* (Aligarh: Faiż-i 'Ām, n.d.), 21, 23–25; cf. Thomas Carlyle, *On Heroes, Hero Worship, and the Heroic in History* (Lincoln: The University of Nebraska Press, 1966), 42–43.

2. The reference to the academy (madrasat al-'ulūm [lit., madrasa of sciences]) is to the Mohammedan Anglo-Oriental College at Aligarh, where Shiblī taught Arabic and Persian. Mr. Arnold is Thomas Walker Arnold (see Appendix 1).

3. Persian: "Let be what will be, I have cast my boat into the water." A line of Persian verse used proverbially in Urdu, typically at times of fear and hope. Shiblī incorporates the line into an original Persian poem in the travelogue. Sayyid Mas'ūd Ḥasan Riẓwī, *Farhang-i amṡāl* (Allahabad: Shāntī Press, 1939), 227.

4. *wasṫan hoṫal.* Contemporary publications by the Thomas Cook & Son Company, Shiblī's travel agency, include advertisements and coupons for a newly expanded Great Western Hotel in Bombay, two minutes from the Apollo Bunder (port), "fully open to the breeze" and featuring "an unrivaled view." It is likely that the reservations were made through the company. Cook & Son, *Cook's Oriental Traveler's Gazette*, November 1892, 25.

5. Maulawī (also, Maulwī). A person learned in Arabic and the Islamic sciences.

6. Thomas Cook & Son, also known as the Cook Company, began to establish offices in India in 1880, when the Italian government offered the company commission on bookings between India and Bridisi to promote overland travel in Europe through Italy. John Mason Cook (the "son") traveled to India that year to make arrangements. The Marquess of Salisbury, Robert Arthur Talbot Gascoyne-Cecil (1830–1903), who had been secretary of state to India from 1866 to 1867 and 1874 to 1878, supported the program in hopes that it would encourage "wealthy Englishmen" to visit and appreciate India's value to England, and inspire a small number of "wealthy Indians" to see "who and what the people are . . . who govern them." Swinglehurst, *The Romantic Journey: The Story of Thomas Cook*

and Victorian Travel (London: Pica Editions, 1974), 134; Lynne Withey, *Grand Tours and Cook's Tours: A History of Leisure Travel, 1750–1915* (New York: W. Morrow, 1997), 284–85; *Oxford Dictionary of National Biography*, s.v. "Cecil, Robert Arthur Talbot Gascoyne-, third marquess of Salisbury (1830–1903)," by Paul Smith, accessed Jan 2011, http://www.oxforddnb.com/view/article/32339.

7. Arabic: "In the name of God is its course and its anchoring" (Quran 11:41). Quoted as the words spoken by Noh (Nūḥ) upon the embarkation of the ark.

8. *qaum* (community, nation); *nasl* ([from a verb meaning to beget] offspring; descent, lineage, race).

9. *quflī* (ice cream) the etymon of *kulfi*, a special kind of ice cream. *Qufl* comes from an Arabic root meaning to close or seal; quflī being that which is closed or sealed; kulfi is traditionally prepared by freezing cream in small, sealed containers (hence the name).

10. *żabḥ* (slaughter; sacrifice). The protocols for slaughter as prescribed by Islamic jurisprudential traditions. As Shiblī indicates in the anecdote, the exact protocols for slaughter vary among the jurisprudential schools.

11. Samī'ullāh Khān (see Appendix 1).

12. *żabīḥah* (that which is slaughtered according to the laws of żabḥ).

13. Ode: qaṣīdah (panegyric poem). The genre is typically defined in terms of both form and content. It typically follows an AA, BA, CA rhyme-refrain pattern and is conventionally written in praise of a patron. The word is related both to *qaṣd* (intention) and *qāṣid* (messenger).

14. Arabic. "Arise, O 'Umar!" 'Umar ibn Khaṭṭāb, the second caliph of Sunnī Islam, is remembered for overseeing the expansion of Islam through military conquests and the establishment of political institutions. Shiblī greatly admired him as a statesman and counted him among the Heroes of Islam (q.v.). He also studied him in a lengthy biography published in 1899. See Shiblī Nu'mānī, *al-Fārūq* (Kanpur: Nāmī Press, 1899).

15. *qaṣīdah-i safariyah* (travel qaṣīdah). (See anon).

16. This poem is in Persian. See Appendix 5 for a transliteration in roman script.

17. *baniyā* (typically Hindu) merchant, esp. of grain or provisions; *baqqāl* (grocer).

18. Arabic: "Where are you going? What do you seek (want)?"

19. Shams al-Dīn (al-)Muqaddasī (fl. 965–90). Geographer and traveler. His name (also interpreted as Maqdisī) reflects the city of his birth, Bait al-Muqaddas, or Bait al-Maqdis (Jerusalem). His *Aḥsan al-taqāsīm fī ma'rifat al-aqālīm* is described as an innovative "atlas of Islam." Miquel, "al-Muḳaddasī." *Encyclopaedia of Islam*, 2nd ed., edited by P. Bearman T. Bianquis, C. E. Bosworth, E. van Donzel, and W. P. Heinrichs. BrillOnline. https://referenceworks.brillonline.com/browse/encyclopaedia-of-islam-2.

20. Arabic: masculine.

21. Almost certainly Friedrich Bohndorff (1848–94) (see Appendix 1).

22. Primate speech was an emergent field of academic enquiry and popular interest in the 1890s. Much of the debate revolved around the work of the American primatologist

R. L. Garner recorded in *The Speech of Monkeys* (1892) and his subsequent journey to Africa to record and analyze monkey speech in 1892–93. For more, see Gregory Radick, *The Simian Tongue: The Long Debate about Animal Language* (Chicago: The University of Chicago Press, 2007).

23. *Ḥaramain-i sharīfain* (lit., the two noble harems or sanctuaries; Mecca and Medina). Shiblī made the ḥajj in 1876. Sayyid Sulaimān Nadwī, *Ḥayāt-i Shiblī* (Azamgarh: Dār al-Muṣannifīn, 1943), 91.

24. al-ḥamdu lillāh (praise be to God).

25. Persian: "*ba-har zamīn kih rasīdīm āsmān paidāst.*" A Persian line of verse and common aphorism in Urdu. The sky being the source of misfortune, the aphorism means that no matter where we have gone, we have encountered affliction.

26. *taẕkirah* (Arabic: passport). Shiblī uses and glosses the Arabic. In Urdu, the word is used in various senses (mention; remembrance, recollection; biography; biographical dictionary).

27. Madrasah-i Ḥarbiyah (Military School). The Ottoman military academy (see Shiblī's account of his visit). Founded by Sulṭān Mahmud II (r. 1808–39) in the 1830s shortly after the abolition of the Janissary military, the Madrasah-i Ḥarbiyah imitated European military academies and trained officers in the modern sciences. To this end, it was one of a few institutions in the Ottoman Empire that commissioned translations of scientific literature from European languages. Ekmeleddin İhsanoğlu, "education." In *Encyclopedia of the Ottoman Empire*, edited by Gábor Ágoston and Bruce Masters (New York: Facts on File, 2009), 199–204. Selçuk Akşin Somel, *The Modernization of Public Education in the Ottoman Empire, 1839–1908* (Leiden: Brill, 2001), 26, 188.

28. Arabic: "No! By God! Is this the hat of a Muslim?"

29. Mu'āwiyah I (d. 680). Founder of the Umayyad dynasty (ruled 661–680). Mu'āwiyah, whose father had fought against the Prophet and whose sister had married him, eventually embraced Islam and is said to have served as one of the Prophet's scribes. After the death of the Prophet, he was a military commander and civic administrator under the Sunnī caliphs (Abū Bakr, 'Umar, and 'Uṡmān). Shiblī rarely gives references for the historical information in the travelogue, but here and elsewhere, the *Fatḥ al-Buldān* (Conquest of Countries) by Balāẕurī is a likely source. Shiblī cited the European edition of Balāẕurī (Leiden: Brill, 1863–66) in his writings in the 1890s. Shiblī Nu'mānī, *Rasā'il-i Shiblī* (Amritsar: Roz Bāzār Steam Press, 1898); Shiblī Nu'mānī, *al-Fārūq* (Kanpur: Nāmī Press, 1899); Groot, "Ḳubrus" and Hinds, "Mu'āwiya I." *Encyclopaedia of Islam*, 2nd ed.

30. The Russo-Turkish War (1877–78).

31. *Shirwānī achkan* (a knee-length frock buttoned in front).

32. qaẓā (Islamic judicature; the judgment of a qāẓī [judge]). In the Ottoman Empire, the term referred not only to the judgment itself, but also to the judge's district of authority. Nagy, "ḳaḍā." *Encyclopaedia of Islam*, 2nd ed.

33. Shiblī likely refers to William Wilkinson, *'Ilm-i Jughrāfiyah* (Aligarh: Scientific Society, 1869).

34. Hisar Mosque.

35. *maktab-i i'dādī* (similar to high school).

36. Ṣabrī Āfandī may be Hoca Hafiz Ahmet Sabri; Maulānā Sa'īd is likely Mehmet Sait, also known as Kürt (Kurdish) Said Hoca, who taught Arabic and Persian at the Izmir i'dādī school. If Ḥusnī Āfandī was the former secretary of education, it is likely that he held the position outside of Izmir, since the present secretary was named Amrullāh and, before him, the position was held by Taḥsīn Bey. For more on intellectual culture at Izmīr, see Erkan Serçe, *İzmir'de kitapçılık* (Bookselling in Izmir) (Izmir: Akademi Kitabevi, 1996); Sibel Zandi-Sayek, *Ottoman Izmir: The Rise of a Cosmopolitan Port, 1840–1880* (Minneapolis: University of Minnesota Press, 2012); Selçuk Akşin Somel, *The Modernization of Public Education in the Ottoman Empire 1839–1908* (Leiden: Brill, 2001).

37. *mut'ah* (temporary marriage). According to some, 'Umar (the second caliph of Sunnī Islam) was the first to prohibit the practice. The issue later became a point of division between Sunnī and Shia scholars, the latter regarding the practice as permissible. W. Heffening, "Mut'a." *Encyclopaedia of Islam*, 2nd ed.

38. Muḥammad II (also known as Mehmet the Conqueror) (1432–81). Conqueror of Constantinople in 1453 and therefore considered the "ultimate founder" of the Ottoman Empire, which he inherited from his father. İnalcık, "Meḥemmed II." *Encyclopaedia of Islam*, 2nd ed.

39. 'Abd al-Fattāḥ (see Appendix 1).

40. Khālid Naqshbandī (see Appendix 1).

41. Mirzā Maẓhar Jān-i Jānān (1700–1781). Naqshbandī and Qādirī Ṣūfī; Persian and Urdu poet. The Naqshbandī tradition was known to advocate relatively sober and traditionalist forms of piety and devotion. Mirzā Maẓhar Jān-i Jānān himself is said to have been "outspokenly anti-Shī'a," because of which he was ultimately murdered, though this claim is contested. His Persian poetry and letters, as well as a small number of Urdu poems, have survived. Annemarie Schimmel, *Classical Urdu Literature from the Beginning to Iqbal* (Wiesbaden: Harrasowitz, 1975), 167–69. In contrast to what Shiblī reports here, Khālid is said to have made the journey to Delhi in 1809 and to have been initiated into the Naqshbandī order by Mirzā Maẓhar's successor, Ghulām 'Alī (d. 1824). Weismann, "Ghulām 'Alī Shāh." *Encyclopaedia of Islam*, 3rd. ed.

42. *Iskāt al-mu'tadī 'alā inṣāt al-muqtadī* (1881) (The Silencing of the Aggressor on the Silence of the Follower). A short (twenty-four-page) treatise in Arabic regarded as Shiblī's first publication. The text examines the question as to whether the person behind the imam should recite the Fāṭiḥah (opening prayer of the Quran) to himself in communal prayer after the imam has recited it. Ḥanafī jurisprudents hold that the person should not recite to himself. Ilyās A'ẓmī, *Āṡār-i Shiblī* (Azamgarh: Dār al-Muṣannifīn,

2013), 50–55; Shiblī Nuʿmānī, *Iskāt al-muʿtadī ʿalā inṣāt al-muqtadī* (Kanpur: Matbaʿ-i Niẓāmī, 1881).

43. Arabic: "May God laud his efforts." The doubling of *k* (*shakkara*) is likely a copyist's error; perhaps a misreading of the diacritical mark pesh/żamma ("u"). In the second edition, the phrase is changed to "shakar allāhu masa'ʿiyahu."

44. Muḥammad Amīn ibn ʿĀbidīn al-Shāmī (1784–1842) (see Appendix 1). *Radd al-muḥṭār ʿalā al-Durr al-mukhṭār* is an influential work of Ḥanafī jurisprudence that challenges, and seeks to reform, authoritative opinion. In 1905, Shiblī wrote a short article summarizing and promoting al-Shāmī's argument, according to which practice had historically provided precedent for changes within Islamic jurisprudence. See Shiblī Nuʿmānī, "Masā'il-i fiqhiyah par żarūratoṅ kā aṡar," in *Maqālāt-i Shiblī*, 1:75–81. For more on al-Shāmī and *Radd al-muḥṭār*, see Itzchak Weismann, "Sufism on the Eve of Reform: The Views of Ibn-i ʿAbidin," in *Ottoman Reform and Muslim Regeneration: Studies in Honour of Butrus Abu-Manneb*, ed. Itzchak Weismann and Fruma Zachs (London, New York: I. B. Tauris: 2005), 69–80.

45. Darwesh Pāshā (see Appendix 1). Shiblī spends time at Darwesh Pāshā's mansion and befriends his son-in-law.

46. This poem is in Persian. See Appendix 5 for the transliteration into roman script.

47. *fann* (subject, field [of learning]; art).

48. *gabr* (Guebre; fire worshipper; Zoroastrian; Christian) and *tarsā* (fire worshipper; Zoroastrian; Christian). In Urdu, these categories, especially when invoked together, suggest any group other than the Muslim community. Here, they seem to refer to the Hindu merchants whom Shiblī encountered in Aden.

49. Maʿd (also, Maʿadd) is the name of an ancestor of northern Arabs and the namesake of a group of Arab tribes from which important tribes later claimed descent. The Prophet is said to have forbidden tracing genealogies beyond him. Mużar is said to be Maʿd's grandson. Maʿd and Mużar are both said to be the ancestors of the Quraish (the tribe of the Prophet). Kindermann, "Rabīʿa and Muḍar," and Watt, "Maʿadd." *Encyclopaedia of Islam*, 2nd ed.

50. Ḥabash (cognate with the English Abyssinia) is the name applied in Islamic Arabic geographical writing to Eastern Africa. Beckingham, "iii.—al-Ḥabash in Muslim Geographical Works" in "Ḥabash, Ḥabasha." *Encyclopaedia of Islam*, 2nd ed.

51. Ferdinand de Lesseps (1805–94).

52. Muʿāwiyah I, founder of the Umayyad dynasty (r. 661–680), oversaw the military campaign in Cyprus against the Byzantine Empire ca. 647 and organized a second campaign in 653–54. Groot, "Ḳubrus." *Encyclopaedia of Islam*, 2nd ed.

53. Sakz (Chios).

54. *mutʿah* (lit., pleasure). Temporary marriage considered permissible by some Islamic jurisprudents. ʿUmar, the third caliph of (Sunnī) Islām, is said to have prohibited the practice. Later, mutʿah came to be seen as a line of division between Sunnī and Shīʿah

jurisprudential traditions. Heffening, "Mut'a." *Encyclopaedia of Islam*, 2nd ed., edited by P. Bearman T. Bianquis, C. E. Bosworth, E. van Donzel, and W. P. Heinrichs. BrillOnline. https://referenceworks.brillonline.com/browse/encyclopaedia-of-islam-2.

55. *adab* (good conduct, courtesy; literature).

Constantinople

1. Bizanṭāyan (Byzantium); Qusṭanṭiniyah (Constantinople).

2. Ibn-i Baṭūṭah (1304–77). World traveler. He visited Asia Minor and Constantinople around 1330, and from there traveled to India. Shiblī does not cite the edition of Ibn-i Baṭūṭah's travelogue that he is reading, but it is likely that he was using the bilingual Paris edition (1853–58), which Thomas Arnold cites in *The Preaching of Islam*. Shiblī mentions in the travelogue that he had studied some French with Arnold, and Arnold had begun to study Arabic. It seems likely that they would have studied this edition together, which includes the Arabic critical edition above the French translation on each page. Thomas W. Arnold, *The Preaching of Islam: A History of the Propagation of the Muslim Faith* (Westminster: Archibald Constable & Co., 1896), 377.

3. Cf., Ibn-i Baṭūṭah, *Voyages d'Ibn Batoutah* (Paris: Imprimerie Impériale, 1854), 2:431–33. Battuta scholar Ross E. Dunn describes his account of the city as being "offered in a spirit of tolerance, objectivity, and indeed wonder," but also as misleading, as it diverts attention from an empire that was "slowly crumbling to bits" outside the walls of the city; a state "living on borrowed time and past glory." By contrast, this excerpt suggests that Baṭūṭah, far from "sens[ing] little of this" or "refrain[ing] from twisting the knife" was acutely aware of the tenuousness of authority in the capital and, despite flourishing trade, the crumbling infrastructure and low standard of living at the capital. Ross E. Dunn, *The Adventures of Ibn Battuta* (Berkeley: The University of California Press, 2005), 171–72.

4. 'Abdullāh bin al-Muṭṭalib is also the name of the father of the Prophet and may be a copyist's error. The military campaigns of 'Abdullāh al-Baṭṭāl (d. 740), the spelling of whose name somewhat resembles al-Muṭṭalib in the Arabic script, is well documented in the early Arabic sources that Shiblī often used in his writings, and it is likely that al-Baṭṭāl is meant. In some early sources, the career of al-Baṭṭāl is said to have begun ca. 705, during the reign of the Ummayad Caliph 'Abd al-Malik, the father of Walīd, in which al-Baṭṭāl is reported to have led campaigns against the Byzantines. Some sources record that al-Baṭṭāl was present during the second siege of Constantinople (717). Though described as an ordinary general in the earliest histories, by the tenth century, some sources had begun to elevate him to the status of a "legendary hero." Athamina, "al-Baṭṭāl, 'Abdallāh." *Encyclopaedia of Islam, Three*, edited by Kate Fleet, Gudrun Krämer, Denis Matringe, John Nawas, and Everett Rowson. BrillOnline. https://referenceworks.brillonline.com/browse/encyclopaedia-of-islam-3.

5. al-Walīd bin ʿAbd al-Malik (d. 715). Umayyad caliph (r. 705–15) remembered for military expansion, architectural patronage, and domestic welfare programs. Jacobi, "al-Walīd." *Encyclopaedia of Islam* 2nd ed., edited by P. Bearman T. Bianquis, C. E. Bosworth, E. van Donzel, and W. P. Heinrichs. BrillOnline. https://referenceworks.brillonline.com/browse/encyclopaedia-of-islam-2.

6. Arabic: "A good land" (Quran 34:15). As a chronogram, the phrase yields the date 857 Hijrī.

7. *sunahrī sīng* (lit., golden horn [an animal's horn]). In the 1901 edition (and subsequent editions) of the travelogue, the phrase *sunahrī sīng* is replaced with the Persianized *shākh-i zarīn* (lit., golden horn).

8. Arabic: "With what do you amuse yourselves?"

9. Ḥusain Ḥasīb (see Appendix 1).

10. Hill stations initially developed as summer retreats for British officials and their families. By the end of the nineteenth century, Shimlā had become the perennial home of a large number of British officials and therefore something like a de facto capital of the British Raj. Dane Kennedy, *The Magic Mountains: Hill Stations and the British Raj* (Berkeley: University of California Press, 1996).

11. *injās* (Arabic: pear). The word is spelled with an *s* rather than *ṣ* in the travelogue. According to lexicographers, the word *injāṣ* belongs to the Syrian dialect of Arabic. Shiblī's use of the term offers a glimpse of the influence that the community of Damascene Arabic speakers whom Shiblī befriended in Constantinople had on his experiences there. Hans Wehr, *A Dictionary of Modern Written Arabic* (Ithaca: Spoken Language Services, 1976), 30.

12. *mishmish* (apricot). This word is found in Arabic dictionaries, but Ottomanist James W. Redhouse does not include it in his Ottoman Turkish dictionary. Instead, he gives two words for apricot: *qaissī* (*kàssi*), and; *zardālū* (*zèrdāli*). The former remains standard in Modern Turkish as *kayısı*. This suggests that Shiblī's exposure to the fruits was, like so many of his experiences inat Constantinople, mediated by the community of Arabic speakers from Syria with whom he lived. J. W. Redhouse, *Redhouse's Turkish Dictionary*, ed. Charles Wells (London: Bernard Quaritch, 1880).

13. *Jāmun* is also valued for its medicinal properties. Apricots (Urdu: *khūbānī*) are commonly found in South Asia. One therefore wonders why Shiblī did not recognize the fruit.

14. One can only wonder if Shiblī refers here to the lengthy *Mirʾāt-i Maktab-i Ḥarbiyah* (1892–93), which was published by the Ottoman military academy and contains information about the college's history, curriculum, and officers, among other subjects.

15. Khair al-Dīn Pāshā (see Appendix 1).

16. Urkhān (Orkhan, Orhan) (d. March 1362). Son of the founder of the Ottoman dynasty, ʿUṡmān I. Historians remember him for his expansion of Ottoman territory and

founding of educational and religious institutions. Zachariadou, "Orkhan." *Encyclopaedia of Islam*, 2nd ed.

17. (*Musalmānoṅ kī*) *Guẓishtah ta'līm* (The Past Education of Muslims). First presented at the second annual Muhammadan Educational Congress (later, Conference) at Lucknow in 1887, then published as a separate tract in 1888. By Shiblī's own account, this was his first major work of modern scholarship in Urdu. The essay surveys the history of translation and intellectual institutions in the first centuries of Islam with special focus on the translations commissioned by the Abbasid court. One of the objectives of the work was to trace Muslims' contributions to the development of knowledge. Shiblī Nu'mānī, *Musalmānoṅ kī guẓishtah ta'līm* (Lucknow: Qaumī Press, 1888), 1–10.

18. Maḥmūd II (r. 1808–39). His early reign was dominated by attempts to restore central authority, which had been weakened, as well as domestic uprisings and foreign conflict. In 1826, he abolished the Janinssaries, an elite corps that had been in existence since the fourteenth century. The new army was trained according to western models and engaged in conflicts and alliances with European militaries. Levy, "Maḥmūd." *Encyclopaedia of Islam*, 2nd ed.

19. *mujaddid* (modernizer, reformer, renewer, the active participle of *tajdīd* [renewal]). The word is printed in the first edition with diacritical markers to facilitate recognition and pronunciation, suggesting that Shiblī or his editors assumed that readers would not be familiar with the term, or might suspect, given the typical context in which the term was used, that another word with the same spelling was intended. The word *mujaddid* neither appears in Platts' 1884 Urdu-English dictionary nor in the *Farhang-i Āṣafiyah* (1908). In the Islamic tradition, scholars have used the word since at least the ninth century to designate political and intellectual figures of divine guidance and revival. In South Asia, the term is often associated with Shaikh Aḥmad Sirhindī, called *mujaddid-i alf-i s̱ānī* (modernizer, renewer of the second millennium). The Mujaddidī Naqshbandī tradition takes its name from him (Shiblī's teacher in jurisprudence, Irshād Ḥusain Rāmpūrī, is remembered as a Mujaddidī, though Shiblī never claimed to be part of any Ṣūfī tradition). Shiblī later used the term *mujaddid* to describe the theologian Ghazālī (d. 1111) as a great reformer of the Islamic intellectual tradition. See van Donzel, "Mudjaddid" and Jansen, "Tadjdīd." *Encyclopaedia of Islam*, 2nd ed.; Shiblī Nu'mānī, *al-Ghazālī* (Azamgarh: Ma'ārif, 1928), 166–69; Sayyid Shāhid 'Alī Riẓwī Jamālī, *Maulānā Irshād Ḥusain Mujaddidī Rāmpūri* (Rampur, 1989), 10–13.

20. For the Military College (Maktab-i Ḥarbiyah), see note 14 above.

21. 'Abd al-Majīd I (Abdülmecid) (r. 1839–61). Ottoman sulṭān, reformer, and son of Maḥmūd II. Deny, "'Abd al-Madjīd I." *Encyclopaedia of Islam*, 2nd ed.

22. *rushdiyah* (*rüştiye*). a class of "government secondary schools" or "advanced primary schools." These schools were established in 1849 as part of broad educational reforms within the Ottoman Empire. The schools, organized by class, were initially conceived

as a bridge between traditional Quranic schools and university education, and soon expanded to offer four years of higher-primary education. According to one historian, the rushdiyah schools became increasingly obsolete during the reign of ʿAbd al-Ḥamīd II as they gave way to a new structure involving elementary and *idādī* schools, even as they remained, as higher-primary intuitions, a part of the system of education. Selçuk Akşin Somel, *The Modernization of Public Education in the Ottoman Empire 1839–1908* (Leiden: Brill, 2001), 8, 15, 35, 37–49.

23. The British colonial educational system in India comprised a series of standardized examinations based on standard curricula. The first examination was entrance, then middle, then first examination in arts, then on to bachelors, masters, and doctoral examinations.

24. The nineteenth century witnessed educational institutionalization and expansion on a large scale in the Ottoman Empire. Primary education for boys aged seven to eleven and girls aged six to ten was made mandatory in 1876. *Rüştiye* schools (middle schools between primary [*sibyan*] and high [*idadi*] schools) spread from Istanbul to rural areas. Ekmeleddin İhsanoğlu, "education." *Encyclopedia of the Ottoman Empire*, ed. Gábor Ágoston and Bruce Masters (New York: Facts on File, 2009), 203.

25. *khāṣ* (elite; private; special). The ambiguity of the word, used in contradistinction to *ʿām* (common; public; general) admits of multiple interpretations. When the two terms are used in parallel (*khāṣ o ʿām*), as appears here, the suggestion is of totality; that is, all the schools, khāṣ and ʿām alike.

26. *al-Muʾayyid*. Established in December 1889 by Shaikh ʿAlī Yūsuf (1863–1913), who was educated at Azhar. It was the first Arabic newspaper in Egypt, and was also the first major Muslim-run newspaper to compete with the influential contemporary newspapers run by Syrian Christians. ʿAbbās Ḥilmī II (Egyptian Khedive from 1892–1914) subsidized its publication. Prime Minister Muṣtafā Riyāẓ (premier 1888–91 and 1893–94) was also a major patron. In the 1890s, Ḥilmī and Riyāẓ were outspoken critics of British involvement in Egypt, and, when Ḥilmī became Khedive in 1892, the paper became an official voice for anti-British perspectives. It carried articles from notable Egyptian intellectuals, including Muḥammad ʿAbduh, whom Shiblī met at Cairo, and ʿAbduh's pupil Rashīd Riẓā, with whom Shiblī later corresponded. Scholars have noted that the paper's anti-British edge softened in the late 1890s when ʿAbbas Ḥilmī II softened his own stance. Shiblī continued to read the paper after his return to India, and it was a major source for his thinking about contemporary politics. He considered the paper as an alternative to media on British politics that was available in India and drew from it in his discussion of the conflict between the Ottoman Empire and the Armenian community. Shiblī Nuʿmānī, *Maqālāt-i Shiblī* (Azamgarh: Maʿārif, 1930–38), 8:185–89; Shiblī Nuʿmānī, *Makātīb-i Shiblī* (Azamgarh: Maʿārif, 1927), 2:181; Arthur Goldschmidt Jr., *Biographical Dictionary of Modern Egypt* (Boulder: Lynne Rienner, 2000), 2, 168–69, 230–31; Bearman, "Yūsuf, ʿAlī." *Encyclopaedia of Islam*, 2nd ed.

27. Kāghaż-khānah (Kağıthane) (lit., paper house). An industrial center in the late nineteenth century.

28. Turkish: "Long live my *bādshāh*!" (*Badşahım çok yaşa*). Shiblī translates the possessive pronominal suffix *im* (my) as *hamārā* (our), which can also be used as a singular first-person possessive pronoun in Urdu.

29. Maktab-i 'Ashāyir (lit., school of the [bedouin] tribes). Established in Istanbul in 1892 (opened in October) to "integrate tribal populations in the Arabic provinces into the Ottoman political system by providing Ottoman education to sons of selected notable tribal families and shaping them into Ottoman loyalists." Selçuk Akşin Somel, *The Modernization of Public Education in the Ottoman Empire 1839–1908* (Leiden: Brill, 2001), 238–40.

30. Dār al-Shafaqah (Darüşşafaka). Founded in 1873. Selçuk Akşin Somel, *The Modernization of Public Education in the Ottoman Empire 1839–1908* (Leiden: Brill, 2001), 53–54.

31. Platts and Fallon give the same definition for both terms: *munṣif* (subordinate judge); *ṣadr-i ṣudūr* (subordinate judge; head ṣadr). Fallon tells us that ṣadr al-ṣudūr used to be a principal, but ca. 1880s had become a subordinate judge. Redhouse tells us that in Ottoman Turkish, the munṣif carried the general meaning of a just, equitable person "holding an office," and that *ṣadr* is the title of administers of canon law. J. W. Redhouse, *Redhouse's Turkish Dictionary*, ed. Charles Wells (London: Bernard Quaritch, 1880), 634.

32. The Civil Engineering College at Roorkee (founded ca. 1848).

33. The Zahur Ḥusain Ward. According to Theodore Morison, principal of the college from 1899 to 1905, the ward functioned as a space in which the schoolboys were placed in "distinct and comparatively small areas, where they [could] be efficiently supervised by a resident master, upon the analogy of the different houses in which the boys of an English Public School are lodged." Theodore Morison, *The History of the M.A.O. College, Aligarh*, ed. Shyam Krishna Bhatnagar (Bombay, 1969), 23. G. R. Batho, "Morison, Sir Theodore (1863–1936)," *Oxford Dictionary of National Biography*, Oxford University Press, 2004, http://www.oxforddnb.com/view/article/35108.

34. *Irādah-i sunnah*. In the nineteenth century, the term *irādah* (*irade*) was used by Ottoman officials to designate decrees issued in the name of the sulṭān. The use of *sunna* is especially interesting, since although its general meaning is that of "custom" or "practice," its dominant connotation is that of the traditions of the Prophet and his companions, especially those recognized as part of the sunnī traditions of Islam. Ed., "Glossary and Index of Terms: irāda." *Encyclopaedia of Islam*, 2nd ed.

35. (Ghāzī) 'Uṡmān Pāshā (see Appendix 1).

36. Persian: "I am not authorized in the Military (Academy)."

37. Shiblī's use of *jīnā* is regarded by linguists as colloquial, Levantine Arabic, once again gesturing to the influence of the community of Damascene Arabic speakers with whom he lived in Constantinople. Leslie J. McLoughlin, *Colloquial Arabic (Levantine)* (London, New York: Routledge, 2009), 69.

38. Likely ʿAlī Rażā Bey. In the official calendar of the academy, he is named both Rażā Afandī and ʿAlī Rażā Bey from Qabātāsh (Kabataş). Few details are recorded, but he is said to have been promoted to the *piyādah ṣinfī* (infantry) at the Military Academy in 1300 Hijrī (1882–83) and to have been in the Internal Royal War Arts Academy (Maktab-i Gunūn-i Ḥarbiyah-i Shāhānah-i dākhiliyah). Muḥammad Asʿad, *Mirʾāt-i Maktab-i Ḥarbiyah* (Istānbūl: Ārtīn Āṣādūryān Shirkat-i Murattib-i Matbaʿah-sī, 1310 [1892–93]), 637. Biographical sources list an ʿAlī Rażā Bey, who may be the same person. He studied at the Military Academy in Istanbul before entering the military, then taught history in military schools (*askeri mektepler*), eventually rising to the rank of *miralay*. His historical writings include *Khulāṣat al-tawārīkh* (Abridgment of the Histories) (1910–11). He died in 1919. Mehmet Zeki Pakalin, *Sicill-i Osmani zeylī* (Ankara: Türk Tarih Kurumu, 2008–9), 3:7.

39. Arabic: "If you please, O *maulānā*." As in Urdu, the term *maulānā* is a respectful form of address in Ottoman for scholars trained in Arabic and the Islamic sciences.

40. *baq* (Turkish: *bak*; look!).

41. This word appears in both the first and second (1901) editions. It may be read as polygraphy, paleography, or, assuming a copyist's error, perhaps topography (*ṭabūghrāfiyā*).

42. In the first edition, *fannī* appears, but this must be a copyist's error since the curriculum of fannī studies has already been discussed. In the 1901 edition, *fannī* has been changed to *ʿaskarī* (military).

43. Maktab-i Sultanī. Modern Turkish: Metkteb-i Sultani (Imperial College). Renamed Galatasaray Lisesi (High School) after the proclamation of the Republic of Turkey. It was founded by French and Ottoman officials in order to give advanced education in the French language and European subjects. It was run by two administrators: a Turkish principle and a French assistant principal. Ekmeleddin İhsanoğlu, "education." *Encyclopedia of the Ottoman Empire*, ed. Gábor Ágoston and Bruce Masters (New York: Factson File, 2009), 203.

44. Shiblī uses the English word *secretary*, as well as *nāʾib* (assistant) *secretary*. In Turkish, the principal of the academy was titled *mudīr*, and the assistant principal, the *mudīr-i ṡanī*. When Shiblī visited, the mudīr was Ismāʿīl Bey, who held the position from 1880 to 1894. The mudīr-i ṡānī was a *Monieur* Dūlīs, who held the position from 1876 until his death in 1904. *Mekteb-i Sulṭānī* (Istanbul: Matbaʿah-i ʿāmirah, 1918), 11, 22.

45. ʿAbd al-ʿAzīz (Abdülaziz) (r. 1861–76). Ottoman sulṭān. Although he made major reforms in education, the military, political administration, and economics, he was deposed in 1876 on account of the state of the Ottoman economy. Karal, "ʿAbd al-ʿAzīz." *Encyclopaedia of Islam*, 2nd ed.

46. Afżal al-Dīn Khūnajī (1194–1248), Arabic logician whom Ibn-i Khaldūn identified as extremely influential in the field. He is most widely known as the author of *Kashf al-asrār*. El-Rouayheb, "al-Khūnajī." *Encyclopaedia of Islam, Three*. ʿAlā al-Dīn ʿAlī Qūshjī (d. 1474), astronomer and mathematician. Born and educated in Samarqand, where he

established himself as a scientist and writer, he traveled to Istanbul during the reign of Sulṭān Muḥammad II and eventually settled there, where he taught at the madrasa in the Aya Sofia. Adivar, "'Alī b. Muḥammad al-Ḳūshdjī." *Encyclopaedia of Islam*, 2nd ed. The reference to Chalabī is ambiguous, as it is the name of a number of Ottoman writers of the period under discussion. Ḥājī Khalīfah, whom Shiblī names here, was also known as Kātib Chalabī. Shiblī may refer to 'Āshiq Chalabī (b. 1520; d. ca.1570), the author of a widely circulated biography of poets, or to Fatḥallāh Chalabī (d. 1561–62), an Ottoman historian. Ménage, "'Āshıḳ Čelebi." *Encyclopaedia of Islam*, 2nd ed.; Yazici, "ČELEBĪ, FATḤ-ALLĀH 'ĀREF." *Encyclopaedia Iranica*, http://www.iranicaonline.org/. Khwājahzādah (d. 1488), Ottoman scholar and tutor to the sulṭān. His best-known work, *Taḥafut al-falāsifah* was commissioned as part of a competition to see who could write the best comparative study of Ghazālī and Ibn-i Rushd, specifically the latter's attempt to refute of the former. The sulṭān declared his work the winner, and it continued to be read into the fifteenth century. Rudolph, "Khōdjā-Zāde." *Encyclopaedia of Islam*, 2nd ed. Shiblī later wrote about both Ibn-i Rushd and Ghazālī in his series of theological texts, and his interest in Ghazālī was spurred by his conversations with Sayyid Aḥmad Khān. Ḥājjī Khalīfah (1609–57), bibliographer and historian. He composed original works in Arabic and translated into Turkish. His massive bibliographic encyclopedia, *Kashf al-ẓunūn*, has been immensely influential. Şaik Gökyay, "Kātib Čelebi." *Encyclopaedia of Islam*, 2nd ed. Shiblī used it as a major source for his early writing on translation into Arabic, *Guẕishtah Ta'līm* (mentioned in the travelogue), and continued to cite it throughout his career.

47. The names of two elementary logic textbooks. The original text of *Īsāghūjī* (*Isagogue*), by Porphyry, was translated and adapted into Arabic a number of times. The most popular version in India was that of Aśīr al-Dīn Abharī (d. ca. 1263–64). Akhtar Rāhī, *Taẕkirah-i Dars-i Niẓāmī* (Lahore: Maktabah-i Raḥmāniyah, 1978), 41; Ed., "Īsāghūdjī" and Brockelmann, "al-Abharī." *Encyclopaedia of Islam*, 2nd ed. *Shamsiyah* is a logic textbook by Najm al-Dīn al-Kātibī (al-Qazwīnī) (d. 1276–77). Mohaghegh, "al-Kātibī." *Encyclopaedia of Islam*, 2nd ed.

48. *Ṣiḥāḥ sittah* (lit., authentic six). A reference to the six collections of hadith considered reliable. Robson, "Hadīth." *Encyclopaedia of Islam*, 2nd ed.

49. *mujtahidānah* (adj. of mujtahid; mujtahid-like; innovative). In a narrow sense within the Islamic jurisprudential context, *mujtahid* refers to someone who can form original judgments by the use of exertion (*ijtihād*) and reason based on basic principles. More broadly, the term has been used to refer to anyone who uses the intellect to benefit Islam or the Muslim community. Shiblī seems to use it in a similar sense to the latter, but perhaps even broader, meaning an innovative thinker in general. The word *mujtahid* is often used in contradistinction to *muqallid* (imitator), or one who follows authoritative jurisprudential opinion. The terms have not always been seen as mutually exclusive. Even within the relatively narrow context of Islamic jurisprudential epistemology, the two terms are not mutually exclusive. Indeed, a *mujtahid-e maẕhab* (innovator of the

tradition) acknowledged the authority of founding mujtahids, but did not submit to them blindly. Calder, "Taḳlīd" and Calmard, "Mudjtahid." *Encyclopaedia of Islam*, 2nd ed.

50. Ibn-i Khaldūn (1332–1406), Tunis-born historian and philosopher, and author of an Arabic *Muqaddamah* (prolegomena), which outlines a sociological theory of history; Abū Jaʿfar Muḥammad (al-)Ṭabarī (839–923), the author of a voluminous universal history in Arabic; Ibn-i Khallikān (1211–82), the author of an Arabic biographical dictionary compiled in Cairo; Taqī al-Dīn (al-)Maqrīzī (1364–1444), historian and geographer who knew and was inspired by Ibn-i Khaldūn. Talbi, "Ibn-i Khaldūn," Bosworth, "al-Ṭabarī;" Fück, "Ibn-i Khallikān;" and Rosenthal, "al-Maḳrīzī." *Encyclopaedia of Islam*, 2nd ed. Shiblī relied on Ibn-i Khaldūn and Ibn-i Khallikān in his earliest writing on Islamic history, *Guẕishtah Taʿlīm* (v.s.). He used Maqrīzī as a source for his historical discussions of Egypt in the travelogue and relied on all four historians in his discussions of Islamic history, theology, and Persian literary aesthetics throughout his career.

51. *rijāl* (lit., men). A branch of historical scholarship that records the biographies of transmitters of hadith (traditions of the Prophet). Juynboll, "Ridjāl." *Encyclopaedia of Islam*, 2nd ed.

52. *rijāl* (lit., men; since the late eighth century, the biographical study of hadith transmitters); *tarājim* (pl. of *tarjumah* [representation; an entry in a biographical dictionary]).

53. *Qāmūs al-aʿlām*, a six-volume encyclopedia by Shams al-Dīn Sāmī (Şemseddin Sami Fraşeri) (1850–1904). Balim, "Sāmī." *Encyclopaedia of Islam*, 2nd ed.

54. Nāmiq Kamāl, ʿAbd al-Ḥaqq Ḥāmid and Muʿallim Nājī (see Appendix 1). Shiblī's remarks about Nājī are surprising, since scholars describe him as a neoclassicist highly critical of modernist Turkish literature and literary figures, including Ḥāmid.

55. Ármin(ius) Vámbéry (see Appendix 1).

56. *malik al-shuʿarā* (king of the poets). The title of poet laureates in Seljuk, Safavid, Qajar, and Mughal courts. de Bruijn, "Malik al-Shuʿarā." *Encyclopaedia of Islam*, 2nd ed.

57. Aḥmad Midḥat (see Appendix 1).

58. *Mudāfaʿah-i Islāmiyah* (3 vols., 1883–85).

59. Aḥmad Jaudat (Ahmet Cevdet) (see Appendix 1). From 1886 to 1890, he was minister of justice on the Council of Ministers, a post that he had held previously. During the same time he was part of a small committee that advised the sulṭān on political matters. Bowen, "Aḥmad Djewdat Pasha." *Encyclopaedia of Islam*, 2nd ed.

60. This may be the story that Shiblī heard from Jaudat, though another version has it that he resigned in 1890 due to interpersonal differences with the Grand Wazīr. Bowen, "Aḥmad Djewdat Pasha." *Encyclopaedia of Islam*, 2nd ed.

61. Aḥmad Jaudat spent part of his career in Syria, which may explain his preference for and fluency in Arabic.

62. In December 1893, following a bombing at the National Assembly in Paris, the French government passed a law restricting freedom of the press and allowing censorship.

63. This heading only appears in the second edition (1901).

64. ʿAbd al-Raḥmān al-Hamadānī, *Alfāẓ al-Kitābiyah* (Beirut: Jesuit Press, 1885). The book was edited and published by the Arabic scholar Louis Cheikho, who was based at the Jesuit college Université Saint-Joseph, which Shiblī visited during his travels.

65. Arabic: "God said."

66. Arabic: "As is in the Glorious Quran."

67. Arabic: "As it was said."

68. Arabic: "As the Quran said."

69. *Sharḥ-i ʿAqā'id-i Nasafī*. A commentary by Saʿd al-Dīn Taftazānī (1322–90) on *ʿAqā'id* (Tenets) by Najm al-Dīn al-Nasafī (d. 1142). Heffening, "al-Nasafī" and Madelung, "al-Taftazānī." *Encyclopaedia of Islam*, 2nd ed. Shiblī later listed *Sharḥ-i ʿAqā'id-i Nasafī* among the standard madrasa textbooks that should be removed from the curriculum of studies at the Arabic-Islamic academy that he administered. Shiblī Nuʿmānī, *Makātīb-i Shiblī* (Azamgarh: Maʿārif, 1927), 1:162–63.

70. Arabic: "The imams [leaders] are from the Quraish [the tribe of the Prophet]." A hadith that plays a central role in debate over caliphal succession. The hadith was instrumental in suppressing claims of the Anṣārī community to the right to succeed the Prophet and in garnering acceptance for the succession of Abū Bakr (the first caliph of Sunnī Islam). Watt, "Ḳuraysh." *Encyclopaedia of Islam*, 2nd ed.

71. *Maʿārif* was the least expensive of a handful of illustrated magazines widely available in the Ottoman Empire in the 1890s. Ahmet A. Ersoy, "Ottomans and the Kodak Galaxy: Archiving Everday Life and Historical Space in Ottoman Illustrated Journals," *History of Photography* 40, no. 3 (2016): 330–57.

72. *Rasamlī Ghazatah* (Ressimli Gazetta; Resimli Gazete), a weekly illustrated review first published in March 1889. Early numbers carried articles on science, current events, and history written for popular audiences. See *Rasamlī Gazatah* 1–5 (Constantinople, 1889–93); Syed Tanvir Wasti, "Süleyman Nazif—A Multi-Faceted Personality," *Middle Eastern Studies* 50, no. 3 (2014): 493–508. *Muṣawwar Jahān* (Musavver Cihan), published from 1891, was an illustrated journal that played an important role in the promotion of European science in Turkish. *Śarwat-i Funūn* (Servet-i Fünun), published from 1891 to 1944, was a weekly journal and a major platform for French aesthetics in Turkish. It was edited by Aḥmad Iḥsān (1868–1942), a graduate of the Maktab-i Mulkiyah who began his career in journalism translating French literature, especially the novels of Jules Verne, into Turkish. Like Fāṭimah's works ʿAliyah's *Niswān-i Islām*, *Śarwat-i Funūn* was also featured at the 1893 Chicago Exposition. Syed Tanvir Wasti, "Ahmed İhsan and the 'Wealth of Sciences,'" *Middle Eastern Studies* 52, no. 2 (2016): 359–74. One scholar identifies these journals as among those published during "the golden age of the illustrated [Ottoman] journal," which began in the 1890s. Ahmet Ersoy, "Ottomans and the Kodak Galaxy: Archiving Everyday Life and Historical Space in Ottoman Illustrated Journals," *History of Photography* 40, no. 2 (2016): 330–57.

73. ʿAbū al-Żiyā (see Appendix 1).

74. Nawal Kishore (d. 1895). Publisher and founder of the largest publishing house in British India. The press turned out large numbers of texts in Arabic, Persian, Sanskrit, and Urdu in the nineteenth century. Ulrike Stark, *An Empire of Books: The Naval Kishore Press and the Diffusion of the Printed Word in Colonial India* (Ranikhet: Permanent Black, 2007); Shscheglova, "Lithography II. In India." *Encyclopaedia Iranica.*

75. Muḥammad ibn Ismāʿīl (al-)Bukhārī (810–70), collector of hadith. The name given to his collection, *Ṣaḥīḥ Bukhārī* (*ṣaḥīḥ* meaning authentic, true), points to its high regard in Sunnī intellectual history. Badr al-Dīn (al-)ʿAinī (1361–1451), historian and hadith critic. Shiblī refers to ʿAinī's *ʿUmdat al-qārī li sharḥ Ṣaḥīḥ al-Bukhārī*, an authoritative commentary on Bukhārī's hadith collection. It was published by the al-Sharikat al-Saḥāfiyah al-ʿUsmāniyah in eleven volumes in 1892. Marmon, "al- ʿAynī, Abū Muḥammad Badr al-Dīn" and Melchert, "al-Bukhārī" in *Encyclopaedia of Islam, Three.*

76. *kharq-i ʿādat.* Also translatable as "a miracle," although Shiblī, following other Islamic thinkers, distinguishes it from "miracle" (*muʿjizah*) in his theological writing. Shiblī Nuʿmānī, *al-Ghazālī* (Azamgarh: Maʿārif, 1928), 138–42; Shiblī Nuʿmānī, *al-Kalām* (Kanpur: Nāmī Press, 1904), 64–130.

77. Qaṣr-i Humāyūn. Modern Turkish: Kasrı Hümayun (royal or blessed palace).

78. Modern Turkish Spellings: Ayasofya Camii; Beyazıt Camii; Yol Camii; Eski Hamidiye; Şeyhülİslam Aşırefendi; Nakibül'l-eşraf Esad Efendi; Fatih Camii; Yeni Hamdiye; Şehid Ali Paşa; Nur-i Osmaniye; Laleli; Hekimoğlu Alipaşa; Köprülü Mehmet Paşa; Kılıç Ali Paşa; Veliyyüddin Efendi; Selimiye; Feyzullah Effendi; Kadızade Sultan Mehmet; Valide Sultan Camii; Atıf Efendi; Damat İbrahim Paşa; Hüsrev Paşa; Mihrişah; Mehmet Efendi; Mustafa Efendi; Tevfik Efendi; Süleymaniye; Mehmet Murat Efendi; Ragıb Paşa. See Şibli Numani, *Anadolu, Suriye ve Mısır Seyahatnamesi*, trans. Yusuf Karaca (Istanbul: Risale, 2002), 90.

79. Also known as the Thornhill-Mayne Memorial Library (1878). The building was designed by Richard Roskell Bayne of the East Indian Railway. Art historians characterize its style as "Scottish baronial" and describe its roof as elaborate. Jonathan Bloom and Sheila Blair, ed., "Allahabad." *The Grove Encyclopedia of Islamic Art and Architecture* Oxford University Press, 2009, http://www.oxfordreference.com.

80. ʿAbd al-Qāhir al-Jurjānī (d. 1078) was a scholar of Arabic language and literature. *Asrār al-balāghah* is celebrated by later scholars as the foundational text of *ʿilm al-bayān* (the science of description) a subfield of rhetoric. The book focuses largely on figurative language. Deeb, "al-Djurdjānī." *Encyclopaedia of Islam*, 2nd ed. *Asrār al-balāghah* was part of the curriculum of studies in theology that Shiblī later developed for the Nadwat al-ʿUlamā academy at Lucknow. Shiblī Nuʿmānī, *Bāqiyāt-i Shiblī* (Lahore: Majlis-i Taraqqī-i Adab, 1965), 102–3.

81. *zarīn* (golden) and *zar-afshān* (gold-scattering). Technical terms used to describe styles of calligraphy and paper ornamentation. See Ḥamīd Riżā Qalīchkhānī, *Farhang-i wāzhigān o iṣṭilāḥāt-i khwush-nawīsī o hunar-hā-yi wābastah* (Tehran, 1994), 110–111.

82. For Shiblī's detailed studies of Arabic translation during the Abbasid period, see Shiblī Nu'mānī, *Musalmānon kī Guzishtah Ta'līm* (Lucknow, 1888) and Shiblī Nu'mānī, "Tarājim" in *Rasā'il-i Shiblī* (Amritsar, 1898), 200–345.

83. Muḥammad ibn Ḥayyān Ṣadaqah al-Żabbī (d. 918). Author of *Akhbār al-Quẓāt* (a biographical dictionary of qāẓīs), first published in 1950. Reinhart, "Wakī'." *Encyclopaedia of Islam*, 2nd ed.

84. Shiblī may refer to *I'jāz al-Qur'ān* by Abū Bakr Muḥammad Baqillānī (d. 1013), theologian and jurisprudent. The book studies the themes and rhetoric in Arabic poetry and discusses the inimitability of the rhetoric of the Quran. In November 1894, Shiblī recommended that the book be sought from the Khedival Library in Cairo and published from Hyderabad. His recommendation was based both on the strength of his own judgment that it was the finest of all books written on the subject and on the strength of the opinion of Abū Bakr 'Arabī (Ibn 'Arabī), who claimed that no one had written its equal. He later appealed for funding to purchase and publish the text. By 1910, he had introduced the text into the curriculum of literary studies at the Nadwat al-'Ulamā academy. Shiblī Nu'mānī, *Bāqiyāt-i Shiblī* (Lahore, 1965), 141–42; Shiblī Nu'mānī, *Maqālāt-i Shiblī* (Azamgarh: Ma'ārif, 1930–38), 8:45–47; Shiblī Nu'māni, ed., *Rūdād-i dār al-'ulūm Nadwat al-'Ulamā . . . 1907, 1908, 1909* (Lucknow: Āsī Press, 1909), 6–7.

85. Abū 'Alī Sīnā, also Ibn(-i) Sīnā (980–1037); also known as Avicenna. Polymath remembered especially for his writings in philosophy and medicine. Goichon, "Ibn Sīnā." *Encyclopaedia of Islam*, 2nd ed. Abū Sa'īd Abū al-Khair (967–1049), mystic from Khurāsān. Scholars suggest that the correspondence between Abū al-Khair and Ibn-i Sīnā may be authentic. Böwering, "Abū Sa'īd Abi'l-Ḵayr." *Encyclopaedia Iranica*. Shiblī records that the correspondence is available in the form of a *risālah* (tract; booklet; magazine).

86. Salomon Munk (see Appendix 1).

87. Shiblī relied on *Tārīkh al-ḥukamā* in his study of Persian poetry (first published in 1909), specifically in his biographical study of 'Umar Khayyām. The work was published from Leipzig in 1903. Shiblī Nu'mānī, *Shi'r al-'Ajam* (Azamgarh: Ma'ārif, 1920), 1:227–28.

88. In 1909, Shiblī wrote a review of the Gibb Memorial Series' edition of *Tajārub al-'umam*. Shilbi, *Maqālāt*, 4:19–28. Shiblī drew from Miskawaih throughout his career. His closest study of Miskawaih is found in his dense historical study of the Islamic theological tradition, first published in 1902. Shiblī used the European critical edition of Tajārub al-'umam. He also used a Beirut edition of *al-Fauz al-aṣghar*, another of Miskawaih's works. The edition was published by the Catholic Press, which Shiblī visited and discusses in the travelogue. It included a preface by Ṭāhir al-Jazā'irī (also known as al-Maghribī), whom Shiblī met at Beirut and discusses in the travelogue. See Shiblī Nu'mānī, *'Ilm al-kalām* (Aligarh: Maṭba'-i Aḥmadī, 1910), 125–45.

89. Shiblī used the European edition of al-Ḥamawī's history, *Mu'jim al-buldān*, in his earliest works on translation into Arabic, Islamic intellectual culture, and the Abbasid caliph Māmūn, all of which he had published before his journey.

90. In 1896, Shiblī spoke about the recent committee formed in Europe whose objective was to compile a critical edition of this work by Ibn Sa'd, which compiles the biographies of early hadith transmitters. Shiblī's cousin, Ḥamīd al-Dīn Farāhī, then a student at Aligarh, translated a portion of the book from Arabic into Persian at the request of Mahdī 'Alī Khān (known as Muḥsin al-Mulk), an affiliate and supporter of the college and a close friend of Sayyid Aḥmad Khān. One of the editors of the European edition, Josef Horovitz (1874–1931), was later hired as professor of Arabic at Aligarh. Farāhī was soon hired as assistant professor, a position he held from 1907 to 1908, during which time he is said to have assisted Horovitz on the project. Sharf al-Dīn Iṣlāḥī, *Żikr-i Farāhī* (Azamgarh: Dā'irah-i Ḥamīdiyah, 2001), 220–23.

91. Shiblī relied on this book in his biography of 'Umar, the second caliph of Sunnī Islam, for information about 'Umar's character.

92. Shiblī cites Jāḥiẓ's book in his discussion of the speeches of 'Umar ibn Khaṭṭāb in his study of 'Umar (see note 91 above).

93. Shiblī recommended to the Dā'irat al-Ma'ārif that *Dalā'il-i i'jāz* be acquired from the As'ad Āfandī library in Constantinople and published from Hyderabad. Shiblī Nu'mānī, *Bāqiyāt-i Shiblī* (Lahore, 1965), 142.

94. This text was available, at least in manuscript form, in India. Shilbī's Arabic teacher, Faiż al-Ḥasan Sahāranpūrī, who worked under Gottlieb Leitner at the Oriental College in Lahore, had used the text as a source in his own lengthy (eight-hundred-page) study of al-Ḥamāsah (the name of Abū Tammām's collection of Arabic poetry). Faiż al-Ḥasan's work was published in 1877 by Nawal Kishore. See Faiż al-Ḥasan Sahāranpūrī, *Sharḥ al-Ḥamāsah al-ma'rūf bal-Faiżī* (Lucknow: Nawal Kishor, 1977).

95. The Egyptian edition of this text lists its author as Abū Sa'īd Muḥammad ibn Aḥmad al-'Ubaidī. See 'Ubaidī, *al-Ibānah sirqāt al-Mutanabbī lafaẓā wa ma'nī* (Cairo: al-Maṭba'ah al-'Aṣabiyah, n.d.).

96. This list of texts offers unique insight into Shiblī's broad and overlapping interests in Arabic literature. Most of the works are historical in nature: universal histories; travel literature; biographical literature; genealogy. Others concern issues of aesthetics, especially poetry and eloquence, or are themselves collections of verse. The works belong to the eighth through fourteenth centuries and cover a range of fields: the biographical dictionary of hadith transmitters by Bukhārī; the general and biographical history of Islam by Żahabī (which is modeled on Jauzī); the biographical dictionary of physicians, philosophers, and astronomers by Qibṭī; and the collections of Arabic poetry. Further, Shiblī may have had in mind to do some kind of comparative study of Arabic aesthetics, for which this list would have been an excellent point of departure. Indeed, Shiblī had studied Abū Tammām's collection in his youth and was aware if its importance in Arabic aesthetics. He may also have been aware that al-'Askarī in *Ṣinā'atain*, criticizes the ideas about aesthetics put forth by Jāḥiẓ in *Kitāb al-bayān*.

97. *Log* (people) is changed to *bāshindoṅ* (obl. pl. of *bāshindah* [resident]) in the second edition.

98. Standard textbooks in the Arabic curriculum nineteenth-century India commonly called the Dars-i Niẓāmī. Shiblī discusses teaching the *Īsāghūjī to students at Constantinople in the travelogue. Later, he proposed removing Mukhtaṣar al-ma'ānī* from the curriculum at his own academy. Shiblī Nu'*mānī, Makātīb-i Shiblī* (Azamgarh, 1927), 1:162–63.

99. Abū Ja'far Muḥammad (al-)Ṭabarī (839–923). Ṭabarī's universal history in Arabic. Shiblī refers to the edition published from Leiden, *Anneles quos scripsit Abu Djafar Mohammed ibn Djarir at-Tabari* (1879–1901) (15 vols.), which was compiled by a team of scholars led by the Orientalist Michael Jan de Goeje. Bosworth, "al-Ṭabarī." *Encyclopaedia of Islam*, 2nd ed.

100. Shāh 'Abd al-'Azīz (1746–1824). Reformer, hadith scholar, and son and successor of the influential Indian theologian Shāh Walīullāh (1703–62).

101. Dā'irat al-Ma'ārif (the Circle of the Sciences). An organization founded around 1888 whose purpose was, along with the Āṣafiyah library, to collect, edit, and publish rare works of Arabic literature. Iqbāl Yār Jang (see Appendix 1) was among its founders, which also included Sayyid Ḥusain Bilgrāmī (1842–1926, statesman at Hyderabad). Shiblī had severely criticized in print a piece by Bilgrāmī on Ibn Rushd and the Arabic historical tradition not long before coming to know him through Sayyid Aḥmad Khān.

102. *zawāyā* (pl. of *zāwiyah*). An Arabic word whose basic meaning (angle or corner, hence nook) is common in Urdu. In modern Arabic, the word also means "small mosque . . . erected over the tomb of a Muslim saint with teaching facilities and a hostel attached to it, usually the establishment of a religious order." The word that Shiblī uses for *hostel* is *khānqāh* (hostel; a lodge, often associated with communities of Ṣūfīs). *Takyah* (pl. *takāyā*) meaning site of repose, from Arabic, is used in Urdu, where its primary denotation is "a pillow," though both Urdu and Persian dictionaries also gloss it as "a house of mendicants." In modern Arabic, the primary denotation is a monastery (especially of a Muslim religious order), hostel, home, or asylum (for the invalid or needy). In Ottoman Turkish, the primary denotation is likewise a convent of dervishes, asylum, or place of repose. See dictionaries by Hans Wehr, John T. Platts, James W. Redhouse, and Ghiyāṡ al-Dīn Rāmpūrī.

103. In the nineteenth century, British stereotypes about decadence and corruption in Lucknow were popularized through best-selling English fiction and reinforced by ongoing discussions in Urdu newspapers. In the twentieth century, these stereotypes were reified, most famously by a short story by Prem Chand, later adapted to film by Satyajit Ray. Other writers, however, while not rejecting notions of decadence entirely, later looked back to Lucknow with eyes of nostalgia. See "Nawabi Dastaan" and "That Famous Touch of Decadence" in *Shaam-e Awadh*, ed. Oldenburg (New Delhi: Penguin Books, 2007), 19–28, 95–158.

104. *śurayyā* (Urdu: the Pleiades).

105. The names of the first four caliphs of Sunnī Islam.

106. *müzehane* (museum).

107. *qadāmat* (seniority, oldness; conservatism; traditionalism).

108. Shaikh al-Islām (Shaikh of Islam). An honorific title given to the muftī (a person who writes fatwās) of Istanbul, in use since the fifteenth century. As the head of the Islamic intellectual community at the capital and an advisor on political and religious affairs to the sulṭān, the Shaikh al-Islām influenced religious life at the city and throughout the Ottoman territories. Following the dissolution of the Janissaries and the reorganization of the Ottoman government, the Shaikh al-Islām was given an official office in Istanbul. Repp, "Shaykh al-Islām." *Encyclopaedia of Islam*, 2nd ed.

109. Steingass gives a different etymology of the word: *khwan-kār*, from *khwand* (lord) and *gār* (genitive or possessive suffix). Francis Joseph Steingass, *A Comprehensive Persian-English Dictionary* (London: Routledge & K. Paul, 1892).

110. Maqrī kūī (Makrıköy). In contrast to what Shiblī records here, Makrıköy was the name of an area of the city later renamed Bakırköy.

111. Muḥarram, the first month of the Islamic calendar, commemorates the death of Ḥusain (grandson of the Prophet). Ḥusain was the son of ʿAlī (son-in-law of the Prophet, fourth caliph of Sunnī Islam and rightful successor to the Prophet in the eyes of Shias) and Fāṭimah (daughter of the Prophet). Ḥusain, members of his family, and his companions were killed at Karbala on 10 Muḥarram 61 Hijrī (680) by the army of the Ummayad ruler Yazīd. The martyrdom of Ḥusain and his family and companions is the subject of Muḥarram mourning rituals.

112. ʿAjam (Persia). This Arabic word relates to the Arabic *ʿujamah* (incomprehensible speech), an indication of the attitudes of Arabs in the pre-Islamic and Umayyad periods toward Persia. According to scholars, after the victory of the Abbasids, the term lost its deeply pejorative sense in Arabic and Persian, and came merely to denote ethnic difference. Shiblī used it to refer to the Persian literary ecumene in general in his study of Persian poetry, *Shiʿr al-ʿAjam* (*The Poetry of ʿAjam*).

113. Wālidah Khānah (Valide Hanı).

114. *soz* (lit., burning); *taḥt al-lafẓ* (lit., under [according to] the word). Two manners of reciting Urdu *marśiyah* poetry, which typically commemorates the death of the Prophet's grandson, Ḥusain, at Karbala. The former often refers to recitation in the form of a mournful dirge; the latter suggests spoken recitation (without melody). For Shiblī's take on both, see Shiblī Nuʿ*mānī, Muwāzanah-i Anīs o Dabīr* (Agra: Mufīd-i *ʿĀm, 1907),* 13.

115. *janāb-i amīr* (janāb [sir]; amīr [leader, nobleman]). A title of ʿAlī (the fourth caliph in the Sunnī and the first Imām in the Shīʿah Islamic traditions).

116. Shiblī's description of the narrative reading portion of the performance, as brief as it is, is especially interesting. Many of the accounts of the Muḥarram rituals in Istanbul were written by foreigners who did not understand the language and therefore wrote little

about the recitation of the Karbala narrative (Raużah-khwānī). Thus, their interest lay almost exclusively in the (often bloody) flagellar mourning rituals. These rituals attracted European and Levantine tourists, including women, some of whom stood on chairs to observe. Unlike other travelers, Shiblī does not record witnessing melodic recitation. Fifteen eyewitness accounts of the ceremonies by European travelers are surveyed by Glassen. Erika Glassen, "Muharram-Ceremonies ('Azādārī) in Istanbul at the End of the XIXth and Beginning of the XXth Century," in *Les Iraniens d'Istanbul*, ed. T. Zarcone and F. Zarinebaf-Shahr (Istanbul-Tehran, 1993), 113–29.

117. *shab-i shahādat* (eve of martyrdom). The ninth night of Muḥarram, the morning after which Ḥusain was killed.

118. According to one scholar, Muḥarram mourning rituals were not held publically in Istanbul until the 1860s, and the bloodier sword beating rituals, which initially took place in tents set up in Wālidah Khānah (which was not the center of the Iranian community in the city late in the nineteenth century), did not begin until the 1870s. Erika Glassen, "Muharram-Ceremonies ('Azādārī) in Istanbul at the End of the XIXth and Beginning of the XXth Century," in *Les Iraniens d'Istanbul*, ed. T. Zarcone and F. Zarinebaf-Shahr (Istanbul-Tehran, 1993), 113–129.

119. Ḥusain Ḥasīb kept records of the subscriptions that he collected from India during the Russo-Turkish War. Azmi Özcan, *Pan-Islamism* (Leiden: Brill, 1997), 112–13.

120. Arabic: "O God, aid and give victory to this sulṭān. The sulṭān, who is the son of the sulṭān, emperor, who is the son of the emperor, Sulṭān 'Abd al-Ḥamīd Khān.»

121. Persian: "My eye is open, but still I am dreaming." Shiblī uses the line in his Persian poem in praise of the sulṭān.

122. See "Eid Maśnawī" (pp. 100–104).

123. This poem is in Persian. See appendix for the transliteration into roman script.

124. The date is slightly confusing, since Eid began on 10 Żū al-Ḥijjah 1309 (July 6, 1892).

125. The first half of the first line is in Persian. The last word of the first line and the entire second line are in Arabic.

126. Hadith.

127. *fann* (subject; art).

128. *gulbāng* (the warbling of a nightingale; a cry or shout; the war cry, "Allah, Allah!"). See Francis Joseph Steingass, *A Comprehensive Persian-English Dictionary* (London: Routledge & K. Paul, 1892).

129. *khwān* (a cloth spread on the floor around which people sit to eat).

130. An allusion to the mark that forms on the foreheads of those who regularly touch their heads to the ground in prayer. The suggestion is that the sun and moon worship him.

131. A play on a conventional dichotomy between *daulat* (government; worldly prosperity, wealth, power) and *dīn* (creed, religion, faith).

132. Fātiḥah (lit., "opening;" the name of the first sura of the Quran). The implication is that the sulṭān's place in the realms of worldly power and religion is primary, and the connotations of the words bring the two realms together: *fāthah* (religious connotations) of worldly power (*daulat*); royal heading (worldly connotations) of religion (*dīn*).

133. Arabic: "May Allah support him with increased assistance [more victories]."

134. Two major battles in which the Prophet and his army emerged victorious. Badr (March 624) was the first major battle of the Prophet's military career. The victory at Ḥunain (630) was both overwhelming and against terrible odds. Shiblī's use of the word *tāzagī* (freshness; prosperity; joy) is also motivated by a pun on *tāz* (hastening; making an assault) and its related *tāzī* (an assault; an Arabian horse; Arabic).

135. A cliché that remains interesting. *Anjum-sipāh* (star army), said of kings whose armies have as many soldiers as there are stars in the sky.

136. *shar'* (lit. way, path; sharia).

137. *samdhī* (father-in-law of one's child).

138. Arabic: "Do not enter homes other than your [own] homes until you become familiar." (Quran 24:27). Classical and later Quranic scholars proposed that the final verb in this quotation, *tasta'nisū* (you become familiar; variously translated as "announcing your presence" [Pickthall]; "ascertain welcome" [Sahih International]) was a scribal error, and that the verb should be *tasta'ẕinū* (you ask permission), which orthographically resembles the former. Devin J. Stewart, "Notes on Medieval and Modern Emendations of the Qur'ān," in *The Qur'ān in its Historical Context*, ed. Gabriel Said Reynolds (London, New York: Routledge, 2008), 225–48; Hussein Abdul-Raof, *Theological Approaches to Qur'anic Exegesis: A Practical Comparative-Contrastice Analysis* (London, New York: Routledge, 2012), 210.

139. Aḥmad Jawād Pāshā (Ahmet Cevat Paşa) (Grand Wazīr 1891–95).

140. *sipah-sālār-i kul* (lit., army commander of all). Shiblī seems here to refer to 'Alī Riẓā Pāshā (1860–1932), who was staff lieutenant colonel (*kaimmakam kurmay yarbay*) in 1890, staff colonel (*miralay*) in 1895, and eventually became Grand Wazīr.

141. Falaknumā. A royal palace of the Niẓām built between 1884 and 1893. Bashīr Bāgh was the residence of the Hyderabadi prime minister. Shiblī visited both palaces in 1891 with Sayyid Aḥmad Khān and other affiliates of Aligarh. Muhammed Abdul Nayeem, *The Royal Palaces of the Nizams* (Hyderabad: Sai Likhitha Printers, 2009), 248; Sayyid Sulaimān Nadwī, *Ḥayāt-i Shiblī* (Azamgarh: Ma'ārif, 1943), 182–84.

142. Mahdī 'Alī Khān, Muḥsin al-Mulk (see Appendix 1).

143. Four Muslim dynasties: 'Abbāsī (750–1258), Fāṭimī (909–1171), Umawī (661–750), and Taimūrī (1370–1507).

144. *haiwān-i insān-numā*.

145. *shurafā* (noble; upper class).

146. The Dār al-Mu'allimāt (Darülmuallimat) (The House of Women Teachers), founded in 1869. Students included the daughters of Turkish aristocrats, some with ties

to the Topkapı Palace. Rafīqah Khānam (Refika Hanım) taught music there and later became its director. She also taught piano lessons privately to Fāṭimah ʻAliyah. Fanny Davis, *The Ottoman Lady: A Social History from 1718–1918* (Westport: Greenwood Press, 1986), 51; *Dünden Bugüne İstanbul Ansıklopedısı* (Ankara, 1993–95), 2:566–67.

147. *kız sanayi mektebi* (industrial or arts and crafts school for girls). The students at kız sanayi mektebi schools were trained in childcare, education, music, and practical crafts such as sewing and embroidery. They worked in factories, producing both fine decorative items as well as underwear and bandages for the military. Fanny Davis, *The Ottoman Lady: A Social History from 1718–1918* (Westport: Greenwood Press, 1986), 52; Elif Ekin Akşit, "Girls' Institutes and the Rearrangement of the Public and the Private Spheres in Turkey," *A Social History of Late Ottoman Women: New Perspectives*, ed. Duygu Köksal and Anastasia Failerou (Leiden: Brill, 2013), 137; *Dünden Bugüne İstanbul Ansıklopedısı* (Ankara, 1993–95), 5:12–13.

148. Madanī ʻAzīz Āfandī (Medeni Aziz Efendi) (see Appendix 1).

149. Annie Hanly (1857–1907) (see Appendix 1).

150. Founded as a small school for girls in 1878, this became an official *kız sanayi mektebi* in 1881. For further discussions of women's education at Istanbul, see Fanny Davis, *The Ottoman Lady: A Social History from 1718–1918* (Westport: Greenwood Press, 1986), 45–60; Elif Ekin Akşit, "Girls' Institutes and Public and Private Spheres in Turkey," in *A Social History of Late Ottoman Women*, ed. Duygu Köksal and Anastasia Failerou (Leiden: Brill, 2007), 133–49.

151. Khairiyah Khānam (Hayriye Hanım) (see Appendix 1).

152. The Arabic translation, titled *Nisā' al-Muslimīn*, was first published in the Beirut-based Arabic journal, *Ṡamarāt al-funūn*, then as a separate volume in 1309 Hijrī (1891–92). The Urdu translation was based on the Arabic, not the Turkish, and even retained the Arabic title, *Nisā' al-Muslimīn* (Fāṭimāh Khānam, *Nisā al-muslimīn*, trans. Saʻīd Aḥmad (Aligarh: Muhammadan Press, n.d.]). Fāṭimah ʻAliyah remained a part of discussions of women in Islam in the following decades in Urdu. *Khawātīn*, a collection of biographical articles on "Islamic ladies" (*Islāmī khawātīn*) published in 1914, brought together entries originally published in the Aligarh-based magazine by the same name. The collection ends with an entry on her. Aslam Jairājpūrī, ed., *Khawātīn* (Aligarh: Faiż-i ʻĀm, 1914), 237–40.

153. This style of covering in public, said to have been borrowed from Syria, gained currency in Istanbul in the last decades of the nineteenth century. Members of the Turkish aristocracy, including women, viewed it as uncouth, foreign and, at times, dangerous, at least at first. Indeed, Sulṭān ʻAbd al-Ḥamīd II briefly banned it in April 1892, but later promoted it as a means of protection in public. Fanny Davis, *The Ottoman Lady: A Social History from 1718–1918* (Westport: Greenwood Press, 1986), 187, 197–198.

154. Shiblī's perspective on women's appearance in public spaces differs from that of his acquaintance, Aḥmad Jaudat Pāshā (see Appendix 1), who lamented the change,

which he saw as ruinous to chastity and Islamic ethics, financially irresponsible, and motivated by a desire to imitate European women. Fanny Davis, *The Ottoman Lady: A Social History from 1718–1918* (Westport: Greenwood Press, 1986), 197.

155. Nuṣrat ʿAlī (see Appendix 1). Here, Shiblī refers to the short-lived journal, *Paik-i Islām* (The Messenger of Islam). First published from Istanbul in 1880, one aim of the paper was to strengthen ties between Indians and the Ottoman state. Ottoman pan-Islamic rhetoric typically described ʿAbd al-Ḥamīd as the caliph of Islam, but the first issue of *Paik-i Islām* shifted from religious to political authority, declaring him to be the caliph of India. This caused alarm, and pressure from British officials soon led to the closure of the paper. Seema Alavi, *Muslim Cosmopolitanism in the Age of Empire* (Cambridge: Harvard University Press, 2015), 296–97; Kemal H. Karpat, *The Politicization of Islam: Reconstructing Identity, State, Faith, and Community in the Late Ottoman State* (New York: Oxford University Press, 2001), 211–14. Alavi writes that Nuṣrat ʿAlī fraudulantly claimed to be Sayyid Nuṣrat ʿAlī, the editor of the paper *Nuṣrat al-akhbār* of Delhi. Sayyid Nuṣrat ʿAlī was also a correspondent of Sayyid Aḥmad Khān. Pānipatī mentions nothing about the fraud in his brief biographical sketch of Sayyid Nuṣrat ʿAlī, but he does say that Sayyid Nuṣrat ʿAlī's knew Turkish well. Sayyid Aḥmad Khān, *Maktūbāt-i Sir Sayyid* (Lahore, 1976), 2:210. Sayyid Nuṣrat ʿAlī Dihlawī collected subscriptions for Turks in the Russo-Turkish War (many Muslims in India did). Ahmad Saeed, *Muslim India, 1857–1947: A Biographical Dictionary* (Lahore: Institute of Pakistan Historical Research, 1997), 260. Sayyid Nuṣrat ʿAlī Dihlawī also appears to have studied English, and wrote works in lexicography, ethics, and theology. ʿAbd al-Ḥayy, *Nuzhat al-Khawāṭir* (Beirut, 1999), 1393. None of these sources mention the Nuṣrat ʿAlī whom Shiblī met in Constantinople or his fraudulent claim to be Sayyid Nuṣrat ʿAlī of Delhi.

156. Roger A. Deal paints a very different picture of Mirzā Muḥammad's character and his association with Ḥasan Āfandī. In 1898, Mirzā Muḥammad was accused of murdering another émigré from India named ʿAbd al-Waḥīd. Apparently, ʿAbd al-Waḥīd had insulted Mirzā Muḥammad in a private letter. In the trial, it was said that Ḥasan ʿAlī had invited ʿAbd al-Waḥīd to his home, where Mirzā Muḥammad had murdered him with a sword. Ḥasan ʿAlī was wounded in the process. Ḥasan ʿAlī's son was put on trial for wounding Mirzā Muḥammad. Mirzā Muḥammad claimed at his own trial that Ḥasan ʿAlī's son and a group of armed men had ambushed him and ʿAbd al-Waḥīd in the room where they had been seated, and that he had wounded Ḥasan ʿAlī during the fight in self-defense. The prosecution read a translation of the letter insulting Mirzā Muḥammad and claimed that Ḥasan ʿAlī and his family had been wounded while attempting to subdue Mirzā Muḥammad. In the end, the court convicted the eighty-five-year-old Mirzā Muḥammad. The motive was likely financial. During the trial, it was reported that Mirzā Muḥammad was in the habit of wearing a sword at his waist. Ḥasan ʿAlī was said to have developed friendly relationships with his neighbors. Roger A. Deal, *Crimes of Honor,*

Drunken Brawls and Murder: Violence in Istanbul under 'Abdülhamid II (Istanbul: Libra Kitapçılık ve Yayıncılık, 2010) 177–81.

157. Ḥasan 'Alī Faiżī (1838–1903) and Badr al-Dīn Ṭayyibjī (1844–1906) (see Appendix 1).

158. *na'am* (Arabic: yes); *hāṅ* (Urdu: yes). That is, Shiblī responded in Arabic.

159. Mujauhar Badastān (Mücevher Bedesten) (lit., jewelry market). The Grand Bazaar in Istanbul. The travelogue records the address (in Ottoman Turkish) with the affix *dah* (*de*; in). This is changed to *inde* in the Turkish translation.

160. Khalid ibn al-Walīd (d. 642). Military commander who fought under the Prophet and Abū Bakr (the first caliph of Sunnī Islam). Crone, "Khālid b. al-Walīd." *Encyclopaedia of Islam*, 2nd ed.

161. The allusion seems to be to the Shihāb (Chehab) family, which held political authority in the Lebanese mountains in the eighteenth and early nineteenth centuries. The Lebanese side of the family gradually converted to Marionism, but the side of the family centered at Hasbaya remained Muslim. As Shiblī records, the family traced its lineage to Khālid b. al-Walīd (q.v.). The family's political control in the region is said to have ended with the exile of Bashir III in 1841. However, Shiblī's discussion of Fawād suggests that the family remained influential, perhaps in part by means of its ties to Ottoman institutions. Mikhail Mishaqa, *Murder, Mayhem, Pillage, and Plunder: The History of Lebanon in the 18th and 19th Centuries*, trans. Wheeler M. Thackston (Albany: State University of New York Press, 1988), 23; Bruce Masters, "Shihab family." *Encyclopedia of the Ottoman Empire*, edited by Gábor Ágoston and Bruce Masters. Facts on File, 2009.

162. *Īsāghūjī* (*Isagogue*) (see note 47 above).

163. Tamghah-i Majīdiyah (Majīdī Medal). Named after Sulṭān 'Abd al-Majīd (Abdülmecid), the Majīdī (Mecidi) Order was created in 1852 shortly following the reform of Ottoman distinctions and the recall of all previous Ottoman medals. Unlike the old orders, the Madjīdī was systematically organized, and its distinctions were clearly defined in detailed, official statutes. In line with Ottoman economic reforms, the medals themselves were to be more inexpensively produced; the old custom of diamond-set badges was replaced by metal ones. The number of medals that could be awarded was limited in each class, but these limitations did not apply to foreigners. The fourth-class medal, which Shiblī received, was to be pinned on the left side of the chest. Higher degrees were to be worn around the neck. According to one historian, medals of the lower orders were "relatively easy to come by." This seems to have been especially true in the case of foreigners like Shiblī. The award was given to European statesmen and artists, including Austrian royalty and a Russian artist. Edhem Eldem, *Pride and Privilege: A History of Ottoman Orders, Medals and Decorations* (Istanbul: Ottoman Bank Archives and Research Centre, 2004), 147, 176–91. One Shiblī scholar suggests that Shiblī's being awarded the Majīdī was not so remarkable, as it had often been awarded to Indians who, like Shiblī,

had raised funds during the Russo-Turkish war of 1876–77, and that the award may have been given because of Shiblī's relationship with Aligarh, which, in part because of its ties to the British state, had long shown support for the Ottoman Empire. Amīn Zubairī, *Żikr-i Shiblī* (Lucknow, 1946), 48–54.

164. *ṭarīqat-i sunnat* (lit., way of; tradition, orthodoxy). The word *sunnat* (related to Sunnī) carries connotations of the traditions tied to the Prophet. It therefore suggests a religiously orthodox greeting, specifically *salām 'alaik*, *salāmu 'alaikum*, and so on, sometimes called *salām-i masnūn*.

165. Writing around 1940, Sayyid Sulaimān Nadwī (Shiblī's student and most influential biographer) records an anecdote that he attributes to Ḥabīb al-Raḥmān Shirwānī, who was Shiblī's colleague and correspondent from the 1890s until 1914. According to the anecdote, when the hand of one was in the other, Shiblī asked (Ghāzī) 'Uṡmān Pāshā for permission to kiss the hand with which he had slain the *kuffār* (pl. of *kāfir*: nonbelievers, heretics, infidels). In response, the pāshā said that Shiblī's hand, which had performed intellectual services, was worthy of kissing, and kissed Shiblī's hand. Sayyid Sulaimān Nadwī, *Ḥayāt-i Shiblī* (Azamgarh: Ma'ārif, 1943), 210.

166. *mābain* (*mabeyn*) (lit., what is in between; offices at the sulṭān's palace that attended to private and official matters).

167. Arabic: "O Shiblī! By Allah! Indeed, a medal has appeared for you!"

168. The British ambassador to Constantinople in 1892 was Francis Clare Ford (1828–1899). Ford's tenure in Constantinople was unwanted and short. He arrived in January of that year, and, according to his biographer, "found himself unequal to the strain of so difficult a position." He transferred to Rome in December, 1893. See Matthew and Seccombe, "Ford, Sir (Francis) Clare" in *Oxford Dictionary of National Biography*, Oxford University Press, 2004, http://www.oxforddnb.com/view/article/35108.

169. *'ulamā aur fużalā*.

170. "This photograph of me was given as a gift to Shiblī Nu'mānī. Muḥarram 1310 Hijrī [July/August, 1892]" (*İş bu fotoğrafım Şibli Numani Efendi'ye hediye edilmiştir*). Şibli Numani, *Andolu, Suriye ve Misir Seyahatnamesi (Sefername-i Rum u Şam u Mısır)*, trans. Yusuf Karaca (Fatih: Risale, 2002), 129.

171. Karaca transliterates the decree into modern Turkish as follows: "*Hindistan'ın Aligarh nâm mahallinde kâin dârü'l-ülûm muallim-i evveli Şiblî Nûmanî Efendi'nin şayân-ı iltifat-ı seniyye-i şahanem olduğuna binâen şeref-efzâ-yi sünûh ve südûr olan emr ü ferman-ı meâli-ünvan-ı padişahanem mûcib-i âlîsi üzre kendisine mecîdî nişân-ı zîşânın dördüncü rütbesinden bir kıt'ası inayet ve ihsan kılınmış olduğunu mutazammın işbu berât-ı âlî-şânım tasdîr olundu. Muharremü'l-haram ayının 14'ünde bu berât yazıldı. Sene Hicrî 1310.*" The final section begins with an Arabic formula, *ḥurrira fī* (written on the day of). Şibli Numani, *Andolu, Suriye ve Misir Seyahatnamesi (Sefername-i Rum u Şam u Mısır)*, trans. Yusuf Karaca (Fatih: Risale, 2002), 129–30.

172. 14 Muḥarram 1310 (August 8, 1892).

173. Shiblī convinced Sayyid Aḥmad Khān to use the medal as leverage to convince British officials to award him the title of *Shams al-'ulamā* (Sun of the Scholars), and the award was announced in January 1894. Sayyid Aḥmad Khān corresponded the British administration about the award, and on February 16, 1894, wrote to request that the British commissioner Harington present Shiblī with the certificate and ceremonial cloak in person. Roper Lethbridge, *The Golden Book of India: A Genealogical and Biographical Dictionary of the Ruling Princes, Chiefs, Nobles, and other Personages, Titled or Decorated, of the Indian Empire* (London, S. Low, Marston & Company Limited, 1900), 291; Sayyid Aḥmad Khān, *Sir Syed's Correspondence: Selected Documents from the Sir Syed Academy Archives* (London: Published for the Department of History, Aligarh Muslim University, by Asia Publishing House, 167), 181.

174. 26 Muḥarram 1309 Hijrī (September 1, 1891) is surely a copyist's error, though it remains unchanged in the second edition, too. If we assume that the month and date are correct, then Shiblī left on 26 Muḥarram 1310 (August 20, 1892).

175. Larnaca and Limassol were standard stops en route to Constantinople in the late nineteenth century. For comparisons with a visit in 1878, see Annie Brassey, *Sunshine and Storm in the East: Or, Cruises to Cyprus and Constantinople* (New York: H. Holt, 1890).

176. *ra'īs* (Urdu: governor; nobleman). In Ottoman Turkish, the word meant a ship's captain or seaman. Soucek, "Ra'īs." *Encyclopaedia of Islam*, 2nd ed.

177. August 27, 1892.

Beirut

1. Arabic: "*wa 'iqāb Lubnān wa kaif bi-qaṭ'ihā / wa hiya al-shatā' wa ṣaifuhunna shitā'*." Shiblī does not translate or gloss the couplet.

2. Shiblī discusses the poetry and character of Khansā (fifth to sixth century) in his discussion of veiling in Islam. Shiblī, *Maqālāt*, 1:115.

3. Jāhiliyah (lit., period of ignorance; the pre-Islamic period)

4. Farazdaq (d. ca. 730) and Jarīr (d. ca. 728–29). Two Arabic poets. Jarīr was the rival of Akhṭal and Farazdaq. Anṭūn Ṣāliḥānī, whom Shiblī met in Beirut, edited the standard critical edition of the poetry of Akhṭal and later published the Naqā'id (rivalrous poems) of Jarīr and Akhṭal. Blachère, "al-Farazdaḳ" and Gäthe an Schaade, "Djarīr." *Encyclopaedia of Islam*, 2nd ed., edited by P. Bearman T. Bianquis, C. E. Bosworth, E. van Donzel, and W. P. Heinrichs. BrillOnline. https://referenceworks.brillonline.com/browse/encyclopaedia-of-islam-2. See also Anṭūn Ṣāliḥānī (see Appendix 1).

5. Vikor Romanovich Rozen (also Victor von Rosen) (1864–1908). Russian Orientalist and professor at St. Petersburg University. For a brief overview of Rozen's career and a discussion of his influence on Russian Orientalism in the twentieth century, see Vera Tolz, *Russian's Own Orient: The Politics of Identity and Oriental Studies in the Late Imperial and Early Soviet Periods* (Oxford, New York: Oxford University Press, 2011), 1–13.

6. *Raużat al-adab fī ṭabaqāt shu'arā' al-'Arab* (1858) by Iskandar ibn Ya'qūb Abkāriyūs (d. 1885); *Majānī al-adab* and *Sharḥ-i Majānī al-adab* by Louis Cheikho (Jesuit priest, faculty member at the Université Saint-Joseph in Beirut). Both books by Cheikho were used as course books in Arabic literature. *Majānī al-adab* is an anthology in six volumes and *Sharḥ-i Majānī al-adab* (Commentary on Majānī al-adab) is in three (and also includes an index). Ed., "Iskandar Agha" and Pouzet, "Luwīs Shaykhū." *Encyclopaedia of Islam*, 2nd ed.

7. Both texts were published by the Catholic press and comprise writings by Badī' al-Zamān Hamażānī (968–1008). *Maqāmāt-i Badī' (Maqāmāt Abī al-Fażl Badī' al-Zamān al-Hamażānī)* (pub. 1889) was critically edited and annotated by Muhammad 'Abduh (see Appendix 1), whom Shiblī met in Cairo. *Kashf al-ma'ānī wal-bayān 'an] Rasā'il-i Badī'* (1890) was compiled and annotated by Ibrāhīm al-Aḥdab (1827–91), an Islamic scholar of the Ḥanafī tradition. Hamażānī's *Maqāmāt* is credited with inaugurating the genre of *maqāmah* or *maqāmāt* (assemblies) literature in Arabic, which includes enlightening speeches and stories related to history, legend, grammar, philology, and poetry, among other topics. The most famous maqāmāt in Arabic are those of Ḥarīrī (1054–1122). These were included in the curriculum of studies in colonial India, and Shiblī therefore almost certainly taught them to his students. Brockelmann and Pellat, "Maḳāma;" Blachère, "al-Hamadhānī;" Ed., "Ibrāhīm b. 'Alī al-Aḥdab." *Encyclopaedia of Islam*, 2nd ed. The press praised 'Abduh's edition as a great service to Arabic letters. *L'Imprimerie catholique de Beyrouth et son oeuvre en Orient (1853–1903)* (Bruxelles: Polleunis et Ceuterick, 1903), 92.

8. In this and the following sentences it is not clear if Shiblī refers to the taste of the poet whom he met or the literary society at Beirut in general. The translation assumes the latter.

9. The typical progression of standard examinations administered by the university system in British India was the entrance examination, then first examination in arts (FA), then bachelor of arts (BA).

10. Cornelius Van Dyck (see Appendix 1).

11. *Naqsh fī al-ḥajar* (*A Mark in the Stone*). The name appears slightly differently on the covers of the original volumes (*al-Naqsh fī al-ḥajar* [*The Mark in the Stone*]). These texts included an introductory textbook by Van Dyck on Astronomy, *Fī 'Ilm al-Hai'ah* (On the Science of Forms/Astronomy) (Beirut, 1888).

12. It is not clear in this sentence if Shiblī refers here to Van Dyck or to Beirut-based scholars in general. The translation assumes the former.

13. Buṭrus al-Bustānī (see Appendix 1). Salīm Āfandī (1846–84) was a novelist, journalist, and reformer. Najīb al-Bustānī (1862–1919) wrote for Arabic journals and practiced law at Cairo. Yūsuf Sarkīs, *Mu'jam al-maṭbū'āt al-'Arabiyah wal-mu'arrabah* (Egypt, 1928–31), 561; 'Abdel-Nour, "al-Bustānī." *Encyclopaedia of Islam*, 2nd ed.

14. *Āṡār al-adhār* (*Traces of the Ages*). An encyclopedia of history and geography begun in 1875 and edited by Salīm Shiḥādah (1848–1907) and Salīm al-Khūrī (1834–75). The Egyptian writer Muḥammad 'Abduh, whom Shiblī met a Cairo, also contributed.

15. Two works by Naufal Ni'mat Allāh Naufal Ṭarābulusī (1812–1887). *Ṣannājat al-ṭarab fī taqaddumat al-'Arab* is a history of Arab civilization published by the American press at Beirut. *Zubdat al-ṣaḥā 'if fī uṣūl al-ma'ārif*, which was also published from Bombay in 1308 Hijrī (1891–92) by a Christian press, is a handbook of geographies, communities, and sciences. For a brief, introductory discussion of Naufal's influence on Arabic intellectual history, see Abdul Latif Tibawi, *A Modern History of Syria, Including Lebanon and Palestine* (London: Macmillan; New York: St. Martin's Press, 1969), 197–98.

16. Arabic: "So take heed, you who have vision!" (Quran 59:2).

17. *kulliyah* (Arabic: college, university; Urdu: generalization, general principle; related to kull [all, complete])

18. In French and English, the institution is typically called the Université Saint-Joseph.

19. 'Abd al-Bāsiṭ Āfandī (see Appendix 1).

20. Ilyās (see Appendix 1).

21. Abū al-Żiyā (see Appendix 1).

22. Anṭūn Ṣāliḥānī (see Appendix 1).

23. Established in 1870, the journal *al-Bashī*r was the organ of the Université Saint-Joseph in the last half of the nineteenth century. In the 1880s, it engaged in anti-Darwinian polemics, largely in response to publications by scholars affiliated with the Protestant College (later American University of Beirut). It was censored by the Ottoman government, which Anṭūn Ṣāliḥānī and others challenged in Istanbul. According to the official history of the press, the number of subscriptions in 1903 was two thousand, mostly from Lebanon, Syria, Palestine, Galilee, Mesopotamia, Egypt, and Cyprus. *L'Imprimerie catholique de Beyrouth et son oeuvre en Orient (1853–1903)* (Bruxelles: Polleunis et Ceuterick, 1903), 45–63.

24. Shiblī relied on this work by Qairawānī in his discussions of Arabic, Persian, and Urdu poetics. In appraising the value of Qairwānī's work and its status in the tradition, Shiblī appeals to judgments made by Ibn-i Khaldūn. Shiblī Nu'*mānī, Muwāzanah-i Anīs o Dabīr* (Agra: Mufīd-i *'Ām, 1907)*, 2; Shiblī Nu'mānī, *Shi'r al-'Ajam* (Azamgarh: Ma'ārif, 1920), 1:1–15, 4:1–113; Shiblī Nu'mānī, "Shi'r al-'Arab" in *Maqālāt-i Shiblī* (Azamgarh: Ma'ārif, 1930–38), 2:29–48.

25. ṭibbī (medical; related to the work of a physician) is Shiblī's gloss for the English word *medical*.

26. Arabic: "*Ijtim'anā fī hāżihi al-ayām 'alā ḥażrat al-'ālim al-Shaikh Shiblī al-Nu'mānī al-mu'allim al-awwal li-l-'ulūm al-'Arabiyah fī balda 'Alīgaḋh min bilād al-Hind fa-ra'ainā fīhi rajulā kaṡīr al-ma'ārif wa huwa jāyiz al-nishān al-majīdī min al-rutbat al-rābi'a.*

Aqāma fī al-āsitāna al-ʿaliya mudda 3 ashhar wa hażara ilā Bairūt wa tawajjaha hāżā al-nahār ilā ziryāra Bait al-Muqaddas śumma minhā ilā Miṣr śumma ilā bilād al-Hind."

27. The word *jamʿīyah* would have been familiar to Urdu readers because the Urdu equivalent, *jamʿīyat*, was frequently used, both in literal senses (collection) and idiomatic ones (peace of mind (e.g., *jamʿīyat-i khāṭir*).

28. *al-Nashrat al-asbūʿiyah* (The Weekly Bulletin), edited by Henry Harris Jessup, a founder of the Presbyterian College (later the American University of Beirut). For more on Arabic journalism, the freedom of the press, print culture in Beirut, see Ami Ayalon, *The Press in the Arab Middle East: A History* (New York: Oxford University Press, 1995); Abdul Latif Tibawi, *A Modern History of Syria, Including Lebanon and Palestine* (London: Macmillan; New York: St. Martin's Press, 1969), 141–144.

29. Robert Haldane West (see Appendix 1).

30. Ṭāhir al-Maghribī (see Appendix 1)

31. Al-Maktabat al-Unsiyah. According to the official catalogue, the bookshop was founded in 1308 Hijrī (1890–91). By 1908–9, al-Unsī owned both the shop and a small printing press, the Matbaʿat al-Maʿārif. The bookshop promoted itself as selling religious and sharia books as well as rare books in the rational sciences and arts. His printing press published poetry collections. It also sold al-Unsī's writings, which included manuals of style in correspondence, accounting for business, and an introduction to Ottoman Turkish. It also published his magazine, *al-Iqbāl*. ʿAbd al-Bāsiṭ al-Unsī, *Qāʾimat al-kutub al-wujūdah fī al-Maktabat al-Unsiyah* (Beirut: Maktabat al-Unsī, 1908), 1–5.

32. ʿUmar Jubailī (see Appendix 1). His name is spelled *Jailī* (or *Jīlī*) in the travelogue, but *Jubailī* (or *Jabīlī*) in the pages of *al-Ṣafā*. The stated aim of *al-Ṣafā* (1886–90) was to publish studies and translations of European, especially French, scholarship in Arabic to gain insight into European progress (*taqaddum*) while purifying (*ṣafā*) Lebanon of "troubling political impurities" and encouraging "national pride and enthusiasm for Arabic." Issues comprised sections on the arts and sciences, literature, editorials, poetry, intellectual puzzles, history, and stories. In the course of its four years of publication, the magazine carried articles on Arabic grammar, poetry, prose, editorials advocating educational reform, lectures, articles on socially relevant subjects (e.g., gambling and marriage), a long series about madness, and articles on photography, inter alia. It also published translations of Darwin, sketches of the Earth seen from other planets (centered on Europe), and a lengthy article titled "Animal Magnetism" ("al-maghnaṭīsiyat al-ḥaiwāniyah"). For information on the journal, see ʿAlī Nāṣir al-Dīn, "al-Muqaddamah," *al-Ṣafā* 1, no. 1 (1886): n.p. For Jubailī, see ʿUmar Jubailī, "Iʿlān," *al-Ṣafā* 4, no. 10 (April 1890): 149/640, both in ʿAlī Nāṣir al-Dīn, ed. (inter alios), *al-Ṣafā* (Beirut, 1886–90).

33. "He has merits and faults."

34. "Good [deeds] remove evil [ones]" (Quran 11:114).

35. Little is known about ʿAbd al-Raḥmān. His residence in Beirut, rather than Damascus, may explain why a recent biographical entry on the Damascene branch of the

al-Jazā'irī family does not list him among 'Abd al-Qādir's descendants. Muḥammad Sharīf al-Ṣawwāf, *Mausū'at al-usar al-Dimashqiyah: Tārīkhahā, Ansābahā, A'lāmahā* (Damascus: Bait al-Ḥikmah, 2010), 3:527–37. For 'Abd al-Qādir al-Jazā'irī (1807–83), see Appendix 1.

36. *man tashabbaha bi-qaum (fahuwa minhum)* (Arabic: "Whoever imitates a community [is from them]). A hadith found in the canonical collection by Abū Dawūd. The permissibility of dining in the English style was advocated by Sayyid Aḥmad Khān and challenged by others on the strength of this hadith. The issue of dining with the English was a related hot-button issue in late nineteenth-century colonial India and became the focus of influential writers, many of whom had close ties to Shiblī. Sayyid Aḥmad Khān, while advocating for certain changes in dining practices that did not lead to censure on the grounds of the hadith, also mentioned those of "the Arabs" by way of comparison to those of other communities. In the same series of discussions, Sayyid Aḥmad Khān also mentioned the work by Khair al-Dīn Pāshā discussed by Shiblī elsewhere in the travelogue. Sayyid Aḥmad Khān, "Tarīqah-i tanāwul-i ta'ām," "Hadith-i tashabbuh," "Tashabbuh," in *Tahżīb al-Akhlāq* (Lahore 1896), 78–80, 223–26, 319–22; Sayyid Aḥmad Khān, *Aḥkām-i ta'ām-i ahl-i kitāb* (Kanpur: Nawal Kishore, 1868); Mahdī 'Alī Muḥsin al-Mulk, "Ta'ām-i ahl-i kitāb," "Ahl-i kitāb ke sāth khānā," *Tahżīb al-Akhlāq* (Lahore: Nawal Kishore, 1910), 216–59, 275–76.

37. 'Abd al-Raḥmān is described in 'Abd al-Bāsiṭ's guidebook to Beirut as having acquired general renown (*al-shuhrat al-'āmmah*) as a doctor. 'Abd al-Bāsiṭ al-Unsī, "I'lānāt," *Dalīl Bairūt* (Beirut: Jarīdat al-Iqbāl, 1908), 1.

38. Soon after returning to India, Shiblī became attracted to the writing of Tripoli-based scholar Ḥusain al-Jisr (1845–1909), whose ideas included, inter alia, that the basic ideas about the universe in the Quran were compatible with Darwinism. Shiblī judged that Jisr's theological work, (*Al-risālah al-*) *Ḥamīdiyah* had laid the foundation for a new series of works that could "breathe new life into the souls of Ghazālī and Rāzī" (two original Islamic theologians and philosophers whom Shiblī admired). Jisr was also an early teacher of Islamic reformer Rashīd Riżā, who worked with Muḥammad 'Abduh to found the reformist journal *al-Manār* in Cairo in 1898. Albert Hourani, *Arabic Thought in the Liberal Age, 1798–1939* (London, New York: Oxford University Press, 1962), 223; Shiblī Nu'mānī, *Rasā'il-i Shiblī* (Amritsar: Roz Bāzār Steam Press, 1898), 122; Ende, "Rashīd Riḍā." *Encyclopaedia of Islam*, 2nd ed. For al-Jisr and the Ḥamīdiyah, see Marwa Elshakry, *Reading Darwin in Arabic, 1860–1950* (Chicago: The University of Chicago Press, 2013), 131–59.

39. Muḥammad Sharīf Ẓabyān (d. 1927). Poet, mystic, and leader of the Qādirī Ṣūfī community in Damascus. Muḥammad Sharīf al-Ṣawwāf, *Mausū'at al-usar al-Dimashqiyah: tārīkhahā, ansābahā, a'lāmahā* (Damascus: Bait al-Ḥikmah, 2010), 2:591–93

40. Arabic: "*tamatta' min shamīm 'arār najd / fa-mā ba'da al-'ashiyat min 'arār.*" A line of verse found in the Ḥamāsah, a compilation by Abū Tammām (d. 845). Abū Tammām attributes it to al-Ṣama ibn 'Abdullāh al-Qushairī (d. 714). The *Ḥamāsah* was part of the

curriculum that Shiblī taught in British-colonial universities in India. Shiblī's teacher, Faiż al-Ḥasan Sahāranpūrī (d. 1887), wrote an extensive Arabic commentary on it titled *al-Faiżī* (Nawal Kishore, 1877), and Shiblī almost certainly studied it with him. Shiblī is said to have been especially fond of the poetry in the text and to have recited couplets from it until the end of his life. Sayyid Sulaimān Nadwī, *Ḥayāt-i Shiblī* (Azamgarh, 1943), 83.

41. The word that Shiblī uses is *maghnā* or *maghnī*. It may also be read as *mughannī* (singer), though the latter is in use in Urdu (indeed, Shiblī uses it in his other writings) and it is unlikely that Shiblī would feel the need to gloss it the way that he does here. Since, as Shibli tells us, it refers to the house, I read it as the locative noun of the root *gh-n-y*, which carries the relevant senses of singing (as in *ghinā'* [song])—hence, a place of song or cabaret—or "to be satisfied or free from want"—thus, a site of satisfaction or free from care. The term is not used in the sense of brothel or cabaret in the standard, *A Dictionary of Modern Written Arabic*, though *maghnan* (orthographically identical) is glossed as a villa. Edward William Lane, *An Arabic-English Lexicon* (Edinburgh: Williams and Norgate, 1877), 2304; Hans Wehr, *A Dictionary of Modern Written Arabic*, edited by J. Milton Cowan (Ithaca, New York: Spoken Language Services, Inc.: 1976), 687.

42. A hadith: "We seek refuge in God from the evils of ourselves and from our bad actions."

43. Karaca transliterates the name as Bellini, but surely Shiblī refers to the Roman historian Pliny the Elder, who, in his *Natural History*, reports that Jaffa "existed, it is said, before the deluge of the earth." Pliny the Elder, *The Natural History of Pliny* (London: George Bell & Sons, 1893), 426. Assuming that the spelling of Pliny as Bliny is in fact Shiblī's spelling and not a copyist's error, the substitution of *b* for *p* in the name suggests that Shiblī was reading Pliny (or about him) in Arabic, since Arabic lacks the letter *p* and regularly transliterates it as *b*. Shiblī was not the only nineteenth-century traveler to discuss Pliny's description of Jaffa. It is also discussed in the historical portion of the Cook Company's guidebook for tourists. See *Cook's Tourists' Handbook for Palestine and Syria* (London: Thomas Cook & Son, 1876), 69.

44. Under construction since 1890, the Jerusalem-Jaffa railway opened in September 1892 just a few weeks after Shiblī's visit.

Jerusalem

1. *Madsī* seems to be a copyist's error. The word *yabūsī* (Jebusite), the Arabic word for the ancient residents of Jerusalem, seems more likely. The two words, while certainly orthographically distinct, are just similar enough that a copyist unfamiliar with the word might misread the latter and write the former.

2. Either a copyist's error or Shiblī's mistake. According to the travelogue, he arrived in early September.

3. ʻAbd al-Malik ibn Marwān (b. 646–47; d. 705) (r. 685–705). Fifth caliph of the Umayyad dynasty. Gibb, "ʻAbd al-Malik b. Marwān." *Encyclopaedia of Islam*, 2nd ed., edited by P. Bearman T. Bianquis, C. E. Bosworth, E. van Donzel, and W. P. Heinrichs. BrillOnline. https://referenceworks.brillonline.com/browse/encyclopaedia-of-islam-2.

4. Ṣalāḥ al-Dīn (Saladin) (1138–93). Founder of the Ayyubid dynasty famous for his battles against Crusaders. Shiblī intended to write a biography of Salāḥ al-Dīn as the representative "hero" of the Ayyubis, but never did. Shiblī Nuʻmānī, *al-Māmūn* (Azamgarh, n.d.), 12.

5. Shams al-Dīn ʻAbd Allāh Muḥammad al-Muqaddasī al-Bashshārī (b. ca. 940–41; d. after 990–91), geographer, merchant, and traveler born in Jerusalem. He was the descendant of master builders, and his observations on architectural aesthetics are therefore especially celebrated. Richter-Bernburg, "al-Muqaddasī." *Encyclopedia of Arabic Literature*, ed. Julie Scott Meisami and Paul Starkey (London, New York: Routledge, 1998), 551; Miquel, "al-Muḳaddasī." *Encyclopaedia of Islam*, 2nd ed.

6. Muḥyī al-Dīn ibn (al-)ʻArabī (1165–1240), known as Ibn-i (also Ibn al-)ʻArabī and Shaikh al-Akbar. Traveler, mystic, philosopher, theologian, and Ṣūfī. He traveled to Jerusalem around 1202. Ateş, "Ibn al- ʻArabī." *Encyclopaedia of Islam*, 2nd ed.

7. *waḥy* (revelation) and *ilhām* (divine inspiration). Islamic theologians have argued that waḥy is limited to prophets while ilhām can be given to anyone sufficiently prepared to receive it. MacDonald, "Ilhām" in *Encyclopaedia of Islam*, 2nd ed. Shiblī, however, had a different reading in his later theological writings. Arguing on the authority of an explication of the mystical Persian Maśnawī of Rumi by the Indian scholar ʻAbd al-ʻAlī (known as Baḥr al- ʻUlūm) (1731–1810), Shiblī argues that waḥy was not exclusive to prophets, and that Ṣūfīs used the term in the phrase *waḥy al-qalb* (revelation of the heart) to address broad audiences. Shiblī also argues the same point with reference to the Quran itself, in which the word *waḥy* is used when speaking of Moses's mother (who was not a prophet). He finds further evidence to support these arguments in the work of Ibn Hazm and Muḥy al-Dīn Ibn-i ʻArabī. Shiblī Nuʻmānī, *Sawāniḥ-i Maulānā Rūm* (Kanpur: Nāmī Press, 1906), 121–25.

8. *sādah-dilī* (lit., plain-heartedness). This word has two relevant and contradictory senses, allowing for some ambivalence in the interpretation of Shiblī's comment: naiveté, credulity; artlessness, sincerity.

9. *peshwāz* (full gown).

10. Ṭāhir al-Ḥusainī (see Appendix 1).

11. Arabic: "Sir, perhaps you are from [among] the people [possessed] of knowledge" (i.e., scholars).

12. Arabic: "No, rather, I am from [among] the seekers of knowledge" (i.e., students). Shiblī has made a witty pun on *ʻālim* (lit., one possessing knowledge; idiom., a scholar) and *ṭālib al-ʻilm* (lit., seeker of knowledge; a student).

13. This exchange plays on an untranslatable pun designed to convey Shiblī's wit and humility. Shiblī was asked if he was a scholar (*'ālim*; lit., one who possesses *'ilm* [knowledge]). In response, he said he was not—rather, he was from among the "seekers of knowledge (*'ilm*)," which idiomatically means a student.

14. Arabic: "O shaikh, sir. We were discussing an issue before. So if it pleases you, let us present it [to] you."

15. "Have you not seen how your lord dealt with Iram of the pillars?" (Quran 89:6–7). The travelogue omits "'Ād(in) ['Ād]," between *bi-* and *Iram(a)*. The verses in standard versions of the Quran read, "[6] Did you not see how your lord dealt with 'Ād [7] [and] Iram of the pillars?" In the 1901 edition of the travelogue, the *r* of Iram is changed to *d* (p. 144). Karaca reinserts *bi-'Ād* (biad) in his translation (155). Cf. Arthur J. Droge, *The Qur'ān: A New Annotated Translation* (Sheffield, Bristol: Equinox, 2013), 433.

16. Urdu: *rūyat* (sight, seeing). This is the verbal noun related to the word *tara* (you see) in the quotation from the Quran above.

17. "Have you not seen how your Lord dealt with the companions of the elephant?" (Quran 105:1). The word *aṣḥāb* (companions) has been variously translated as "owners" (Pickthall), "possessors" (Shakir), "people" (Sarwar), "men" (Arberry), and "possessors" (Droge).

18. Shiblī uses the word *muqaddas* (sacred, holy) to describe him. This word also carries the broader sense of "religious" or "observant."

19. Arabic: "We heard that Shaikh, sir, went out without a laffah."

20. Arabic: "By God! You were right!"

21. Sayyid ṣāḥib. (Sir) Sayyid Aḥmad Khān (Sir Syed) (1817–98). Indian educational reformer, theologian, founder of the Muhammadan Anglo-Oriental College at Aligarh; also, Shiblī's boss, landlord, patron, mentor, and collaborator (see Appendix 1). He traveled to England in 1869–70 and, after his return to India, published his diary in installments in the Urdu magazines (of which he was the editor) *Tahżīb al-akhlāq* and the *Aligarh Institute Gazette*. These were later collected and published as *Musāfirān-i Landan* (Lahore, 1961). The work has been translated into English. Sayyid Ahmad Khan, *A Voyage to Modernism*, trans. Mushirul Hasan and Nishat Zaidi (Delhi: Primus Books, 2001), ix–xi, 1–45.

Cairo

1. Jauhar al-Ṣiqillī (d. 991). Military commander and statesman; among the founders of the Fatimid Empire in Egypt; founder of Cairo as the capital; founder of the Azhar mosque. Monés, "Djawhar al-Ṣiḳillī." *Encyclopaedia of Islam*, 2nd ed., edited by P. Bearman T. Bianquis, C. E. Bosworth, E. van Donzel, and W. P. Heinrichs. BrillOnline. https://referenceworks.brillonline.com/browse/encyclopaedia-of-islam-2.

2. Imām Ḥusain (625–80). The grandson of the Prophet. 'Abd al-Qādir Jīlānī (b. 1077–78; d. 1166). Theologian, mystic, and eponym of the Qādirī order of Ṣūfism. The

Qādirī order had been influential in Egypt for centuries before Shiblī arrived. One of Jīlānī's most influential biographers, Shaṭṭanaufī (d. 1324) was from the region. His biography of Jīlānī, as well as other Qādirī literature, was published from Cairo in the nineteenth century. Chabbi, "'Abd al-Qādir al-Jīlānī." *Encyclopaedia of Islam, Three*, edited by Kate Fleet, Gudrun Krämer, Denis Matringe, John Nawas, and Everett Rowson. BrillOnline. https://referenceworks.brillonline.com/browse/encyclopaedia-of-islam-3.

3. 'Alī Pāshā Mubārak (see Appendix 1).

4. Shams al-Dīn al-Inbābī (d. 1895–96) (see Appendix 1).

5. *hạdīṡ* (hadith; the traditions of the Prophet and the principles of their criticism); *tafsīr* (exegesis of the Quran), *uṣūl-i fiqh* (the principles of Islamic law jurisprudence), fiqh (Islamic law [jurisprudence]), *ṣarf* ([Arabic] morphology), and *naḥw* ([Arabic] syntax).

6. Ḥamzah Fatḥullāh and Ḥasan al-Ṭawīl (see Appendix 1).

7. Aḥmad Bey Naẓīm and Aḥmad al-Qūṣī (see Appendix 1). According to institutional records, the director of the academy in 1892 was Ibrāhīm Muṣṭafā Bey, who held the position from 1890 until 1895. Muḥammad 'Abd al-Jawād, ed., *Taqwīm Dār al-'Ulūm* (Cairo: Dār al-Ma'ārif, 1950s), 1:13.

8. Arabic:

Muḥammad anta Shiblī al-ma'ālā
La-qad fuqta al-warā wa 'alauta qadrā

Wa qad aulaitanā sharafan wa fażlā
Bi-tashrīf ziyārat arż Miṣrā

Fa-lā zulnā narāk bi-kull uns
Tazīdu tafażżulan wa nazīdu shukrā.

9. *iqwa'* (verse ending in irregular vowels). Stoetzer, "Prosody" in *Encyclopedia of Arabic Literature*, ed. Julie Scott Meisami and Paul Starkey (London, New York: Routledge, 1998), 620. Although Shiblī was not entirely impressed by Qūṣī's work, another graduate of the Dār al-'Ulūm, 'Abd al-Muṭṭalib (d. 1931), achieved wide renown as an Arabic poet and later taught at the academy. Still another graduate, Ḥifnī Nāṣif, was also highly regarded as a poet. Lois Armine Aroian, "Education, Language and Culture in Modern Egypt: Dar al-'Ulum and its Graduates" (Ph.D. diss., University of Michigan, 1978), 132.

10. *tauḥīd* (lit., unity; a branch of Islamic learning and theology concerned with affirming the unity of God; the science of monotheism).

11. The travelogue reads *mīkro-ḥabranī*, which is orthographically nearly identical to *mīkrū-jarāfī* (the logical transliteration of micrography into Arabic). Karaca (169) translates the word as microbiology, perhaps assuming that the meaningless *ḥabrānī* is a mistake for *ḥaiwānī* (animal), which orthographically resembles the former. However, the fact that Shiblī uses the word *ḥaiwānāt* in the same line of text to refer to the biological

sciences strengthens the likelihood that *mīkro-jarāfī* (micography) is intended. The term had been used in English to mean examination by means of microscope since the mid-nineteenth century.

12. Ruṙkī (Roorkee) College. A well-known engineering school. The small town saw civic development in the nineteenth century. In 1845, Lieutenant Governor Thomason instituted a class to train "native youths" in engineering and assist in public works projects. In 1848, the Thomason Engineering College was established for this purpose. *Imperial Gazetteer of India* (Oxford: Claredon Press, 1908–31) 21:324–25, http://dsal.uchicago.edu/reference/gazetteer/.

13. *'ām* (general; public) Here, Shiblī seems to use the term in the former sense, but the latter is also possible.

14. Taufīqiyah: A French-language school for teachers. See Hilary Kalmbach, "Training Teachers How to Teach," in *The Long 1890s in Egypt: Colonial Quiescence, Subterranean Resistance*, ed. Marilyn Booth and Anthony Gorman (Edinburgh: Edinburgh University Press, 2014), 87–116.

15. 'Alī Pāshā Mubārak (b. 1823–24; d. 1893) (see Appendix 1). Egyptian statesman, educational reformer, and author. He founded the Dār al-'Ulūm as well as the Khedival Library, both of which Shiblī visited while in Cairo.

16. Al-Mu'izz li-Dīnillāh (also li-Dīn Allāh) (931–75) (r. 953–75). Fourth Fatimid caliph remembered for his military exploits, especially his conquest of Egypt. F. Dachraoui, "al-Mu'izz li-Dīn Allāh." *Encyclopaedia of Islam*, 2nd ed.

17. Al-'Azīz Billāh (955–96) (r. 976–96). Fifth Fatimid caliph remembered for his wisdom and territorial expansion. M. Canard, "al-'Azīz Bi'llāh." *Encyclopaedia of Islam*, 2nd ed.

18. Al-Ḥākim bi-Amrillāh (also bi-Amr Allāh) (r. 996–1021). Sixth Fatimid caliph whose mysterious reign remains the subject of much confusion and controversy. Paul E. Walker, "al-Ḥākim bi Amr Allāh." *Encyclopaedia of Islam, Three*.

19. Shams al-Dīn al-Inbābī (d. 1895–96) (see Appendix 1).

20. *Kāfiyah* is a work on Arabic grammar by Ibn Ḥājib (1175–1249), who studied mostly in Cairo and taught jurisprudence in Damascus. Akhtar Rāhī, *Tażkirah-i Muṣannifīn-i Dars-i Niẓāmī* (Lahore: Maktabah-i Raḥmāniyah, 1978), 24–26.

21. Muḥammad ibn 'Alī al-Ṣabbān (d. 1791–92). Author of many marginal commentaries on earlier works. Ṣabbān's writings were regularly printed in Egypt in the nineteenth century, perhaps owing to his prominence in the curriculum at Azhar.

22. Ja'far-i Ṣādiq (b. ca. 700; d. 765). The final imām recognized by both the "twelver" and Ismā'īlī Shī'ī Muslim communities. Sunnī scholars also recognize him as a dependable transmitter of hadith. Among the scholars who collected hadith from him was Abū Ḥanīfah, who is the eponym of the Ḥanafī school of jurisprudence, the source of Shiblī's adopted epithet (Nu'mānī), and a celebrated scholar of Sunnī Islam in South Asia. Hodgson, "Dja'far al-Ṣādiḳ." *Encyclopaedia of Islam*, 2nd ed.

23. Karl Vollers (1857–1909), a German Orientalist, was the director of the library from 1886–96. He attended the Ninth International Congress of Orientalists in London and sat on a panel with Aḥmad Zakī (whom Shiblī did not meet, but does discuss in the travelogue). *Transactions of the Ninth International Congress of Orientalists (Held in London, 5th to 12th September 1892)* (London: Printed for the Committee of the Congress, 1893), lvii, lii, xxviii.

24. The Arabic notes in the list of titles, as well as the list's Arabic style, suggest that Shiblī had consulted the library catalogues printed from Cairo. (Catalogue of the Arabic Manuscripts and Printed Books in the Khedival Library at Cairo; 7 vols.)

25. One of the books that Shiblī wanted to have printed by the Dā'irat al-Ma'ārif and cited earlier. Shiblī's inclusion of the text in the list here makes it seem less likely that he also consulted it in the library in Istanbul.

26. Shiblī had been searching for works by Mu'tazilī philosophers on behalf of Sayyid Aḥmad Khān (and perhaps for himself as well) while in Constantinople (see Appendix 2).

27. 'Abd al-Ḥaqq Ishbīlī (d. 1185), known asa Ibn al-Kharrāṭ, hadith scholar in Andalusia. The name is misspelled in the travelogue.

28. Perhaps Ibn Durustawaih (871–957), though *akhbār* is not listed in standard sources. Vadet, "Ibn Durustawayh." *Encyclopaedia of Islam*, 2nd ed.

29. Ḥājjī Khalīfah (1609–57). Author of *Kashf al-Ẓunūn*, an extensive bibliographical dictionary in Arabic. *Kashf al-Ẓunūn* was published from Leipzig from 1835 to 1858 and was a major source in Shiblī's work on Islamic intellectual history.

30. Arabic: "Among the ṣāḥibs of the fifth century."

31. Arabic: "Copied from the original manuscript written by Kāfūr al-Akhshīdī."

32. Quṭb mīnār in Delhi. Erected by Quṭb al-Dīn Aibak (d. 1210–11) in 1193 shortly after capturing the city. It stands 238 feet tall. The tower is said to be named after Khwājah Quṭb al-Dīn Bakhtyār Kākī (d. 1235), a mystic in Delhi. Arnold and Fischer, "Quṭb Mīnār." *Encyclopaedia of Islam*, 2nd ed.

33. Malik al-'Azīz (1172–98). Second Ayyubid ruler in Egypt and son of Ṣalāḥ al-Dīn (the founder of the Ayyubid dynasty).

34. "Gaz . . . an instrument for measuring with; a yard measure; a foot-rule; a yard (of measure, varying formerly from about thirty-two English inches upwards; and now fixed by Government at thirty-three inches)." John T. Platts, *A Dictionary of Urdu, Classical Hindi, and English* (London: W.H. Allen & Co., 1884), http://dsal.uchicago.edu/dictionaries/platts/.

35. 'Abd al-Laṭīf Baghdādī (b. 1162–63; d. 1231–32), polymath, philosopher, Egyptologist. Here, Shiblī refers to Baghdādī's study of Egypt, *al-Ifādah wal-i'tibār*. Stern, "'Abd al-Laṭīf al-Baghdādī." *Encyclopaedia of Islam*, 2nd ed.

36. The reference is to a story in the Quran. When Joseph is sent to prison after refusing the advances of the governor's wife, he is accompanied by two young men, who ask him to interpret their dreams. Joseph does so, and this eventually leads to his exoneration.

(Quran 12:35–49). See Arthur J. Droge, *The Qur'ān: A New Annotated Translation* (Sheffield, Bristol: Equinox, 2013), 144–45.

37. The language in this section suggests that Shiblī based his discussion of Egyptian museums partly on the work of scholars connected to the Egyptian archaeological society. The Urdu word that Shiblī uses for museum, *'ajā'ib-khānah* (lit., house of wonders), is common in Urdu. Shiblī knew that the Arabic term that he uses, *antīk-khānah* (antique house) would not be familiar to his readers ("The Arabic Language of the Present Day" at the end of the travelogue). Aḥmad Zakī (q.v.) used the word in his Arabic translation (1889) of a French book by the Orientalist Frédéric Bonola (also Frederico Bonola; a member of the Khedival Geographical Society), which discusses the history of the museum founded by the Egyptian Khedive Muḥammad 'Alī in 1835. Zakī mentioned the translation in his book on slavery (which Shiblī discusses in the travelogue; q.v.), and the relevant passage in the translation of Bonola bears a striking resemblance to Shiblī's discussion of the history of Egyptian museums here. See Aḥmad Zakī, *Miṣr wal-jughrāfiyah* (Bulāq: al-Maṭba'at al-Amīriyah, 1892), 21. Frederico Bonola, *l'Egypte et la géographie: Sommaire historique des travaux géographiques éxecutés en Égypte sous la dynastie de Mohammed Aly* (Cairo : Imprimerie Nationale, 1889), 22.

38. Persian: «*dar chaman būd Zulaikhā o ba-ḥasrat mī guft / yād-i zindān kih dar ū anjuman-ārāe hast.*» The "one who adorns the assembly" is an allusion to the beautiful Joseph. Zulaikhā is the name given to the governor's wife, not named in the Quran, who attempts to seduce him.

39. Maqrīzī (1364–1442). Historian, geographer, and author of *Khiṭāṭ wal-āṡār* (a geographical and historical study of Egypt). Shiblī used the book as a source in the travelogue, and also in his writings on Islamic history, philosophy, and theology. See Shiblī Nu'mānī, *Rasā'il-i Shiblī* (Amritsar: Roz Bāzār Steam Press, 1898); Shiblī Nu'mānī, *'Ilm al-kalām* (Aligarh: Maṭba'-i Aḥmadī, 1910).

40. 'Umar ibn al-Khaṭṭāb (d. 644) (r. 634–44), remembered as (al-)Fārūq in Urdu, the second caliph of Sunnī Islam. Shiblī's biography of 'Umar, al-Fārūq (1899) is celebrated as a classic in Urdu literature. Shiblī prided himself on the work. 'Amr bin al-'Āṣ (d. 662–64), a companion of the Prophet and leader of the conquest of Egypt under 'Umar in 642. Keshk, "'Amr b. al-'Ās." *Encyclopaedia of Islam, Three.*

41. Ḥasan (r. 1347–51 and 1354–61). Mamluk sulṭān of Egypt whose reign and life were cut short by his murder. The Sultān Ḥasan madrasa is perhaps the most famous relic of his reign, which also witnessed the outbreak of the plague. J. Wansbrough, "Ḥasan." *Encyclopaedia of Islam*, 2nd ed.

42. That is, scholars of Islamic law. The four imāms refer to the eponyms of the four most influential schools of Islamic jurisprudential reasoning, Abū Ḥanīfah (d. 767) (Ḥanafī), Mālik ibn Anas (d. 796) (Mālikī), Abū 'Abdullāh Muḥammad Shāfi'ī (d. 820) (Shāfi'ī), and Aḥmad ibn Ḥanbal (780–855) (Ḥanbalī).

43. *mazār* (lit., site of visitation, pilgrimage); *mashhad* (lit., site of witnessing/martyrdom; the site of the mausoleum of a religious figure).

44. *shirk* (association, inclusion; often translated as polytheism) The literal meaning alludes to the practice of associating anything with God, which is criticized in the Quran. Gimaret, "Shirk." *Encyclopaedia of Islam*, 2nd ed.

45. Persian: "*zi-pāe tā ba-sarash har kujā kih me nigaram / karishmah dāman-i dil mī kashad kih jā īn jā-st.*" A famous couplet by Naẓīrī Nīshāpūrī, one of Shiblī's favorite Persian poets. The first line is often given as "*zi farq tā qadamash har kujā kih mī nigaram* (from the crown of his head to his feet, every place I look)."

46. *Musalmānōṅ kī guzishtah ta'līm* (q.v.).

47. Abū Yūsuf (731–98). Central figure in the Ḥanafī jurisprudential tradition and Abbasid qāẓī (judge). Kitāb al-Kharāj, which was written for Hārūn al-Rashīd, deals with taxation, finance, law, and criminal justice. Schacht, "Abū Yūsuf." *Encyclopaedia of Islam*, 2nd ed.

48. Sayyid 'Abd al-Wāḥid al-Ṭūbī (see Appendix 1).

49. Lajnat al-Adab (Committee of Literature). Administrative reports describe Lajnat al-Adab and its Urdu counterpart led by Thomas Arnold, Ikhwān al-Ṣafā (Brethren of Purity; named after the authors of a collection of epistles written in the tenth century by an anonymous group of Neoplatonist Islamic philosophers), as flourishing in the mid-1890s. Khaliq Ahmad Nizami, ed., *Theodore Beck Papers from the Sir Syed Academy Archives* (London: Published for the Department of History, Aligarh Muslim University, by Asia Pub. House, 1967), 104. *Al-Hilāl* was founded in 1892 by Jurjī Zaydān (1861–1914). Zaydān was from Beirut, studied at the Protestant College under Cornelius Van Dyke, and eventually left the college and Beirut to settle in Cairo. Shiblī and Zaydān were in contact in the 1900s, when Shiblī asked Zaydān to recommend an Arabic lexicon to facilitate translations of scientific literature from English into Urdu. Eventually, Shiblī severely criticized Zaydān in the pages of the Egyptian Arabic journal, *al-Manār*, leading to tensions between them. *Al-Hilāl* included articles on European history, Arabic literature, Islamic history, and regional politics. Walther, "Djurdjī Zaydān." *Encyclopaedia of Islam*, 2nd ed.

50. Ismā'īl Pāshā (1830–95). Khedive of Egypt, 1863–79. Vatikiotis, "Ismā'īl Pāshā." *Encyclopaedia of Islam*, 2nd ed.

51. Arabic: "How can we accept this humiliation and shame?"

52. Arabic: "Life is complete, prosperity is common because of the revered Khedive."

53. An Urdu couplet by Momin Khān Momin (b. 1800–1801; d. 1850–51).

54. *żikr* (lit., utterance). The text, context, and style of żikr varies, but the practice typically involves the recitation of the profession of the faith, "There is no God but God and Muhammad is the Prophet of God" or the names of God. The practice is typically associated with Ṣūfī traditions. Gardet, "Dhikr." *Encyclopaedia of Islam*, 2nd ed.

55. *faqr* (poverty, mendicancy; renunciation); *taśawwuf* (sufism; mysticism).

56. The name of ranks among mystics: *ghauṡ* (redresser); *quṭb* (axis, pole); *abdāl* (lit., substitutes, placeholder; mystical discourse holds that this refers to a special class of mystics responsible for safeguarding the order of the universe); *autād* (lit., pegs; a class of four mystics charged with overseeing one of four "cardinal points"). Goldziher, "Abdāl" and "Awtād." *Encyclopaedia of Islam*, 2nd ed.

57. Arabic: "The people find paths in what they love." Here, the word *mażhab* can be read either in its broad sense (path) or in its narrow one (religious tradition or school; in Islam, typically a jurisprudential tradition).

58. *al-Mawā'iẓ wal-i'tibār fī żikr al-khiṭaṭ wal-āṡār*, a geographical study of Egypt by Maqrīzī (see note 42 above). Rosenthal, "al-Maqrīzī." *Encyclopaedia of Islam*, 2nd ed.

59. 'Alī Pāshā Mubārak died on November 14, 1893.

60. Shiblī almost certainly refers to Muḥammad Durrī, *Tārīkh ḥayāt al-maghfūr lahu 'Alī Mubārak Bāshā* (Miṣr: al-Matba'at al-ṭibbiyat al-Durriyah, 1894).

61. Amīn Bey Fikrī, *Irshād al-alibbā ilā maḥāsin urūbbā* (Cairo: al-Muqtaṭaf, 1892).

62. The topic of slavery in Islam was one that interested Shiblī and Sayyid Aḥmad Khān, who wrote about it in his Urdu journal, *Tahżīb al-akhlāq*. Sayyid Aḥmad Khān's essays were later collected and published as *Ibṭāl al-ghulāmī* (Refutation of Slavery) (Agra: Mufīd-i 'Ām, 1893).

63. Shiblī and Aḥmad Zakī did not meet in Cairo. Zakī had left for the conference on August 13 or 14, 1892. The conference took place September 5–12, 1892. Zakī attended as delegate of the Egyptian government, translating speeches and poetry by his Egyptian colleagues in attendance. He also spoke about Arabic language and pedagogy on a panel that included Karl Vollers (1857–1909), then director of the Khedival Library in Cairo (cf.), and George Tindall Plunkett (1842–1922), the author of Arabic and Hindi-Urdu-Persian-Pashtu vocabularies and phrase books for English readers. Plunkett used the occasion to pass a resolution to petition the British secretary for foreign affairs for better instruction in modern Arabic in Egypt. After the conference, Zakī visited Paris, then traveled through Spain and Portugal, back to France, then through Italy, finally returning to Egypt via Brindisi. He recorded his experiences in a travelogue, *al-Safar ilā al-mu'tamar* (*The Journey to the Congress*). Shiblī included a detailed review of the travelogue in his collected articles (*Rasā'il-i Shiblī* [1898]). In the article, he criticized Zakī for the European style of his Arabic prose. In contrast to Urdu, which had benefited from European influence, Arabic, with its "exalted status" was "not complemented by any other language." Shiblī also criticized the travelogue for paying too much attention to Paris and London and not enough attention to Andalusia. He judged that modern readers would be more interested in Arab influence in Spain than in accounts of London and Paris. Still, insofar as the soul of travelogues of Europe lay in discussions that sought to discover the causes of European progress, he judged Zakī's work valuable. *Al-safar* detailed Europeans' preoccupation with timeliness, their feelings of civic duty, the advanced status of women in academic positions (though Shiblī felt that women's general social freedoms

were regrettable), the great number of museums in Paris that served as sites of public intellectual culture, the quality and innovative character of European education evinced by Paris's schools for the deaf and blind, and the prevalence of government-funded charitable organizations for poor pregnant women, orphans, unemployed professionals, and unmarried women. Shiblī, "Al-naẓar fī al-safar alā al-mu'tamar," in *Rasā'il-e Shiblī* (Amritsar, 1898), 133–49; Anouar Louca, *Voyageurs et écrivains Égyptiens en France au XIXe siècle* (Paris: Didier, 1970), 209–17; *Transactions of the Ninth International Congress of Orientalists (Held in London, 5th to 12th September 1892)* (London: Printed for the Committee of the Congress, 1893), lvii, lii, and xxviii; Anwar al-Jindī, *Aḥmad Zakī* (Cairo, 1964), 23–43; Zakī, *al-Safar ilā al- mu'tamar* (Bulāq: al-Matba'ah al-Kubrah al-Amīriyah, 1893), 394.

64. *Maqāmat al-Badī'* by Badī' al-Zamān Hamażānī (968–1008), which is said to have inaugurated the *maqāmāt* genre (enlightening speeches) in Arabic. The text, along with 'Abduh's commentary, was published by the Catholic Press in Beirut, which Shiblī discusses in the travelogue. Badī' al-Zamān Hamażānī, *Maqāmāt Abī al-Fażl Badī' al-Zamān al-Hamażānī*, ed. Muḥammad 'Abduh (Beirut: Maṭba'ah al-Kaśūlīkiyah, 1889). Blachère, "al-Hamażānī" in *Encyclopaedia of Islam, Second Edition.*

65. Jamāl al-Dīn Afghānī (see Appendix 1).

66. The passage that follows is copied in Arabic without translation or gloss. It is excerpted from Muḥammad 'Abduh's biographical study of Afghānī. Shiblī presents it as one continuous paragraph, but in fact it is an edited bricolage taken from two subsections. The first part of the excerpt is taken from a section titled *Akhlāq Jamāl al-Dīn* (The Ethics of Jamāl al-Dīn). The second is *Manzilatuhu min al-'ilm* (his status in knowledge). Shiblī's praise for 'Abduh's language seems to inhere in the double-entendres implied in the Arabic. 'Abduh describes Afghānī's physical appearance, but he uses words that also convey ideas about his personality. For example, the phrase raḥb al-ṣadr (lit., "broad-chested") idiomatically denotes "magnanimity." 'Muḥammad Abduh, *al-Śā'ir al-Islāmī: Jamāl al-Dīn al-Afghānī wa risālat al-radd 'alā al-dahriyīn* (Cairo: Dār al-Hilāl, 1973), 28–30.

67. Arabic:

> Ammā khalquhu fa-maśala li-nāẓir 'arabīyā maḥażā. Rab'a fī ṭūlihi, wasaṭ fī binyatihi. Qamḥī fī launihi. 'Asabī damawī fī mizājihi. 'Aẓīm al-ra's fī i'tidāl. 'Arīż al-jabhah fī tanāsub. Wāsi' al-'ain. Żakhm al-wajanāt. Raḥb al-ṣadr. Hashshbashsh 'ind al-liqā'. Ammā akhlāquhu fa-salāmat al-qalb sāyidah fī ṣifātihi wa la-hu ḥilm 'aẓīm yasa' māshā Allāh an yasa' ilā an yadnū minhu aḥad li-yamass sharafahu au dīnahu fa-yanqalibu al-ḥilm ilā ghażab fa-bainamā huwa ḥalīm awwāb iżan huwa asad wa hābb. Wa huwa karīm yabżil mā bi-yadihi qawī al-i'timād 'alā Allāh lā yubālī mā ta'tī bi-hi ṣurūf al-dahr. sahl liman lāyanahu. Ṣa'b 'alā man khāshanahu. Wa la-hu sulṭah 'alā daqāyiq al-ma'ānī wa taḥdīdihā

wa ibrāzihā fī ṣūratihā al-lāyiqah la-hā ka-anna kull maʿnā qad khuliqa la-hu. Kull mauẓūʿ yulqā ilaihi yadkhalu li-l-baḥṡ fīhi ka-annuhu ṣanʿ yadaihi fa-yaʾtī ʿalā aṭrāfihi wa yuḥītu bi-jamīʿ aknāfihi.

68. An allusion to a phrase in the Quran: "They are [even] farther astray from the way" (Quran 25:44).

69. Hamzah Fatḥullāh, *Bakūrat al-kalām ʿalā ḥuqūq al-nisāʾ fī al-Islām* (Cairo, 1890–91).

70. Ḥamzah Fatḥullāh (1849–1918) (see Appendix 1). Commissioned by the state and published by the official press at Būlāq, the book engages European Orientalism and Islamic jurisprudential traditions. See Marilyn Booth, "Writing Women's History in 1890s Egypt," *The Long 1890s in Egypt: Colonial Quiescence, Subterranean Resistance*, ed. Marilyn Booth and Anthony Gorman (Edinburgh: Edinburgh University Press, 2014), 383–93.

71. *maulawiyānah*. The sense in which Shiblī uses the term here is not clear. Booth characterizes Fatḥullāh's worldview as "conventional," as he argues in favor of "gendered seclusion" and relegation to the domestic sphere. He also argues that men have an obligation to make sex enjoyable for women. *Maulawiyānah* seems to suggest that Shiblī found Ḥamzah Fatḥullāh to be old fashioned. Marilyn Booth, "Writing Women's History in 1890s Egypt," *The Long 1890s in Egypt: Colonial Quiescence, Subterranean Resistance*, ed. Marilyn Booth and Anthony Gorman (Edinburgh: Edinburgh University Press, 2014), 383–93.

72. Shiblī brought copies of the book back to India and gave one to Mumtāz ʿAlī, who soon thereafter wrote a book on the same subject in Urdu. Shiblī Nuʿmānī, *Maktūbāt-i Shiblī* (Azamgarh: Adabī Dāʾirah, 2012), 70–71.

73. Niẓārat al-Maʿārif.

74. The phrase "most detestable of sounds" is an allusion to the Quran (31:19): "Truly, the most disagreeable of sounds is the sound of the donkey."

The End of the Journey

1. Arabic: "What have you done? What have you done?"

2. Arabic: "By God, he should sell his beard and pay!"

3. *hawālah karnā* (to turn over; to consign). In Islamic jurisprudential discourse, *hawālah* refers to the case in which one transfers one's debt to another person by means of written document or deed of surety. İnalcık, "Ḥawāla." *Encyclopaedia of Islam*, 2nd ed., edited by P. Bearman T. Bianquis, C. E. Bosworth, E. van Donzel, and W. P. Heinrichs. BrillOnline. https://referenceworks.brillonline.com/browse/encyclopaedia-of-islam-2.

4. *jubbah* (robe or gown considered the uniform of a religious scholar).

5. Arabic: "That which is hoped from you is that you will veil our faults, for verily it is among the habits of the noble."

6. Arabic: *Bi-l-raʾs wal-ʿain* (lit., "With head and eye;" gladly, at your service).

Modern Arabic

1. Arabic: "I do not say."
2. Arabic: "I do not know.
3. Arabic: "He takes."
4. All letters representing distinct phonemes in classical and Modern Standard Arabic: *hamzah* (glottal stop; '); *qāf* (voiceless uvular plosive; *q*); *gāf* (voiced velar plosive; *g*); *jīm* (voiced palato-alveolar sibilant affricate; *j*); *dāl* (dental stop; *d*); *żāl* (voiced dental fricative; *dh*); ʿain (voiced pharyngeal fricative; ʿ).
5. Arabic: "He came from Friday [prayers]."
6. *astaghfirullāh* (I ask Allāh for forgiveness). In Urdu, this phrase is typically spoken to emphasize denial. Sayyid Masʿūd Ḥasan Riżwī, *Farhang-i amṡāl* (Allahabad: Shāntī Press, 1939), 12.
7. *amān* (safety). In Urdu, the phrase *al-amān* is commonly used as a call for God's help, especially to express the severity of one's situation. Riżwī also notes that the word is used in Urdu, though infrequently, to express surprise. Sayyid Masʿūd Ḥasan Riżwī, *Farhang-i amṡāl* (Allahabad: Shāntī Press, 1939), 19.
8. Arabic: "What need of yours is it?"
9. Arabic: "It is unavoidable."

Translator's Afterword

1. An early tract in Urdu on jurisprudence exists and is attributed to Shiblī, but its authorship is contested.
2. Muʿtazilah refers to a heterogeneous tradition of rationalist theology that emerged in the eighth century and gained prominence partly through promotion by the Abbasid court of Māmūn, but whose influence later waned with the loss of official support and eventually ceased to exist as a school, though it continued to influence theological traditions in Islam and Judaism. Muʿtazilah scholarship was, in the words of one scholar, "'rediscovered' at the beginning of the 20th century" when it was especially popular among Egyptian intellectuals. Gimaret, "Muʿtazilah." *Encyclopaedia of Islam*, 2nd ed., edited by P. Bearman T. Bianquis, C. E. Bosworth, E. van Donzel, and W. P. Heinrichs. BrillOnline. https://referenceworks.brillonline.com/browse/encyclopaedia-of-islam-2.
3. Sayyid Aḥmad Khān, foreword to *al-Māmūn*, by Shiblī Nuʿmānī (Aligarh, 1889), 4.
4. Shiblī Nuʿmānī, *al-Māmūn* (Azamgarh, n.d.), 4.
5. Ed., "Russia and England," *Malwā Akhbār*, Dec. 19, 1877, in *Selections from the Vernacular Newspapers Published in the Panjab, North-Western Provinces, Oudh, and Central Provinces* (Allahabad: N.W.P. and Oudh Government Press, 1878), 4–5.
6. Ed., "The Policy of Turkey in the Event of War between England and Russia," *Qaisar-ul-Akhbar*, June 2, 1878, in *Selections from the Vernacular Newspapers Published*

in the Panjab, North-Western Provinces, Oudh, and Central Provinces (Allahabad: N.W.P. and Oudh Government Press, 1878), 478.

7. Ed, "Lord Northbrook and the Muslims of India," *Aligarh Institute Gazette*, Aug. 31, 1878, in *Selections from the Vernacular Newspapers Published in the Panjab, North-Western Provinces, Oudh, and Central Provinces* (Allahabad: N.W.P. and Oudh Government Press, 1878), 771.

8. Gail Minault, *The Khilafat Movement: Religious Symbolism and Political Mobilization in India* (Delhi: Oxford University Press, 1982), 1–64; Barbara Daly Metcalf and Thomas R. Metcalf, *A Concise History of India* (Cambridge: Cambridge University Press, 2002), 60, 178–79.

9. Muḥammad Wāṣil ʻUṡmānī, *Shiblī bilād-i Islāmiyah meṅ* (Karachi: Khurshīd Publishers, 1982), 20–21.

10. Muḥammad Amīn Zubairī, *Żikr-i Shiblī* (Lucknow: Adabī Press, 1946), 48.

11. Swinglehurst, *The Romantic Journey: The Story of Thomas Cook and Victorian Travel* (London: Pica Editions, 1974), 134; Lynne Withey, *Grand Tours and Cook's Tours: A History of Leisure Travel, 1750–1915* (New York: W. Morrow, 1997), 284–85; Paul Smith, "Cecil, Robert Arthur Talbot Gascoyne-, third marquess of Salisbury (1830–1903)." *Oxford Dictionary of National Biography*, Oxford University Press, 2004, http://www.oxforddnb.com/view/article/35108.

12. Azim Nanji, "Nāṣir-i Ḵẖusraw," Encyclopaedia of Islam, 2nd ed.

13. Muzaffar Alam and Sanjay Subrahmanyam, *Indo-Persian Travels in the Age of Discoveries, 1400–1800* (Cambridge: Cambridge University Press, 2007), 1–44; Mirza Abu Taleb, *Westward Bound: Travels of Mirza Abu Taleb*, trans. Charles Stewart (New Delhi: Oxford University Press, 2005).

14. See Yusuf Khan Kambalposh, *Between Worlds: The Travels of Yusuf Khan Kambalposh*, trans. Mushirul Hasan and Nishat Zaidi (New Delhi: Oxford University Press, 2014).

15. Khālid Maḥmūd, *Urdū safarnāmoṅ kā tanqīdī mutālaʻah*, (Delhi: Maktabah-i Jāmiʻah, 2011), 92–129.

16. Deborah Manley, ed., *A Cairo Anthology: Two Hundred Years of Travel Writing* (Cairo: The American University in Cairo Press, 2013); T. J. Gordon, ed, *A Beirut Anthology: Travel Writing through the Centuries* (Cairo: The American University in Cairo Press, 2015).

17. Ibrāhīm Muawiliḥī, *Spies, Scandals, and Sultans: Istanbul in the Twilight of the Ottoman Empire*, trans. Roger Allan (Lanham: Rowman & Littlefield Publishers, Inc., 2008).

18. Tim Youngs, *The Cambridge Introduction to Travel Writing* (Cambridge: Cambridge University Press, 2013), 1–18, 53–67, 87–101.

Appendix 1. Biographies

1. Mark J. Sedgwick, *Muhammad Abduh* (Oxford, New York: Oneworld, 2010); von Kügelgen, "Muḥammad ʻAbduh." *Encyclopaedia of Islam, Three*, edited by Kate Fleet,

Gudrun Krämer, Denis Matringe, John Nawas, and Everett Rowson. BrillOnline. https://referenceworks.brillonline.com/browse/encyclopaedia-of-islam-3.

2. Sayyid Aḥmad Khān, *Khuṭūṭ-i Sir Sayyid* (Badayūn: Niẓāmī Press, 1931), 116.

3. Goldziher and Jomier, "Djamāl al-Dīn al-Afghānī." *Encyclopaedia of Islam* 2nd ed., edited by P. Bearman T. Bianquis, C. E. Bosworth, E. van Donzel, and W. P. Heinrichs. BrillOnline. https://referenceworks.brillonline.com/browse/encyclopaedia-of-islam-2; Nikki R. Keddie, *An Islamic Response to Imperialism* (Berkeley: University of California Press, 1968); Nikki R. Keddie, *Sayyid Jamāl ad-Dīn "al-Afghānī"* (Berkeley: University of California Press, 1968).

4. Minault, "Sayyid Mumtaz Ali and Huquq un-Niswan: An Advocate of Women's Rights in the Late Nineteenth Century," in *Gender, Language, and Learning: Essays in Indo-Muslim Cultural History* (Ranikhet: Permanent Black, 2009), 35–63.

5. For more on Nuṣrat 'Alī and Paik-i Islām, see Kemal H. Karpat, *The Politicization of Islam: Reconstructing Identity, State, Faith, and Community in the Late Ottoman State* (New York: Oxford University Press, 2001), 212–13 and Seema Alavi, *Muslim Cosmopolitanism in the Age of Empire* (Cambridge: Harvard University Press, 2015), 296–97.

6. M. A. Stein, "Thomas Walker Arnold," *Proceedings of the British Academy XVI* (1930), 439–74; H. A. R. Gibb, "Arnold, Sir Thomas Walker (1864–1930)," rev. Christine Woodhead, *Oxford Dictionary of National Biography*, Oxford University Press, 2004, http://www.oxforddnb.com/view/article/30457/; Katherine Watt, "Thomas Walker Arnold and the Re-Evaluation of Islam, 1864–1930," *Modern Asian Studies* 36, no. 1 (2002): 1–98.

7. Yilmaz Öztuna, *Türk Bestecileri Ansiklopedisi* (Istanbul: Hayat, 1969), 63; Sadun Aksüt, *Türk Musikisinin 100 Bestekarı* (Istanbul: İnkilap Kitabevi), 210–11.

8. Charles Edward Buckland, *Dictionary of Indian Biography* (London: Sonnenschein, 1906), 33.

9. Yves Boulvert, "Friedrich Bohndorff (1848–1894): Primier explorateur européen parvenu en Centrafique," in *Hommes et destins Tome XI Afrique noire*, ed. Jacques Serre (Paris: L'Harmattan, 2011), 95–97; Conrad Weidmann, *Deutsche Männer in Afrika* (Lübeck, B. Nöring, 1894), 16, 183; Franz Stuhlmann, *Mit Emin Pascha ins Herz von Afrika* (Berlin: D. Reitmer, 1894), 14; F. Jentink and H. Schegel, *Notes from the Leyden Museum* (Leyden: Brill, 1885), 7:35; *The History of the Collections Contained in the Natural History Departments of the British Museum* (London: Longmans & Co.) 2:313.

10. Nour, "al-Bustānī." *Encyclopaedia of Islam*, 2nd ed.

11. Yūsuf Sarkīs, *Mu'jam al-maṭbū'āt al-'Arabiyah wal-mu'arrabah* (Egypt, 1928–31), 561; 'Abdel-Nour, "al-Bustānī." *Encyclopaedia of Islam*, 2nd ed.

12. 'Abdel-Nour, "al-Bustānī." *Encyclopaedia of Islam*, 2nd ed.

13. Ghada Yusuf Khoury, *The Founding Fathers of the American University of Beirut: Biographies* (Beirut: The American University of Beirut, 1992), 179–232; van Dyck's Astronomy textbooks published in the al-Naqsh al-ḥajar series include works on

metaphysics, physics, geography, geology, astronomy, biology, and logic. Cornelius Van Dyck, *Kitāb al-naqsh fī al-ḥajar* (Beirut, 1886–91).

14. Arthur Goldschmidt Jr., *Biographical Dictionary of Modern Egypt* (Boulder: Lynne Rienner, 2000), 55–56; Marilyn Booth, "Writing Women's History in 1890s Egypt," *The Long 1890s in Egypt: Colonial Quiescence, Subterranean Resistance*, ed. Marilyn Booth and Anthony Gorman (Edinburgh: Edinburgh University Press, 2014), 365–98.

15. Muḥammad Sharīf al-Ṣawwāf, *Mausū'at al-usar al-Dimashqiyah: tārīkhahā, ansābahā, a'lāmahā* (Damascus: Bait al-Ḥikmah, 2010), 3:616; Weismann, "'Abd al-Majīd b. Muḥammad al-Khānī." *Encyclopaedia of Islam, Three.*

16. For more on 'Atiyā Faiẓī and her relationship with Shiblī, see Siobhan Lambert-Hurley and Sunil Sharma, eds., *Atiya's Journeys: A Muslim Woman from Colonial Bombay to Edwardian Britain* (New Delhi: Oxford University Press, 2010), 17–21. Shiblī's letters were published as Shiblī Nu'mānī, *Khuṭūṭ-i Shiblī* (Agra: Shamsī Steam Press, 1930); Fyzee, introduction to "The Autobiography of Tyabjee Bhoymeeah, Merchant Prince of Bombay 1803–1863)," *Journal of the Asiatic Society of Bombay* 36–37 (Supplement) (1962): 1–24; Abdul Gafoor Noorani, *Badruddin Tyabji* (Delhi: Publications Division, Ministry of Information and Broadcasting, Govt. of India, 1969).

17. Arthur Goldschmidt Jr., *Biographical Dictionary of Modern Egypt* (Boulder: Lynne Rienner, 2000), 59.

18. Ilyās A'ẓmī, *'Allāmah Shiblī ke nām ahl-i 'ilm ke khuṭūṭ* (Lahore: Maktabah-i Jamāl, 2015), 157–65.

19. Azmi Özcan, *Pan-Islamism* (Leiden: Brill, 1997), 23–63; Landau, "Pan-Islamism." *Encyclopaedia of Islam*, 2nd ed.

20. Deny, "'Abd al-Ḥamīd II." *Encyclopaedia of Islam*, 2nd ed.

21. Tanpinar, "'Abd al-Ḥaḳḳ Ḥāmid." *Encyclopaedia of Islam*, 2nd ed.

22. Ed., "Obituary, Annie Hanly (1857–1907)," *Lincolnshire Chronicle* (Lincolnshire, England), February 15, 1907.

23. Mehmet Zeki Pakalin, *Sicill-i Osmani zeylī* (Ankara: Türk Tarih Kurumu, 2008–9), 9:103–4; Azmi Özcan, *Pan-Islamism* (Leiden: Brill, 1997), 112–13.

24. Muḥammad 'Umar Ḥamādah, Mausū'ah a'lām Filasṭīn (Damascus: Dār al-Waśā'iq, 2000) 4:197–98; Ilan Pappe, *The Rise and Fall of a Palestinian Dynasty: The Husaynis 1700–1948)* (Berkeley: University of California Press, 2010).

25. *L'Imprimerie catholique de Beyrouth et son oeuvre en Orient (1853–1903)* (Bruxelles: Polleunis et Ceuterick, 1903), 31–32.

26. Indira Falk Gesink, *Islamic Reform and Conservatism: Al-Azhar and the Evolution of Modern Sunni Islam* (London, New York: Tauris, 2010), 116–18; Marwa Elshakry, *Reading Darwin in Arabic, 1860–1950* (Chicago: The University of Chicago Press, 2013), 199–200.

27. 'Alī Nāṣir al-Dīn. "al-Muqaddamah," *al-Ṣafā* 1, no. 1 (1886); 'Umar Jubailī, "I'lān," *al-Ṣafā* 4, no. 10 (April 1890): 149/640; Rondot, "Djānbulāt." *Encyclopaedia of Islam*, 2nd

ed.; Firro, "Al-Shūf." *Encyclopaedia of Islam*, 2nd ed.; Findley, "Mutaṣarrif." *Encyclopaedia of Islam*, 2nd ed.

28. Haywood, "Maẓhar." *Encyclopaedia of Islam*, 2nd ed.

29. David Dean Commins, *Islamic Reform: Politics and Social Change in Late Ottoman Syria* (New York: Oxford University Press, 1990), 27–42, 89–94; Joseph H. Escovitz, "He Was the Muḥammad 'Abduh of Syria," *International Journal of Middle East Studies* 18, no. 3 (August 1986): 295–97; Muḥammad Sharīf al-Ṣawwāf, *Mausū'at al-usar al-Dimashqiyah: tārīkhahā, ansābahā, a'lāmahā* (Damascus: Bait al-Ḥikmah, 2010), 2:527–37; Itzchak Weismann, *Taste of Modernity: Sufism Salafiyya, and Arabisim in Late Ottoman Damascus* (Leiden, Boston: Brill, 2001), 197–98, 234–35.

30. Muḥammad Kabīr al-Dīn, *Iqbāl Yār Jang: 'Ilmī o Samājī Khidmāt* (Hyderabad: Abul Kalam Azad Oriental Research Institute, n.d.), 105–15.

31. Bowen, "Aḥmad Djewdet Pasha." *Encyclopaedia of Islam*, 2nd ed.; Neumann, "Ahmed Cevdet Paşa." *Encyclopaedia of Islam, Three.*

32. Tansel, "Kemāl, Meḥmed, Nāmiḳḳ." *Encyclopaedia of Islam*, 2nd ed.

33. Muḥammad Żakā'ullāh, *Sawāniḥ-i 'Umrī Ḥājī Maulawī Muḥammad Samī'ullāh Khān Bahādur Sī Em Jī* (Hyderabad: Anwār al-Islām, 1909).

34. Robinson, "Aḥmad Khān, Sayyid." *Encyclopaedia of Islam, Three.* For more on Aligarh, see David Lelyveld, *Aligarh's First Generation: Muslim Solidarity in British India* (Princeton: Princeton University Press, 1978).

35. Muḥammad Amīn Zubairī, *Tażkirah-i Muḥsin al-Mulk* (Aligarh, 1935); Muḥammad Amīn Zubairī, *Ḥayāt-i Muḥsin* (Aligarh, 1934); Ahmad Saeed, *Muslim India: A Biographical Dictionary* (Lahore: Institute of Pakistan Historical Research), 232–33.

36. Serpil Çakır, "ALİYE, Fatma (1862–1936)," in *Biographical Dictionary of Womens Movements and Feminisms*, ed. Krassima Daskalova, et al., (New York: Central European University Press, 2006), 21–24.

37. Yunus Özger, "Osmanlı'da Kadınların Memuriyette İstihdamı Meselesi Ve Sicill-i Ahvalde Kayıtlı Memurelerin Resmi Hal Tercümeleri: The Issue of Women's Employment in State Service in the Ottoman Empire and Women in the Sicill-i Ahval Records," *History Studies* 4, no. 1 (2012): 436.

38. Ahmet Mithat, *Fatma Aliye Hanım yahut Bir Muharrire-i Osmaniye'nin Neş'eti*, (Istanbul: İsis, 1998), 52.

39. Ḥāzim Zakariyā Muḥyī al-Dīn, *al-Shaikh Ṭāhir al-Jazā'irī* (Damascus: Dār al-Qalam, 2001); 'Abd al-Laṭīf Shāh al-Farfūr, *A'lām Dimashq fī al-qarn al-rābi' 'ashar al-hijrī* (Damascus, 1987), 149–51; Joseph H. Escovitz, "He Was the Muḥammad 'Abduh of Syria," *International Journal of Middle East Studies* 18, no. 3 (August 1986): 295–97; David Dean Commins, *Islamic Reform: Politics and Social Change in Late Ottoman Syria* (New York: Oxford University Press, 1990), 27–42, 83–94; Itzchak Weismann, *Taste of Modernity: Sufism Salafiyya, and Arabisim in Late Ottoman Damascus* (Leiden, Boston: Brill, 2001), 197–98, 234–35, 284–86.

40. Lewis, "Aḥmad Midḥat." *Encyclopaedia of Islam*, 2nd ed.

41. Arthur Goldschmidt Jr., *Biographical Dictionary of Modern Egypt* (Boulder: Lynne Rienner, 2000), 131; Agai, "'Alī Mubārak." *Encyclopaedia of Islam, Three.*

42. Isidore Singer, *The Jewish Encyclopedia* (New York: Funk and Wagnalls, 1901–6), 9:110–11.

43. Shiblī Nu'mānī, *al-Ghazālī* (Azamgarh: Ma'ārif, 1928) 39–42. For more on Munk and Jewish philosophy in Europe, see Chiara Adorisio, "The Debate between Salomon Munk and Heinrich Ritter on Medieval Jewish and Arabic History of Philosophy," *European Journal of Jewish Studies* 6, no. 1 (2012): 169–82.

44. Esen, "Mu'allim Nādjī." *Encyclopaedia of Islam*, 2nd ed.

45. Albert Hourani, "Shaikh Khalid and the Naqshbandi Order," in *Islamic Philosophy and the Classical Tradition*, ed. Vivian Brown et al. (Columbia: University of South Carolina Press, 1972), 96–97; Hakan Yavuz, "The Matrix of Modern Turkish Islamic Movements: The Naqshbandi Sufi Order," in *Naqshbandis in Western and Central Asia*, ed. Elisabeth Özdalga (Istanbul, 1999), 129–34; Algar, "Naḳshbandiyya." *Encyclopaedia of Islam*, 2nd ed.

46. Muḥammad 'Abd al-Jawād, ed., *Taqwīm Dār al-'Ulūm* (Cairo: Dār al-Ma'ārif, 1950s), 1:13; Khair al-Dīn Ziriklī, *al-A'lām* (Cairo, 1954–59), 1:264.

47. Christoph Herzog and Barbara Henning, "Derviş İbrahim Paşa: Views on a Late 19th-Century Ottoman Military Commander," in *Occasional Papers in Ottoman Biographies* 1 (Bamberg: OPUS, Otto-Friedrich-Universität, 2012), 1–21, http://opus4.kobv.de/opus4-bamberg/solrsearch/index/search/searchtype/series/id/; Tekindağ, "Ibrāhīm Derwīsh Pasha." *Encyclopaedia of Islam*, 2nd ed.; Ess-Bremer, "Fehmī." *Encyclopaedia of Islam*, 2nd ed.; Marie Luise Bremer, *Die Memoiren Des Türkischen Derwischs Aşçi Dede Ibrāhīm* (Walldorf-Hessen: Verlag für Orientkunde, 1959), 118–19.

48. Selçuk Akşin Somel, *Historical Dictionary of the Ottoman Empire* (Lanham: Scarecrow Press, 2003), 95–96.

49. Krieken, "Khayr al-Dīn Pasha." *Encyclopaedia of Islam*, 2nd ed.

50. Mehmet Zeki Pakalin, *Sicill-i Osmani zeylī* (Ankara: Türk Tarih Kurumu, 2008–9), 19:80.

51. Khair al-Dīn Ziriklī, *al-A'lām* (Cairo, 1954–59), 1:249.

52. Philippe de Tarrazi, *Tārīkh al-ṣaḥāfat al-'Arabiyah* (Beirut, 1933), 156–59; Kamīl Ḥushaimah, *al-Mu'allifūn al-'Arab al-Masīhiyūn min qabl al-Islam ilā ākhir al-qarn al-'ishrīn* (Beirut: Dār al-Mashriq), 6:122–24; Dossier personnel d'Antoine Salhani, AFSI (Archives Français de la Societas Iesu), Archives de la Province de Lyon; *L'Imprimerie catholique de Beyrouth et son oeuvre en Orient (1853–1903)* (Bruxelles: Polleunis et Ceuterick, 1903).

53. Ed., "Ibn 'Ābidīn." *Encyclopaedia of Islam*, 2nd ed.; Itzchak Weismann, "Sufism on the Eve of Reform: The Views of Ibn-i 'Abidin," in *Ottoman Reform and Muslim Regeneration: Studies in Honour of Butrus Abu-Manneb*, ed. Itzchak Weismann and Fruma

Zachs (London, New York: I.B. Tauris: 2005), 69–80; Muḥammad Mutīʿ al-Hāfiẓ, *Faqīh al-Ḥanafiyya Muḥammad Amīn al-ʿĀbidīn: ḥayātuhu wa āṡāruhu* (Damascus: Dār al-Fikr, 1994).

54. Lois Armine Aroian, "Education, Language and Culture in Modern Egypt: Dar al-ʿUlum and its Graduates" (Ph.D. diss., University of Michigan, 1978), 96, 99; Muḥammad ʿAbd al-Jawād, ed., *Taqwīm Dār al-ʿUlūm* (Cairo: Dār al-Maʿārif, 1950s), 1:23.

55. Abdul Gafoor Noorani, *Badruddin Tyabji* (Delhi: Publications Division, Ministry of Information and Broadcasting, Govt. of India, 1969); Fyzee, introduction to "The Autobiography of Tyabjee Bhoymeeah, Merchant Prince of Bombay 1803–1863)," *Journal of the Asiatic Society of Bombay* 36–37 (Supplement) (1962): 1–24; Husain Badruddin Tyabji, *Badruddin Tyabji: A Biography* (Bombay: Thacker, 1952).

56. *"Innā lillāh wa innā alaihi rājiʿūn,"* *al-Ahrām*, December 4, 1927; *"Huwa al-Ḥaī al-Bāqī, al-Ahrām," al-Ahrām*, February 2, 1920.

57. Sources differ on the date of his death. Kaḥḥālah gives 1928; Marʿashlī (citing Dāʿūq, *ʿUlamāʾunā fī Bairūt*, 146–48) gives it as March 22, 1940. ʿUmar Riżā Kaḥḥālah, *Muʿjam al-muʾallifīn* (Beirut, n.d.), 2:40; Yūsuf Marʿashlī, *Naṡr al-Jawāhir* (Beirut: Dār al-Maʿrifah, 2006), 1: 619–20.

58. ʿAbd al-Bāsiṭ al-Unsī, *Qāʾimat al-kutub al-wujūd fī al-Maktabat al-Unsiyah* (Beirut, 1890–91).

59. ʿAbd al-Bāsiṭ al-Unsī, *Abdaʿ al-asālīb fī inshā al-rasāʾil wal-makātīb* (Beirut, 1912–13). Library catalogues also list printings in 1906 and 1931; ʿAbd al-Bāsiṭ al-Unsī, *Hidāyat al-sāʾil ilā inshāʾ al-rasāʾil* (Beirut, 1913–14).

60. ʿUmar Riżā Kaḥḥālah, *Muʿjam al-muʾallifīn* (Beirut, n.d.), 2:40; Yūsuf Marʿashlī, *Naṡr al-Jawāhir* (Beirut: Dār al-Maʿrifah, 2006), 1:619–20; Shiblī Nuʿmānī, *Bāqiyāt-i Shiblī* (Lahore: Majlis-i Taraqqi-i Adab, 1965), 140–44.

61. Michael Knüppel, *Ármin(ius) Vámbéry (1832–1913): Versuch einer Personalbibliographie,* (Nordhausen: Verlag Traugott Bautz GmbH, 2015); Ármin Vámbéry, *The Coming Struggle for India: Being an Account of the Encroachments of Russia in Central Asia and of the Difficulties Sure to Arise therefrom to England* (London: Cassell & Co., 1885); Lory Adler and Richard Dalby, *The Dervish of Windsor Castle* (London: Bachman and Turner, 1979); David Mandler, *Arminius Vambéry and the British Empire: Between East and West* (Lanham: Lexington Books, 2016).

62. Stephen B. L. Penrose, *That They May Have Life: The Story of the American University of Beirut, 1866–1941* (Beirut: American University of Beirut, 1970), 61–2; *General Catalogue of Princeton University 1746–1906* (Princeton: The University, 1908), 267.

63. Muḥammad Sharīf al-Ṣawwāf, *Mausūʿat al-usar al-Dimashqiyah: tārīkhahā, ansābahā, aʿlāmahā* (Damascus: Bait al-Ḥikmah, 2010), 2:591–93; Abū al-Ḥasan ʿAlī Nadwī, *Mużakkirat sāʾih fī al-Sharq al-ʿArabī* (Beirut, 1975).

64. C. F. Andrews, *Zaka Ullah of Delhi* (Cambridge: W. Heffer & Sons, 1929); Mushirul Hasan, "Maulawi Zaka Ullah: Sharif Culture and Colonial Rule," in *The Delhi College:*

Traditional Elites, the Colonial State, and Education before 1857, ed. Margrit Pernau and Muhammad Ikram Chughtai (New Delhi: Oxford University Press, 2006), 261–98.

65. (Listed as Ahmad Zeki Effendi), *Transactions of the Ninth International Congress of Orientalists (Held in London, 5th to 12th September 1892)* (London: Printed for the Committee of the Congress, 1893), xii; Anouar Louca, *Voyageurs et écrivains Égyptiens en France au XIXe siècle* (Paris: Didier, 1970), 209–21.

66. *Transactions of the Ninth International Congress of Orientalists (Held in London, 5th to 12th September 1892)* (London: Printed for the Committee of the Congress, 1893), lvii, lii, xxviii.

67. Anwar al-Jindī, *Aḥmad Zakī* (Cairo, 1964), 23, 43; Arthur Goldschmidt Jr., *Biographical Dictionary of Modern Egypt* (Boulder: Lynne Rienner, 2000), 236.

68. Abdullah, "Ebüzziya Tevfik." *Encyclopaedia of Islam*, 2nd ed.

Appendix 2. Letters

1. The letter opens with the short poem in Persian, which begins "*Chūn kamar bastam*" (When I girded my loins), which is copied in the travelogue.

2. qiblah (the direction faced while praying; also a term of respect used when addressing someone, especially in a letter).

3. Shiblī Nuʻmānī, *Maktūbāt-i Shiblī* (Azamgarh: Adabī Dā'irah, 2012), 22–23. May 8, 1892 was a Sunday.

4. *ʻUmdat al-qārī li sharḥ Ṣaḥīḥ al-Bukhārī* (Istanbul: al-Sharikat al-Saḥāfiyah al-ʻUśmāniyah, 1892) Badr al-Din Maḥmūd ʻAinī (1351–1451).

5. Ḥamīd al-Dīn Farāhī (1860–1930). Shiblī's cousin. In 1892, he was a student at the Mohammedan Anglo-Oriental College in Aligarh. He passed the Bachelor of Arts examination administered by the University of Allahabad in 1895, spent the next two decades writing and teaching, and eventually retired to a life of seclusion. While a student at the college, he translated the *Tabaqāt* of Ibn-i Saʻd from Arabic into Persian (published in 1891).

6. Established in 1876, *Akhtar* was patronized by the Persian ambassador in Istanbul as a "weapon against the idle talk of Ottoman newspapers" (quoted by Pistor-Hatam, 142). The paper was suspended in Iran in 1892 for siding against the Iranian state in the Persian Tobacco Protest of 1891–92, and was eventually shut down in 1896. The paper was also important for the attention it drew from the Orientalist Edward Granville Brown, who subscribed to it from Cambridge in 1888. Anja Pistor-Hatam, "The Persian Newspaper Akhtar as a Transmittor of Ottoman Political Ideas," in *Les Iraniens d'Istanbul*, ed. T. Zarcone and F. Zarinebaf-Shahr (Istanbul-Tehran, 1993), 141–47; John Gurney, "E. G. Browne and the Iranian Community at Istanbul," *Les Iraniens d'Istanbul*, ed. T. Zarcone and F. Zarinebaf-Shahr (Istanbul-Tehran, 1993), 149–75; For a lengthy study of *Akhtar*, see Tanya E. Lawrence, *Akhtar: A Persian Language Newspaper Published in Istanbul and*

the Iranian Community of the Ottoman Empire in the Late Nineteenth Century (Istanbul: Libra Kitap*çılık*, 2015).

7. In a marginal note, Nadwī writes in his biography of Shiblī that Ḥabīb al-Raḥmān Khān Shirwānī once told him that when Shiblī met (Ghāzī) Uṡmān Pāshā, "when the hand of one was in the other's hand, [Shiblī] asked [(Ghāzī) Uṡmān Pāshā] for permission to kiss the hand with which he had slain the *kuffār* (pl. of *kāfir*; nonbelievers). The pāshā said, "Your hand is worth kissing, which has performed scientific services and, having said this, he kissed [Shiblī's] hand." Sayyid Sulaimān Nadwī, *Ḥayāt-i Shiblī* (Azamgarh, 1943), 210.

8. *Akmal al-akhbār*. An Urdu newspaper based in Delhi.

9. *Sīrat al-Nu'mān* (1889). Shiblī's biography of Nu'mān b. Ṡābit, also known as Abū Ḥanīfah, an influential jurist and teacher, and the eponym of the Ḥanafī school of jurisprudence in Sunnī Islam.

10. Shiblī lived in a bungalow at the rear of Sayyid Aḥmad Khān's large home on the grounds of the college in Aligarh.

11. William C. Horst. headmaster at the Mohammedan Anglo-Oriental College, Aligarh.

12. Theodore Beck (1859–99), principal of the MAO College from 1883 until his death.

13. Khwushī Muḥammad Nāẓir (1872–1944). One of Shiblī's students at Aligarh. Eventually, a statesman in Kashmir and Ladakh. He also wrote poetry in Persian and Urdu. Under Shiblī's tutelage, he passed the BA examination with honors in Persian from Allahabad University in 1893.

14. Sayyid Mumtāz 'Alī (see Appendix 1). Shiblī brought him a copy of a book on women's rights in Islam by Ḥamzah Fatḥullāh, whom Shiblī met in Cairo.

15. *Akmal al-akhbār* (Delhi-based Urdu newspaper). Maulawī Zain al-'Ābidīn (1832–1905) was a friend and supporter of Sayyid Aḥmad Khān. Khān Bahādur was a ceremonial title given to Muslims in British India.

16. Shiblī copies the first eighteen couplets of his maṡnawī. The only difference between the maṡnawī copied here and that copied in the travelogue is that instead of the couplet "*bazm-i khwushī būd tamāshā chih kard / kār base būd az ān hā chih kard*?" (Was it a joyful affair? What did you see? There were many tasks. What of them did you accomplish?), Shiblī writes "*sharḥ dih ākhir kih dar ānjā chih dīd / sair khwushī būd ba-farmā chih dīd*?" (Explain at last what did you see there? Was it a joyful visit? What did you see?).

17. *Shams al-'ulamā* (Sun of the Scholars). An order of the British government given to Muslims in recognition of "great Oriental learning." It was announced in 1887 on the occasion of Jubilee Day celebrating the fiftieth anniversary of the reign of Queen Victoria. Zakā'ullāh (see Appendix 1), an associate of Aligarh and Sayyid Aḥmad Khān, was among the first to receive the title. Ceremonial markers were modeled on British knighthood, but a turban and cloak took the place of ribbons and stars. In the ceremonial *darbār*

(court), Shams al-'ulamā sat in the rank immediately after nawābs (deputy administrators), and were said to be analogous to the privy councilor in the United Kingdom. Lord Dufferin and Harrriot Ava, *Our Viceregal Life in India* (London: J. Murray, 1889), 115–16; Roper Lethbridge, *The Golden Book of India: A Genealogical and Biographical Dictionary of the Ruling Princes, Chiefs, Nobles, and other Personages, Titled or Decorated, of the Indian Empire* (London: S. Low, Marston & Company Limited, 1900), xiii; Sayyid Sulaimān Nadwī, *Ḥayāt-i Shiblī* (Azamgarh: Maʻārif, 1943), 259.

18. *charāgh tale andherā* (Urdu: lit., darkness under a lamp; said when a person pays attention to the accomplishments of others, but ignores those of the people near him, such as family members).

19. Shiblī Nuʻmānī, *Maktūbāt-i Shiblī* (Azamgarh: Adabī Dā'irah, 2012), 23–27.

20. Shaikh Ḥabībullāh (see Appendix 1). Shiblī's father.

21. Badr al-Dīn (al-)ʻAinī (1361–1451). Historian and hadith critic. As elsewhere in the travelogue, Shiblī refers to *ʻUmdat al-qārī li sharḥ Ṣaḥīḥ al-Bukhārī*, which was published by al-Sharikat al-Saḥāfiyah al-ʻUsmāniyah in eleven volumes in 1892. Marmon, "al- ʻAynī, Abū Muḥammad Badr al-Dīn" and Melchert, "al-Bukhārī." *Encyclopaedia of Islam, Three*, edited by Kate Fleet, Gudrun Krämer, Denis Matringe, John Nawas, and Everett Rowson. BrillOnline. https://referenceworks.brillonline.com/browse/encyclopaedia-of-islam-3.

22. *Fatḥ al-bārī*. A commentary by Ibn Ḥajar al-ʻAsqalānī (1372–1449) on the authoritative hadith collection often called *Ṣaḥīḥ Bukhārī* by Abū ʻAbdullāh Muḥammad al-Bukhārī (810–870). Written between 1410–38, *Fatḥ al-bārī* is considered by Melchart to be "the most important commentary on the *Ṣaḥīḥ* (*Bukhārī*)." Melchart, "al-Bukhārī." *Encyclopaedia of Islam, Three*; Rosenthal, "Ibn Ḥadjar al-ʻAsḳalānī." *Encyclopaedia of Islam* 2nd ed., edited by P. Bearman T. Bianquis, C. E. Bosworth, E. van Donzel, and W. P. Heinrichs. BrillOnline. https://referenceworks.brillonline.com/browse/encyclopaedia-of-islam-2

23. Shiblī's brother, a lawyer in Allahabad. Died in 1914.

24. *munṣif* (Urdu: a low-level judge in British India involved in minor civil suits.)

25. Shiblī Nuʻmānī, *Makātīb-i Shiblī* (Azamgarh: Maʻārif, 1927), 1:12–14.

26. Khwājah ʻAzīz al-Dīn. Professor at Canning College, Lucknow; respected Persian poet and author; and a good friend of Shiblī's.

27. Perhaps a copyist's error. This should be *maʻrifat*. Shiblī did visit Maʻārif in Istanbul, but the remainder of his letters suggest that he was receiving mail "care of" (*maʻrifat*) the office of the Persian newspaper *Akhtar*.

28. Shiblī Nuʻmānī, *Makātīb-i Shiblī* (Azamgarh: Maʻārif, 1927), 1:14–15.

29. *maqṣūrah* (an enclosure in a mosque for the use of the sulṭān).

30. Arabic: "O God, aid and give victory to our lord the sulṭān. Sulṭān, ghāzī (warrior) ʻAbd al-Ḥamīd Khān.» This version differs slightly from that given in the travelogue.

31. Abu Bakr and ʻUmar, the first two caliphs of Sunnī Islam.

32. Arabic: "God be pleased with them both."

33. Shiblī Nu'mānī, *Makātīb-i Shiblī* (Azamgarh: Ma'ārif, 1927), 1:15–17.

34. *Mukhtār al-ṣiḥāḥ* by Muḥammad ibn Abī Bakr al-Rāzī (fl. 1261). A rearrangement, selection, and extension of the Arabic lexicon *Tāj al-lughah wa ṣiḥāḥ al-'Arabiyah* (often shortened to al-Ṣiḥāḥ) by al-Jauharī (d. ca. 1002–10). According to one scholar, the latter was "for centuries . . . the most widely used Arabic dictionary." Kopf, "al-Djawharī." *Encyclopaedia of Islam*, 2nd ed.

35. It is not clear what Shiblī means here, but he seems to use *examination* metaphorically to refer to the questions that he anticipates answering. Mumtāz 'Alī soon after completed a book on women's rights in Islam, *Ḥuqūq-i Niswān*, and his exchange with Shiblī was probably related to the book project.

36. Shaikh Ḥamzah Fatḥullāh (see Appendix 1).

37. Shiblī Nu'mānī, *Maktūbāt-i Shiblī* (Azamgarh: Adabī Dā'irah, 2012), 70–71.

Appendix 3. Contemporary Reviews of the Travelogue

1. *safar dar watan* (travel in *watan*); *watan* (homeland; dwelling; self). A technical term in mystical discourse closely associated with the Naqshbandī tradition, it refers to the journey within oneself toward ideal virtue or the divine.

2. The allusion is to the prophet Joseph (Yūsuf), celebrated for his beauty, who was cast into a well and abandoned by his brothers, then eventually found and purchased by Zulaikhā (the wife of Potiphar in the Islamic tradition), who lusted after him.

3. Ḥabīb al-Raḥmān Shirwānī, *Maqālāt-i Shirwānī* (Aligarh: Shirwānī Printing Press, 1946), 30–32.

4. Waḥīd al-Dịn Salīm Pānīpatī (1869–1928). Teacher, secretary, editor, and professor. Educated at the Oriental College in Lahore, he became secretary to Sayyid Aḥmad Khān in 1894. Ahmad Saeed, *Muslim India, 1857–1947: A Biographical Dictionary* (Lahore: Institute of Pakistan Historical Research, 1997), 333.

5. *al-Jiziyah* (The Jiziyah Tax) (1891) and *Kutub-khānah-i Iskandariyah* (The Alexandrian Library) (1892). Two short tracts written in Urdu by Shiblī largely in response to orientalist debates about Islamic history. Both were translated into English shortly after their publication in Urdu and published as Shiblī Nu'mānī, *Jiziya: Capitation Tax* (Aligarh, 1894); Shiblī Nu'mānī, *An Enquiry into the Destruction of the Alexandrian Library*, trans. Muhammad Ghouse Sayeed (Madras: Vest & Co., 1893).

6. Reprinted in Ẓafar Aḥmad Ṣiddīqī, *Shiblī mu'āṣirīn kī naẓar meṅ* (Lucknow: Uttar Pradesh Urdu Academy, 2005), 328–32.

Appendix 4. Newspaper Reports

1. Persian: "I have traveled the way of mountains and wilderness, Shiblī / Now I am a wayfarer of the path of the sea."

2. Shiblī copies the short poem, in Persian, that he later includes in the travelogue (p. 20).

3. May 8, 1892, was a Sunday.

4. The postcard is in Arabic.

5. Shiblī copies the first eighteen couplets of his maśnawī. One couplet differs from the published version (see Appendix 2 note 17).

6. Aḥmad Zakī (cf.) (see Appendix 1).

Appendix 5. Transliterations of Persian Poems

1. See p. 20 for the English translation.

2. See pp. 36–40 for the English translation.

3. *ʿīdiyah* (adj. of ʿīd [Eid; celebration]). ʿĪd al- Ażḥā (Eid ul-Adha), celebrated from 10 Żū al-Ḥijjah. The date is slightly confusing, since Eid that year began on 10 Żū al-Ḥijjah 1309 (July 6, 1892). For the English translation, see pp. 100–104.

Index

Shiblī Nu'mānī (1857–1914) was an Indian educator, historian, and writer. His travelogue of the Ottoman Empire and Egypt, his critical studies of Urdu *marṡiyah* poetry and Persian poetry, and his biographies of the Abbasid caliph al-Māmūn, Nu'mān bin Ṡābit (Abū Ḥanīfah), 'Umar ibn al-Khaṭṭāb, Abū Ḥāmid al-Ghazālī, Jalāl al-Dīn Rūmī, and the Prophet Muḥammad are considered classics in Urdu.

Gregory Maxwell Bruce was educated at the University of California, Santa Cruz and the University of Texas at Austin. He is currently a lecturer in Urdu at the University of California, Berkeley.